ACUA
Underwater Archaeology Proceedings
2018

edited by

Matthew Keith and Amanda Evans

AN ADVISORY COUNCIL ON UNDERWATER ARCHAEOLOGY PUBLICATION

2018 © Advisory Council on Underwater Archaeology

Made possible in part through the support of the
Society for Historical Archaeology

Cover Image: Title; Attribiution

Forward..iii

Contributing Authors

Identifying Gun Carriage Components from *Queen Anne's Revenge*: A Preliminary Review......................1
    Stephen B. Atkinson

Conserving and Interpreting a Mechanical Jack from Blackbeard's Flagship,
Queen Anne's Revenge 7
    Arianna M. DiMucci

On the Verge: The Pocket Watch from *Queen Anne's Revenge*..15
    Karen E. Martindale

The Investigation of the Anniversary Wreck, a Colonial Period Shipwreck Lost off St.
Augustine, Florida: Results of the 2017 Excavation Season..21
    Chuck Meide

Ceramics of the Anniversary Wreck: A Preliminary Analysis...31
    Sam Turner, Allyson Ropp, Chuck Meide, Roger Arrazcaeta, Marcos Acosta,
    Yoser Martínez

Way Hay and Up She Rises: The Recovery, Conservation, and Documentation of an
Historic Admiralty Anchor from the Gulf of Mexico..37
    John R. Bratten, Christopher E. Horrell, Stephen B. Atkinson, Andrew T.
    Willard

Phosphate, Potassium, Pisces, Poop and Pollution: Surveying the Pacific Guano
Company Anchorage of Woods Hole, MA, USA..45
    Raymond L Hayes

Preserved Meat Supplies or Slaughterhouse Waste Disposal? Zooarchaeology of the
Valparaiso Fiscal Mole, Chile...55
    Isabel Cartajena, Diego Carabias, Ana Carolina Barrera, Renato Simonetti,
    Carla Morales

Landing for Water and Wood can leave a Mark: Ship Graffiti as Evidence of Visitation
to Cocos Island, Costa Rica..63
    Jason T. Raupp, Anne E. Wright, Omar Fernández López

Impressions, Itineraries and Perceptions of a Coastscape: The Case of Medieval Paphos
(A.D. 12th–16th Century)...71
    Maria Ktori

Routes of Removal: Vessel Biographies and the Island Transfer of Aboriginal and Torres
Strait Islander Peoples, Queensland, Australia..85
    Madeline Fowler

The Plantation Boat Accommodation: A Maritime Icon of the American Southeast 93
    Daniel Mark Brown, Kathryn L. Cooper M.A., Lynn B. Harris

Chebacco: The Boat that Built Essex 103
    Leland S. Crawford

Mapping the Sacramento River in 1837 111
    Glenn J. Farris

Computer Vision Photogrammetry as a Tool for Three-Dimensional Archaeological
Recording of a Sixteenth Century Spanish Shipwreck in the Dominican Republic 117
    Kirsten M. Hawley, Matthew M. Maus, Charles D. Beeker, Samuel I.
    Haskell

The Backyard Shipwreck: The 2017 Lake Champlain Maritime Museum Field School
Exploration of a Shipwreck in Basin Harbor 123
    Allyson Ropp

Analysis of Québec Shipwrecks: the Necessity of Integrating Local Divers to Improve
the Management of Maritime Heritage 133
    Carolane Veilleux

Indiana's Maritime Heritage: Ongoing Investigations and Management Strategies for the
1910 *Muskegon* (aka *Peerless*) Shipwreck (12LE0381) 139
    Samuel I. Haskell, Matthew J. Maus, Charles D. Beeker, Kirsten M. Hawley

Past and Present Research in the Underwater Archaeology of Saint-Pierre, Martinique, (FWI) 149
    Jean-Sébastien Guibert, Max Guérout, Laurence Serra

Parallels in History: Shipwreck Salvage and Exploitation of Archaeological Resources in
Florida and Aruba 155
    Melissa R. Price

War on the Homefront: A Survey of South Africa's WWII Heritage at Risk 163
    Ian Harrison

Shore to Ship: The application of KOCOA to a Maritime Military Environment 170
    Terence Christian, Kristen McMasters

"Unidentified Planes Sighted": The Application of KOCOA Military Terrain Analysis to
Aerial Combat 181
    Madeline Roth, Jennifer McKinnon

Lost at Sea: The Archival and Archaeological Investigation of Two Submerged F8F Bearcats 187
    Hunter W. Whitehead

Foreword

Landscapes, Entrepôts, and Global Currents

The year 2018 marked the city of New Orleans, Louisiana's Tricentennial. Throughout its history, New Orleans has been an important entrepôt in the Atlantic World, a bustling port city where merchants and smugglers exchanged commodities from the interior of North American and around the globe. Known for its cuisine and as the birthplace of Jazz, New Orleans has also played a significant role in military struggles, from the Battle of New Orleans, through the American Civil War, and World War II. The Society for Historical Archaeology celebrated the 300th anniversary of the founding of New Orleans while hosting its 51st Annual Conference on Historical and Underwater Archaeology from January 3-6, 2018. New Orleans' history and culture inspired the conference theme Landscapes, Entrepôts, and Global Currents. This theme was embraced by conference participants, many of whom critically examined how our discipline perceives and interprets historical landscapes and considered how current and global trends affect our examination of the past.

The robust program saw a total of 1,011 abstracts submitted. Underwater and maritime submissions accounted for a significant portion of the program and included: 100 of 582 abstracts submitted within organized symposia; 69 of 212 general abstract submissions; 10 of 65 posters; and 3 of 8 panel discussions. Underwater program elements also included workshops and roundtable luncheons and the always popular ACUA Photo Competition. The ACUA Proceedings have been prepared for the 12th consecutive year.

This year's Proceedings contains 24 papers. Contributors covered a diverse array of topics and this volume has been organized with a focus on keeping papers that were presented within organized sessions together; individual contributions have been organized thematically, where possible. The volume begins with a series of papers that focus on artifact analysis. These include papers from an organized session on Queen Anne's Revenge submitted by Stephen Atkinson, Arianna DiMucci, and Karen Martindale. John Bratten's chapter (with Chris Horrell) discusses the discovery, conservation, and subsequent research of a 19th century anchor found in the Gulf of Mexico, while papers by Chuck Meide and Samuel Turner (with Allyson Ropp, Chuck Meide, Roger Arrazceta, Marcos Acosta, and Yoser Martínez) discuss investigations into St. Augustine's Anniversary Wreck and its ceramic assemblage. Isabel Cartajena's chapter (with Diego Carabias, Ana Carolina Barrera, Renato Simonetti, and Carla Morales) discusses 19th and early 20th century faunal assemblages discovered offshore of Valparaiso, Chile. Papers by Daniel Brown (with Kathryn Copper and Lynn Harris) and Leland Crawford delve into vernacular vessel types used in North Carolina and Massachusetts, respectively. Several papers focused on site documentation methods and mapping strategies. Glenn Farris' paper digs into archival sources to reassess the early mapping expeditions of the Sacramento River. Allyson Ropp's chapter discusses the Lake Champlain Maritime Museum's 2016 and 2017 Field School investigations of an unidentified shipwreck and the importance of community involvement. Papers by Samuel Haskell (with Matthew Maus, Charles Beeker, and Kirsten Hawley) and Kirsten Hawley (with Matthew Maus, Charles Beeker, and Samuel Haskell) summarize results of investigations performed by Indiana University on an early 20th century vessel in Indiana and a 16th century shipwreck in the Dominican Republic with an emphasis on the use of photogrammetry for mapping. Caroline Veilleux and Jean-Sébastien Guibert (with Max Guérout and Laurence Serra) tackle heritage management issues in French-speaking Quebec and Martinique, respectively. Raymond Hayes discusses investigations offshore of Woods Hole, Massachusetts that provide insight into the 19th century guano trade, while Maria Ktori looks at the potential for heritage management and education to promote preservation of medieval sites in Cyprus. Chapters by Melissa Price, Jason Raupp (with Anne Wright and Omar Fernández López), and Madeline Fowler cover diverse topics from a historical and cultural perspective. Price discusses the history of shipwreck salvage in Florida and Aruba; Raupp et al. discuss potential functions of historic graffiti found in remote Cocos Island, Costa Rica; and Fowler discusses the historical and archaeological evidence of forced removals of native peoples in 19th and 20th century Australia. The final four papers all have a focus on conflict. These include Ian Harrison's survey of World War II South African sites; Terrance Christian and Kristen

McMaster's discussion of the utilization of military terrain analysis on maritime battle fields using the Civil War Battle of Mobile Bay as a case study; and Madeline Roth's (with Jennifer McKinnon) use of military terrain analysis in looking at the submerged remains of aerial battles. The volume concludes with Hunter Whitehead's discussion of research on submerged aircraft related to the Naval Air Station in Pensacola, Florida.

The ACUA Proceedings could not be completed each year without the invaluable assistance and support of the PAST Foundation, especially the hard work and dedication of Sheli Smith, and the preparation of final proofs performed by Jim Bruner. The editors would like to acknowledge the entire conference committee in putting on a highly successful event, especially Conference Chairs Christopher Horrell and Andrea White. Finally, the editors would like to thank the authors for contributing their work for publication.

MATTHEW E. KEITH
AMANDA M. EVANS

Identifying Gun Carriage Components from *Queen Anne's Revenge*: A Preliminary Review

Stephen B. Atkinson

This paper aimed to identify gun carriage components recovered from North Carolina state shipwreck site 31CR314, Queen Anne's Revenge (1718). The investigation used in situ locations of cannon and gun carriage hardware recovered from concretion to better understand the construction of the carriages present on QAR. Artifacts identified as gun carriage components included cleaned hardware, artifacts in concretion identified via x-radiography, and pieces identified as rigging elements analogous to gun carriage tackle. Evidence for nationality and date range for QAR carriages were also investigated, by comparison of French and English carriages from the late 17th and early 18th centuries.

Introduction

This research aimed to identify gun carriage components recovered from North Carolina state shipwreck site 31CR314, identified by researchers as *Queen Anne's Revenge (QAR)*, flagship of the pirate Blackbeard which ran aground and was abandoned at Beaufort Inlet, in June 1718. Prior to its capture and renaming by the pirates the ship was *La Concorde*, a French slave ship out of Nantes (Wilde-Ramsing and Ewen 2012). North Carolina state archaeologists investigating the site have so far found 30 cannon, of which 24 have been recovered. Seventeen of these are in various stages of conservation, documentation, and investigation at the NC Department of Natural and Cultural Resources' (DNCR) *Queen Anne's Revenge* Conservation Laboratory (*QAR* Lab). The *QAR* Lab has been located at East Carolina University (ECU) since 2002. Seven cannon have so far completed conservation and are on display at various museums in North Carolina.

Previous research, by members of the *QAR* Project team, in relation to artillery recovered from site has focused mainly on dating and identifying the cannon and iron shot variants (Henry 2009; 2011). Other artillery-related research includes Schnitzer's (2012) investigation of lead cannon aprons from the site. These were used originally to cover a cannon's vent, but none were found in place on cannon. Additional cannon accessories found on *QAR* include wooden tompions, a gun worm, and a powder scoop.

This paper focuses on new discoveries in relation to the hardware of the gun carriages themselves, while also discussing some newly cleaned tools that may have been used to manipulate carriage-mounted artillery. The potential presence of gun carriage components had been considered in previous research, but many new discoveries have necessitated a more detailed analysis.

The de-concretion of a well-preserved strip of iron (QAR1771.016) proved to be what is commonly referred to as a trunnion band, trunnion strap, or cap-square (Moody 1952:304). This led to a decision to focus work (2016 to 2018) on concretions from three blocks of contiguous excavation units which had contained the highest number of cannon clustered together. This association of the concretions with multiple guns raised the chances of identifying gun carriage components based on context in situ. None of the cannon had been recovered attached to its gun carriage, but it was hypothesized that gun carriage components were more likely to be found near the locations of known cannon. Many concretions including the aforementioned capsquare, were also recovered from these areas.

Through identification of naval gun carriage components, the aim was to better understand the construction, nationality, and dating of gun carriages on *QAR* at the time of its wrecking. Potential gun carriage components identified by the author included cleaned hardware, artifacts in concretions observed via x-radiography, as well as possible identification of examples of rigging analogous to gun carriage tackle. The nature of nationality and date range were addressed by comparison with historically and archaeologically known features of French and English naval gun carriages from the late 17th and early 18th centuries and what variations through time they may have, to better identify the components present from the site.

Historical Background: Gun Carriage Construction

Most European naval gun carriages of the late 17th to early 18th centuries were characterized by a handful of common construction traits. The carriages were based on a full sole (also referred to as a bed or table), a flat platform resting on two solid wood axle trees each with two solid wheels (trucks). The fore trucks were at times larger to compensate for the camber of the deck, and the aft axle trees and trucks were sometimes replaced with half circle wooden blocks to increase friction and reduce recoil from lighter guns (Boudriot 1993:321).

The cheeks, or side walls of the carriage, were affixed to the top face of the sole, with a front breast/transom bolted to the bed and the cheeks supporting and tying the carriage together. The upper aft of these cheeks were stepped to permit the use of hand spikes (or crowbars) to adjust the breech of the gun, supplemented using the quoin block or stool bed to adjust and hold the desired height of the breech in place (Moody 1952:304). In most cases, semi-circular recesses were cut out of the top of the cheeks on either side to accept the trunnions, directly over an internal supporting brace. The transition away from this type of platform seems to have occurred around the 1720s, as the full sole and cheeks had a habit of retaining more moisture on the bed, leading to rot. This basic form was used by many nationalities at the time, with only minor variances in carriage construction. For example, research indicates that French-built carriages of this period employed the use of distinctive cleats on the sides of their cheeks as part of the carriage hardware (Boudriot 1993:323).

Elm seems to have been the preferred wood for gun carriages, as it splintered less in battle and thus assumedly reduced casualties, although oak may also have been used out of necessity (Martin 2004:87). Various orientations of breeching hardware and tackle have been observed, but the standard layout included at least one ring bolt affixed to either side, as well as advancing hooks or cleats, used to bring the gun back to ready (Moody 1952:306). The tackle used to breech the gun was comprised of generic assemblages of rope, eye hooks, ring bolts, blocks, and deadeyes, therefore making them difficult to identify as related to gun carriages without exceptional context. It was these iron implements that were sought in this research, along with the capsquares and their associated fastening methods.

QAR Excavation Unit Blocks

All artifacts recovered from the QAR site are assigned a unique find number. The exact provenience of each is recorded in relation to the site datum, and to

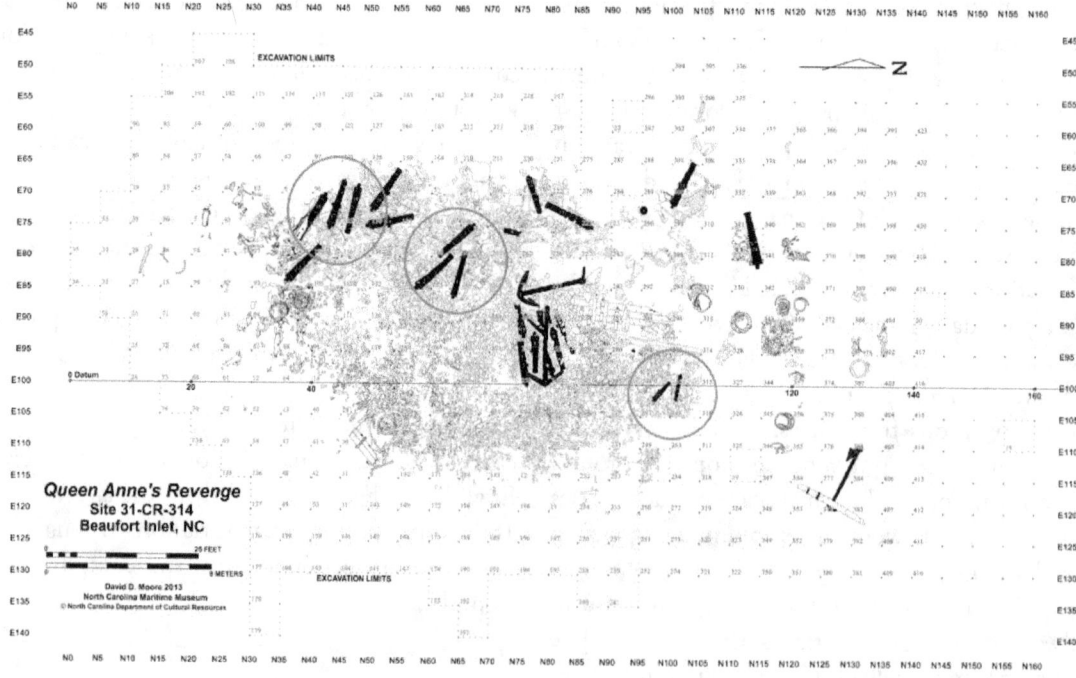

Figure 1: Site Plan of Queen Anne's Revenge Indicating Research Areas (Site Plan by David Moore, 2013.)

the five-foot x five-foot numbered excavation unit it was recovered from. Documentation of their context in situ includes site plan mapping. To discern possible yet unidentified gun carriage hardware already recovered from site the author scrutinized the *QAR* Site Plan (Moore 2013, Figure 1), and interrogated records in the *QAR* Artifact Database. Three main areas of the site were thus "surveyed" for gun carriage hardware due to their high concentration of cannon resting muzzle to button. All the cannon located in the unit blocks being assessed in this research had been raised, with half of the cannon cleaned or in the process of being cleaned. The first group of cannon (referred to by number designations beginning with "C") includes C1 (QAR3385.000), C2 (QAR0232.000), and C3 (QAR0233.001), all of which are six-pounders. C2 and C3 have been fully cleaned. The second group of cannon included C16 (QAR2300.000), C17 (QAR2299.000), and C18 (QAR1875.000), with only C16 in the process of being actively cleaned. The final cluster included C26 (QAR0363.008) and C27 (QAR3650.000), both of which had been cleaned and were undergoing desalination treatment (Figure 1).

Thus far, this research has focused mainly on concretions containing capsquares, as they are the most unique piece of associated carriage hardware and are readily identifiable. Four capsquares have been definitively identified, in various states of preservation. Most of these capsquares remain in concretion, while one remains in situ on the right trunnion of C16. The iron artifacts included in concretion with these capsquares comprise much of the iron hardware one would expect from gun carriages at the time. The concretions investigated are as follows:

Concretion QAR1771.000

This concretion was found on site between cannons C17 and C18, and recovered from site in 2007. It was investigated and broken down by the author and found to contain the first capsquare (QAR1771.016) to be identified and conserved from *QAR*. This concretion also included the remains of a large fore-locked eye bolt, rope fragments, nails, and a trunnion staple. The capsquare itself exhibits traits that suggest French manufacture, such as basic, flat ends that do not curl back in the aft (Figure 2).

It also matched the trunnion diameter of a four-pound gun. The presence of a staple also suggests a French-built carriage, in that French gun carriages used a staple to affix the rear of the capsquare to the top of the cheek on which to pivot when folding the straps back to remove or install a gun in place (Boudriot 1993:321).

Figure 2: Capsquare from Concretion QAR1771.000 (Photo by author)

Concretion QAR3105.000

Concretion QAR3105.000 was in Unit 204, near C1, C2, and C3. All three cannon are six-pounders. C3 the closest gun to the concretion has been identified as being of Swedish manufacture and C2 is possibly English (although unmarked) (Henry 2009). C1 has yet to be cleaned.

Concretion QAR3105.000 contained several iron artifacts that can readily be identified as gun carriage hardware. The gun carriage components residing within this concretion compose what appears to be one whole side of a gun carriage minus the wooden cheek. This includes a capsquare, its forward and aft fastenings, an eye hook, a small deadeye frame, as well as a six-pound cannon ball. The width of the capsquare found within QAR3105.000 matches the trunnion widths of a six-pound gun, and was found associated with a six-pound cannon ball.

These gun carriage components exhibit traits that more closely align with English manufacture. French style capsquares have a flat, basic aft, whereas English capsquares tend to curl up and back at the aft, creating a rounded tip on which to pivot when being loosened to remove a gun (Gardiner 1992:155). This trait is apparent on the capsquare in concretion QAR3105.000. French capsquares were fastened in the aft with a staple (Boudriot 1993:323). The capsquare in QAR3105.000, however, appears to be affixed through with an eye bolt, which then would have been fastened through the entire side of the cheek and the bed of the carriage.

The guns closest to this hardware assemblage have been tentatively identified as English and Swedish. The third has tentatively been identified as Swedish, but has yet to be de-concreted. The distinct differences in carriage construction mentioned earlier suggest that the remains of the carriage found in QAR3105.000, which was almost certainly used by one of the nearby six-pound guns, stylistically and typologically appears to be of English manufacture (Gardiner 1992:155). C2 seems the most likely candidate as it is the only nearby cannon identified as English, but at present this remains speculative.

Concretion QAR3105.000 also contained a tapered iron artifact with a broadened end, shaped into a slight hook (QAR3105.008). A nearly identical artifact was discovered in concretion QAR1724.000, along with a crowbar which will be discussed below. A similar but smaller tapered bar with a hooked end was found in concretion QAR1106.000. Based on comparative examples (Bryce 1984: 43-44), it is now believed that these small tapered bars are lynch pins for the axle trees, used to hold the trucks onto the gun carriage.

Concretion QAR2565.000

Concretion QAR2465.000, found in Unit 165, is included in the same block of units containing cannon C1, C2, and C3, and concretion QAR3105.000. X-radiographs suggest that the gun carriage components contained in this concretion mirror those in QAR3105.000; a capsquare, most likely for a six-pounder, fastened in the rear with an eye bolt affixed through the aft of the capsquare. This marks the second collection of a contextual conglomerate of gun carriage components exhibiting non-French characteristics.

Concretion QAR2300.000 (C16)

The *QAR* Lab team began cleaning of cannon C16 (QAR2300.000) in summer of 2017. The first task was to remove the concreted remains of what was believed to have once been a box, edged with strips of lead and containing many cannon balls and other objects that have yet to be identified. The surface of the gun is covered with iron concretions that all have potential to be carriage-related, but no conclusions can be made until they are extracted and x-rayed. However, cleaning of the trunnion on the right-hand side of the gun revealed a capsquare in situ, resting in what would have been its original location, (Figure 3). Assessment of the surface concretion on the left-hand trunnion suggests the presence of its matching counterpart.

Artillery Implements

In discussing the *QAR* artillery assemblage so far identified, besides the cannon it is pertinent to reference the small collection of other artillery-related items found on site. These include approximately 13 lead cannon aprons recovered from the site that were investigated for the Master's thesis research by Schnitzer (2012). Other objects include wooden tompions, found in varying sizes, which would have been used to keep the bore of a cannon dry when not in use. Wood tompions removed from C19 and C21 have been identified as European pine and a species of fir respectively (Newsom 2005). Insofar as tools are concerned, only one large gun worm (QAR 2549.002) and a powder scoop (QAR 3831.000) have been identified thus far as being definitively artillery-related. Removal of prying implements from concretions, and as well as discovering their presence in artillery treatises, highlights their use maintaining and aiming QAR's artillery properly.

Crowbars

Since Henry's (2009, 2011) review of artillery and associated objects, several possible artillery-related tools have been discovered via x-ray and subsequently de-concreted. Of note with respect to gun carriages is the growing collection of iron crowbars. Two of these crowbars exhibit traits analogous to those depicted in Boudriot's Artillerie de Mer, France 1650-1850, which outlines the standard gunners tool kit. Of these tools, Boudriot exhibits multiple hand tools which were used to lift the breech of the gun using the carriage cheek crenellations, to allow the adjustment of the quoin block, or to aid in bringing the gun to the ready by prying the wheels, among other tasks (Boudriot 1992:70).

Use of crowbars or similar hand spike tools in relation to artillery has been noted in several French treatises from the period, such as Dictionnaire de Marine (Aubin 1702). Such tools are described as fanged instruments, used to bring the cannons back to the portholes and keep them there (Aubin 1702:203). L' art de Bâtir

Figure 3: Capsquare In Situ on the Trunnion of C16 (QAR2300.000)

(Mortier 1719) also describes this tool as a split and bent iron bar, used as a strong lever to return the cannon to portholes (Mortier 1719:46). Images included in these documents match the features of at least two of the crowbars in the *QAR* assemblage (QAR3443.010 and a crowbar that is only partially de-concreted in concretion QAR1955.000).

Of the seven known crowbars from the site, two (QAR3443.010 and the crowbar present in concretion QAR1955.000) can almost certainly be attributed to these functions of artillery handling. These crowbars are made entirely of wrought iron, and exhibit a widened, flat face on the end with the tines and a square profile that tapers to a rounded haft. The tines on the squared end are flat and broad as well, with the other end of the crowbar coming to a point. The crowbars also exhibit a pattern of sorts, forged into the flat face exhibited in Figure 4. The pattern can be interpreted as a chevron shape of six "V"s with a line down the center, creating a series of arrows or "crow's feet". The purpose of this surface feature is thus far unknown.

Conclusion

As the number of de-concreted artifacts recovered

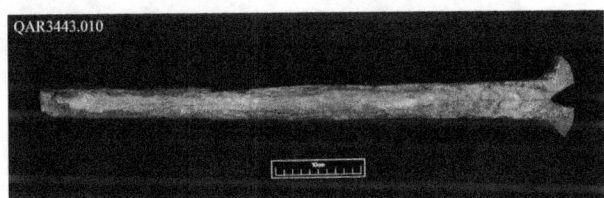

Figure 4: Crowbar (QAR3443.010) Featuring a Broad Surface with Chevron Pattern

from *Queen Anne's Revenge* increases, so too does our understanding of the QAR assemblage. This in turn changes the quantifiable amount of artifact typologies drastically, as seen in this research. The presence of capsquares and other definitive gun carriage components indicates that there are indeed remains of gun carriages present on site, undoubtedly with more yet to be found. Many of the carriages did not float away post deposition as has been theorized in the past, but rather stayed with the wreck and the guns. Although the wood has largely deteriorated, many iron components such as the capsquares, staples, eye bolts, and lynch pins have survived in concretion. Gun carriage components are often overlooked when it comes to the research of artillery, but they nevertheless play an important role in the archaeological record. This summation of known gun carriage components from Queen Anne's Revenge will continue to grow, and provide another facet of our research on this storied vessel.

References

AUBIN, NICOLAS
1702 *Dictionnaire de Marine Contenant les Termes de la Navigation et de L'architecture Navale,* Enrichi des Figures etc. Chez P. Brunel. Bibliothèque nationale d'Autriche.

BRYCE, DOUGLAS
1984 Weaponry from the *Machault*: An 18th-Century French Frigate. Studies in Archaeology Architecture and History, National Historic Parks and Sites Branch, Parks Canada, Ottawa, ON.

BOUDRIOT, JEAN, H. BERTI
1992 *L'Artillerie de Mer: Marine Francaise* 1650-1850. Ancre, Paris.

BOUDRIOT, JEAN
1993 *The History of the French Frigate: 1650-1850*, David H. Roberts, translator. Jean Boudriot Publications, England.

GARDINER, ROBERT, BRAIN LAVER.
1992 *The Line of Battle: The Sailing Warship* 1650-1840. Naval Institute Press, Annapolis, MD.

HENRY, NATHAN C.
2009 Analysis of Armament from 31CR314: *Queen Anne's Revenge* Site.In *Queen Anne's Revenge* Shipwreck Project Research and Report Bulletin Series, QAR-B-08-02, North Carolina Department of Cultural Resources, Raleigh. NC.

HENRY, NATHAN C.
2011 *Queen Anne's Revenge* Site Iron Shot Report. In *Queen Anne's Revenge* Shipwreck Project Research Report and Bulletin Series, QAR-B-11-1, North Carolina Department of Cultural Resources, Raleigh, NC.

MARTIN, COLIN J. M.
2004 An Iron Bastard Minion Drake Extraordinary by John Browne from the Pinnace Swan (1641–53). In *The International Journal of Nautical Archaeology* 33(1):79–95.

MOODY, J. D.
1952 OLD NAVAL GUN CARRIAGES. IN T*IHE MARINER'S MIRROR* 38(4):301-311.

MORTIER, DAVID
1719 L'ART DE BATIR LES VAISSEAUX, ET D'EN PERFECTIONNER LA CONSTRUCTION; DE LES GARNIR DE LEURS APPARAUX, LES METTRE EN FUNIN, LES MANOEUVRER, &c. AMSTERDAM.

NEWSOM, LEE A. AND REGIS B. MILLER
2005   Wood Species Analysis of Ship Timbers and Wooden Items Recovered from North Carolina Shipwreck Site 31CR314. Manuscript on file, North Carolina Underwater Archaeology Branch, Kure Beach, NC.

SCHNITZER, LAURA KATE
2012   Aprons of Lead: Examination of an Artifact Assemblage from the Queen Anne's Revenge Shipwreck Site. Masters Thesis, Department of History, East Carolina University, Greenville, NC.

WILDE-RAMSING, MARK U. AND CHARLES R. EWEN
2012   Beyond a Reasonable Doubt: A Case for Queen Anne's Revenge. In Historical Archaeology 46(2):110-133.

· · · · · · · · · · · · · · · ·

Stephen B. Atkinson
North Carolina Department of
Natural and Cultural Reources
Queen Anne's Revenge Conservation Laboratory
East Carolina University
1157 VOA Site C Road
Greenville, NC 27834

Conserving and Interpreting a Mechanical Jack from Blackbeard's Flagship, *Queen Anne's Revenge*

Arianna M. DiMucci

The in-progress conservation of a mechanical jack recovered from North Carolina state shipwreck site 31CR314, identified as the early 18th century shipwreck Queen Anne's Revenge, *is presented here. Designed to lift or pry apart heavy objects, the jack was likely part of the ship carpenter's tool kit and worked much like its modern hydraulic counterpart. The implementation of a successful treatment strategy is complicated by the variable condition of the iron and by numerous corrosion-filled cavities where the rack teeth once were. Innovative conservation techniques help document the conservation process and augment our current understanding of this tool.*

Introduction

With their familiar slotted racks, curved cranks, and internal gearing mechanisms concealed between thin iron plates, jacks are at once instantly recognizable and yet rarely discussed in scholarly sources. Described in mechanical and shipbuilding treatises, depicted on trade cards advertising the services and workshops of various smiths and ironmongers, and found in association with 19th century Conestoga wagons, jacks were ubiquitous tools. In addition to these historical descriptions, jacks have been found archaeologically on a variety of shipwreck sites, including North Carolina's state shipwreck site 31CR314, identified by researchers as *Queen Anne's Revenge* (Wilde-Ramsing and Ewen 2012). While their use as generic lifting devices explains their recovery from a variety of contexts, this pervasiveness is not reflected in existing published material. For instance, while comparative examples from other underwater sites including *Henrietta Marie* (c.1697-1700), the *Cabin Wreck* (1715), and Indian River county in Florida (1715) exist, very little has been written specifically on the jacks from those sites (Moore and Malcom 2008; Jeremy Vause 2017, pers. comm.).

Mechanical jacks were used for a variety of purposes by a variety of tradesmen. As generic lifting devices, these tools likely served many utilitarian purposes aboard a ship, from moving cargo to lifting the wheels of gun carriages. Two mechanical jacks have been recovered by North Carolina state archaeologists from *Queen Anne's Revenge (QAR)*. The ship was originally *La Concorde*, a French slave ship out of Nantes that was captured by Blackbeard in November of 1717 and renamed *Queen Anne's Revenge* (Wilde-Ramsing and Ewen 2012). The first jack, QAR60.000, was recovered from in between two cannons, six-pounders QAR3385.000 and QAR232.001, in 1997 (Moore and Welsh 2012). While conservation was begun it was never finished and the jack remains in wet storage. The second jack, QAR1319.000 (Figure 1), was raised from the site in 2006. Its conservation, begun by the author in 2017, is the focus of this paper and is ongoing.

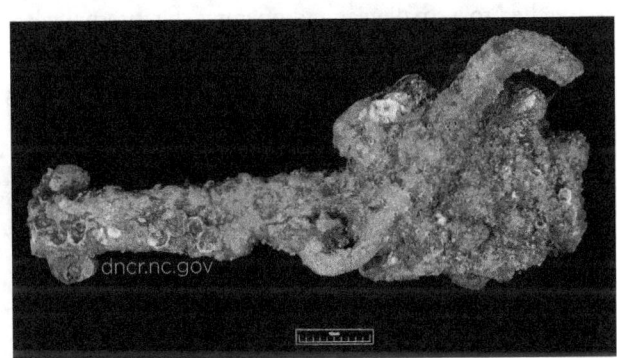

Figure 1: QAR1319.000 prior to beginning conservation. (Image by NC Department of Natural and Cultural Resources, date.)

Historical Context

Historical references to jacks are predominately found in mechanical or shipbuilding treatises. Joseph Moxon's (1703) mechanical treatise, for example, lists jacks alongside other carpentry tools used for lifting. A 1702 French dictionary of naval architecture, the *Dictionaire de Marine Contenant Les Termes De La Navigation et de L'architecture Navale*, describes a jack, or cric, as a device in which a toothed wheel, or gear, is operated by a crank to raise and lower a toothed iron bar, or rack (Aubin 1702). A revised edition of this dictionary, dated to 1736, expands on the usefulness of the device and states that jacks were used to help build and lift gun carriages and to service artillery (Mortier and Cóvens 1736). A

1719 French source on shipbuilding, *L'art de batir les vaisseaux*, reiterates that jacks, used to lift all kinds of burdens, were valuable devices to have onboard vessels (Mortier 1719). The tool was supposedly so useful in ship construction that a well-supplied workshop might have 'twenty to twenty-five jacks' (Mortier 1719:52). William Sutherland's (1729:140) treatise on shipbuilding mentions them only briefly, and he calls the tools 'hand screws.' Thomas Blanckley (1750:70), who also refers to jacks as 'hand screws,' merely notes that they were used for canting timber and lifting other heavy items.

Jacks are invariably described as compact devices made up of a vertical, toothed iron bar or rack which is raised and lowered through the rotation of gears inside a gearbox (Shumway and Frey 1968, Horsley 1978, Gawronski et al. 1992, Mercer 2000). Iron front and back plates bolted together would have housed the internal gearing mechanism (Shumway and Frey 1968). The crank, clearly visible on the jack raised from *Queen Anne's Revenge* as an S-shaped bar positioned over the gearbox, is attached to a small gear and operates the internal gearing mechanism. Turning the crank rotates the small gear which intersects with and rotates the larger gear, raising and lowering the rack. The mechanics of this internal gearing mechanism seem somewhat variable, however. Shumway and Frey (1968), for instance, place three gears in the gearbox: a small, four-toothed gear that attaches to the crank and two gears, one large and one small, that are fastened on the same shaft and intersect with the rack. Mercer (2000:53-55), in contrast, only describes two gears in the gearbox. This may be what makes the device either "single-power or double-power" (Horsley 1978:227-230). Jacks also would have had a wooden housing that extended up along the sides of the gearbox. This could have been oak (Shumway and Frey 1968) or elm (Horsley 1978) or even ash or hickory (Sloane 1964). The device also typically had a locking mechanism to hold it in a set position, the "back-stop ratchet" Mercer (2000:53-55) mentions in his description.

Where jacks are mentioned they are also typically illustrated. Joseph Moxon's mechanical treatise includes one such illustration. The *Dictionaire de Marine: Contenant les termes de la Navigation et de L'architecture Navale* includes another. Thomas Blanckley (1750:70) includes a sketch of a jack in his work as well; the words 'double' and 'single' – referring to the gearing – are written in parentheses near the illustration. Diderot illustrates the tool, including the internal gearing mechanism and intersecting rack, in the carpentry plates of his *Encyclopedia* (Gillispie 1993). He also depicts the tool in an engraving of a wheelwright's workspace. Jacks also appear on several 18th century trade cards. One of these, housed in the British museum and dated to between 1760 and 1818, belonged to William Clark, an anchor and ship smith. A jack is depicted in the lower right-hand corner of the card opposite an anchor. Another trade card, also dating to 1760, includes a jack and a mill, underneath which reads: 'Richard Hughes at the Mill, Hand-Screw, & Blue Ball in Crooked Lane, near the Monument, London, makes all sorts of Mills, Single and Double Hand Screws for Home and Foreign Trade of any Dimension.' Hughes' trade card underscores that he made these tools whereas Clark's does not specify. London directories name several other 'handscrew-makers' including a 'White Wm.,' a 'Cawthorn Geo.,' and an 'Ely J. Mill' – whose trade card is also housed in the British Museum and dates to 1770 (Kent 1803).

A jack is also listed in the Dutch East India Company's (VOC) equipment books, or Lyste, among the carpentry tools typically carried onboard VOC vessels (Gawronski et al. 1992:127). The replica of the VOC ship *Amsterdam*, on display in front of the city's National Maritime Museum, substantiates this and features a jack positioned near a cannon. Authors Gawronski, Kist, and Stokvis-van Boetzelaer additionally illustrate the tool in their lexicon though one was not found aboard the vessel they focus on, *Hollandia* (Gawronski et al. 1992).

Another valuable resource is Sellens' (2002:250) pictorial dictionary of hand tools, which includes several illustrations of jacks likely reproduced from a late-19th-century illustrated catalog of railway and machinists' tools. Finally, black and white images of a wagon jack dated '1865' and initialed 'C.B' on its rack and a 19th century 'fire engine jack' that belonged to the Union Fire Company are additional examples of the pervasiveness of these tools (Schiffer et al. 1979:120, 317).

While Shumway's and Frey's focus on Conestoga wagons and the jacks used to lift them may seem tangential to a discussion of jacks carried on ships, the lack of a comprehensive history regarding the development and use of this tool makes their research worth consulting. Most noteworthy is their assertion that "almost all [jacks] bear the date of manufacture and a small amount of ornamentation" (Shumway and Frey 1968:208). Chisel-cut dates are typically found on the rack alongside decorative, cross-hatched patterns and punch marks (Shumway and Frey 1968:210; Mercer 2000:53-55).

Comparative Examples

Comparable jacks and jack components have been recovered from a handful of underwater contexts, notably the English slave ship *Henrietta Marie* (c.1697-1700), the *Cabin Wreck* (1715), and Indian River county (1715) in Florida. However, little research on these pieces has been completed or made widely accessible. The jack from *Henrietta Marie*, for instance, is only mentioned in passing as having been recovered during field investigations of the site (Moore and Malcom 2008). The jacks and jack pieces associated with the *Cabin Wreck* (8IR23) include one complete jack recovered in 1974, another in 1979, and one partial jack that is in pieces as the gearbox did not survive (Jeremy Vause 2017, pers. comm.). The jack recovered from Indian River county – an area full of 1715 material, and which contains the *Corrigans, Cabin, Rio Mar,* and *Green Cabin* wrecks – includes a gearbox with three gears, supposedly for more lifting power, and rack; most of the crank and all wooden components are gone (Jeremy Vause 2017, pers. comm.). This jack was disassembled, conserved, and reassembled (Jeremy Vause 2017, pers. comm.). Such comparative examples have been invaluable as the conservation of QAR1319.000 has progressed since few published illustrations show precisely what the gearing mechanism looks like.

One of the best comparative collections of antique mechanical jacks is held by the Maison de l'Outil et de la Pensée Ouvrière in Troyes, France. The museum has seven jacks on display, which are thought to have been used in quarry work and stone carving (Agathe Colombié 2017, pers. comm). Several of these have a variety of markings on them, including decorative diamond patterns, what appear to be initials, and even dates. One of these bears the date 1779 (Agathe Colombié 2017, pers. comm). Another, with three fleurs-de-lis on the rack, has a date of 1785 (Agathe Colombié 2017, pers. comm). While these date to more than sixty years after the sinking of *Queen Anne's Revenge*, it is worth noting how similar they are to the two jacks recovered from the shipwreck site.

Conserving a Mechanical Jack

All artifacts recovered from the shipwreck site are taken to the North Carolina Department of Natural and Cultural Resources' (DNCR), *Queen Anne's Revenge* Conservation Laboratory (*QAR* Lab) for conservation, documentation, and investigation. As the entity charged with the conservation of materials from *Queen Anne's Revenge*, the *QAR* Lab has developed a set of tools and methods for the preservation of the more than 400,000 artifacts so far recovered from excavation of the shipwreck site since its discovery more than two decades ago. Prior to beginning conservation, x-radiographs are taken of concretions at the *QAR* Lab to determine what might be inside the layers of corrosion and marine deposits. These concretions are then kept in wet storage, in 2.5% sodium carbonate, until conservation can begin.

X-radiographs of QAR1319.000 (Figure 2) revealed

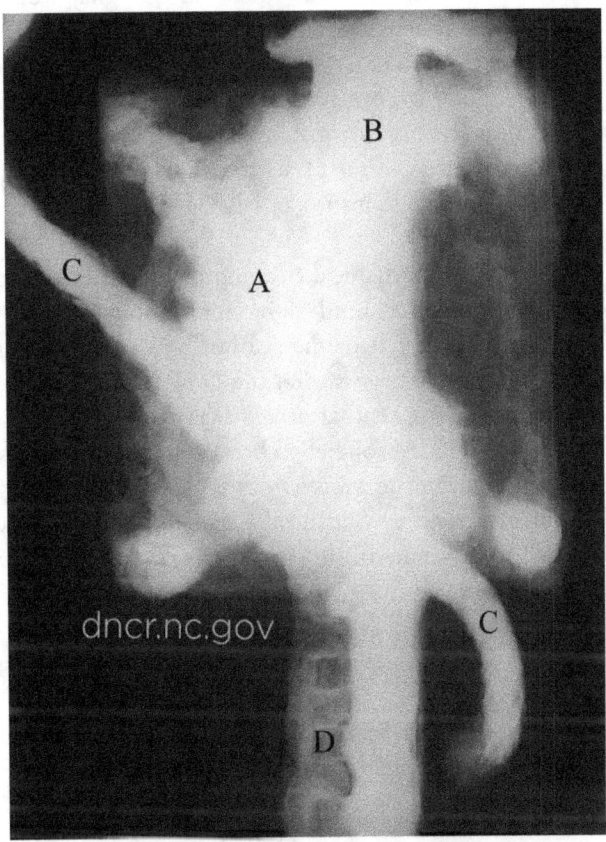

Figure 2: X-radiograph image of the jack, including the internal gearing mechanism (a), interior section of the rack (b), the crank (c) (positioned over the front plate), and the exposed rack teeth (d). (Image by NC Department of Natural and Cultural Resources, date.)

some of the components and their condition, including a large, geared wheel, slotted rack, and well-preserved, S-shaped metal crank. The iron plates that conceal the internal mechanism are very faint, almost invisible in x-ray. Concretion along both plates and along the sides (where fragments of the wooden housing have been discovered) has obscured the interior components of the jack. This has limited the usefulness of the radiographs as a guide during the concretion breakdown process and made it necessary to repeatedly x-ray the device as work on the jack has progressed.

It was initially hoped that the gearbox could be disassembled to thoroughly de-concrete the interior components of the jack (DiMucci 2017). Surface cleaning of the exterior front plate using an air scribe, however, revealed fasteners attaching the two plates together that could damage the plates if the fasteners were drilled out to facilitate disassembly. Careful cleaning of the front plate also revealed the largely intact, wrought-iron crank. The crank intersects the small gear that would have moved when the crank was turned and which worked in conjunction with the larger gear to drive the movement of the toothed rack. Small wooden fragments found near the back of the rack and along the sides of the gearbox attest to the presence of a wooden housing; unfortunately, these insubstantial fragments are all that remain.

During the mechanical cleaning of the gearbox and crank, voids were found along the back of the rack where it extends out of the gearbox and in the center of the crank. Casting, used at the *QAR* Lab to preserve the shape of artifacts that have otherwise disintegrated, was done alongside concretion breakdown, with the jack kept wet during the process. Voids were cleaned using dental picks and a windshield wiper blade, repeatedly flushed with water, and then irrigated with acetone to allow the void to dry sufficiently for casting. Hysol RE 2039 (resin) mixed with 30% Hysol HD 3561 (hardener) by weight was then poured in and allowed to set, typically overnight.

The concretion breakdown process of the jack has necessitated the development of multiple treatment alternatives. As the conservation of the jack has progressed it has become increasingly apparent that the fasteners in each corner of the iron plates are quite fragile. Initially it appeared that they were in good condition on the front plate (where the crank is located) and worsened partway through, almost to the point of complete deterioration by the time they reached the rear plate. Multiple solutions were considered, from cleaning out what little remained of each fastener and casting them, to encasing the extant iron in epoxy, to possibly reconstructing them in the future. In the end, a more variable approach has become necessary. The two fasteners nearest the exposed rack could be carefully de-concreted, while the other two have required casting. One of these could only be cast with the jack 'upside-down,' in other words positioned directly on its crank. Since this could damage the crank, a wood two-by-four support to distribute the weight of the tool along the front plate had to be temporarily built to avoid placing any of the weight of the device on such a diagnostic feature. This was done while keeping the entire jack wet as the epoxy set.

Additional concretion removal has revealed another challenge: while the rack teeth inside the gearbox plates are still present (Figure 3), those exposed are voids and need to be cast. Two of the missing rack teeth have been found so far; these voids have been cleaned out and cast. Casting will continue as more of the teeth are found.

From one end of the rack to the other, QAR1319.000 measures approximately 30.5 in. (77.47 cm) in length. This is an approximation as one end of the rack is currently still concreted (Figure 4). The rack is approximately 2.5 in. (6.35 cm) wide and about 1.0 in. (2.54 cm) thick. The number of rack teeth have been

Figure 3: Close-up of the jack gearbox. (Image by NC Department of Natural and Cultural Resources, date.)

Figure 4: In-progress conservation of QAR1319.000 with de-concreted gearbox and crank and partially exposed rack. (Image by NC Department of Natural and Cultural Resources, date.)

estimated at 16; there are likely six teeth preserved in the gearbox (the large gear and crank obscure the rack teeth in x-radiographs, making it difficult to obtain an accurate count) with up to 10 teeth in the exposed rack. As conservation progresses this estimate can be reevaluated. The gearbox measures 9.0 in. (22.86 cm) in length and 8.5 in. (21.59 cm) in width, with a height of 3.5 in. (8.89 cm). The plates are thin and vary between 0.25 in. (0.63 cm) and 0.38 in. (0.96 cm) thick. The large gear wheel, with the rack on one side and the crank on the other, is similarly obscured in x-radiographs. Only six gear teeth are clearly visible in x-ray. However, these six teeth are in a 135° arc. Dividing the 360° in a circle by the visible 135° arc and multiplying this by the six visible teeth provides an estimate of 16 teeth for the geared wheel.

Documentation: 3D-Modeling

Documentation practices at the *QAR* Lab routinely employ radiography and digital photography prior to and during treatment, but in the case of this tool photogrammetry was used to create three-dimensional models during the conservation process. Pretreatment images with photogrammetry targets at set positions around the artifact were taken to generate a model using Agisoft Photoscan, with a second model created several months later. This process will be repeated once QAR1319.000 is completely de-concreted to have a 'final' model of the jack. In addition to tracking concretion breakdown, the photogrammetry models provide a detailed, rotatable and manipulatable model that helps augment current understanding of the jack.

Future Conservation and Research

The conservation of the jack from *Queen Anne's Revenge* has been a multi-year project and it remains a work-in-progress as of January 2018. A fair amount of concretion removal remains to be done around the gearbox mechanism and along the rack. Only two of the rack teeth have been cast to date – the others will hopefully be cast in the next few months. Once thoroughly cleaned of concretion the jack will go into electrolytic reduction to expedite the desalination process. It will then need to dry and receive protective coatings before it can eventually be displayed at the NC Maritime Museum in Beaufort, NC.

The condition of the gearing mechanism and its complexity has been a focus from the beginning, however this was initially out of a conservation concern. Whether the gearbox could be or needed to be taken apart, whether the rack teeth were accessible from either side if disassembling the jack wasn't an option – these were all important considerations for successfully de-concreting, and eventually desalinating, the device. As the interior becomes more and more visible, however, it is becoming apparent that the large gear is not positioned directly in line with the rack. Instead, it is almost flush with the interior of the front plate whereas the rack is equidistant between the plates. This raises questions regarding how jacks were constructed. While available shipbuilding and mechanical treatises, illustrations, and comparative examples have all helped inform the concretion breakdown process, it is worth noting that none of these tell researchers how the jack was put together. The presence of rack guides, to keep the rack in place as it moved up and down, is also not discussed in the literature despite it being a key component of the functionality of the tool. Comparative examples at the Maison de l'Outil et de la Pensée Ouvrière in Troyes, France, have also not been exhaustively studied. The museum has seven jacks in their collection, at least two of which are from the 18th century. It would be remiss to not examine these thoroughly. Finally, there are a number of concretions found in the same five-by-five-foot grid square that the jack was recovered from that have not yet been broken down. Conserving these, along with reevaluating the jack recovered in 1997 and which has since been placed back into wet storage, may reveal more clues about who used the device or what it was used for.

Concluding Thoughts

As discussed throughout this paper, jacks were generic lifting devices utilized by a variety of tradesmen. They may have helped in "raising heavy mast parts," been used to service the artillery onboard the ship, or even assisted with moving cargo (Horsley 1978). Despite references in a variety of sources from naval dictionaries to VOC equipment records, there remain many unanswered questions concerning the origins of this tool and how they were constructed. The jack discussed here, QAR1319.000, is still in the process of being conserved and will need several more years before it can be displayed. Its conservation and research, which has focused on contextualizing the day-to-day operations of the tool and its role in shipboard life, needs to be expanded to include the wider context of other tools so far recovered from *Queen Anne's Revenge*, ultimately augmenting our understanding of this shipwreck.

Acknowledgments

I would like to thank all *QAR* Project staff, especially my colleagues at the *QAR* Lab, all of whom have contributed significant time and effort to the preservation of these artifacts, along with staff at the North Carolina Maritime Museum and the North Carolina Office of State Archaeology. I would also like to thank Agathe Colombié, communications officer at the Maison de l'Outil et de la Pensée Ouvrière, for images of the jacks in the museum's collection, and Jessica Stika, head conservator at the Florida Bureau of Archaeological Research, and Jeremy Vause, collections technician at the Florida Bureau of Archaeological Research, for providing information on the jacks and jack components from the *Cabin Wreck* and Indian River County.

References

AUBIN, NICOLAS
1702   *Dictionaire de Marine Contenant Les Termes De La Navigation et de L'architecture Navale.* Pierre Brunel, Amsterdam, NLD.

BLANCKLEY, THOMAS R.
1750   *A Naval Expositor, Shewing and Explaining the Words and Terms of Art Belonging to the Parts, Qualities, and Proportions of Building, Rigging, Furnishing, & Fitting a Ship for Sea.* E. Owen, London, UK.

DIMUCCI, ARIANNA
2017   Conserving and Interpreting the Mechanical Jacks from Blackbeard's Flagship, *Queen Anne's Revenge* (1718). Poster presentation at the 45th American Institute for Conservation Conference, Chicago, Ill.

GAWRONSKI, JERZY, BAS KIST, AND ODILIA STOKVIS-VAN BOETZELAER
1992   *Hollandia Compendium: A Contribution to the History, Archaeology, Classification and Lexicography of a 150 ft. Dutch East Indiaman (1740-1750).* Elsevier, Amsterdam, NLD.

GILLISPIE, CHARLES C. (EDITOR)
1993   *A Diderot Pictorial Encyclopedia of Trades and Industry: Manufacturing and the Technical Arts in Plates Selected from "L'Encyclopédia, ou Dictionnaire Raisonné des Sciences, des Arts et des Métiers" of Denis Diderot. Volume Two.* Dover Publications, Inc., New York, NY.

HORSLEY, JOHN E.
1978   *Tools of the Maritime Trades.* David & Charles, Newton Abbot, UK.

KENT, HENRY
1803   *Kent's Directory for 1803. Being An Alphabetical List of the Names and Places of Abode of the Directors of the Merchants And Traders of London, And Parts Adjacent Other Eminent Traders in the Cities of London and Westminster, And Borough of Southwark.* H. Kent, London, UK.

MERCER, HENRY C.
2000   *Ancient Carpenters' Tools: Illustrated and Explained, Together with the Implements of the Lumberman, Joiner, and Cabinet-Maker in Use in the Eighteenth Century.* Dover Publications, Inc., Mineola, NY.

MOORE, DAVE AND COREY MALCOM
2008   Seventeenth-Century Vehicle of the Middle Passage: Archaeological and Historical Investigations on the *"Henrietta Marie"*. In *International Journal of Historical Archaeology,* 12(1):20-38.

MOORE, DAVID AND WENDY WELSH
2012   Preliminary Report Relating to Hand-Screws or Mechanical Jacks Recovered from *Queen Anne's Revenge.* Manuscript, NCDNCR QAR Lab, Greenville, NC.

MORTIER, CORNEILLE AND JEAN CÓVENS.
1736   *Dictionnaire de Marine: Contenant les termes de la navigation et de l'architecture navale avec les régles [et] proportions qui doivent y être observées : ouvrage enrichi de figures.* Second Edition. Jean Cóvens and Corneille Mortier, Amsterdam, NLD.

MORTIER, DAVID
1719   *L'Art de Batir les Vaisseaux, et d'en Perfectionner la Construction; de les Garnir de Leurs Apparaux, les Mettre en Funin, les Manoeuvrer, &c.* Amsterdam.

MOXON, JOSEPH
1703   *Mechanick Exercises: or, The Doctrine of Handy-Works.* 3rd Edition. London, UK.

SCHIFFER, HERBERT, PETER SCHIFFER, AND NANCY SCHIFFER
1979   *Antique Iron: Survey of American and English Forms, Fifteenth through Nineteenth Centuries.* Schiffer Publishing Ltd., Atglen, PA.

SELLENS, ALVIN
2002   *Dictionary of American Hand Tools: A Pictorial Synopsis.* Schiffer Publishing Ltd., Atglen, PA.

SHUMWAY, GEORGE AND HOWARD C. FREY
1968   *Conestoga Wagon 1750-1850: Freight Carrier for 100 Years of America's Westward Expansion.* Third Edition. York, PA: George Shumway, Publisher.

SLOANE, ERIC
1964   *A Museum of Early American Tools.* Wilfred Funk, Inc., New York, NY.

SUTHERLAND, WILLIAM
1729   *Britain's glory: or, Ship-building unvail'd. Being a general director, for building and compleating the said machines.* Second Edition.

WILDE-RAMSING, MARK U. AND CHARLES R. EWEN
2012   *Beyond a Reasonable Doubt: A Case for Queen Anne's Revenge.* Historical Archaeology 46(2):110-133.

. . . .

Arianna M. DiMucci
North Carolina Department of Natural
and Cultural Resources
Queen Anne's Revenge Conservation Laboratory
East Carolina University
1157 VOA Site C Road
Greenville, NC 27834

On the Verge: The Pocket Watch from *Queen Anne's Revenge*

Karen E. Martindale

Since the development of the verge escapement in the 13th century, mechanical timekeepers steadily became more accurate and portable. The late 17th century marks a point in the evolution of pocket watches from unique ornaments for the wealthy to accurate tools for broader use. It is not uncommon to find documentation of pocket watches on ships during the 17th and 18th centuries, but few have survived in the archaeological record. Several artifacts from North Carolina state shipwreck site 31CR314, Queen Anne's Revenge, have been identified as components of a verge fusée pocket watch, each providing more information about its manufacture.

Introduction

Full excavation of North Carolina state shipwreck site 31CR314, identified as Blackbeard's flagship *Queen Anne's Revenge*, began in 2006 under the direction of North Carolina's Office of State Archaeology (OSA) within the North Carolina Department of Natural and Cultural Resources (NCDNCR) (Wilde-Ramsing and Ewen 2012). All recovered artifacts, normally in the form of conglomerates of sediment and artifacts called concretions, are sent to OSA's *Queen Anne's Revenge* Conservation Laboratory (*QAR* Lab) for conservation and documentation. Given the turbulent nature of the site, it may be surprising to discover that many small artifacts have been recovered, including glass beads, sewing pins, and even pocket watch components.

Although it is not uncommon to find mention of pocket watches in documents such as mariners' probate records (Earle 1998:58–59), it is rare to find pocket watches in archaeological sites dating prior to 1800. Intact pocket watches have been found on the following waterlogged sites: one from the site of *Swan* in the Sound of Mull, Scotland, dating between 1646 and 1653 (Troalen et al. 2010); one from the Thames foreshore at the site of Custom House quay in London, England, dating between 1670 and 1675 (Meehan et al. 1996); three from the site of *Kronan*, which sank in the Battle of Öland in 1676 (Lars Einarsson 2018, pers. comm.); one from the section of Port Royal, Jamaica sunken by an earthquake in 1692, stamped with the date 1686 (Link 1960:157,173,178–181); and one from the site of HMS *Pandora*, stamped with the date 1786 (Queensland Museum 2010:8). In addition, pocket watch components have been found on the site of *La Belle* in Texas, which wrecked in 1686 (Waselkov et al. 2017:661–662), and on the site of *L'Auguste* in Ottawa, which wrecked in 1761 (Environment Canada 1992:44).

Like the pieces from *L'Auguste* and *La Belle*, the pocket watch from *Queen Anne's Revenge* is not intact. As of February 2018, five components from four concretions originating from the section of the site identified as the stern have been identified by the author.

Queen Anne's Revenge ran aground in June 1718. Given this date, if researchers had been searching for a pocket watch or pocket watch components among the artifacts, there are certain features they would have expected to find: a round case made of gold, silver, or brass; brass inner workings such as the fusée, gears, or the crown wheel; and a circular balance cock table with a pierced design set inside a solid border and a D-shaped foot. The components discussed here belong to a watch that predates the wrecking event by several decades.

Balance Cock

The first piece identified as a pocket watch component by the author was QAR1263.019 (Figure 1a), the table of a balance cock. According to analysis by a Bruker Tracer III-SD X-Ray Fluorescence (XRF) spectrometer, this small, delicate component is composed of gilt brass, with trace amounts of mercury, tin, lead, and silver. The balance cock from *Queen Anne's Revenge*, though broken—it is missing part of the table, and the part of the balance cock called the foot—is noticeably oblong in shape, not circular, and there is no border around the symmetrical floral design.

Even though it is not fully intact, the balance cock is one of the most diagnostic features of an early pocket watch, and the distinct features of QAR1263.019 allowed for an approximate identification of the style and period of the pocket watch movement. "Based on the shape of the cock, the open piercing, the lack of border, and the symmetrical design" the balance cock most likely belongs to a pre-balance spring verge fusée pocket watch made between 1660 and 1675 (Laura Turner 2017, pers.

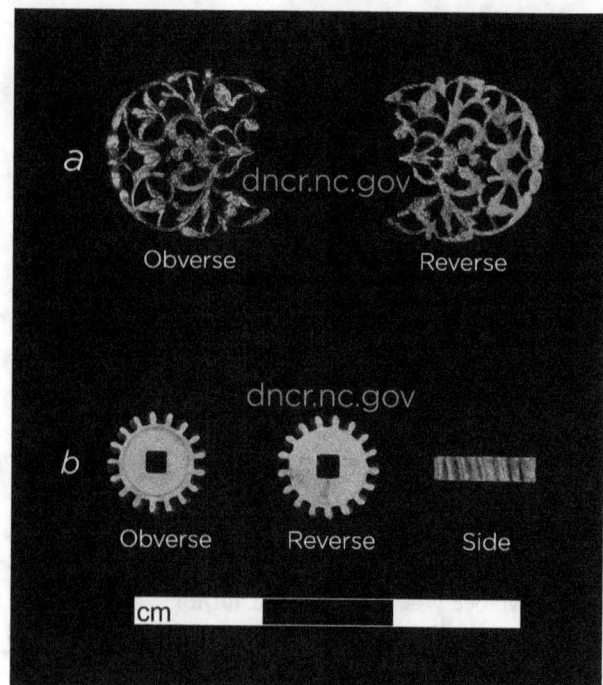

Figure 1: Movement components. QAR1263.019 (a) is the balance cock table. QAR1210.009 (b) is the balance arbor setup wheel (NC Department of Natural and Cultural Resources).

comm.). Such an early date is surprising for the site, but not for pocket watch ownership, as they could be kept in a family for decades. Lost and found columns from the 17th and 18th centuries often describe lost pocket watches with features in use a century prior, or as simply "very old" or "very large and old" (Jagger 1988:38). As with many artistic and technological developments, this date range is not absolute. Floral designs in the symmetrical style of QAR1263.019 became popular in the mid-17th century (*The American Jeweler* 1907: 378,380). The balance spring, developed by Christiaan Huygens and Robert Hooke, was first used in a pocket watch in London in 1675, though several years may have passed until the new technology was found in all new pocket watches throughout Europe (Baillie 1929:160–162; Cuss 1971:31–32; Cardinal 1985: 78–79). The development of the balance spring lead to the change in shape of the balance cock from an oval to a circle to protect the delicate component (Baillie 1929:360–361; Cardinal 1985:167; Cuss 1996:14).

The movement—the inner workings—of a verge fusée pocket watch (Figure 2) combines three important technologies: the verge and crown wheel escapement (Figure 2c), the mainspring (Figure 2a), and the fusée (Figure 2b).

The verge and crown wheel escapement is comprised of the verge—a stick, or arbor, with two angled pallets—and the crown wheel—a wheel with an odd number of sawtooth-shaped teeth that interact with the pallets. It allowed for the first fully mechanical clocks to be built, and was in use from the 13th century and not fully superseded until the mid-19th century (Cuss 1971:20; Cardinal 1985:70). The mainspring mechanism is comprised of the mainspring—a coiled ribbon of metal—which sits inside the mainspring barrel. The development of the mainspring in the 15th century allowed for clocks to be made portable, relying on the tension from the coiled mainspring rather than weights to drive the gears (Cardinal 1985:13; Cuss 1996:11). The fusée is a tiered, cone-shaped pulley attached to a cord made of animal gut or a metal chain, and serves to equalize the force of the mainspring and prevent the watch from slowing as the mainspring unwinds. Though it existed prior to its use in clocks, it is first described in relation to clocks in the late 15th century (Cardinal 1985:15). By the early 16th century, portable clocks became small enough that

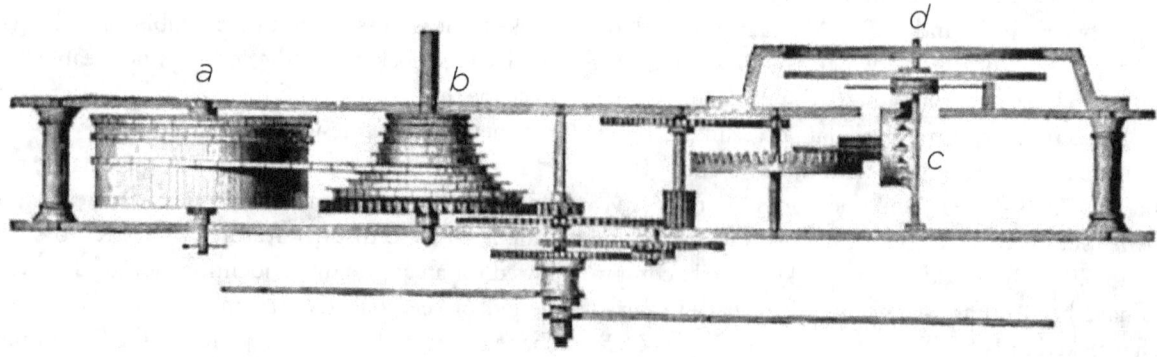

Figure 2: The verge fusée movement, featuring (a) the mainspring, (b) the fusée, (c) the verge and crown wheel, and (d) the location of the balance cock table (Benjamin 1891:903).

they became what people today would consider watches: timekeeping devices that can be carried around on one's person.

Movement mechanics are described in detail by several well-respected horologists (Thiout 1741:321–327; Baillie 1929:74–89; Cardinal 1985:69–75). When a watch is wound, the key winds the arbor of the fusée, unwinding the fusée chain from the mainspring barrel and winding it around the fusée. This chain is attached to the mainspring barrel by a hook, so that as the fusée is wound, the mainspring barrel turns, and the mainspring inside the barrel coils. When the watch key is removed, the mainspring begins to uncoil, causing the mainspring barrel to turn. The turning action of the mainspring barrel unwinds the fusée chain from the top of the fusée to the wider base, winding the fusée chain back around the mainspring barrel. This energy is transferred through a series of gears from the base of the fusée to the crown wheel. Because of the orientation of the verge's pallets to the teeth of the crown wheel, the crown wheel—and thus the entire movement, beginning with the mainspring—is only able to advance in set increments, visible in the regulated movements of the watch hands. The hole in the central flower of QAR1263.019 would have had a plug in which the top of the balance arbor—the verge—was supported, so that the balance cock table (Figure 2d) acts as a pivot point for the verge.

Balance Arbor Setup Wheel

In addition to the balance cock, one other movement component has been identified. QAR1210.009 (Figure 1b) is a small gear with a square central hole, an impressed circle on one surface, and 17 teeth. The teeth are slightly askew, but given that they are uniformly angled, and the lack of evident damage, it was most likely manufactured this way. According to XRF analysis, the gear is brass, with traces of lead and tin. It has been identified as a balance arbor setup wheel, also known as a regulator, a type of worm gear that has been used in fusée watches from about 1630 to put a small amount of initial wind, or setup, on the mainspring, which was then fully wound by turning the fusée arbor (Baillie 1929:87; Cuss 1971:21; Laura Turner 2017, pers. comm.). It would have been attached to the mainspring arbor and wound or unwound using a tangent screw; a numbered disk, commonly made of blued steel, was sometimes mounted on these worm gears to use as a guide (Baillie 1929:87). By the end of the 17th century, regulators of this type had largely been phased out of watch movements (Baillie 1929:167–169, 361).

Watch Case

The last group of artifacts, though found in concretions several feet apart, together comprise what is believed to be the outer watch case. X-radiographic images of concretions QAR1466.000 (Figure 3a) and QAR1794.000 (Figure 3b–c) show that each of the possible case halves is composed of three concentric, tiered rings that were initially believed to be composed of copper or iron. In addition to the rings, the X ray of QAR1466.000 shows what appears to be a watch chain with a hook. If any organic materials such as leather or tortoiseshell were present, they would not have been visible in an X ray.

Information gleaned by studying the balance cock (QAR1263.019) and balance arbor setup wheel (QAR1210.009) may not be applicable to the watch case, as cases were often manufactured separately from the movement and a case or movement could be replaced independently as fashions changed and technology improved (Cardinal 1985:35–36; Jagger 1988:14). What is certain is that the case would have been made prior to June 1718. Although specific styles of decoration—including engraving, piercing, repoussé, enamel painting, and piqué—are numerous in the century leading up to 1718, the materials used are much more limited (Cardinal 1985:111–155; Cuss 1996:55–109). Cases of gold, silver, or brass, which was normally gilt, make up a large part of the 17th and 18th century watch

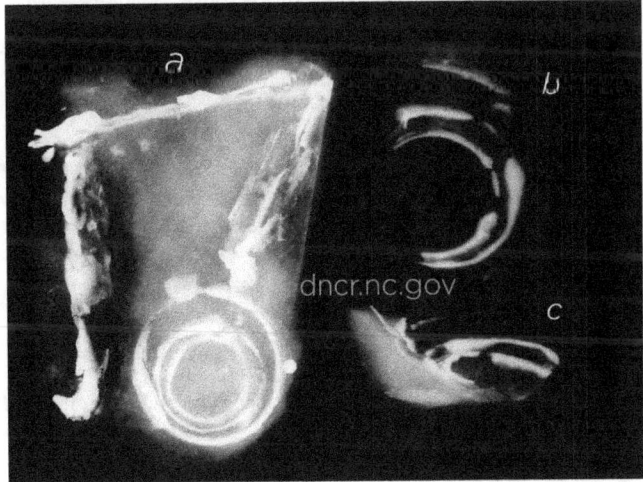

Figure 3: X-radiographic images of (a) QAR1466.000 and (b) QAR1794.000 from the top and (c) QAR1794.000 from the side (NC Department of Natural and Cultural Resources).

cases that are described in historic inventories and lost and found advertisements, and found in existing collections (Cardinal 1985:111–155; Jagger 1988:74–82); the author has only found one example of an iron case, dated 1665 (Cuss 1996:74), and one mention of an iron case from a 16th century inventory (Cardinal 1985:16), though more instances of iron cases might be expected since the earliest clock and watch makers were locksmiths and blacksmiths (Baillie 1929:69,80,238; Cuss 1996:11). Non-metal materials used included leather, shagreen, tortoiseshell, horn, stone, and rock crystal, with decorations or practical components made of gold, silver, or brass (Cuss 1971:39; Cardinal 1985:111–155; Cuss 1996:15–16).

The rings from QAR1794.000, which had broken prior to treatment, were too degraded to draw additional conclusions. As concretion was removed from the rings in QAR1466.000, the presence of thin sections of the rings extending up to the next tier revealed that these rings were not originally made as separate pieces, but rather they represent the thickest parts of a single dome, and the thinnest sections have corroded away over time (Figure 4). Impressions in the concretions left by the original, degraded artifacts corroborate this theory.

The rings are circular in shape, and the impressions left in the concretion by the original artifacts do not show any obvious decoration. A certain style of watch, known as the Puritan watch, was very popular in England in the mid-17th century; the cases were almost exclusively silver, smooth, and without decoration (Cardinal 1985:127–128; Cuss 1996:18). Watch cases covered in organics such as hardened leather or shagreen would often be attached to a plain metal support—usually gold or silver—with gold or silver pins in a style of decoration called piqué (Baillie 1929:152–153; Jagger 1988:49; Cuss 1996:15, 21, 318).

No organic material was found in QAR1466.000 or QAR1794.000, indicating that either the material degraded before concretion formed over it, or that the two halves of the case were composed of metal only. Despite expectations, according to XRF analysis the rings are composed not of copper or iron, but primarily of lead and tin— most likely a pewter alloy with a high lead content. The chain is composed of the same material as the rings, except for the iron hook.

At the time of publication, the author has found no other mention or examples of a pewter watch case, or a corresponding pewter chain. While it is possible that these pewter artifacts are associated with another instrument aboard the ship, or a personal item such as a locket, the possibility of a pewter watch case cannot be excluded. More unlikely materials, such as amber, glass, porcelain, and puddingstone, have been made into watch cases (Baillie 1929:151–152; Jagger 1988:110–114).

Explanations for the existence of a pewter watch case can be grouped into three categories: that the use of pewter was a short-lived experiment in case materials, perhaps by a provincial watchmaker (including any who may have emigrated to colonies) with no association with an horological guild; that the original case was separated from the movement and pewter, being a very versatile material, was simply the easiest material to use for a replacement case; or that the pewter case was made or commissioned to imitate a silver case. Though the first two explanations are alluded to, the third is the focus of this discussion.

Pocket watches were produced throughout Europe in the 17th and 18th centuries, but the examples here focus on France and England, the most prominent watchmaking centers of the period (Cardinal 1985:27–44). In both countries, civil unrest affected the watchmaking industry. For example, it may be that a shortage of silver bullion and the diminishing finances of the aristocracy leading up to the English Civil War lead to the rise of smooth, undecorated Puritan cases and other simple designs found in England during the mid-17th century (Cardinal 1985:127–128; Priestly 2000:3). The end of King Louis XIV's reign in 1715 was marked by decades of emigration by Huguenots—many wealthy artisans, including watchmakers, goldsmiths, and jewelers, among them—the disastrous War of Spanish Succession, and famine, all leading to the ruin of the treasury (Cardinal 1985:38–41). Sumptuary laws halted production of

Figure 4: Partially exposed "rings" from QAR1466.000 (NC Department of Natural and Cultural Resources).

luxury goods such that, by 1720, French watchmakers could not even assemble a watch without importing parts from London or Geneva (Cardinal 1985:38–41). In this socioeconomic climate, a pewter watchcase may have been deemed acceptable in the short term, or could have been used as a passable imitation of silver for a once-wealthy aristocrat keeping up appearances.

Imitations of precious metals were not unheard of at the time. Priestly (2000:3) posits that a method of making a case from a "fire-gilded…brass alloy covered with a variety of cheaper materials, rather than using precious gold or silver" may have been developed to avoid registering a mark at the highly regulated Goldsmith's Hall. Other cheap, copper-based gold substitutes include tombac, Prince Rupert's metal, and pinchbeck (Baillie 1929:257; Jagger 1988:76–77). Some watch case makers simply found the standards for gold and silver inadequate for everyday use and would avoid sending their "substandard" gold and silver works to the assay office (Priestley 2000:47).

These imitations were not up to the standards of the clock and watchmaker's guilds that controlled the trade in wealthy towns such as London and Paris. The Worshipful Company of Clockmakers, upon viewing a watch by John Wyeth, banned the use of "spelter metal" in 1656, "considering it deceitful 'being in Imitation of Gould'" (Loomes 1981: 23–24; Priestley 2000:1–2). Membership and quality of workmanship of both the Company of Clockmakers in London and the Corporation of Horologers of Paris was highly regulated, and within their chartered territory, they sought to destroy or confiscate any work not up to their standards (Cardinal 1985:19–22,27–30,35–37; Loomes 1981:23–24; Priestley 2000:37).

The guilds controlled the production of watches in their chartered territories—within ten miles of London for the Worshipful Company of Clockmakers—but would not have had such control outside their limits, even within their own countries, so unassociated watchmakers who were not required to follow such stringent regulations could conceivably ply their trade outside a guild's territory, though not necessarily without harassment (Cuss 1971:13, Loomes 1981:20; Cardinal 1985:28; Priestley 2000:1). On a larger scale, the guilds lacked the power to regulate the international import or export of watches outside their territories, the quality of which varied. By the early 18th century, French and Genevan makers were forging London makers' names, or using "fictitious, English-sounding names," on their poor-quality watches (Cuss 1971:40–41). A 1719 article complains that many English watchmakers, "sheltered by the reputation the English have so rightly acquired," exported only their "Waste Goods," which in turn were copied in Geneva, Germany, and Holland, flooding the market with bad watches (Cardinal 1985:41). In the mid- to late-18th century, these became known as "Dutch forgeries," since much of this work was marketed through Amsterdam (Cuss 1971:41).

Conclusions

Although the pocket watch components found so far have revealed an astonishing amount of information, several questions remain. Who owned this pocket watch? When did it board the ship? When, and how, did it break?

The only way to answer these questions is to find more components. Any iron or steel parts—screws, hands, springs, and the fusée chain—would not have survived, but anything made of brass, silver, or gold—the fusée, gears, and potence and pillar plates—have a much better chance of survival. Any component found has the potential to reveal how the watch broke, whether it was purposefully taken apart, violently shattered when *Queen Anne's Revenge* ran aground, or slowly corroded and drifted apart in the current.

Four pocket watch parts are particularly diagnostic: the balance cock, the watch case, the dial, and the potence plate. Watch cases, especially gold and silver cases, were commonly stamped with a maker's mark and, less commonly, hallmarks, neither of which are present on the surviving pieces from QAR1794.000 and QAR1466.000 (Jagger 1988:75–76; Priestley 2000:3, 5–7,46). Until a more likely candidate has been found, it is assumed that these artifacts compose the two halves of the watch case. Dials could be plain or highly decorated with techniques such as enamel or repoussé, and the style could be used to determine a terminus post quem for the watch movement; the most dramatic and lasting change in dial appearance was the addition of minutes shortly after the development of the balance spring (Baillie 1929:199,201; Cuss 1996:37–38). By far, the most diagnostic feature of a verge fusée pocket watch is the potence plate, opposite the pillar plate and dial, where makers would engrave their name and often their location and the year. Any of this information would prove invaluable in finding the original owner of the watch, and discovering how it came to be on *Queen Anne's Revenge*.

Acknowledgements

I would like to thank all *QAR* Project staff from the *QAR* Lab, the North Carolina Maritime Museum, and the North Carolina Office of State Archaeology. I would also like to thank Dr. Linda Carnes-Mcnaughton for her help in reviewing the *QAR* collection for artifacts that could be associated with the pocket watch, and Laura Turner, Curator of Horological Collections at the British Museum, for her help in identifying the artifacts and suggesting sources to continue my own research.

References

THE AMERICAN JEWELER
1907   *Determining the Age of Antique Watches*. American Jeweler 27(8):375–382. Chicago, IL.

BAILLIE, G.H.
1929   *Watches: their history, decoration, and mechanism*. Reprinted 1979 by T & A Constable, Edinburgh, Scotland.

BENJAMIN, PARK
1891   *Appleton's Cyclopaedia of Applied Mechanics Vol 2*. D. Appleton and Company, New York, NY.

CARDINAL, CATHERINE
1985   *The Watch from its Origins to the XIXth Century*. Tabard Press, New York, NY.

CUSS, T.P. CAMERER
1971   *Early Watches*. The Hamlyn Publishing Group, Hong Kong.

1996   *The Camerer Cuss Book of Antique Watches. Expanded and revised from 1976 edition*. Antique Collectors' Club, Woodbridge, UK.

EARLE, PETER
1998   *Sailors: English Merchant Seamen 1650–1775*. Reprinted 2007 by Methuen Publishing, London, UK.

ENVIRONMENT CANADA
1992   *The Wreck of the Auguste*. National Historic Sites, Parks Service, Environment Canada, Ottowa, Canada.

JAGGER, CEDRIC
1988   *The Artistry of the English Watch*. Charles E. Tuttle Company, Rutland, VT.

LINK, MARION CLAYTON
1960   Exploring the Drowned City of Port Royal. In *National Geographic* 117(2):151–182.

LOOMES, BRIAN
1981   *The Early Clockmakers of Great Britain*. N.A.G. Press, London, UK.

MEEHAN, PETER, PAUL BUCK, AND LORNA LEE
1996   The Investigation and Conservation of a 17th Century Watch Retrieved from the River Thames. In *The Conservator* 20(1):45–52.

PRIESTLEY, PHILIP T.
2000   *Early Watch Case Makers of England 1631 to 1720*. National Association of Watch and Clock Collectors, Special Order Supplement #3. Lititz, PA.

QUEENSLAND MUSEUM
2010   Conservation of *Pandora* Artefacts. Queensland Museum <http://www.qm.qld.gov.au/Find+out+about/Histories+of+Queensland/Transport+Maritime+History/HMS+Pandora#/pandora-conservation.pdf>. Accessed 7 February 2018.

THIOUT, ANTOINE
1741   *Traité de L'Horlogerie Méchanique et Pratique, Tome Second*. Paris, France. <https://bibdig.museogalileo.it/Teca/Viewer?an=979351>. Accessed 7 February 2018.

TROALEN, LORE G., DARREN COX, AND THEO SKINNER
2010   Three-Dimensional Computed Tomography X-Radiographic Investigation of a 17th-century Watch from the Wreck of the *Swan*, off Duart Point, Mull, Scotland. In *International Journal of Nautical Archaeology* 39(1):165–171.

WASELKOV, GREGORY A., BONNIE L. GUMS, AND HELEN DEWOLF
2017   Domestic Artifacts. In *La Belle: The Archaeology of a Seventeenth-Century Vessel of New World Colonization*, James E. Bruseth, Amy A. Borgens, Bradford M. Jones, and Eric D. Ray, editors, pp. 660–718. Texas A&M University Press, College Station.

WILDE-RAMSING, MARK U., AND CHARLES R. EWEN
2012   Beyond Reasonable Doubt: A Case for *Queen Anne's Revenge*. In *Historical Archaeology* 46(2): 110-133.

• • • • • • • • • • • • • • • • •

Karen E. Martindale
North Carolina Department of Natural and Cultural Resources
Queen Anne's Revenge Conservation Lab
East Carolina University
1157 VOA Site C Road
Greenville, NC 27834-2018

The Investigation of the Anniversary Wreck, a Colonial Period Shipwreck Lost off St. Augustine, Florida: Results of the 2017 Excavation Season

Chuck Meide

In July 2015, a buried shipwreck was discovered off St. Augustine, Florida by the St. Augustine Lighthouse Archaeological Maritime Program (LAMP), the research arm of the St. Augustine Lighthouse & Maritime Museum. Excavations that year and the following summer revealed a remarkable amount of material, dating to 1762-1800 and suggesting an English or perhaps Spanish merchant ship laden with cargo. In the summer of 2017 LAMP researchers returned to the site, though excavations were limited by poor visibility, logistical issues, and weather. This paper summarizes the results of the 2017 fieldwork and analysis of material collected over two excavation seasons.

Introduction

The colonial shipwreck site known as the Anniversary Wreck (8SJ6461) was discovered by LAMP archaeologists in 2015 when testing targets originally identified during a 2009 remote sensing survey (Turner and Kennedy 2010; Meide et al. 2016; McDaniel et al. 2017; Meide 2017). The magnetic target was initially designated "Silver Surfer," but upon confirmation as a historic shipwreck the site was named in honor of the 450th anniversary of the founding of the city being celebrated that year. Depending on the tide, the shipwreck lies in about 5.79 to 7.01 m of water. The Anniversary Wreck is located about 0.7 km from the beach, and some 2.7 km from St. Augustine's other two known 18th-century shipwrecks, the 1764 Industry and the 1782 Storm Wreck (Meide 2015). Interestingly, the Anniversary Wreck is situated well to the north of the relict channel, around which all other St. Augustine 18th- and 19th-century shipwrecks have been found to date. Its position places it inside the historically charted location of St. Augustine's infamous North Breakers, suggesting the captain of this vessel was considerably off course, perhaps with no control over his vessel at the time of wrecking, or possibly ignorant of the local environment and rashly attempting to enter the port through an insufficient channel or without the aid of a pilot.

The physical nature of the site can be described as a very dense scatter of buried concretions and other artifacts covering an area of unknown extent. Hydraulic probing over a 7 by 4 m area conducted in 2015 suggests the scatter becomes more sporadic further away from the currently understood center of the site, where excavations have taken place (McDaniel et al. 2017:Figure 4). Every unit excavated to date, within an area measuring 5 by 4 m, seems to contain an abundance of artifacts, often so closely positioned that many have concreted together into large masses. This material culture is relatively deeply buried, covered by as much as 1.2 or more meters of sand.

No articulated hull remains have been encountered to date, though a few individual fragments of well-preserved wood have been unearthed. When first discovered, all wreckage was buried and there were no signs that divers had ever visited the site before, though some modern beverage cans have been encountered among the historic material.

Investigations were carried out over 21 days in June, July, and August of 2017, from the 36 ft. research vessel Roper and the 29 ft. research vessel Mombo. A total of 365 dives were logged, totaling just one minute shy of 281 hours of bottom time. Four new 1 x 1 m units were partially excavated, along with four units worked in the prior year. Conditions on this wreck can be adverse, with frequent heavy surge and poor visibility, complicating diving activity, and the constant threat of sudden storms which can unexpectedly shut down operations for the day. These challenges were especially stringent during the summer of 2017. For the first time in around a decade of LAMP field seasons there was not a single day of visibility good enough to see anything at the bottom, and recording was done in the blackness with the diver rising in the water column to read a tape measure, write, or draw. Storm activity was particularly active in 2017, with two nor'easters and Hurricane Irma, which curtailed the field season. Furthermore, the completion of a newly constructed Maritime Archaeology and Education Center on the Lighthouse grounds necessitated the temporary suspension of fieldwork to move the contents from the old headquarters into the new laboratory complex. In addition, there were two episodes of mechanical breakdowns on one research vessel that prevented fieldwork for multiple days during repairs.

The cumulative effect of these delays, unfortunately, was that 2017 was the least efficient field season LAMP has conducted in over a decade. Eight 1 x 1 m units were excavated in 2017 compared to twelve the previous season, and only a single one was drawn to scale in 2017, compared to nine units completed the year before. This was due to not just the hampering visibility but the poor timing of weather and logistical delays. It can take days of excavation to clear enough sand to expose cultural material, and an unexpected hiatus due to storm or breakdown allowed sand to slump back in and refill the excavation area. Twice this entailed having to dig out the project dredges which had been buried along with the gridded units. The end result was that despite a substantial amount of time spent excavating (actually with more bottom time and more individual dives than the year before), there was only a very narrow window available for recording exposed wreckage.

Another result of the logistical and environmental obstacles faced in 2017 was that relatively few artifacts were collected. Only 16 finds were recovered by divers, not including 39 sediment samples and four core samples. This is quite a low number considering that 87 artifacts were recovered in 2016, along with 40 sediment samples and three core samples. An additional 68 numbered specimens were encountered when sorting the 2016 dredge spoil and sediment samples, an activity that has not yet been completed with the 2017 dredge spoil. The low number of collected artifacts in 2017 was not necessarily an unwelcome outcome considering that LAMP conservation activities have been suspended for over a year's time during the construction and outfitting of the new conservation laboratory.

The archaeological data collected to date has led to the tentative identification of this shipwreck as a merchant vessel loaded with cargo that wrecked while attempting to enter St. Augustine sometime between 1762 and 1800. The following discussion presents a review of the methodology and results of archaeological fieldwork and analysis conducted on the Anniversary Wreck since its discovery.

Methodology

A thorough overview of the methodology used on the Anniversary Wreck to establish a grid system, maintain vertical control, excavate by suction dredge, record exposed features, and recover artifacts is included in Meide 2017(12-14). Additional activities undertaken in 2017 are described below.

Systematic sediment sampling has been employed by LAMP researchers on the Storm and Anniversary Wrecks since 2015 (Shidner 2016; Veilleux and Meide 2016:128). Subsequent analysis has produced tiny faunal remnants, including insect, fish, and rodent remains (Shidner 2016). Samples were collected by hand in each excavated unit at the beginning of each arbitrary level, and at the bottom of the final level. Divers simply filled a pre-labeled, gallon-sized (3.79 L) sealable bag. The elevation of each sample was recorded in cmbd (cm below datum). All Anniversary Wreck samples collected in 2016 and all except for two collected in 2017 were sent to Jacob Shidner, a doctoral student at the University of Arkansas, for analysis. The remaining two samples from 2017 were transferred to Lee Newsom at Flagler College for analysis, which is still underway.

Core samples were also collected in both 2016 and 2017, in an attempt to better discern geological stratigraphy on the shipwreck site. The site is characterized by deep deposits of shifting sand with little stratigraphy discernable to divers, even when visibility allows observation. Clay deposits have been noted around and coating some concretions, and in some cases divers have encountered dark layers of more organic sediment. These are believed to represent mud deposited by tidal currents from St. Augustine's estuarine rivers which have filled voids scoured naturally or created by previous archaeological excavation. A more thorough discussion of site formation processes on St. Augustine shipwrecks is presented by Burke (2016).

Seafloor sediment coring has become an increasingly useful tool for better understanding the geological properties and site formation processes of shipwreck sites (Horlings 2009, 2011; Keith and Evans 2016:60-62). A simple coring methodology was utilized on the Anniversary Wreck, with the diver hammering transparent 1.22 m long plastic tubes with 2.54 cm inner diameters directly into the seafloor at several predetermined locations. Micro layers of stratigraphy could be viewed with the naked eye and measured in each core sample. All core samples from the 2016 and 2017 seasons have been provided to environmental archaeologist Lee Newsom of Flagler College for analysis, which has not yet been completed.

In 2017 a metal detecting survey was begun to delineate buried wreckage and better understand site boundaries. Four survey areas were completed covering parts of the northeastern, southeastern, and southwestern quadrants of the site. Divers used methods that proved successful on the Storm Wreck (Veilleux and Meide 2016:128), following a series of 10 m long transect lines spaced 2 m apart and marking noticeable hits on a pre-drawn template. A total area of 240 m² was surveyed in this manner. Unfortunately, very few positive returns were indicated by the metal detector, even when it was deployed directly over the reburied excavation area known to feature dense and substantial concentrations of iron. This is likely due to the buried depth of cultural material, which is significantly greater on Anniversary Wreck than on Storm Wreck. While more experimenting with the metal detector may be attempted in the future, the 2017 survey proved inconclusive.

Summary of 2017 Fieldwork

The 2017 excavation of Anniversary Wreck encompassed a single day in June and the entire months of July and August. Diving commenced to assess the current condition of the site and to confirm the positions of datum, grid, baseline, and mooring systems. Most of the 2016 grids were buried, with only a few portions of some exposed. Metal detecting began while dredges were set up and pre-disturbance elevation measurements were recorded. In order to remove overburden and expose the buried grid system, excavation was initially carried out in two general proveniences: the northern and southern halves of the 2016 excavation area. As the prior year's excavation grids, defining Units 1-12, became exposed, new grids were deployed to delineate Units 13-18, to the west and north of the previous excavation area (Figure 1). Core samples were collected in four undisturbed locations just outside the boundaries of the 2016 excavation area (Figure 1).

From this point, excavation proceeded in individual 1 by 1 m units. In the 2016 area, excavation was limited to Units 2, 10, 11, and 12, with most dredging taking place in the latter two. These two had been only partially excavated the year before, and in 2017 they were more thoroughly dredged so a dense concentration of artifacts were exposed and sketched (but not yet drawn to scale). Dredging also took place in four new units, 14-17, with most excavation limited to Units 14-16. While artifacts were exposed in all three units, only Unit 15 was drawn to scale (Figure 1). Limited artifact recovery occurred in Units 10-11 and 15-16.

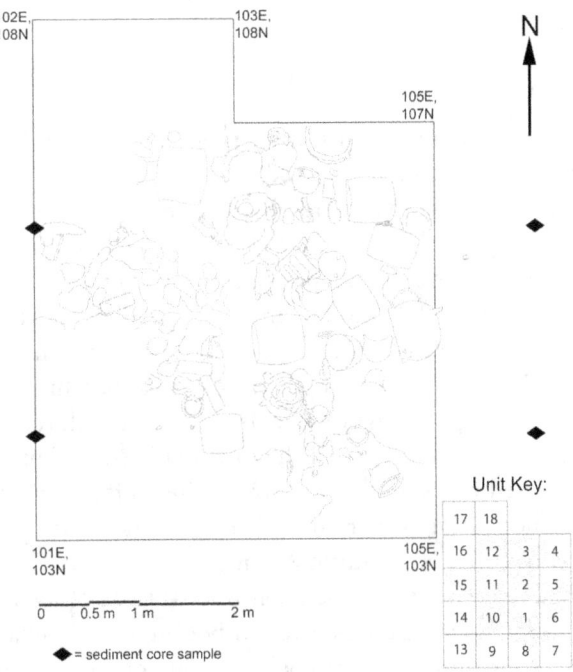

figure 1: The Anniversary Wreck main excavation area site plan, 2017. Note that Units 11 and 12 are based on diver sketches and have not yet been drawn to scale. The sediment core samples shown were the ones collected in 2017 (Chuck Meide, Tim Jackson and Allyson Ropp; courtesy LAMP).

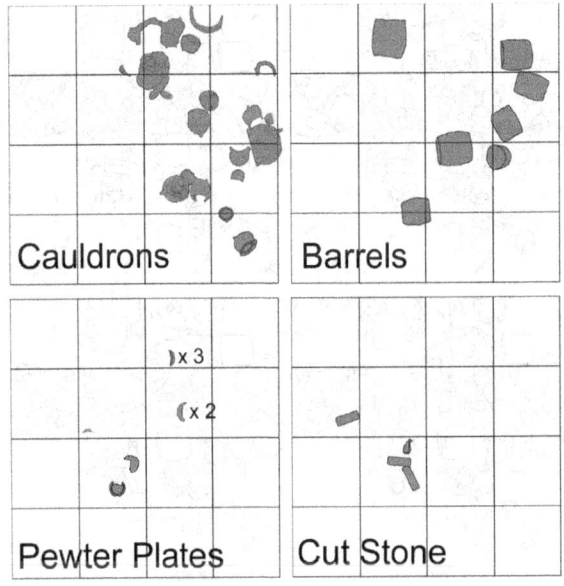

Figure 2: Artifact distribution maps showing the spatial arrangement of cauldrons, barrels or casks, pewter plates, and cut stone encountered on Anniversary Wreck in the 2016-2017 seasons. Units 17 and 18 were omitted from these maps as excavation has not yet reached material culture in those units. (Allyson Ropp and Chuck Meide; courtesy LAMP).

Artifacts

Cauldrons

The most ubiquitous artifact on the shipwreck is the cast-iron cauldron or cooking pot. As many as 28 individual cauldrons were observed in 2016, most of them apparently intact, and often stacked or nested inside each other. One more specimen was unearthed in 2017, in Unit 11. The cauldrons are distributed across the eastern half of the excavation area, largely confined to Units 1-7 (Figure 2, top left). It is clear that this ship was carrying, among other items, a cargo of cauldrons.

All of the cauldrons were heavily concreted, and often concreted to each other or surrounding objects, and to date none have been recovered. Representative samples may be collected in future seasons.

All of the observed specimens appear to be of identical form, that of the classic round-bodied, round-bellied pot, narrowing at the top before flaring out at the rim (Noël Hume 1969:175-177; Neumann 1984:176; Eveleigh 1997:15). Each has three legs, allowing them to stand stably in a fire, a feature common by the medieval period and lasting into the 19th century, when iron hobs and kitchen ranges required flat bottomed cookware (Eveleigh 1997:17). All display opposing pairs of "ears" on their rims, from which an arched wrought-iron bail or handle was once placed to hang the pot over a fire. The ears appear to be pointed or squared, a style that predates the rounded ears introduced in the 19th century (Neumann 1984:176). Casting seams and other surface details are not visible due to concretion.

Concretion also prevents entirely accurate measurements, but Table 1 presents a selection of eight cauldrons which have been measured in situ, representing the general size range of the assemblage. The largest of these, which had three smaller specimens nested inside, is considerably larger than the biggest Storm Wreck cauldron, while the smallest is still somewhat larger than the smallest Storm Wreck cauldron (Meide et al. 2018:Table 21).

The Anniversary Wreck cauldrons display a rounded rather than oval shape, which according to Neumann (1984:175-177) suggests a date range of 1740-1780. This should be considered a general temporal range, as cauldrons of this older form were still used after the newer styles were introduced in the 19th century, especially in more rural or remote kitchens (Everleigh 1997:17). Likewise, Noël Hume (1969:175) notes that neither cauldrons nor skillets "can be dated at all closely, as traditional shapes continued to be made in a great many places over a long period of time."

These cauldrons are identical or very close in form to the nine recovered from the 1782 Storm Wreck (Carter 2014, 2016; Meide et al. 2018:216-218) and one recovered on the nearby Industry lost in 1764 (Meide 2015). Port records indicate cast-iron cookware was a regular import into St. Augustine under both Spanish and British rule. For example, in or shortly after April 1760 the sloop Cornelia arrived from Hampton, Virginia with "53 Iron Potts;" in September 1766 the 20-ton sloop St. Augustine Packet arrived from Philadelphia with 61; in February 1767 the 25-ton schooner Florida Packet arrived from Charleston with 4; in June 1767 the 25-ton schooner Margaret arrived from Georgia with 7; in May 1768 the 30-ton schooner Ruby arrived from Philadelphia with 27 and the 70-ton schooner Grant arrived from Philadelphia with 53; in October 1768 the 30-ton schooner Thorogood arrived from Charleston with 50 and the 20-ton sloop Speedwell arrived from Philadelphia with 87; in November 1768 the schooner Ruby brought in another 27 from Philadelphia; in December 1768 the 20-ton schooner Juno arrived from Charleston with 30; in January 1769 the 35-ton schooner John & Phebe arrived from Philadelphia with 38 while Margaret returned with another 6, this time from Charleston; and in June 1769 the 20-ton schooner Expedition arrived from Charleston with 21 (BNA 1765-1769:CO5/573; Harman 1969:59,91). Cauldrons were in such demand in early 19th-century St. Augustine that they were frequently stolen from the

Description of Cauldron	Diameter across rim	Max. Diameter	Height	Comments
Large cauldron straddling Units 5-6	54	61	46	Largest cauldron on site. Leg height 11 cm. Three more cauldrons nested within.
Nested inside above cauldron	40	n/a	n/a	
Nested inside above cauldron	35	n/a	n/a	
Nested inside above cauldron	21	n/a	n/a	
Cauldron in southeast quadrant of Unit 1	21	29	25	
Cauldron in center of Unit 7	31	32	24	One more cauldron nested within.
Nested inside above cauldron	20.5	n/a	n/a	
Small cauldron in southwest quadrant of Unit 6	19	24	20	Smallest cauldron on site. Straddles Unit 6 and Unit 7 border.

Note: Cauldron height does not include legs. Rim measurements are outer diamters. All measurements in cm.

Table 1: Dimensions of selected cauldrons encountered on the anniversary wreck

waterfront after being unloaded from inbound vessels (Patricia Griffon 2011, elec. comm.).

Barrels or Casks

Six barrels or casks were identified during 2016 excavations and a seventh was confirmed in Unit 12 in 2017 (Figure 2, top right). In all cases it appears that the wooden components have deteriorated, leaving the barrel-shaped concreted contents. This phenomenon has been observed before on three St. Augustine shipwrecks, including the Storm Wreck, where two concreted casks were determined to have originally contained wrought iron nails. It is probable that the Anniversary Wreck casks also contained nails or some other iron hardware or tools, most likely cargo intended for the St. Augustine market. There seem to be two general size ranges represented, measuring 40-43 cm (15.75-17 in.) and 47-48 cm (18.5-18.9 in.) in length (Meide 2017:Table 1).

Pewter Plates

A total of seven pewter plates were encountered in 2016, four of which were recovered. An additional plate, mostly complete, and a separate rim section were recovered from Unit 11 in 2017. All were found relatively close to each other, in adjacent Units 10-11 and 2-3 (Figure 2, bottom left). The three in Unit 3 were overlapped and appear to have originally been stacked together. All but one are about the same size, 23.2 to 23.5 cm in diameter. The exception is a larger plate or charger which, while deteriorated, originally would have been somewhat greater than 33 cm in diameter.

Pewter flatware was commonly used throughout the 17th and 18th centuries, and declined in popularity in the early 19th century. The rim styles discernable on several of the plates are temporally diagnostic. Multiple-reeded brims which had been popular in the late 17th century gave way to single-reeded brims and smooth-edged brims in the early 18th-century. Both of these styles are present in the Anniversary Wreck assemblage, and date to ca. 1720-1800 (Neumann 1984:276-277). The recovered pewterware has not yet been cleaned or conserved, which might reveal diagnostic maker's marks.

Shoe Buckles

Twelve whole and partial brass shoe buckle frames were recovered in 2016. They were all located in a very confined area, around the border between Units 1, 8, and 9, and are identical in form. Their spatial proximity and stylistic uniformity suggest they were cargo items rather than personal possessions. This is in contrast to those found on the Storm Wreck, a refugee vessel with many passengers, where shoe buckles varied in material, style, and provenience (Brendel 2016:191).

The Anniversary Wreck buckles are devoid of decoration with a frame shape somewhat more ovoid than rectangular, with rounded edges. The frames are convex to fit the top of the foot, flat in cross-section, and feature a Type 1 pin terminal (White 2005:34). They are described in more detail in Meide 2017 (16-17).

Ceramics

A variety of ceramics, including stonewares, refined and course earthenwares, and brick and tile pieces, have been encountered on the wreck site in the 2015-2017 seasons. A single sherd of creamware has provided the terminus post quem for the shipwreck, 1762. An overview and analysis of the shipwreck's ceramic assemblage is presented in Turner et al., this volume, and will not be further discussed here.

Glass

In 2016, one bottle base fragment was recovered from Unit 5, likely from an English 18th-century liquor bottle. In 2017, a second base fragment was recovered from Unit 11. The cylindrical shape seen in these bottles became the norm by the 1730s. Often referred to as wine bottles, they were also used for beer, cider, and other beverages, and were the dominant container for such liquids until around 1820 (Jones 1986). Similar bottle fragments are commonly found in North American colonial assemblages. While these almost certainly date to the last three quarters of the 18th century, they have not yet been carefully analyzed to narrow their date range.

Other glass fragments were found throughout the excavation area, but appear to post-date the shipwreck and are likely intrusive.

Cut Stone

In 2016 three oblong blocks of dressed or cut stone were unearthed in Unit 10. The two collected measured 37.5 cm by 10.5 cm by 5.6 cm and 39.5 cm by 11 cm by 5.7 cm. The third block was not fully excavated from its surrounding clay matrix but its dimensions seemed similar to the others. A fourth block of stone was encountered in 2017 after excavation in Unit 15 (Figure 2, bottom right). It was recovered and measured 32.5 cm by 10.2 cm by 5 cm. The blocks appear to be sandstone and were likely intended as building material for sale in St. Augustine, for use as sills, thresholds, or other such architectural components (Figure 3). There is no natural

Lead Shot

Numerous tiny lead pellets or birdshot in the 2.5 to 5 mm size range were recovered from the site in 2016-2017. Similar lead pellets are common on other colonial shipwrecks including Belle (1686), Queen Anne's Revenge (1718), Machault (1760), and Storm Wreck (1782) (Meide et al. 2018:161-166). Known as Rupert shot after their alleged inventor, Prince Rupert of the Rhine, they were used from ca. 1665 through the 19th century. These pellets are typically ovoid in shape with a slight dimple, features which are by-products of their manufacturing process. The shot encountered on the wreck could have been intended for either shipboard defense or a cargo item.

Other Artifacts

Other artifacts recovered include numerous concretions which have not yet been x-rayed or cleaned. In one concretion collected in 2017, a brass escutcheon, perhaps from a piece of furniture, is partially exposed. Some wood fragments were collected, at least one with an apparent fastener hole. Three pieces of coal were found in 2016, perhaps representing fuel for cooking or heating. Also in 2016 part of a wooden knife handle was recovered from Unit 8 (Meide 2017:18).

Microfaunal Remains: Results of the 2016 Sediment Sample Analysis

At the time of this writing, all of the 2016 sediment samples have been screened and, while many biological specimens have not yet been positively identified, preliminary analysis has been completed by Jacob Shidner. Screening of the 2017 samples is underway and about halfway completed. All analyzed samples were water-screened through a set of three stacking screens of 2 mm, 1 mm, and 0.5 mm mesh, for subsequent visual examination under a dissecting microscope. The screening and analysis methodology is fully described in Shidner 2016:203-204.

Table 2 displays the preliminary results of Shidner's analysis of the 2016 samples. A variety of insect body parts were identified, including heads, outer protective wings, inner flight wings, mandibles, and thoraxes, some with leg remnants. Of these, two varieties were positively identified: the hide beetle (family Dermestidae) and drugstore beetle (Stegobium paniceum). Both of these are tiny beetles which could have lived on food stores or cargo items such as textiles or leather goods. Both have been found on other historic shipwrecks, including

Figure 3: The three blocks of dressed or cut stone recovered from the Anniversary Wreck. The upper two examples were recovered from Unit 10 in 2016 and the bottom specimen was recovered from Unit 15 in 2017. (Allyson Ropp; courtesy LAMP).

source of building stone in northeast Florida other than coquina, a sedimentary rock formed of bivalve shell fragments, so these would have been valued in St. Augustine.

Another piece of cut stone was encountered in the northeastern quadrant of Unit 11 in 2017. This was significantly smaller than the blocks mentioned above, octagonal in shape with one protruding corner and only a few inches across and one to one and a half inches thick. This object was not recovered or recorded to scale, and it may represent a tile rather than stone.

Brass Tacks and Pins

Two brass straight pins and three small brass tacks were recovered in 2016 from Units 2 and 3. Pins were used for sewing or other crafts, and as wig or clothing fasteners, and are common finds on shipwrecks and other colonial sites (Meide et al. 2018:207,209-210). The tacks could have been used in upholstery or luggage. A concretion recovered in 2016 from the southeastern corner of Unit 2 was recently x-rayed in the new conservation facility, revealing many more tacks, perhaps dozens more.

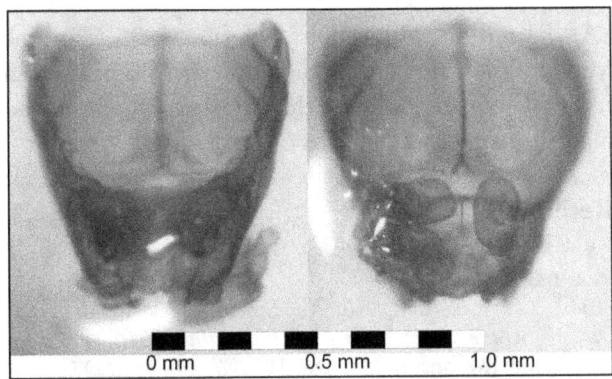

Figure 4: The probable remains of a louse encountered during microscopic analysis of a sediment sample collected from Unit 2 at an elevation of 117 cmbd. Upper and lower views of the thorax with attached leg segments are shown. (Jacob D. Shidner; courtesy LAMP).

the 16th-century Emanuel Point wrecks and the Storm Wreck (Shidner 2016:204-206). The most viscerally interesting find was what appears to be the remains of a louse, comprised of a thorax and leg fragments (Figure 4), a testament to the unpleasant realities of shipboard hygiene. Non-insect remains observed include fish and other bones, including a possible claw from a mouse or small rat. A possible seed was the only botanical remnant cataloged.

Conclusion

A significant amount of data has been amassed after two field seasons, and a better understanding of the Anniversary Wreck is evolving. Excavation has revealed a vast and dense deposit of material culture buried deep beneath the sand, and further excavation promises even more material. The great quantity of cauldrons, barrels,

Field Specimen No.	Description	Tentative ID	Common Name	Scientific Name	Unit	Depth in cmbd
16SS-95.02	UID Insect Head	prob. ant			Unit 2	54.5 cmbd
16SS-95.03	UID Poss. Seed				Unit 2	54.5 cmbd
16SS-98.03	Poss. Insect Head				Unit 1	63 cmbd
16SS-98.04	UID Insect Head		Drugstore Beetle	Stegobium paniceum	Unit 1	63 cmbd
16SS-98.05	UID Insect Mandible	prob. beetle or ant			Unit 1	63 cmbd
16SS-98.06	Beetle Outer Wing		Drugstore Beetle	Stegobium paniceum	Unit 1	63 cmbd
16SS-98.07	UID Insect Fragments	poss. thorax	Hide Beetle	family Dermestidae	Unit 1	63 cmbd
16SS-98.08	UID Insect Head	poss. ant			Unit 1	63 cmbd
16SS-98.09	Beetle Outer Wing		Hide Beetle	family Dermestidae	Unit 1	63 cmbd
16SS-98.10	UID Insect Flight Wings				Unit 1	63 cmbd
16SS-98.11	UID Bone				Unit 1	63 cmbd
16SS-99.02	UID Bone				Unit 1	115 cmbd
16SS-99.03	UID Insect Mandible				Unit 1	115 cmbd
16SS-99.04	UID Insect	Poss. bean beetle	Bean Beetle		Unit 1	115 cmbd
16SS-101.02	UID Insect Fragments				Unit 2	94 cmbd
16SS-101.03	UID Fish Bone				Unit 2	94 cmbd
16SS-102.02	UID Insect Abdomen	prob. louse thorax	Louse	order Phthiraptera	Unit 2	117 cmbd
16SS-104.01	UID Insect Mandible				Unit 3	128 cmbd
16SS-106.02	UID				Unit 5	75 cmbd
16SS-109.02	UID Insect				Unit 8	72 cmbd
16SS-111.02	UID Insect Head				Unit 4	112 cmbd
16SS-112.02	UID Insect Head				Unit 6	91 cmbd
16SS-115.02	UID Bone	poss. rodent claw	Mouse or Rat	family Muridae	Unit 5	84 cmbd
16SS-116.01	UID Insect				Unit 7	71 cmbd
16SS-118.02	UID Bone				Unit 5	97 cmbd
16SS-122.02	UID Insect				Unit 1	125 cmbd
16SS-123.02	UID Fish Bone				Unit 5	138 cmbd
16SS-125.02	UID Insect Wing				Unit 8	141 cmbd
16SS-128.02	UID Insect Part	prob. abdomen			Unit 11	87 cmbd
16SS-128.03	UID Bone				Unit 11	87 cmbd
16SS-129.02	UID Insect Parts				Unit 11	125 cmbd
16SS-130.01	UID Insect Mandible				Unit 9	120 cmbd
16SS-131.01	UID Insect Head				Unit 10	138 cmbd

Note: cmbd = cm below datum

Table 2: Summary of the preliminary analysis of sediment samples collected from anniversary wreck in 2016 (jacob d. Shidner)

plates, and buckles, and their stylistic homogeneity, indicate that this ship was a merchant vessel loaded with cargo, attempting to enter St. Augustine when it ran aground and broke up on the bar. All of the objects unearthed were imports that would have been valued in St. Augustine's markets, and could have been acquired in no other way than by ship.

It appears that most of the diagnostic artifacts are of British origins. This does not necessarily mean that the ship was British, as an early American vessel might be plying similar wares, or a Spanish vessel might have been trading illegally with British colonies (Harman 1969; Deagan 2007). But a strong possibility remains that this ship was English (although see Turner et al., this volume). Many of the artifacts are datable, and suggest with a good degree of certainty a date range of 1762-1800. Much of this analysis is in a preliminary stage, and the date range cannot be further narrowed without continued excavation. This 38-year span was a period of cultural transformations in St. Augustine, as it shifted from Spanish to British and then back to Spanish control. As of yet we do not fully understand the cultural origins of this maritime trading vessel.

It is clear that this shipwreck has immense archaeological potential. This is the first colonial-era merchant vessel that has been discovered in the waters of America's oldest port, and it features a wealth of material culture. Preservation is so good that even microscopic insect remains have been recovered. Further excavation will lead to a greater understanding of the nature and extent of the wreckage and its cultural context. Once the ship's date and nationality are refined, then archaeologists can bring into focus the cargo items and better understand this ship's role in the emerging global capitalist system. The continued archaeology of the Anniversary Wreck will allow us to ask meaningful questions and to explore 18th-century consumerism and the desires and needs of St. Augustine's colonial population during a time of sociocultural transformation.

Acknowledgments

The 2015-2017 seasons were funded by field school students and with grants from the Bureau of Historic Preservation, Division of Historical Resources, Florida Department of State through the Florida Historical Commission. Dave Howe, Mike Potter and Kevin Carrigan have provided research vessels, and the Hutcherson family dock space, to support our research. The project's success ultimately lies with the team of LAMP and St. Augustine Lighthouse & Maritime Museum staff, students, and volunteers who have given time, talent, and passion to this shipwreck. There are too many to name here, but thanks to all of you.

References

BRENDEL, HUNTER
2016 Personal Items from the Storm Wreck. In *ACUA Underwater Archaeology Proceedings 2016*, edited by P. F. Johnston, pp. 187-193, Washington, D.C.

BRITISH NATIONAL ARCHIVES (BNA)
1769 A List of All Ships and Vessels that have entered inwards or cleared outwards the port of St. Augustine in East Florida, Naval Office Shipping Lists for East Florida, 1765-1769. CO5/573, Colonial Office Papers, The National Archives, Kew, United Kingdom.

BURKE, P. BRENDAN
2016 Hidden in Plain Sight: Monitoring Shipwrecks in the Atlantic Waters of St. Augustine, Florida. In *ACUA Underwater Archaeology Proceedings 2016*, edited by P. F. Johnston, pp. 25-34, Washington, D.C.

CARTER, ANNIE E.
2014 *A Wreck of a Site: An Archaeological Examination of Cauldrons from the Storm Wreck, 8SJ5459*. Unpublished Bachelor's Thesis, Department of Anthropology, New College of Florida, Sarasota, FL.

2016 An Archaeological Examination of Cookware from the Storm Wreck, 8SJ5459. In *ACUA Underwater Archaeology Proceedings 2016*, edited by P. F. Johnston, pp. 177-181, Washington, D.C.

DEAGAN, KATHLEEN
2007 Eliciting Contraband through Archaeology: Illicit Trade in Eighteenth-Century St. Augustine. In *Historical Archaeology* 41(4):98-116.

EVELEIGH, DAVID J.
1997 *Old Cooking Utensils*. Shire Album No. 177. Shire Publications Ltd, Buckinghamshire.

HARMAN, JOYCE ELIZABETH
1969 *Trade and Privateering in Spanish Florida 1732-1763*. St. Augustine Historical Society, St. Augustine, Florida.

HORLINGS, RACHEL L.
2009 An Effective Diver-Operated Coring Device for Underwater Archaeology. *Technical Briefs in Historical Archaeology* 4:1-6.

2011   *Of His Bones Are Coral Made: Submerged Cultural Resources, Site Formation Process and Multiple Scales of Interpretation in Coastal Ghana.* Doctoral Dissertation, Department of Anthropology, Syracuse University, Syracuse, New York.

JONES, OLIVE R.
1986   *Cylindrical English Wine and Beer Bottles 1735-1850.* Studies in Archaeology, Architecture and History. Parks Canada, Ottawa.

KEITH, MATTHEW E. AND AMANDA M. EVANS
2016   Sediment and Site Formation in the Marine Environment. In *Site Formation Processes of Submerged Shipwrecks,* edited by M. E. Keith, pp. 44-69. University Press of Florida and the Society for Historical Archaeology, Gainesville, Florida.

MCDANIEL, OLIVIA, P. BRENDAN BURKE AND CHUCK MEIDE
2017   The 450th Anniversary Shipwreck Survey: Applying Updated Methodologies to the Search for Historic Shipwrecks in the Nation's Oldest Port. In *ACUA Underwater Archaeology Proceedings 2017,* edited by J. Albertson and F. H. Hanselmann. Advisory Council on Underwater Archaeology, Forth Worth, TX.

MEIDE, CHUCK
2015   "Cast Away off the Bar": The Archaeological Investigation of British Period Shipwrecks in St. Augustine. In *Florida Historical Quarterly* 93(3):355-387.

2017   The Investigation of the Anniversary Wreck, a Colonial Period Shipwreck off St. Augustine, Florida: Results of the First Excavation Season. In *ACUA Underwater Archaeology Proceedings 2017,* edited by J. Albertson and F. H. Hanselmann. Advisory Council on Underwater Archaeology, Forth Worth, TX.

MEIDE, CHUCK (ET AL)
2018   *First Coast Maritime Archaeology Project 2013: Report on Archaeological Investigations.* Lighthouse Archaeological Maritime Program, St. Augustine Lighthouse & Museum, St. Augustine, Florida.

MEIDE, CHUCK, OLIVIA MCDANIEL, P. BRENDAN BURKE AND SAMUEL P. TURNER
2016   *450th Anniversary Shipwreck Survey: Report on Archaeological Investigations.* Report prepared by the Lighthouse Archaeological Maritime Program, St. Augustine Lighthouse & Maritime Museum, St. Augustine, Florida.

NEUMANN, GEORGE C.
1984   *Early American Antique Country Furnishings: Northeastern America, 1650-1800.* McGraw-Hill, New York.

NOËL HUME, IVOR
1969   *A Guide to Artifacts of Colonial America.* University of Pennsylvania Press, Philadelphia.

SHIDNER, JACOB D.
2016   Life Among the Wind and Waves: Examining Living Conditions on Sailing Vessels Through the Use of Microscopic Remains. In *ACUA Underwater Archaeology Proceedings 2016,* edited by P. F. Johnston, pp. 202-208, Washington, D.C.

TURNER, SAMUEL P. AND KENDRA KENNEDY
2010   LAMP 2009 Remote Sensing Survey. In *ACUA Underwater Archaeology Proceedings 2010,* edited by C. Horrell and M. Damour, pp. 11-16. Advisory Council on Underwater Archaeology, Amelia Island, Florida.

VEILLEUX, CAROLANE AND CHUCK MEIDE
2016   The Archaeological Investigation of the Storm Wreck, a Wartime Refugee Vessel Lost at St. Augustine, Florida, at the End of the Revolutionary War: Overview of the 2010-2015 Excavation Seasons. In *ACUA Underwater Archaeology Proceedings 2016,* edited by P. F. Johnston, pp. 122-132, Washington, D.C.

WHITE, CAROLYN L.
2005   *American Artifacts of Personal Adornment, 1680-1820: A Guide to Identification and Interpretation.* AltaMira Press, Lanham, MD.

....

Chuck Meide
81 Lighthouse Avenue
St Augustine, FL 32080

Ceramics of the Anniversary Wreck: A Preliminary Analysis

Sam Turner, Allyson Ropp, Chuck Meide, Roger Arrazcaeta, Marcos Acosta, Yoser Martínez

The Anniversary Wreck was discovered in 2015, the 450th anniversary of the founding of St. Augustine, Florida. Preliminary analysis of the material recovered dates the site between 1750 and 1800. A closer examination of the ceramic assemblage and a comparison to terrestrial ceramic assemblages from St. Augustine are used to attempt to accurately place the shipwreck within the prevailing historical divisions of Florida's History that span the years 1750 to 1800, that is, the late First Spanish Period, the British Period, or the Second Spanish Period.

Introduction

The current state of research on the ceramic assemblage from the Anniversary Wreck provides a rough date that based on the overall collection of material culture, occurred in the second half of the 18th century (Meide 2017). Additional excavation of the site will hopefully produce more ceramics with which to broaden this study. As described in another paper in these proceedings (Meide, this volume), the Anniversary Wreck was discovered by members of the Lighthouse Archaeological Maritime Museum (LAMP), the research arm of the St. Augustine Lighthouse & Maritime Museum during the summer of 2015, the 450th anniversary of the founding of St. Augustine.

The data consists of ceramic material from three field seasons which took place between 2015 through 2017. The majority of the pieces were recovered in 2016 with only one each for 2015 and 2017. A total of 22 pieces were recovered (Table 2). Ceramics analysis was carried out using the typology collection of the City of St. Augustine housed at the City's archaeology lab on Pellicer Lane in St. Augustine and the typology collection of the University of Florida which may be used on line (University of Florida 2017).

Salt Glazed Stoneware

The majority of the ceramic sherds represent salt glazed stoneware vessels, reflecting at least four individual vessels in number but possibly more. These sherds, ten in total, likely represent English Salt-glazed stoneware of the Fulham-type with a production range of roughly 1690-1775 (University of Florida 2017). The distribution of ceramic material throughout that portion of the site so far explored can be seen in Figure 1.

In Britain, brown stoneware drinking and serving vessels were made in imitation of the popular German, or Rhenish, stonewares. These became known as "Fulham wares" because of their association with John Dwight of Fulham who received a 14 year patent in 1672. John Dwight set about methodically experimenting and producing stone ware with the intent of replacing those imported from the European mainland (Metropolitan Museum of Art 2018). He largely succeeded in his task,

Site	Location	Date	Length	Width	Thickness
La Isabella	Dominican Republic	1490s	n/a	11	5
Concepcion de la Vega	Dominican Republic	Ca. 1500	28.667	13.333	4
Puerto Real	Haiti	Ca. 1520	28	13.667	4
Alleged Rosario	Dry Tortugas	1622	30	14	n/a
Old Mobile (French)	Alabama	1700-1711	18.79	9.39	3.30
Queen Anne's Revenge (French)	North Carolina	1718	18.42	10.785	2.57
Santa Rosa	Pensacola	Ca. 1730	22.667	11.067	3.567
San Jose	Florida	1733	28	13	3
El Nuevo Constante (red)	Louisiana	1766	37.4	19.8	5.5
El Nuevo Constante (yellow)	Louisiana	1766	23	11	3.3
Bateria de San Antonio	Pensacola	1797	28	12.3	4.75

Table 2: Comparative Spanish And French Bricks

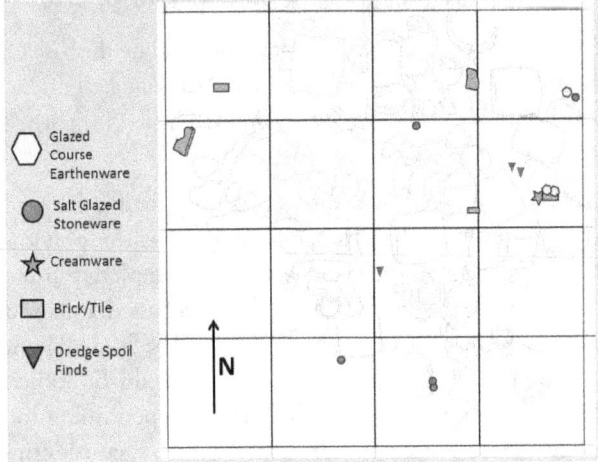

Figure 1: Site map of the Anniversary Wreck showing the distribution of ceramics.

capturing most of the English stoneware market by 1700 (University of Florida 2017). Very similar pieces were made elsewhere in England, including Greater London, Bristol, and Staffordshire and thus the term Fulham-type. By approximately 1730, some American colonial potters began producing brown stoneware that was difficult to distinguish for the English Fulham-Type.

Principal vessel forms for this ceramic type were mugs, jugs, and crocks. Crocks mostly had vertical sides, like a mug but were considerably thicker than mugs. These were used to store just about anything from apples to bread dough. Jugs tended to be more oval in nature, the body of the vessel going from a narrower base to a wider waist before terminating in a narrower neck. These were used to store liquids of all sorts. At least three crocks of varying sizes are represented within the inventory of salt glazed stoneware sherds.

The first, represented by 15SS-001.1, was approximately 20 cm. in diameter derived from a metric diameter template. The second vessel, represented by 16SS-044.1, had a diameter of 18 cm and the third

Figure 3: Creamware shard 16SS 16.6 (left) and Coarse earthenware showing interior glazing (right).

A single sherd of grey salt glazed stoneware (16SS-079.1) is indicative of either a mug or jug given the thickness of the fragment since a crock would likely have had thicker walls. This style of stoneware had a production period that ranged from approximately 1690 to 1775 (University of Florida 2017).

Creamware

A single ceramic sherd is representative of white refined earthenware. Identified as creamware, this sherd likely represents the rim sherd of a gravy boat, bowl, or some other form of specialized tableware (Figure 2, Gesner 2000:105). Creamware was originally derived from experiments by Thomas Astbury and Thomas Whieldon beginning in around 1750 and later developed in a partnership between Whieldon and Josiah Wedgwood. Wedgwood perfected what we know as creamware in 1762. Thus this ceramic type is typically dated to a range of 1762 to about 1820 (Meide et al. 2018:233). However, the 1762 start date postdates the actual development of the ceramic type. Originally, the occurrence of this particular sherd seemed to eliminate the wrecked vessel from dating to the late First Spanish Period which ended in 1763. It is possible that ceramic vessels that would be classified as creamware and dating to the Whieldon and Wedgwood partnership period from 1754 to 1759 and shortly thereafter were landed in St. Augustine before Wedgwood perfected the type in 1762 (Kathleen Deagan:2017, pers. comm.).

Figure 2: Archaeologist Olivia McDaniel holding the base of the salt glazed stoneware jug (left) and Archaeological diver with salt glazed stoneware shards found in Unit 15 (right).

crock, represented by sherd 17SS-238.1, had a diameter of 17 cm. derived in the same manner as the previous two. The single jug, evidenced by a completely intact base with ascending bulging walls had a base diameter of 12 cm. A number of jug body sherds (16SS-044.1) and a fragment of a handle (16SS-158.1) could be indicative of additional vessels or be fragments pertaining to a single vessel, represented by the intact base, considering the similarities in glazing, body thickness, and paste of the individual fragment.

A white salt glaze piece in the city of St. Augustine collection has the same rim and body thickness as this piece suggesting the same vessel form indicating that identical ceramic forms occurred in both white salt glaze and creamware either simultaneously or successively as white salt glazed stonewares gave way to creamware.

Bricks

Another important category of ceramics from the wreck is bricks. These number six, incomplete examples, in total with two of the fragments being so small they have no diagnostic value beyond color and fabric which is in conformity with the other four larger fragments. These larger fragments are detailed in the table below (Table 1). Of these fragments only one is close to being complete (16SS-067.1) being roughly 19 cm by 14 cm where it terminates at a break, and just over 3 cm thick. As a group, however, the brick fragments vary little in thickness and so may be considered all members of like bricks. These are most likely Spanish *ladrillos* (Kathleen Deagan 2017). However, a French origin can't be excluded as shown by some similar examples of bricks from other archaeological contexts (Table 2).

FS #	Unit	Length	Width	Thickness
16SS-015.1 (fragment)	5	9.6	5.1	3.04
16SS-023.1 (fragment)	2 SE	8.5	4.2	3.40
16SS-067.1 (partial)	3 SE	18.6	13.9	3.13
17SS-236.1 (fragment)	16	11.5	6.7	3.08

Table 1: brick/tile

Earthenware

Five sherds recovered from the Anniversary Wreck in 2016 are of an earthenware vessel form with a dark red interior glaze (Figure 3). The exterior of the vessel is unglazed and there appears to be no exterior treatment of any sort what so ever. These fragments appear to pertain to a single vessel and were all collected in 2016 (Table 1). These have an orange paste with black inclusions with smooth exterior surfaces. These have yet to be positively identified. They are consistent with a large earthenware storage container of some variety. The closest type match for these so far is El Moro but the thickness of the sherds and the smoothness of the exterior surface preclude that possibility. Roger Arrazcaeta, the Director of the *Gabinete de Arqueología* based in Havana, Cuba, and one of the co-authors of this paper believes, after examining the ceramics, that these sherds may possibly represent a French ceramic tradition. No such earthenware ceramics have been found in the City of Havana. However, coarse earthenwares, possibly of Flemish or British origin, have also been found on British colonial sites so these cultural affiliations cannot be entirely ruled out at this time (New London Museum 2018).

The French Connection

Given the possible presence of French material culture on this shipwreck in the case of the bricks and earthenware ceramics, it seems reasonable consider possible French culture connections with St. Augustine that date to the second half of the 18th century. As it turns out there is a very interesting one. The American Revolution was followed by that of France beginning in 1789. The ideals of liberty swept through French colonial possessions and most especially the French colony of Saint-Domingue on the Island of Hispaniola which France shared with Spain. These new ideals led to political divisions among white colonial French and free *mulatos* on Saint-Domingue. These issues were quickly overwhelmed by a slave rebellion in 1791 brought about by the same ideal of liberty (Moya Pons 1983:166-167).

One of the principal leaders of this rebellion was a fifty year old slave named Georges Biassou from the Le Cap area on the north coast of Saint-Domingue (Figure 4). He and Jean François, another rebellion leader, entered into Spanish service with their armies of liberated slaves in 1793 when Spain declared war on France (Landers 2010:71). Their combined armies conducted military operations against the French in what is today Haiti. They remained loyal to Spain once France had abolished slavery in Saint-Domingue the next year in 1794. Many slaves and their leaders, especially Biassou's subordinate Toussaint L'Ouverture, who betrayed and fought Biassou to become Haiti's founding father, deserted the Spanish cause.

The war went badly for Spain which in 1795 ceded the Spanish portion of Hispaniola to France. This posed a problem for Spain which feared that their generals Biassou and François would not abide by the terms of the treaty. Therefore they were quickly transferred off the island of Hispaniola with their households and most loyal attendants and staff. They first traveled to Cuba where they were ordered to remain on their ships while they awaited orders from the governor.

Jean François and his contingent were dispatched to Cádiz in Spain. Georges Biassou was dispatched to St. Augustine Florida which at the time was part of the Spanish colonial world. There he assumed command of the black militia stationed at Fort Matanzas near the southern end of Anastasia Island some ten miles south of St. Augustine. He brought with him his "family", which in addition to his immediate family consisted of 25 of his most faithful followers and confidants from Hispaniola. It is likely that these in turn brought members of their own families. He resided on St. George Street in St. Augustine when in town and away from Fort Matanzas. Was one of Biassou's ships lost on the St. Augustine bar?

Conclusions and Avenues of Further Research

One of the original premises of this research was to examine a number of ceramic collections from local terrestrial archaeological sites to see if they could help inform a determination regarding the period of Florida's history to which the wreck pertained. This strategy will continue to be used as this archaeological investigation goes forward. Only one collection could be examined within the time frame of this project to date. This collection, a portion of the material excavated at the Peña Peck house held at the Sue Middleton Archaeology Lab in St. Augustine, was examined with no particularly useful result except producing a definitive example of El Moro that made it clear that the coarse earthenware off the wreck is not that type. The majority of the Peña Peck collection is kept at the Museum of Natural History at the University of Florida and will be consulted in the near future.

Of particular interest is the successful identification of the earthenware sherds. If this is indeed a French ceramic type it should appear on French colonial sites and so an examination of ceramics from archaeological sites in Louisiana and the Caribbean might prove very informative. If there is a connection with Biassou, an examination of any archaeological material from his St. Augustine residence would make an excellent comparison. Also, examination of archaeological material from Santiago in eastern Cuba could also prove valuable as this was one of the principal ports to which colonial French from Saint-Domingue fled beginning in 1791. They would have carried possessions with them, including possibly course earthenware, which may turn up there in the archaeological record. It is still early days in terms of the archaeological investigation of the Anniversary Wreck. It is to be hoped that additional ceramics will be obtained during the upcoming field seasons that can shed more clarity on the nationality and time period for this shipwreck.

References

DEAGAN, KATHLEEN
1987 *Artifacts of the Spanish Colonies of Florida and the Caribbean, 1500-1800*, Volume I: Ceramics, Glassware, and Beads. Smithsonian Institution Press, Washington D.C.

GESNER, PETER
2000 *HMS Pandora, 1791: HMS Pandora Project – A Report on Stage I: Five Seasons of Excavation.* Memoirs of the Queensland Museum, Cultural Heritage Series, Volume 2, Issue 1. Brisbane

LANDERS, JANE
2010 *Atlantic Creoles in the Age of Revolutions.* Harvard University Press, Cambridge

MEIDE, CHUCK
2017 The Investigation of the Anniversary Wreck, a Colonial Period Shipwreck off St. Augustine, Florida: Results of the First Excavation Season. In *ACUA Underwater Archaeology Proceedings 2017*, edited by J. Albertson and F. H. Hanselmann. Advisory Council on Underwater Archaeology, Fort Worth, TX

MEIDE, CHUCK (ET AL)
2018 *First Coast Maritime Archaeology Project 2013: Report on Archaeological Investigations.* Lighthouse Archaeological Maritime Program, St. Augustine Lighthouse & Maritime Museum, St. Augustine

METROPOLITAN MUSEUM OF ART
2018 < https://www.metmuseum.org/art/collection/search/671537 >. Accessed March 31, 2018.

MOYA PONS, FRANK
1983 *Manual de Historia Dominicana*, Universidad Católica Madre y Maestra, Santiago

NEW LONDON MUSEUM
2018 <http://www.newlondonmuseum.org/meads-tavern-a-crossroads-of-american-history/archaeology/>. Accessed February 28, 2018

UNIVERSITY OF FLORIDA
ND *Digital Type Collections,* Florida Museum of Natural History, <www.floridamuseum.ufl.edu/histarch/gallery_types/>.Accessed December15, 2017

Sam Turner
SEARCH, Inc.
12443 San Jose Boulevard #204
Jacksonville, Florida 32223

Allyson Ropp
St. Augustine Lighthouse & Maritime Museum
81 Lighthouse Ave.
St. Augustine, FL 32080

Chuck Meide
St. Augustine Lighthouse & Maritime Museum
81 Lighthouse Ave.
St. Augustine, FL 32080

Roger Arrazcaeta
Gabinete de Arqueología
Mercaderes # 15, e/ O´Reilly y Empedrado.
La Habana Vieja. C.P. 10100.
La Habana, Cuba

Marcos Acosta
Gabinete de Arqueología
Mercaderes # 15, e/ O´Reilly y Empedrado.
La Habana Vieja. C.P. 10100.
La Habana, Cuba

Yoser Martínez
Gabinete de Arqueología
Mercaderes # 15, e/ O´Reilly y Empedrado.
La Habana Vieja. C.P. 10100.
La Habana, Cuba

Way Hay and Up She Rises: The Recovery, Conservation, and Documentation of an Historic Admiralty Anchor from the Gulf of Mexico

John R. Bratten, Christopher E. Horrell, Stephen B. Atkinson, Andrew T. Willard

In 2013, an historic anchor was recovered from the Gulf of Mexico by a contractor working for an offshore energy operator. Because the Bureau of Safety and Environmental Enforcement was not notified, the operator was in violation of regulations protecting submerged archaeological resources. A compromise was reached between the bureau and the operator resulting in the transportation of the anchor to the University of West Florida (UWF) for conservation and long-term study purposes. Conservation revealed markings indicating that the anchor was manufactured by R. Flinn & Company in North Shields, England, sometime in the first half of the 19th century.

Introduction

The Bureau of Safety and Environmental Enforcement's (BSEE) Historic Preservation Program is constantly striving to improve the manner in which submerged archaeological resources are identified and protected on the Outer Continental Shelf (OCS). BSEE's Historic Preservation Program is located in the Gulf of Mexico Regional Office within the Office of Environmental Compliance. The Historic Preservation Program's primary function is to ensure that offshore energy operators adhere to the regulations while conducting work offshore. During the course of operations, there have been many interesting finds. This is the story of one.

One of the offshore operations that BSEE regularly monitors is related to decommissioning. This activity is centered on the removal of a structure, usually an oil or gas production platform or caisson, that is no longer productive or one who's lease has expired. As part of the lease agreement, the oil and gas operator is required to bring the lease back to pre-lease conditions. To accomplish this, the operator will hire a decommissioning service providing company to complete the removal of the structure. Depending on water depth, and as a part of the regulations for decommissioning activities, the operator will also hire a trawling vessel to drag nets on the seafloor to recover any debris that may have been left behind. At the end of operations, the operator is required to supply a report of the activities and to document all materials and debris recovered. In most cases, the debris may be sections of pipe, grating, bumper tires, and random pieces of metal. However, material culture that may be associated with a submerged archaeological resource (e.g. a shipwreck) may be recovered. During one such decommissioning activity an historic anchor was described in the required report that was submitted for review by BSEE to ensure compliance with the regulations. BSEE reviewed the report and requested further information including a photograph which the operator submitted. The photograph depicts the concreted anchor sitting in the operator's backyard next to his swimming pool. (Figure 1). Upon inspection of the photograph, the anchor appeared to be a 19th-century Admiralty anchor. Though the anchor was listed in the report, it was not reported to the bureau within the required timeframe. The documentation also indicated that the recovery of the anchor occurred 40 miles offshore of Louisiana in approximately 69 feet of water. Archaeologists within BSEE recognized that it would be highly unusual for an anchor from this time period to simply be lost in this relatively featureless environment and that the trawling activities of the operator may have encountered the remains of an historic shipwreck.

Figure 1: The Flinn anchor following recovery from Gulf of Mexico (Courtesy Bureau of Safety and Environmental Enforcement.).

Once BSEE received the initial information regarding the anchor, the Bureau requested to know where the anchor was stored and its current condition. The condition of the anchor was significant because any artifact manufactured from a metal other than gold will react with its environment in a variety of ways until more stable compounds are formed. Iron objects recovered from sea water, such as this anchor, could have been subjected to many variables that influenced its corrosion state including temperature, pH, and the presence of aggressive chloride ions (Hamilton 2010:38). Upon removal from the sea, the corrosion process can increase substantially due to environmental changes such as decreased relative humidity and increased oxygen. This would be especially true if the protective encrustation covering the anchor had been removed or the anchor had not been placed in an alkaline inhibitive storage solution following recovery.

BSEE learned that the operator's company representative (an individual who represents the operator during all contracted activities) contacted his boss who expressed interest in acquiring the anchor for his personal collection. The boss then drove to Louisiana, picked up the anchor, and transported it back to Houston, Texas, where it was placed on this individual's property for display (Figure 1). BSEE contacted the operator and informed them that they were out of compliance with the regulations (30 CFR 250.194(c)) for failure to notify BSEE of the recovery of the anchor. As a result, the operator received an Incident of Non-compliance (INC) along with a Corrective Action Order. This order required that the operator provide funds for the transportation, conservation, and long-term curation of the anchor. Additionally, the operator was ordered to conduct a high-resolution remote sensing survey using a magnetometer, side-scan sonar, and sub-bottom profiler to determine if the anchor may have been associated with a shipwreck.

The operator immediately responded and in coordination with BSEE put together a conservation and curation plan for the anchor. BSEE Historic Preservation coordinated the conservation efforts between the operator and the University of West Florida's (UWF) Archaeology Institute where the anchor would receive proper treatment and become a teaching tool for students. UWF would also retain ownership of the anchor.

The operator also conducted the required high-resolution remote sensing survey and several promising targets were identified in the remote sensing data. BSEE archeologists who are members of the Seafloor Compliance Monitoring Assessment Program (SCAMP) and the BSEE Scientific Diving Program, mobilized to investigate the targets. Over the course of two days diver visual inspection of the targets was conducted. Through this work, BSEE Historic Preservation determined that the anchor was an isolated find and that a shipwreck was not present in the area where the trawling activities had occurred.

Conservation and Documentation

In March 2014, the University of West Florida received the anchor. Although the anchor was covered by a thick layer of encrustation, it was obvious that the corrosion process had accelerated during its outdoor storage period in Texas. When exposed to air, the iron experienced a lower relative humidity and a higher O_2 concentration. According to Selwyn, this would allow acidic $FeCl_2$ and other salts to concentrate, causing the corrosions layers to crack (2004:295-296). This in turn, provides oxygen access to new areas of metal. This type of corrosion is sometimes visible in the form of yellow crystals of $FeCl_2$. For this reason, the anchor showed signs of active corrosion and was deteriorating at an increasingly rapid rate in several areas. To preserve as much detail as possible, UWF planned a conservation treatment. The first step was documentation. UWF graduate students, Stephen Atkinson and Andrew Willard recorded the anchor's pre-conservation condition and noted a number of diagnostic features that would aid in analysis and dating (Figure 2). All components of the anchor, including its folding stock, were fashioned entirely of iron. As can be seen in Figures 1 and 2, the anchor's stock is broken. Almost certainly, the stock fractured at the point where it had been fashioned in a ninety-degree angle for ease of storage below deck, but because that portion is missing it cannot be stated with absolute certainty. Remnants of modern netting were found trapped in the anchor's encrustation suggesting that it had been drug along the sea floor during the BSEE compliant trawl operations or prior shrimping activities, an action that probably caused the stock to break. The remaining portion of the stock is round in circumference and tapers to its end. It is secured to the anchor with a washer and cotter pin, supported by a flange on the stock itself.

Situated on the end of the surviving stock arm is a ball or stock nut, a feature designed to prevent the stock from slipping out of its support. The ball includes the stamped numeral "3" on its surface, a designation that may represent the anchor position in a series of anchors. It was in this area that the anchor exhibited the most deterioration. For the reasons mentioned above, the accelerated corrosion process following its recovery caused this rounded end to crack and resulted in an area ready to spall away. Photographic documentation and 3D-scanning were used to record the anchor in its pre-conservation state from two views (Figure 2).

The shank of the anchor is of a flattened and tapered

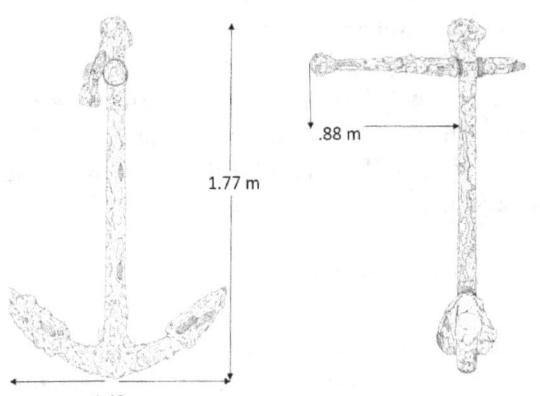

Figure 2: Details of pre-conserved Flinn anchor (Drawing by Stephen B. Atkinson, date.).

form, thinner near the stock and wider near the crown, with rounded edges. Arms angled at approximately 42 degrees spread from the crown. Tipped, spade-shaped flukes were welded onto the end of each arm. The top of the anchor, where the stock mated through the shaft, widens to create a circular opening for the stock. It then transitions upward into a square shape that incorporates a second hole in the stock to accept the anchor's main shackle. The large main shackle was heavily concreted in place, but a smaller shackle found affixed to it was able to move freely. The presence of shackles were also indicative of the anchor's age, a feature that postdated other ways of attaching a cable to an anchor, such as the use of an anchor ring. The uppermost portion of the shank was finished in a diamond-shaped pattern.

Overall length of the anchor is 1.77 m. Width from the tip of each fluke to the center of the crown is 1.13 m. The complete arm of the stock measures 88 cm in length, while the broken section consists of a surviving section 25 cm in length, from the washer and cotter pin designed to hold the stock in place. Circumference of the friable ball at the end of the stock is 30 cm. The stamped number "3" is 4.5 cm in height.

Similar to the two arms of the stock, the condition of the anchor's flukes are uneven. Undoubtedly, the preservation difference is related to the anchor's long-term placement on the seafloor. Presumably, half of the anchor, including the longer arm of the stock, was fully embedded in the sediment, while the bent arm of the stock and the upper fluke were exposed in the water column. Because of this, the encrustation layer was much less pronounced and, as a result, one fluke is 41 cm long and 30 cm wide, while the other is 45 cm long and 32 cm wide. The distance between the tips of the flukes is 1.57 m. The throats, or the arms for the flukes, are 50 cm in length. The length along the bottom of the crown from the tip of each fluke is 1.57 m.

Once the recording portion of the project was completed, the process of conserving the anchor began. The first step was to remove the bulk of the adhering marine encrustation from surface of the anchor by mechanical means. This task was completed with the use of a hand-held pneumatic chisel (i.e. air scribe) as well as a hammer and chisel. Care was taken to remove the encrustation with as little damage to the original surface as possible. The encrustation interface varied greatly, with

Figure 3: UWF Graduate student Stephen B. Atkinson prepping the Flinn anchor for electrolysis (Photo by author, 2018.).

some sections shearing off in large fragments, while others took the precision of an air scribe to remove.

Following the mechanical cleaning process, the anchor was lifted by forklift and placed in a large stainless steel tank for treatment by electrolytic reduction (ER), also known as electrolysis (Figure 3). By angling the anchor, complete submersion was insured. The tank was then filled with approximately 2,000 gallons of fresh water. Placement onto stacked cinder and wooden blocks prevented the object from touching the tank.

ER relies on a DC power source, an alkaline electrolyte, and an anode. In this case, the stainless steel tank acted as the anode. By passing a current between the tank and the anchor, cleaning is performed by the liberation of hydrogen bubbles at the cathode (the anchor and negative terminal). Negatively charged chloride ions are removed by attraction to the positive tank (the anode) and reduction is possible because of the addition of electrons to the corroded iron.

The power source used to power the process was an Epsco model NFB Filtered DC power supply which was placed in a covered shed adjacent to the tank. Conservators used three modified C-clamps attached to Mueller clips and 16 gauge, 2-strand insulated lamp wire to link the C-clamps and 12 gauge wire to attach the leads to the power source, which were then secured to the stock and shank of the anchor. The stainless steel tank served as the positive terminal (anode), while the anchor itself is the negative (cathode).

Once the leads were properly attached and the tank prepped for solution, conservators filled the tank with fresh water (1,820 gallons) and added approximately 758 pounds of sodium sesquicarbonate ($Na_3H(CO_3)_2$) to create a 5% electrolyte solution. Once electrolysis commenced, conservators closely observed the anchor in the following weeks and months to ensure the conservation process was working well and monitor the chloride level in the solution.

Electrolysis began on October 7, 2014 and concluded on December 7, 2015. At that time it was determined that chlorides were not present to a degree that might damage the anchor, less than 100 parts per million. The remaining encrustation adhering to the anchor was sufficiently loosened to the extent that final mechanical cleaning could be accomplished with hand held instruments such as an air scribe, dental picks, and small chisels.

Following UWF environmental health and safety guidelines and the Department of Environmental Protection definition of hazardous waste characteristics, the approximately 1,880 gallons of electrolyte used in the treatment was not considered hazardous waste due to the fact that its pH was less than 12.5 (United States Environmental Protection Agency 2005). In order to conveniently dispose of it and recycle the sodium sesquicarbonate, UWF contracted Progressive Environmental Services to pump out the chemical and transport it to Mobile, Alabama, for processing. Following the removal of the electrolyte solution, the anchor was given the first of three, full-tank rinses in fresh water to remove any residual electrolyte from the iron. Before any new oxidation could begin, the anchor was given a coat of 5 percent tannic acid. Tannic acid reacts with iron ions to form ferric tannate that provide the anchor with a blackish protective film. Two additional coats were applied several days later.

Historical Interpretation

Following removal from the ER tank, a light cleaning revealed that the crown of the anchor had been stamped with the name of its maker, "R. Flinn & Co" (Figure 4). According to the initial few historical sources that could be found, a Robert Flinn manufactured cable chain, harpoons and anchors in North Shields, England during

Figure 4: The maker's name, "R. Flinn & Co." stamped on anchor crown (Photo by author, 2018.).

the first half of the 19th century (The Newcastle Courant 1826). Historical research conducted at National Archives in Kew, England, and at the Discover North Tyneside Libraries in North Shields, England, further revealed that Robert Flinn began working with iron in the late 18th century when he began manufacturing harpoons in Hartley, England, for the Greenland and Davis Straits fisheries (North & South Shields Gazette 1859). Flinn was born in Ireland in 1766/67. His father had garnered notoriety when he fought with British General James Wolfe at the 1759 Battle of Quebec during the French and Indian War. Wolfe succumbed to his battle injuries and died in the senior Flinn's arms on the Plains of Abraham (Page's Engineering Weekly 1904:110).

Robert Flinn is mentioned in numerous historical sources because he was the first person to introduce chain cable to a ship. In 1808, he secured the Ann and Isabella to the shore of the Tyne River and saved the vessel from a "great flood accompanied with much floating ice" (The Nautical Magazine 1890:405). Hempen cables proved no match for the ice, but Flinn's cable protected Ann and Isabella and a row of other vessels. He soon followed this accomplishment with the invention of a proving machine.

When Flinn's business increased, he moved to North Shields, England, a town on the north bank of the River Tyne in North East England, eight miles northeast of Newcastle upon Tyne. His shop was on Bell Street and it was there that he made his first chain cable. At that time, he employed a young clerk by the name of Robert Pow (North and South Shields Gazette 1859). Pow eventually became Flinn's business partner as did Flinn's son-in-law, George Fawcus. Fawcus is listed in the Northumberland Directory as a chain cable maker and anchor smith (Pigot 1829:181). Together the three men made Flinn & Co. into a very successful business that manufactured harpoons, anchor chain, anchors, as well as performing "ship and smith works of all kind" (Newcastle Chronicle 1826). The chain factory was separate from the smith's shop and consisted of "thirty forges (in full employment)" (Tyne Mercury 1826). The smith's shop, known as the North Shields Iron Works, frequently advertised for "workmen of sober and industrious habits" (Northumberland Advertiser: 1832). In addition to iron manufacture, the enterprise included ownership of several ships engaged in passenger transportation and the Canadian timber trade (Northumberland Advertiser: 1832, 1834).

On September 15, 1826, Robert Flinn retired, but the company continued to operate under the name Flinn & Co. for 11 more years. Flinn died on February 27, 1837 and on September 23rd of that year, The Newcastle Journal reported that the "Business in all its branches from this day forward, will be carried on under the firm of Pow & Fawcus." George Fawcus also died in 1837 and Robert Pow continued the operation with Fawcus's widow, Margaret (North & South Shields Gazette :1859). Robert Pow died in 1859.

In addition to the manufacturer's name, the Flinn anchor is also marked on its shank with the numerals "198" followed by an illegible number or letter (Figure 4). It is also possible that a "dash" may have been incorporated between the 9 and the 8, although that is a surmise. Initially, it was thought that these numbers might represent the anchor's weight. The conserved weight of the Flinn anchor is 172.5 kg (380 lbs.), however. The numbers do not reflect an accurate hundred weight (cwt) designation as well. When new, the anchor would have weighed between 3.5 and 5 cwt. If the markings represented stones (19) and pounds (8), the anchor would weigh 274 pounds, a value too low to be representative of the actual weight of the anchor. More likely, the numbers represent some type of production number or proofing designation.

The Flinn anchor is an Admiralty pattern anchor, one of the most recognizable anchors associated with sailing ships. Admiralty anchors incorporating iron stocks were common by the 1830s, but dated examples that still incorporated wooden stocks are noted for 1820 and 1837 (Smith 2000:7). The Flinn anchor was almost certainly manufactured prior to 1837, the year that the company's name changed to Pow & Fawcus. It is known that Pow and Fawcus utilized their own stamp because a Pow & Fawcus anchor is located in Kingston, Ontario (Heeney, undated). This anchor is documented by the presence of three photographs in the North Shields Library holdings. The photographs show the anchor to be somewhat larger than the Flinn anchor. It also differs from the Flinn anchor in that would have utilized a wooden stock as opposed to a folding iron stock. It also possesses an anchor ring instead of a shackle. It is stamped "Pow & Fawcus," and includes the name "North Shields" and a number thought to be a production marking. The anchor depicted in this paper is the only Flinn & Co. anchor located to date. Detailed company records are missing and not available in North Shields. In 1875 the factory experienced a severe boiler explosion which destroyed the works (Shields Daily News 1875:3).

The Flinn anchor appears to have been made very well. It is well proportioned, but not extremely large in overall size and weight. Its size suggests that it might have served as a kedge or stream anchor, although it could have served as a main or bower anchor on a much smaller vessel. Historic anchor tables provided in Curryer's Anchors: An Illustrated History (1999:58-59), suggests that an anchor of this size would be suitable as a kedge anchor for sloops from 268 to 340 tons or a brig of about 313 tons. Considering that the anchor was discovered 40 miles offshore suggests use as a bower anchor or stream anchor rather than a kedge anchor, however. It does not appear to be associated with a shipwreck, but may have been lost during a storm event.

Through the work of BSEE Historic Preservation and the cooperation of the operator, the INC and violation of the regulations was corrected and UWF received an historic piece of ground tackle. Historic research identified its place of manufacture and a possible terminus ante quem. UWF graduate and undergraduate students enrolled in an artifact conservation course gained valuable experience in the treatment of large iron artifacts recovered from a saltwater environment as a result of this project. It is hoped that anchor will soon be placed in an exhibit at the Margaret J. Smith Archaeology Institute on the campus of UWF.

Acknowledgments

The authors wish to thank the following individuals who helped with project: Eric Swanson, Michael Dillon Roy, Hunter W. Whitehead, and the UWF students who assisted in cleaning and moving the Flinn anchor. John Bratten wishes to acknowledge the UWF Office of Research and Sponsored Programs for the Research Stimulus Award Program and Karen Mims and Juliette Moore for travel assistance to England. The staff of the Discover North Tyneside Local Studies Department in North Shields, England were extremely helpful in locating relevant records in their collections.

References

CURRYER, BETTY NELSON
1999 *Anchors: An Illustrated History*. Naval Institute Press, Annapolis, MD.

HAMILTON, DONNY L.
2010 *Methods of Conserving Underwater Archaeological Material Culture. Conservation Files: ANTH 605, Conservation of Cultural Resources I*. Nautical Archaeology Program, Texas A&M University, College Station, Texas <http://nautarch.tamu.edu/class/ANTH605>. Accessed 16 March 2018.

HEENEY, D. H.
Undated letter from D.H. Heeney to North Shields Historical Library, North Shields, England.

PIGOT, JAMES
1829 *Pigot's Directory of Northumberland*. London, UK.

SELWYN, LYNDSIE
2004 Overview of Archaeological Iron: The Corrosion Problem, Key Factors Affecting Treatment, and Gaps in Current Knowledge, In *Proceedings of Metal 2004*. National Museum of Australia, Canberra.

SHIELDS DAILY NEWS
1875 "Alarming and Fatal Boiler Explosion at North Shields," *Shields Daily News*, 7 January. Johnston Press, Tynemouth, Tyne and Wear, England.

SMITH, TIM
2000 *Old Pattern Admiralty Long Shanked Anchor, North Head, Sydney: Conservation Management Plan*, Heritage Office, NSW Australia <http://www.environment.nsw.gov.au/resources/heritagebranch/maritime/anchornorthheadsydney.pdf>. Accessed 2 March 2018.

THE NAUTICAL MAGAZINE
1890 Chain Cables In *The Nautical Magazine*,(59), Brown, Son and Ferguson.

NEWCASTLE CHRONICLE
1826 George Fawcus & Robert Pow, In *Newcastle Chronicle*, 9 September. Newcastle, England.

THE NEWCASTLE COURANT
1826 *The Newcastle Courant*, 23 September. Newcastle, England.

NORTH & SOUTH SHIELDS GAZETTE
1859 *North & South Shields Gazette*, 2 and 9 June. Johnston Press, South Shields, Tyne and Wear, England.

NORTHUMBERLAND ADVERTISER
1832a No title. *Northumberland Advertiser* 5 May. Johnston Press, South Shields, Tyne and Wear, England.

1832b No title. *Northumberland Advertiser* 25 September. Johnston Press, South Shields, Tyne and Wear, England.

1832c No title. *Northumberland Advertiser* 9 October. Johnston Press, South Shields, Tyne and Wear, England.

1833a No title. *Northumberland Advertiser*, 8 January. Johnston Press, South Shields, Tyne and Wear, England.

1833b No title. *Northumberland Advertiser* 7 May. Johnston Press, South Shields, Tyne and Wear, England.

1834 No title. *Northumberland Advertiser* 18 February. Johnston Press, South Shields, Tyne and Wear, England.

PAGE'S ENGINEERING WEEKLY
1904 *Page's Engineering Weekly*, 1 January (4). 1904, Page Publishing Syndicate, Limited.

TYNE MERCURY
1826 *Tyne Mercury*, 5 September. John Mitchell, Newcastle, UK.

UNITED STATES ENVIRONMENTAL PROTECTION AGENCY
2005 *Introduction to Hazardous Waste Identification (40 CFR Parts 261)*, Training Manual, Washington, DC. <https://www.epa.gov/sites/production/files/2015-09/documents/hwid05.pdf.>. Accessed 2 March 2018.

. . . .

John R. Bratten
University of West Florida
11000 University Parkway
Pensacola, FL 32514

Christopher E. Horrell
Bureau of Safety and Environmental Enforcement
Office of Environmental Compliance
1201 Elmwood Park Blvd.
New Orleans, LA 70123

Stephen B. Atkinson
Queen Anne's Revenge Conservation Laboratory
200 N. Harding Street
Greenville, NC, 27858

Andrew T. Willard
University of West Florida
7201 Bruner St. Apt. 8F
Pensacola, FL 32526

Phosphate, Potassium, Pisces, Poop and Pollution: Surveying the Pacific Guano Company Anchorage of Woods Hole, MA, USA

Raymond L Hayes

An 1857 chart of Great Harbor at Woods Hole, Massachusetts originally detailed sailing instructions for ships entering this deepwater anchorage. From 1859-1889 ships carrying seabird guano sailed into Great Harbor to unload at the Pacific Guano Company. We have conducted a maritime archaeological reconnaissance survey of the anchorage and wharves. Submerged artifacts and remote sensing show that seafaring trade brought prosperity to investors, but created health concerns for workers and residents. Analytical data reveal village culture during the era. The U.S. Guano Act of 1856 stimulated the industrialization that re-defined and transformed Woods Hole into a marine science research center.

Introduction

New England merchant shipping to California brought supplies and personnel for the Gold Rush and westward expansion in the mid-19th century. Clipper ships from Boston and other Atlantic ports transferred manufactured goods, supplies, and human resources through maritime trade. However, return trips were without ballast, unless Pacific cargo was found for the return voyage. A solution was to load the hulls of ships with Pacific seabird guano. The US Guano Act of 1856 had encouraged American mariners to claim uninhabited islands for mining guano. The Chincha Islands (Peru) and Howland Island (USA) in the Pacific Ocean and the Swan Islands (Honduras) in the Caribbean Sea were sources of this natural product. Merchant ships sailed back to Woods Hole, MA, to deliver guano to the Pacific Guano Company between 1863 and 1889, satisfying ballast needs and providing raw material to fertilize farms in New England, mid-Atlantic, and southern states.

Recent survey of the historical anchorage within Great Harbor suggests that the Pacific Guano Company transformed Woods Hole village in many ways. Patent medicine bottles among the submerged cultural resources recovered from the harbor indicate that the health of residents, workers, and visitors to Woods Hole may have been affected adversely by industrial air pollution from the factory.

The Historical Anchorage of Great Harbor

A US Coast and Geodetic Service survey map of 1857, redrawn in 1882 (Figure 1), includes sailing directions for ships to reach the area designated for temporary anchorage and access to docks for transferring cargo in Great Harbor. As a natural deepwater site, the Great Harbor anchorage stretches between the base of Long Neck and Ram Island. The harbor is bordered to the north and west by a C-shaped peninsula, Long Neck (now Penzance Point) that extends west of Woods Hole village. The harbor border to the east is Little Neck (now Juniper Point). Dockages are on the northern boundary of the harbor. Great Harbor opens to the south into Vineyard Sound. Remote sensing of the anchorage indicates depths of from 20-30 ft. (7-10 m) to 60-70 ft. (15-20 m). The deep, southern end of the anchorage includes a 100-120 ft. (30-35 m) wide geological kettlehole.

The Pacific Guano Company (1863-1889)

Wealthy shipping agents from Boston and New York incorporated the Pacific Guano Company in 1863. Factory buildings, warehouses, offices, and worker residences were constructed on the narrow peninsula immediately adjacent to the village (Figure 2 from Kilburn 1865). Corporate papers were filed in Boston where company officials and transactions were located. Two experienced shipping captains, Prince S. Crowell and Asa Shiverick, both of Dennis, MA, served as Manager and Supervisor at the factory, respectively. Private investors and Boston banks underwrote over one million dollars as capital for the firm (Pacific Guano Company 1876). Business flourished for twenty years, largely due to extensive advertising and the creation of an innovative admixture of seabird guano (Figure 3) with North Atlantic menhaden (Brevcortia tyrannus) scrap. The product, advertised as "Soluble Pacific Guano", optimized crop yields. Demands for the fertilizer were received from

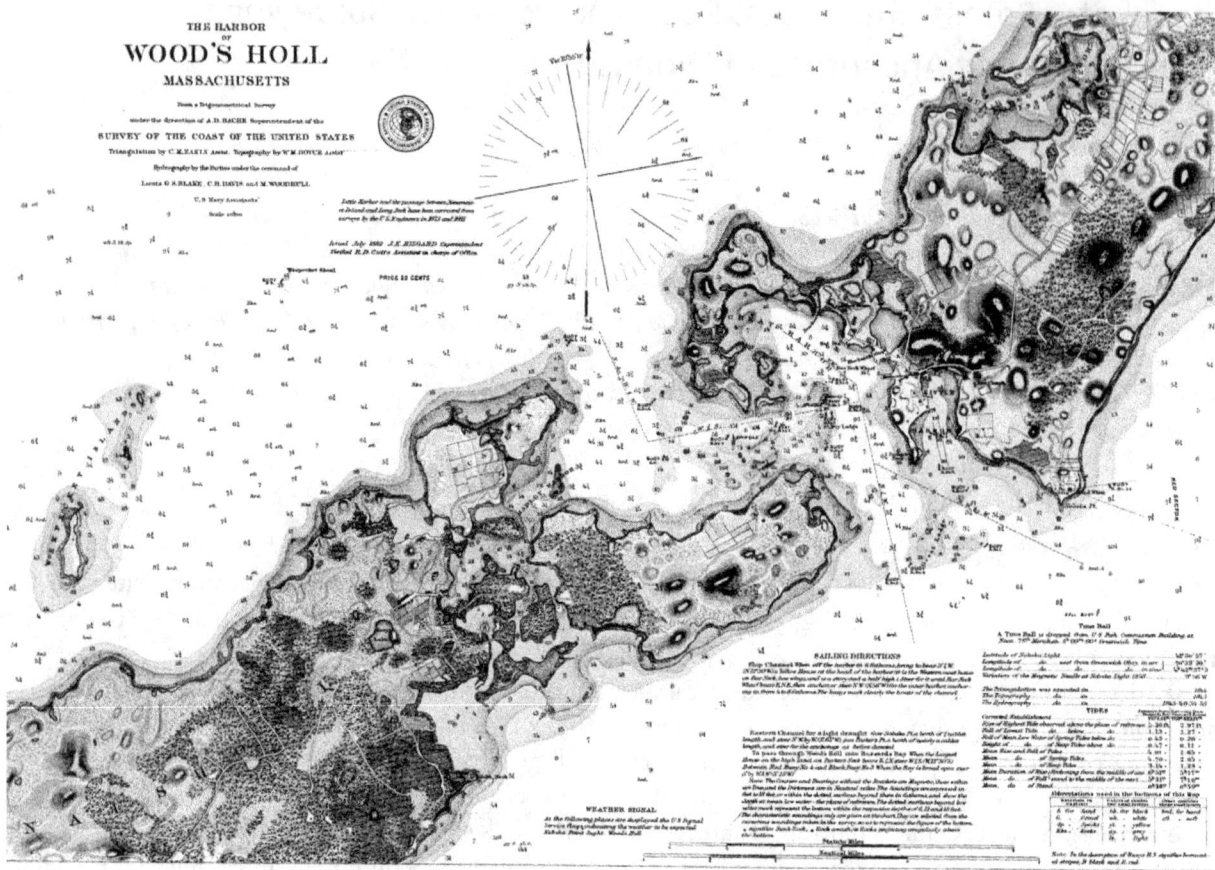

Figure 1: 1857 Coastal survey map of Woods Hole, with sailing directions in the lower right corner for the historical anchorage in Great Harbor at Woods Hole, MA (courtesy of NOAA, public domain).

Figure 2: Engraving of the Pacific Guano Company factory in Woods Hole, by Samuel Smith Kilburn of Boston (public domain).

across New England and throughout Atlantic and Gulf coast states.

For the first few years of operation, the Pacific Guano Company had 33 ships hauling guano after supplying settlers in California (Gaines 2007). Six ships were lost on return voyages; two were captured and burned by Confederate forces. For convenience, seasonal guano mining shifted successively over time from Pacific islands to Caribbean islands. Southern blockades still interfered with fertilizer deliveries to ports servicing cotton, rice, and sugar plantations in Louisiana, Florida, the Carolinas, Alabama, and Georgia.

Dried seabird guano from uninhabited islands of the Pacific and Caribbean was in great demand. Sailing ships from New England merchants delivered raw guano to Woods Hole where it was processed into organic fertilizer. Sea bird guano, from cormorants, pelicans, and boobies, provided the best agricultural fertilizer available between 1850 and 1900. Congress passed the US Guano Acts in 1856, authorizing American merchants to claim, occupy, and mine uninhabited islands for guano. The Pacific Guano Company became one of many firms in this business, and the small New England village of Woods Hole was transformed into an industrial center.

Pre-eminence of the Pacific Guano Company product, Soluble Pacific Guano, was attributable to a massive advertising campaign in newspapers throughout the national agricultural community. Soluble Pacific Guano was unique since it combined seabird guano with local menhaden residue. This idea must have come from an awareness that Native Americans utilized fish as fertilizer. Also, Dr. Spencer Baird, Assistant Director of the Smithsonian Institution, who would later become the first US Fish Commissioner, supported the concept. Coincidently, he first summered in Woods Hole in 1863, the year the Pacific Guano Company opened its factory. By 1871, Baird had established the Northeastern Fisheries Research Laboratory to monitor, restore, and research fish populations in the North Atlantic (Allard 1978).

At the time, menhaden were plentiful catch in waters surrounding Woods Hole, and fish scrap, that would otherwise be discarded after de-oiling, was of value as a supplement for the seabird guano. This mixture provided an exceptional natural organic product, rich in phosphates, nitrates and potassium for growing vegetables, cotton, and sugar cane. Menhaden were mixed with pulverized guano, sulfuric acid was added, and the mixture was boiled, filtered, dried, and packaged for distribution. Burlap bags of fertilizer were transported by carriage, ship, and railroad for sale to farms.

For two decades the Pacific Guano Company operated as a lucrative business that was dependent upon sailing ships to deliver raw materials, also including sulfates from Germany and phosphates from South Carolina, into Great Harbor for transfer to the processing factory. Ships of many nations frequented the waters of Great Harbor in support of this industry. As scientific knowledge advanced, however, essential chemical ingredients of natural fertilizers were elucidated. Synthetic fertilizers of comparable quality were produced quicker and cheaper than via sailing ship trade. Dependency upon guano rapidly disappeared.

After more than 20 years of profitable activity the Pacific Guano Company shut down in March of 1889. Inabilities to repay bank loans and settle financially with shipping agents were responsible for the closure (Gaines 2007). Unsustainable management practices, decisions to allow payment delays, contract negotiations for future crop yields, and deliberate financial misrepresentation (overvaluation of stock and holdings) by Glidden & Curtis as sole agents undoubtedly contributed to the failure.

Extrinsic factors responsible for the failure were the Confederate raiders, the abolishment of slavery, and poverty of southern farmers. The raiders interfered with northern coastal shipping, disrupting sailing routes of guano ships between New England and Pacific ports. Depression of the Atlantic shipping trade began in

Figure 3: Seabird guano from the swan islands was blended with Atlantic menhaden scrap into soluble pacific guano at the woods hole factory (photo by author).

1863 and extended beyond termination of the Civil War (1865). Losses of slave labor and depression among southern plantation owners extinguished the market for fertilizer that the New England shippers relied upon. Traders turned to railroads for support of westward expansion, a cheaper, quicker, and more reliable choice than the clipper ship trade.

Company assets in Woods Hole and Charleston, SC, were sold to pay debts to banks and agents. The property on Long Neck was subdivided into lots and sold to wealthy bankers at high prices beginning in 1890, creating the exclusive, private waterfront development of Penzance Point.

Transformation of Woods Hole Village

The influences of the Pacific Guano Company on the culture rapidly transformed Woods Hole from a small shipbuilding, whaling, and sheep farming village into a single industry factory town (Table 1). Viewed from an economic perspective, the company brought prosperity to the village: high tax revenues were paid to the town of Falmouth, based upon company profits; the village population more than doubled from employment at the factory; male Irish immigrants and workers from many eastern seaboard states moved to the village; and a productive industrial center was created. Many workers brought their families, necessitating schools, churches, and community services. Factory leadership convinced the Old Colony Railroad to extend into the village, providing transportation for distributing fertilizer. Passengers and commerce came to the village, as new local markets developed for food, medicine, beverages, and household goods.

In 1871, Woods Hole emerged as the center for a national fisheries inventory, regulation, and fish culture research agenda. The Northeastern Fisheries Research Laboratory was established there by Dr. Spencer F. Baird (Allard 1978; Rivinus and Youssef 1992). Baird successfully obtained allocations from Congress to initiate marine scientific research in Woods Hole. His popularity among academics in prestigious universities attracted other marine scientists to Woods Hole. This influx eventually resulted in the founding of the Marine Biological Laboratory (established in 1888) and the Woods Hole Oceanographic Institute (established in 1930).

Maritime Archaeological Survey of Great Harbor

A reconnaissance survey of the historical anchorage zone in Great Harbor was proposed in 2007 and a permit was issued by the Massachusetts Board of Underwater Archaeological Resources. The objective of that survey was to evaluate Great Harbor as an historical anchorage. The work included examination of artifacts from Great Harbor and a review of documents about the cultural development of Woods Hole.

Feature of Woods Hole/Falmouth	Before Pacific Guano Co. (1850)	After Pacific Guano Co. (1890)	Transformation
Old Colony RR (arrived in 1872)	shipping or carriage delivery	rapid bulk rail & passenger transfers	increased trade for local/island visits
Population	200	508 (1880)	factory workers
Immigration	< 4% foreign-born sparsely settled by small family units	>18% foreign with 60% Irish, later 48% Cape Verdean (Port.)	population growth with multi-ethnic diversification
Industrialization	maritime (salt, whaling, fishing) & manufacturing (ship-building)	agricultural products guano and menhaden fertilizers, chemicals (e.g., PO_4, H_2SO_4)	cranberry, home gardening, local & regional farming
Resort community of high income	maritime services: marina, dockage, provisions, repairs	many visitors from Boston and north shore, New York and Westchester Co.	Penzance Pt. and Juniper Pt. homes of big bankers; summer tourism
Lodging	private B & Bs, small inns	Breakwater Hotel, Tower Hotel, etc.	seasonal visitors; "American Naples"
Scientific Enterprises	US Fisheries (Spencer Baird), Marine Laboratory (Louis Agassiz)	MBL, WHOI, USN, USGS, USCG, NE Fisheries, SEA, WH Research Center	academic links to the Ivy League; federal gov't labs and research $$
Religion	Quaker, Protestant Baptist, Methodist	Catholic (St. Joseph's) 1882, Episcopal 1888	diversification of preferences
General Economy	subsistence, local, not competitive with large cities in MA, RI, CT	Multi-million dollar assessment with potential for growth & prosperity	multifaceted, broad-based, resourceful and rapidly expansive

Table 1: Characterizations of woods hole village before (1850) and after (1890) the pacific guano company (1863-1889), with transformations that were introduced by this industrialization

Submerged Cultural Resources from Great Harbor

For many years, submerged cultural resources from Great Harbor have been collected by local divers. Examination of those artifacts was made possible once direct communication had been established with collectors. In exchange for access to the collections, computerized databases of their individual collections were prepared for each diver. These data were also shared with the Woods Hole Historical Museum. Spreadsheets with descriptive data and measurements for each artifact were created. Several scaled digital photographs were taken of each artifact.

Four diver collections were used in this study, representing many years of diving within the anchorage and loading docks of Great Harbor. Each collector was an experienced diving professional, employed in marine salvage, underwater construction and repairs, or scientific diving instruction. The cumulative database represents the utilization of the harbor, particularly during the industrialization of the village.

Ceramic dinnerware, clothing, nautical instruments, toys, and assorted bottles were among over 400 artifacts that were photographed, measured, described, classified, and recorded. Computer research was conducted to identify additional historical data about each artifact. Bottles were classified, dated, and original contents ascertained. Several ceramic plates and cups were found with patterns or maker's marks that identified the dinnerware as English whiteware. Other artifacts included a shoe, a child's porcelain toy figurine, several clay smoking pipes, and a deadeye. The nautical artifact of greatest interest was a kedge Admiralty anchor that would have been used to pull a sailing ship into dock for loading or unloading cargo.

Glass Bottles from the Harbor: Typology and Manufacturing Dates

Once discarded, an artifact drifts out of sight, carried by prevailing currents, and descends into deep water. It might collect in a crevice or be temporarily suspended by sediment. When storms disrupt the unconsolidated bottom of the harbor, artifacts are moved around. Over time, extensive mixing of sediment, vegetation and artifacts has occurred.

Water and Soda Bottles

Stoneware bottles were made in Holland and exported for filling with mineral water, soda water, or gin. One bottle with an ear was filled in Schiedam, Germany and stamped "A. Houtman & Co." The Houtman Company opened in 1842 and distilled gin. Ceramic bottles were durable and often re-cycled.

Round bottom glass bottles were also included in the collections. One, embossed with the name COCHRAN, was from Belfast, Ireland. The company bottled aerated water and ginger ale. These bottles were sealed with a cork that remained moist, since the bottle must be rested on its side. These "ballast" bottles were imported on ships.

Beer, Wine and Liquor Bottles

In spite of the lack of specificity about when they were deposited, submerged cultural resources may be classified according to type and vintage. Unlike a shipwreck site, where the timing of an event is known, deposition of artifacts from ship or shore in Great Harbor cannot be determined. However, the typology of glass bottles is based upon shape, size and color (Figure 4 top). Embossed lettering and symbols indicate the company of origin and contents. Date of manufacturing and nationality were found in historical records. Most bottles from Great Harbor date between 1870-1920 (Figure 4 bottom).

Assorted beer and wine bottles were among those collected from Great Harbor. Some dark brown glass beer bottles were imported from Germany; others were

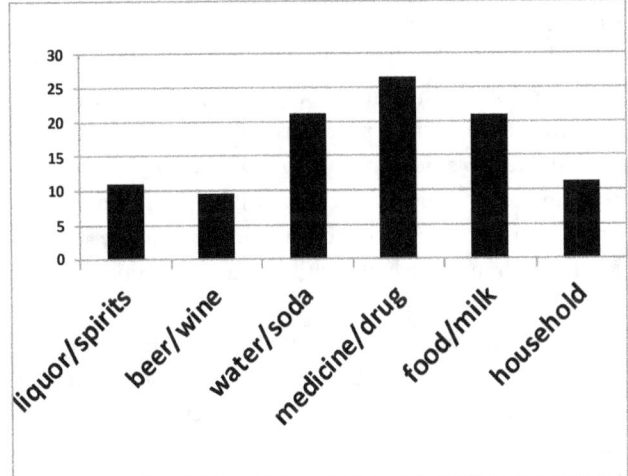

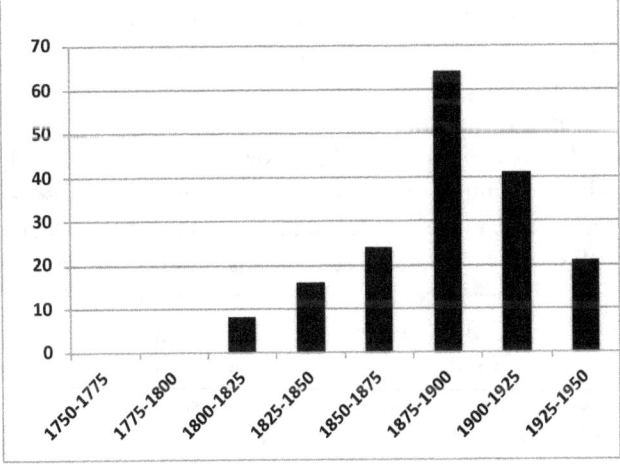

Figure 4: (top) Typologies of bottles (N=284) recovered by local divers from dockages and anchorage in Great Harbor. (bottom) manufacturing dates of bottles (N=164) identified by: brand and contents.

of domestic origin. Wine and champagne bottles were typically dark green glass with high kick-ups at the base. Bubbles or imperfections in the glass suggest a date range of 1860-1900.

Among liquor bottles, a frosted London Dry Gin bottle was found. Also, several side-strapped whiskey bottles, flasks, and embossed liquor bottles were recovered. Since alcohol was considered medicinal in the 1800s, these bottles may indicate treatments for various ailments (Robinson 2015).

Food and Milk Bottles

Unique beehive bottles with stacked and molded concentric rings were retrieved from Great Harbor. These bottles were used from 1878 to 1885 for sauces made by the Durkee Company. Other food bottles resemble those commonly used for ketchup, mustard, and soft drinks.

In the 1890s, Mellin's infant food was the most popular brand sold in the United States. Aggressive marketing used testimonials from parents that Mellin's had brought a child back to a healthy and happy life. The infant food contained malt added to cow's milk. Mellin's may not have improved children's health, but being the face of Mellin's often launched a child's career in modeling or show business.

Milk bottles are a special typology since their contents were highly perishable and bottles were usually returned for refilling. Store bottles of milk were capped with cardboard or foil covers. Store bottles and home delivery bottles required a deposit. This encouraged consumers to return bottles for recycling. The expectation with store bottles was that the contents would be consumed at the site of purchase, and the bottles would never leave the premises.

Bottled milk was distributed over short distances and within a limited time frame. Daily purchase was essential for raw, unpasteurized milk, dairy products available before 1900. The largest milk distributors to Woods Hole were from New Bedford, Falmouth, or local farms on Cape Cod. State law required that milk delivery be limited to a radius of 140 miles. Land delivery via horse and carriage or train assured quick distribution. Stores in Woods Hole were at the base of Little Harbor and on the Bar Neck waterfront. A worker from the Guano factory would purchase milk enroute to work, drink the milk while on break, and discard the bottle by pitching it into the sea. Other drinks would be consumed and the container similarly discarded.

Household bottles

Bottles containing disinfectant, ink, cleaning solution, cosmetics, perfume, and oil were identified by embossed letters or symbols. This bottle type was a minor fraction of the total, but an important indicator of household items used at the time.

Medicine and Drug Bottles

In the 18th century, medicines were unregulated (Dillin 1989; Baker 2006; O'Reilly 2012). Contents and dosages were not listed. Cure-alls were plentiful but had no scientific basis. The U.S. Food and Drug Act was not enacted until 1906. Medicine bottles from Great Harbor indicate the health concerns of local residents who relied on painkillers and alcohol (Figure 4). Coughing, wheezing, congestion, bronchitis and many other respiratory complications that are aggravated by poor air quality appear to have been common.

Opium derivatives (laudanum, cocaine, morphine, and heroin) were commonly included in the medicines available from local sources. Opium and its derivatives were imported by carriage, ship, and railroad. They were sold without prescription or medical supervision. The U.S. Harrison Narcotics Act that required a prescription from a licensed physician was not in effect until 1914. Antibiotics were unknown and pasteurization was not required. Infectious diseases were poorly understood, and patients self-treated symptoms without medical diagnosis.

The prevalence of medicine bottles in Great Harbor confirms that the local population experienced a wide range of discomforts and illnesses. Respiratory diseases, including dyspnea, chronic obstructive pulmonary disease, and asthma, were exacerbated by air pollution. Neurological complications, including headaches, dizziness, fatigue, and depression, were suggested by submerged pain medication bottles. Liniments to treat cuts, sprains, strains, and musculoskeletal pain were also found.

Dr Scott's Emulsion (1879) contained 50% cod liver oil, 6 gr. of hypophosphite of lime (calcium), and 3 gr. of sodium hypophosphite/oz, emulsified with mucilage and glycerine. Fletcher's Castoria (1868), patented in Barnstable, MA, was a cathartic containing senna, sodium bicarbonate, wintergreen, dandelion extract, sugar, and water. As a cure-all mixture, Castoria was purported to dull pain, treat worms, and relieve fever, diarrhea, colic, teething, flatulence, and constipation

Alcohol and toxic ingredients were commonly sold as soda pop (Dillin 1989) in patent medicines (Figure 4).

These were uncontrolled since dosage, age limits, and frequency of administration were unspecified. Hood's Sarsparilla (1875) was advertised as a blood purifier and cure for eczema, cancer, catarrh, rheumatism, consumption, and dropsy. This drink contained 18% ethanol. Johnson's Anodyne Liniment (1906), containing ethyl ether, was administered both externally and internally. It was a cure-all for coughs, colds, grip, colic, asthma, bronchitis, nasal catarrh, cholera, cramping, diarrhea, bruises, sore throat, burns, and scalds, chafing and chapping, chilblains, frostbite, soreness, rheumatism, sprains, and strains. Dr. A Haynes of Braintree, MA, concocted Arabian Balsam (1850) as an expectorant and counter-irritant to relieve colds, coughs, and hoarseness. Balsam was also recommended for sprains, bruises, burns, stiff muscles, and insect stings or bites. Its ingredients included turpentine and thyme in vegetable oil.

Sanford's Jamaica Ginger (1876) was a delicious and stimulating beverage to treat cramps, generalized pain, colds, and cramps. It contained ginger, aromatics, and French brandy with 70-80% ethanol. However, a neurotoxin, tricresyl-phosphate, was included. This toxin caused an upper motor neuron paralysis called "Jake's Leg", in which patients lost balance, had difficulty walking, stumbled around, and required support for locomotion.

Opium and Opiates in Patent Medicines

Dr. Wistar's Balsam of Wild Cherry, Perry Davis' Vegetable Pain Killer and Dr. A. Boschee's German Syrup are among the addictive narcotic medicine bottles from the harbor (Table 2). The Balsam of Wild Cherry was recommended for diseases of the lung. Wistar promoted his balsam as a cure for consumption (TB) and other pulmonary diseases. Davis' Vegetable Pain Killer was advertised as a wonder drug and painkiller of vegetable origin. This "vegetable elixir", formulated in 1840 by a carpenter from Fall River, MA and Providence, RI, contained alcohol and habit-forming opiates. Davis' Vegetable Pain Killer was the first nationally advertised remedy for pain.

German Syrup was taken for upper respiratory ailments, especially coughs and colds. It was advertised as a cure for consumption and chronic diseases of the throat and lungs (Clemmons 2011). Free samples of this addictive mix of opium, laudanum, and morphine were widely available. In addition, German Syrup contained cyanide in the form of hydrocyanic acid.

By 1890, opium and its derivatives had peaked as a national health problem. Distribution of narcotics was especially widespread in Massachusetts and other New England states (Harmon 2003; Leonard et al. 2012; Bebinger 2017). Courtwright (1983) documented narcotic addiction in southern states. A British cartoon advertising the opium derivative, laudanum, was captioned "Opium, the poor infant's nurse" (Kennedy 2001). Opium and opiate derivatives (morphine, heroin, cocaine, paregoric, and laudanum) were added to many proprietary medicines (Brecher 1972; Berridge and Mars 2004). Opium abuses in the 19th century parallel today's synthetic opioid epidemic. However, synthetic opioids today are more powerful and overdoses are more frequent (Musto 1991; Stobbe 2017).

Opiates in patent medicine were taken to control pain. Robust advertising was used to promote these products. Access to addictive medicines was not restricted. Young children and small infants were given these medications by their parents as sedatives to relieve discomfort and induce sleep (Nevius 2016). Many women developed addiction to narcotics for treating "female problems" such as menstrual cramps, "melancholy" (depression), and stress (Aldrich 2017).

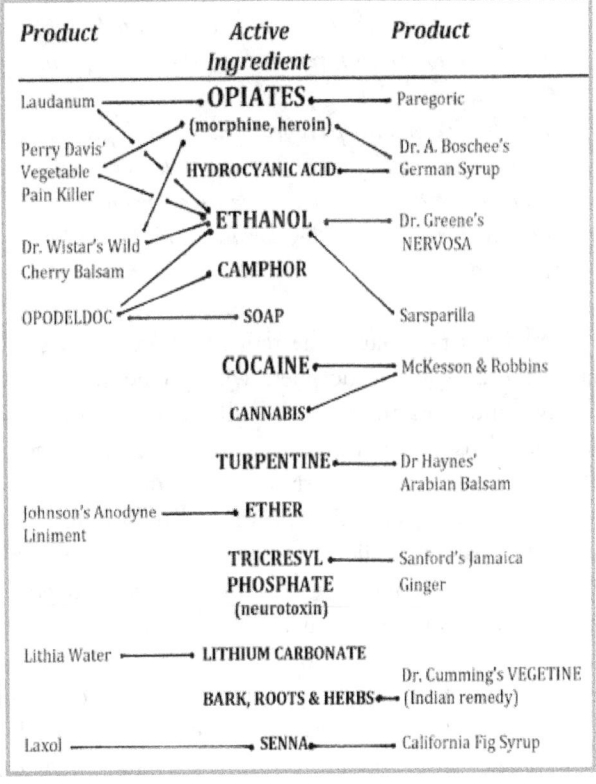

Table 2: Schematic linking the various patent medicines and the harmful ingredients of each for bottles recovered from great harbor

In the 19th century, requirements for listing ingredients on medicine labels and in advertisements were not required. Patent medicines were self-administered, were purchased at nominal cost, and were distributed without any prescription. Not until 1906 did the US Food and Drug Act require listing of components on patent medicine labels. In 1914, the Harrison Narcotic Act required a physician's prescription to purchase any medicine containing narcotics (Nespor 2014).

Industrial Air Pollution

The Pacific Guano Company was the only industry in Woods Hole. When fully operational, effluents from the factory smokestacks accounted for notable odorous and noxious discharges, as indicated in personal diaries (Smith 1986) and in an editorial in the Barnstable Patriot (1873):

> *"The smell of the works is offensive, but not deleterious to health. It will remain for two or three days in the clothes of a visitor. A farm near the establishment would scarcely need a fertilizer, if the wind always blew from the direction of the factory. People interested in building up Woods Hole as a watering place once agitated legal measures to compel removal of the Works, but the general sentiment of the town of Falmouth, in which the company pays heavy taxes, and specially of the many villagers of Woods Hole who earn their living at the Works, made the movement as odious as the factory is odorous, and the subject was dropped."*

Emissions permeated the residential area of the village, polluting the atmosphere with pungent, foul, offensive, and irritating odors of sulfuric acid, rotten and fermented fish, and ammonia-laden seabird excrement. Residents, workers, and visitors to the village could not avoid direct contact with these fumes. The number and variety of patent medicine bottles recovered from Great Harbor suggest that everyone in the village was adversely affected by exposure to heavily polluted air. Those working at the factory may have been most severely influenced because of proximity to the discharge source of micro-particulates and aerosolized industrial chemicals.

Poor air quality coincided with times of full operation of the fertilizer factory, especially when winds blew from the west or when doldrum conditions permeated the atmosphere with stagnant and toxic air. Whenever the wind direction shifted towards the east, the entire landscape was subjected to airborne effluxes that permeated clothing, settled as residues in soil, and adhered to exposed surfaces of people, animals, and objects. Impacts of air pollution extended for several miles beyond the point sources of emission. Recent studies have demonstrated that micro-particulates in industrial emissions impair cognitive brain development and function (Weir 2012; Brockmeyer and D'Anguilli 2016; Rees 2017), disrupt calcium storage in the skeleton (Diddier et al. 2017), irritate sensitive conjunctiva, nasal, oral, and laryngeal membranes, pulmonary and extra-pulmonary airways, and compromise the health of the public (Younan et al. 2017).

Air Pollution as a Public Health Concern

The preponderance of alcoholic and opiate medicine bottles in Great Harbor raises the probability that chronic exposure to air pollution from the Pacific Guano Company may have posed a health threat to the community. Analysis of symptoms supposedly cured by the medicines in medicine bottles from Great Harbor suggests a variety of respiratory, neurological, cutaneous, mucosal, and musculoskeletal ailments. Woods Hole residents relied upon patent medicines to relieve symptoms consequent to exposure to industrial air pollution.

Complaints about air pollution were inconsequential. The town of Falmouth benefitted from taxes paid by the company. The workers enjoyed gainful employment at the company. Since they play outdoors, pre-school and school-aged children were at high risk from factory emissions. However, their concerns were treatable.

Recent clinical studies from UNICEF on the impacts of micro-particulates, volatile toxins, and acidic residues in polluted air from industrial emissions show that the respiratory system is not the only target for air pollution (Rees 2017). Air pollution breaks down epithelial barriers in the brain, increases immunological defenses and activates inflammation. Particulates adversely impact mucous membranes and exposed skin. When inhaled or absorbed, these aerosols can be transported across the blood-brain barrier directly to the central nervous system. If picked up by the blood, they are carried through vascular channels to bone and viscera.

Inhaled airborne pollutants are absorbed through nasal epithelia to exert direct effects upon the frontal cortex, the cortical lobe that controls cognition and executive functions. Micro-pollutants pass through the blood-brain barrier to reach nuclei of the brain stem, including the thalamus and limbic system (Brockmeyer and D'Anguilli 2016). Calcium homeostasis is also affected by micro-pollutants in air. Although calcium mobilization is a complex dynamic, involving the parathyroid glands, vitamin D, and other physiological regulators, absorption of micro-particulates via the lung disturbs mineral retention in bone and contributes to osteoporotic degeneration. Over time, abnormalities in calcium salt deposition result in a skeletal deformations such as scoliosis and kyphosis (Didier et al. 2017).

Conclusions

A natural deepwater harbor is a reservoir for cultural resources. Historical anchorages and their shores represent time capsules, not because of any catastrophic event, but because of where people meet and abandon unwanted objects. Great Harbor at Woods Hole is no exception. Ship crewmen, factory workers, families, and visitors spent time at the harbor's edge and in the anchorage. They discarded empty containers into the sea and out of sight.

The prevalence of medicine bottles among submerged cultural resources retrieved from Great Harbor, coupled with toxic emissions regularly discharged from the Pacific Guano Company, suggest that air quality challenges once affected public health in the village. Although air pollution was not viewed as an environmental health issue at the time, poor air quality would account for treatment of symptoms with opiates and other drugs. Easy access to and advertising for patent medicines, as were common throughout the country, assured marketing of narcotic remedies.

Cultural resources from Great Harbor provide clear evidence that industrialization threatened public health. After 26 years, the Pacific Guano Company collapsed, quality air was restored, and an influx of marine scientists and wealthy property owners ensued to create the Woods Hole village of today.

Acknowledgments

The author expresses his appreciation to the many residents of Woods Hole, MA, who have contributed to this project, especially to the four professional divers who shared their collections of submerged cultural artifacts from Great Harbor. Also, thanks are extended to administrators and staff of the Woods Hole Historical Museum and the Falmouth Historical Society who provided invaluable historical documentation on the early history of the village and harbor. This reconnaissance survey was authorized by permit #07-001 from the MA Board of Underwater Archaeological Resources.

References

ALDRICH, MICHAEL R.
2017   *Historical notes on women addicts.* California AIDS Intervention Training Center, Fitz Hugh Ludlow Memorial Library, San Francisco, California.

ALLARD, DEAN C.
1978   *Spencer Fullerton Baird and the US Fish Commission.* Arno Press, New York, New York.

BAKER, PEGGY M.
2006   *Patent Medicine: cures and quacks.* Pilgrim Society and Pilgrim Hall Museum, Plymouth, Massachusetts.

BARNSTABLE PATRIOT
1873   Pacific Guano Works, Woods Hole. In *Barnstable Patriot.* 21 October:1. Barnstable, Massachusetts.

BEBINGER, MARTHA
2017   *As the Opium Trade Boomed in the 1800s, Boston Doctors Raised Addiction Concerns.* WBUR Common Health, 1 August 2007.

BERRIDGE, VIRGINIA AND SARAH MARS
2004   *History of Addictions.* J. Epidemiol. Comm. Health 58:747-750.

BRECHER, EDWARD M.
1972   Licit and Illicit Drugs. In *The Consumer Union Report on Narcotics, Stimulants, Depressants, Inhalants, Hallucinogens and Marijuana, Including Caffeine, Nicotine and Alcohol,* Little, Brown and Co., Boston, Massachusetts.

BROCKMEYER, SAM AND ARMEDEO D'ANGUILLI
2016   How air pollution alters brain development: the role of neuro-inflammation. Translat. In *Neurosci.* 7(1):24–30.

COURTWRIGHT, DAVID T.
1983   The Hidden Epidemic: Opiate Addiction and Cocaine Use in the South, 1860-1920. In *J. Southern Hist.* LXIX:57-72.

DIDDIER PRADA (ET AL)
2017   Association of air particulate pollution with bone loss over time and bone fracture risk: analysis of data from two independent studies. In *The Lancet Planetary Health* 1:337-347.

DILLIN, JOHN
1989 Roots of US Drug Crisis Run Deep. A century ago, narcotics were found in stores, taverns, patent medicines, and soda pop. In *Addiction in America*. Christian Science Monitor Archives, Boston, Massachusetts.

GAINES, JENNIFER
2007 Pacific Guano Company. In *Spritsail* 21:11-15. Woods Hole Historical Collection, Woods Hole, Massachusetts.

HARMON, KELLY
2003 *A Period of Deceit: the Patent Medicine Business between 1865 and 1906*. Master's Thesis, Univ. North Carolina, Ashville, North Carolina.

KENNEDY, ROBERT
2001 Opium, the Poor Child's Nurse. In *New York Times Co.*, New York, NY. (originally from *Punch, 1849 and Harper's Weekly,* 29 January 1859).

KILBURN, SAMUEL S.
1865 *Specimens of Designing and Engraving on Wood*. Holland Press, Boston MA (plate 35), commissioned by Glidden & Williams, Boston, Massachusetts.

LEONARD, SUSAN H., JEFFREY K BEEMES AND DOUGLAS L ANDERTON
2012 Immigration, Wealth and the "Mortality Plateau" In *Emergent Urban-industrial Towns of 19th Century Massachusetts*. Contin. Change 27:433-459.

MUSTO, DAVID F.
1991 Opium, Cocaine and Marijuana in American History. In *Scientific American* 265 (1):30-37.

NESPOR, CASSIE
2014 *The Great American Fraud: Quacks and Quackery in Medicine*. Melnick Medical Museum, Youngstown, Ohio.

NEVIUS, JAMES
2016 The Strange History of Opiates in America from Morphine for Kids to Heroin for Soldiers. In *The Guardian,* 15 March 2016.

O'REILLY, EDWARD
2012 *Snake oil almanacs: patent medicine advertising in the 19th century.* NY Hist. Soc. Mus. Lib., New York, New York.

PACIFIC GUANO COMPANY
1876 *The Pacific Guano Company: its History, its Products and Trade; its Relation to Agriculture.* (prepared for US Centennial Exhibition in Philadelphia). Riverside Press, Cambridge, Massachusetts.

REES, NICHOLAS
2017 *Danger in the air: how air pollution can affect brain development in young children*. Data Research and Policy, UNICEF, New York, New York.

RIVINUS, E. F. AND E. M. YOUSSEF
1992 *Spencer Baird of the Smithsonian*. Smithsonian Institution Press, Washington, District of Columbia.

ROBINSON, LAUREN
2015 *Hygienic whiskey and little nerve pills: the rise of direct-to-consumer pharmaceutical advertising*. Dig. Proj. Manuscr. Advert. Ephemera, NEH, MCNY. org (https://wp.me/p1kGOJ-30s).

SMITH, MARY L.
1986 *Book of Falmouth*. Elizabeth Spooner Fay (1939) quotation. Falmouth Historical Society, Falmouth, Massachusetts.

STOBBE, MIKE
2017 Opiod epidemic shares chilling similarities with the past. In *Denver Post*. 28 Oct. (Health and Science). Denver, Colorado.

WEIR, KIRSTEN
2012 Smog in our brains. In *American Psychology Association Newsletter* 43:32.Younan, Diana, Catherine Tuvblad, Meredith Franklin, Fred Lurmann, Lianfa Li, Jun Wu, Kiros Berhane, Laura Baker and Jiu-Chiuan Chen

2017 Longitudinal Analysis of Particulate Air Pollutants and Adolescent Delinquent Behavior in Southern California. J. Abnorm. In *Child. Psychology* (https://doi.org/10.1007/s10802-017-0367-5)

. . . .

Raymond L. Hayes
Institute of Maritime History
1010 N Noyes Dr.
Silver Spring, MD 20910 USA

Preserved Meat Supplies or Slaughterhouse Waste Disposal? Zooarchaeology of the Valparaiso Fiscal Mole, Chile

Isabel Cartajena, Diego Carabias, Ana Carolina Barrera, Renato Simonetti, Carla Morales

This paper discusses the zooarchaeological evidence of S3-4 PV, an extensive submerged wharf site located contiguous to the remains of the Fiscal Mole in the port of Valparaiso on the central Chilean coast (32°S). This facility was used by the many line steamers from ca.1884 to 1925. Through underwater archaeology excavations, numerous animal bones were recovered. The data obtained from the zooarchaeological analyses, their comparison with other assemblages recovered near the site, and documentary evidence suggest that the sample represents primarily on-land consumption refuse. We aim to stimulate further discussion on site formation processes of bone assemblages in harbors.

Introduction

In 2011, a dredging project under archaeological monitoring at Terminal No. 1 of the Port of Valparaiso (32° S), on Chile's central coast, designed for handling container and multi-purpose vessels, revealed evidence of an extensive underwater archaeological site (Figure 1). Designated S3-4 PV, the site proved to be an extensive area of activity or refuse deposition situated contiguous to the seaward or exterior line of piles of the Fiscal Mole, a major late 19th century port facility.

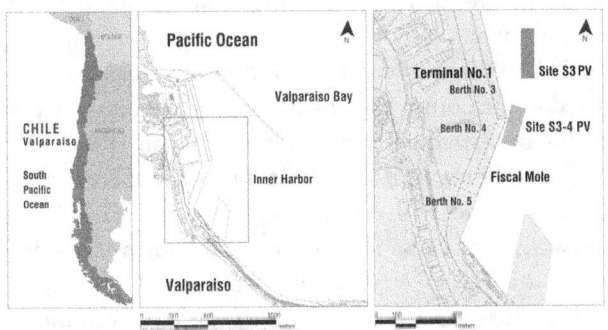

Figure 1. Map showing the location of site S3-4 PV in the inner harbor of Valparaiso, central coast of Chile. (Drawing by Diego Carabias, date.).

As part of a rescue archaeology project in 2012, underwater test excavations revealed artifact rich deposits. Under controlled conditions, a large and diverse assemblage comprising 1,716 finds related to shipping activity in the late 19th and early 20th century was recovered (ÀRKA 2012). Archaeological material included ceramic tableware and other wares, food and beverage glassware and ceramic containers, building materials and personal items, among other items. The vast majority of the material culture was of apparently British origin, most prominently institutional ceramic wares, glassware, and cutlery pertaining to the Pacific Steam Navigation Company (PSNC).

In addition, the excavation yielded abundant animal bones which have undergone preliminary analysis (Barrera 2014). Faunal specimens recovered at wharf and jetty sites are not regularly analyzed. Zooarchaeological studies of underwater historical faunal assemblages derive primarily from wreck sites and while relatively few published studies are known (Migaud 2011:287), a body of descriptive work has been generated during the last few decades providing basis for future analyses (English 1990; Coy et al. 2005; Maclean 2016). In Valparaiso, the best documented collection came from *Infatigable*, a Chilean Navy sailing transport lost in the harbor in 1855 as the result of an accidental fire and subsequent explosion (Carabias 2015; Carabias et al. 2015). The results of the taxonomical and taphonomical analyses concluded that the sample corresponded primarily to preserved meat supplies packed for storage and later consumption (López 2014). The *Infatigable* wreck site, S3 PV, is also located within the inner harbor, approximately 30 m north of S3-4 PV.

Site formation processes affecting wharf and jetty sites have not been thoroughly investigated. However, the factors affecting the archaeological record can include refuse disposal practices in which wastes are intentionally dumped into the sea, along with the loss of material from the waterfront or from moored vessels. The materials deposited on the seafloor are later disturbed by natural and cultural post depositional processes, generating primarily secondary contexts (Nutley 2005:92-95).

Ultimately, the archaeological evidence of site S3-4 PV as an activity area connected to the port of Valparaiso's Fiscal Mole has been highlighted as a primary source of information on food consumption and discarding patterns as well as hygiene standards on board steamships sailing from Europe to South America. In addition, S3-4 PV has provided a more precise understanding of the organization and use of space within the harbor and the historical evolution of Valparaiso's waterfront (Carabias 2015).

The recently available zooarcheological data for *Infatigable*, a well-documented site with and both spatially and temporally close context, provided a basis for new interpretation of the Fiscal Mole faunal assemblage, prompting the authors to reexamine the assemblage and conduct an inter site comparative analysis. Taxonomical and taphonomical data is presented and discussed while considering relevant historical information. Finally, site formation processes of bone assemblages in urban harbors are discussed and the interpretive value of comparative analyses in historical zooarchaeology is highlighted.

Historical Background

From 1873 to 1883, increased shipping activity resulting from Chile's integration into the global capitalist economy led to the construction of the Valparaiso Fiscal Mole, the first major port infrastructure developed in the country. This port facility was preferentially reserved for steamer lines, most notably the Pacific Steam Navigation Company (PSNC), a Liverpool-based company that entered into service in 1840 along the west coast of South America but rapidly became one of the British Empire's leading steamship lines.

The Fiscal Mole infrastructure was only able to partially meet the shipping industry's increasing demand for discharging facilities in Valparaiso at the turn of the century. From 1912 to 1930, major upgrades installed at the port included an extensive breakwater that substantially transformed the waterfront, creating its present inner harbor configuration. At this time, the Fiscal Mole was partly demolished, and the remaining structure, including the massive concrete piles, became embedded in the new pier.

Data and Methods

The remains recovered come from two excavation units covering a total area of 8 m2 with deposits up to 1.2 m deep. In all, 771 animal bones were recovered (Barrera 2014). Once at the laboratory, the recovered bones underwent conservation treatment to remove soluble salts in order to stabilize the material. The soluble salts were removed by rinsing in successive baths of water, starting with 100% seawater and increasing the proportion of freshwater (local tap water) until the rinse contained pure freshwater. Distilled water was then used to rinse the material until the soluble salts were removed. Soft wooden tools and brushes were used to prevent surface damage.

The remains were identified taxonomically through reference collections and age estimations for cattle and small livestock were conducted on the basis of epiphyseal fusion (Schmid 1972) and by dental eruption using the tables assembled by Manhart (1998) and Schmid (1972) for domestic taxa.

In order to compare and contrast the frequencies of skeletal parts, different quantification units were used. NISP (number of identified specimens) were contrasted with MNI (minimum number of individuals) values for each taxa. The MNE (minimal number of elements) was defined as the number of skeletal elements necessary to account for an assemblage of specimens of a particular skeletal element under study, while the MAU (minimal anatomical units) results from dividing MNE values for each anatomical part or portion by the number of times that part or portion occurs in the complete skeleton (Lyman 1994). To obtain the %MAU, each MAU value was divided by the greatest observed MAU in the assemblage and then each resulting value was standardized by multiplying it by 100. One major advantage of using %MAU is that different excavation units can be compared to each other, thereby preventing the bias inherent in different-sized bone assemblages (Lyman 1994).

The taphonomical analyses included the effect of abrasion, as contact with sedimentary particles suspended in the water may cause abrasion in bones during transport or in situ (Fernández-Jalvo and Andrews 2003; Migaud 2011). Abrasion was measured taking into account intensity (low, moderate, and severe), extension (extensive, limited) and rounding of the edges (Fernández-Jalvo and Andrews 2003). Despite considerable abrasion, signs of weathering could still be observed. The effects of weathering on the bone assemblage were measured using the six weathering stages proposed by Behrensmeyer (1978). Other natural taphonomic agents were considered as well, such as the presence of root marks and staining. In addition, modifications resulting from rodent gnawing and carnivore activity (Binford 1981), and bioreosion and encrustation caused by marine organisms (Leonard-Pingel 2005) were recorded. Cultural modifications included cut marks and bone fractures by metal objects such as saws and knives (Bagaloni and Carrascosa 2013).

As a final stage of analysis, an interassemblage comparison of the Fiscal Mole and Infatigable samples was conducted in order to better address research questions. The material comes from eight excavation units that cover an area of 32 m2 and correspond to 297 bone remains (López 2014).

Results

The Fiscal Mole faunal assemblage displays a high taxonomic diversity (large mammals, small livestock, carnivores, rodents, hares, domestic fowl, and fish) while primarily represented by domestic taxa. The NISP is clearly dominated by cattle bones, small livestock (mainly sheep and goats), and domestic fowl (mainly chickens and turkeys). However, when measured through MNI, the taxonomic abundance of cattle and small livestock increase and the latter now represent the majority (Figure 2).

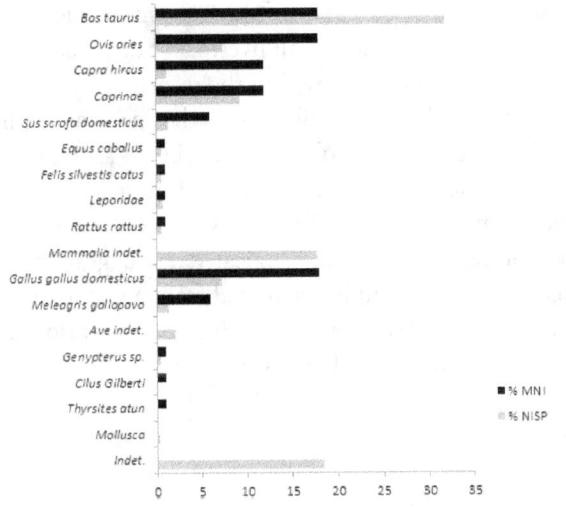

Figure 2. Taxonomic distribution of the site S3-4 PV quantified in terms of %MNI (black bar) and %NISP (grey bar).

In the case of cattle, the distribution of axial and appendicular bone skeletal units was recorded (Table 1). Heads and limbs are highly underrepresented. Several bones correspond to butchering refuse discarded after deboning. The presence of tongue bones suggest that the tongue was cut out for consumption possibly before the hide was delivered to the tanner. Head and lower extremities are generally unlikely to be found since they would have remained with the hide. Most cattle were slaughtered while they were subadults and juveniles, a profile characteristic of meat-oriented cattle production. Sixty percent of the bones exhibit sawing and cut marks resulting from industrial processing of carcasses. The high proportion of sawed bones, the regular size of the pieces, and the representation of skeletal units are in accordance with meat cuts commonly performed by butchers, suggesting that the majority of the units correspond to consumption refuse.

Anatomica Unit	S3-4 PV[a] NISP	MNE	MAU	%MAU	S3-PV[b] NISP	MNE	MAU
Cranium	-	-	-	-	1	1	1
Molar indet.	1	1	0.1	2	-	-	-
Third molar	1	1	0.5	13	-	-	-
Os hyoideum	1	1	0.5	13	-	-	-
Atlas	3	2	2.0	50	3	2	2
Axis	3	3	3.0	75	1	1	1
Cervical vertebrae	6	3	0.4	11	22	12	2.4
Thoracic vertebrae	13	9	0.7	17	13	9	0.7
Lumbar vertebrae	26	11	1.8	46	2	1	0.2
Caudal vertebrae	1	1	0.1	1	-	-	-
Costae	109	39	1.5	38	69	14	0.5
Sacrum	2	2	1.0	25	1	1	1
Scapula	10	4	2.0	50	21	12	6
Humerus	15	5	2.5	63	11	3	1.5
Radius-ulna	9	8	4.0	100	3	2	1
Carpalia	4	4	0.7	17	-	-	-
Metacarpus	1	1	0.5	13	-	-	-
Innominate	10	7	3.5	88	9	8	4
Femur	23	7	3.5	88	19	8	4
Patella	2	2	1.0	25	-	-	-
Tibia	12	8	4.0	100	8	3	1.5
Tarsalia	3	3	0.6	15	1	1	0.1
Astragalus	5	5	2.5	63	1	1	0.5
Calcaneum	7	5	2.5	63	3	2	1
Metatrsus	6	6	3.0	75	-	-	-
Metapodia	2	1	0.3	6	-	-	-
Phal. 1	2	2	0.3	6	-	-	-
Phal. 2	3	3	0.4	10	-	-	-
Phal. 3	4	4	0.5	13	-	-	-

a Source Barrera 2014: Table 8
b Source López 2014: Table 10

Table 1. Distribution of cattle anatomical units for the S3-4 PV and S3-PV sites (source Barrera 2014:table 8; lópez 2014:table 10).

Anatomical Unit	NISP	MNE	MAU	%MAU
Cranium	4	4	4.0	67
Maxilla	7	7	3.5	58
Mandible	13	12	6.0	100
Incisor	2	2	0.3	6
Third Premolar	1	1	0.5	8
Third Molar	1	1	0.5	8
Os hyoideum	2	2	1.0	17
Atlas	2	2	2.0	33
Axis	1	1	1.0	17
Cervical vertebrae	7	5	0.7	12
Thoracic vertebrae	2	2	0.1	1
Lumbar vertebrae	6	6	0.9	14
Costae	38	24	0.9	12
Scapula	3	3	1.5	25
Humerus	4	3	1.5	25
Radius-ulna	11	6	3.0	50
Metacarpus	1	1	1.0	17
Innominate	3	3	1.5	25
Femur	10	7	3.5	58
Tibia	14	9	4.5	75
Matacarpus	1	1	0.5	8
Astragalus	5	5	2.5	42

Source: Barrera 2014: Table 15

Table 2. Distribution of caprinae anatomical units for the S3-4 PV site (source Barrera 2014:table 15).

Sheep are the most frequently occurring small livestock, although some goats and very few pigs are also present. In the case of sheep (MNI 6) and goats (MNI 4), the head (cranium, maxilla and mandible) is most frequently represented, followed by hind legs (femur and tibia), front legs (radius and ulna), and to a lesser degree, vertebrae, ribs and scapular, and pelvic girdles (Table 2).

The processing of caprines (sheep and goats) differs from that of cattle. Fewer bones show saw marks (i.e. ribs), instead long bones were fractured by hacking with

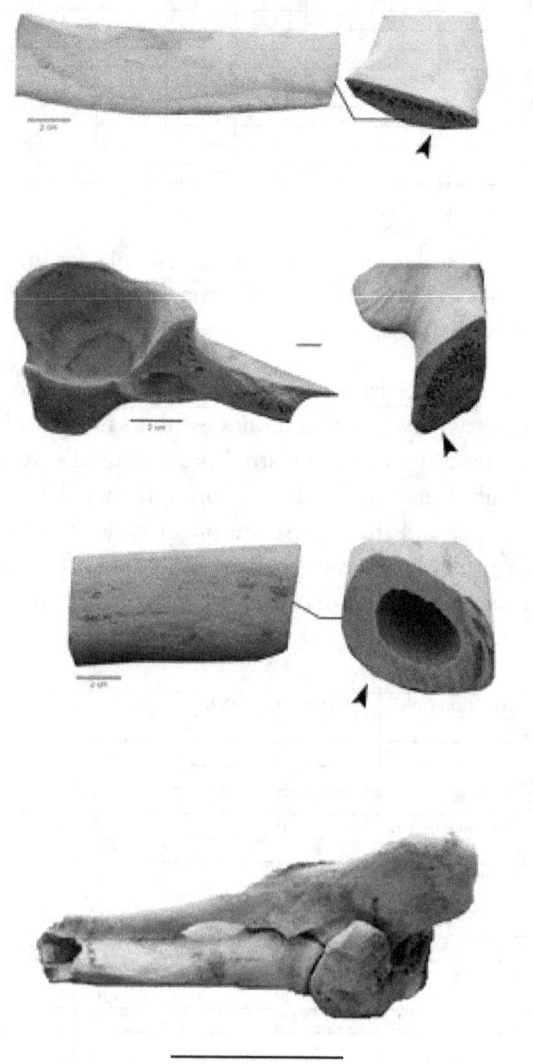

Figure 3. Cattle rib, innominate and humerus diaphisys sawed cuts. Bottom: Caprinae radius-ulna medial and proximal and humerus distal articulated (Photo by Ana Carolina Barrera, edited by Patricio López, date.).

a large butcher knife (Figure 3). As in the case of cattle, the caprine units represented may correspond to the remains of consumption, although unlike in the cattle remains, where heads are quite infrequent, heads are present in this sample, and were probably cooked.

In sum, the analyses of the cattle and caprine bones recovered at the Fiscal Mole site tend to indicate mainly consumption refuse, while retail butchery refuse may also be present. This is also the case for domestic fowl and hare, which have been consumed.

By contrast, the *Infatigable* (S3 PV) site displays one important difference, namely a less diverse faunal assemblage, which is clearly dominated by cattle bones with few small livestock remains (López 2014) (Figure 4 top). The cattle skeletal units of the Fiscal Mole faunal assemblage show less variety, with a high predominance of scapula, radius-ulna, and innominates. It is worth noting that the butchering pattern recorded at the Fiscal Mole site is very similar to that observed at the Infatigable wreck site. Most of the bones feature saw marks. Nonetheless, the sizes of the portions are smaller, showing high homogeneity (standardization) which might be related to the dimension of the casks in which the meat was stored. This is also the case for small livestock, notwithstanding its scarce representation within the record.

Figure 4 (bottom) highlights the natural taphonomic modifications observed in both assemblages. Pre-depositional processes can be inferred from the different modifications observed within the Fiscal Mole assemblage. The zooarchaeological data suggests that a large part of the sample originated from a variety of on-land activities including butchering; consumption and disposal and was later dumped into the sea.

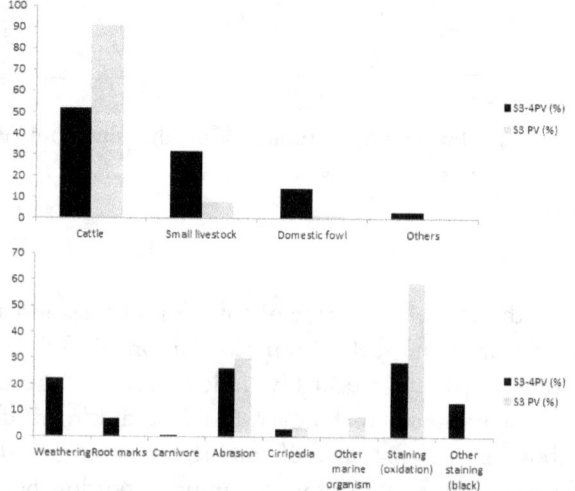

Figure 4. Comparison between the sites S3-4PV and S3 PV. Top: general taxonomic groups (%NISP). Bottom: natural taphonomic modifications. (Sources: Barrera 2014 and López 2014).

By contrast, the animal bones recovered from the *Infatigable* wreck site show no pre-depositional modifications. This taphonomic evidence supports the idea that the material recovered from the wreckage represents primarily preserved meat supplies packed for storage and later consumption.

Discussion

A comparison of the Fiscal Mole and the *Infatigable* wreck site faunal assemblages yields some evident differences. First, the diversity and frequency of the represented taxa at the two sites differ significantly. The animal bones recovered at S3-4PV originated predominantly from on-land activities and are interpreted as food remains related to Valparaiso's urban market system. In effect, the zooarcheological data seems to indicate that the sample corresponds primarily to consumption refuse from the nearby area of the city. Indeed, in 1870 many popular taverns and butcher shops were operating around the neighboring *Recova del Puerto* or Port Market.

In the latter half of the 19th century, the rapid growth of Valparaiso's population and industrial sectors prompted municipal authorities to introduce a regulatory system, normalize urban planning and implement countless public works (Estrada 2000). Public health and sanitation standards, enforced as city ordinances, included regulations for waste disposal. During the 1860s, refuse from slaughterhouses, households, and public and private buildings were to be dumped on beach places washed away by breaking waves (Peña 1872:170). In 1870, the authorities announced the building of small jetties to be located in appropriate places along the coastline to facilitate the disposing of garbage and filth as far off the beach as possible (Lira 1870:61-62). One year later, sanitation officers were operating an experimental jetty on the waterfront close to the Fiscal Warehouses, using wagons on rails to transport and dump waste into the sea (Echaurren 1871:103-104). This historical information is consistent with the Plan of the City of Valparaiso published in 1871 in Paris, which presumably depicts at least one jetty in that location.

The location of this first 'sanitation jetty', approximately 300 m from the Port Market place, was located approximately 125 m from the eventual location of the Fiscal Mole, built in 1873. The waterfront next to the Fiscal Warehouses where the jetty was located would later be modified to accommodate a wharf during the construction of the Fiscal Mole.

The taphonomic trajectories of the examined sample indicates that at least some of the animal bones were disposed of on land and shortly afterwards dumped into the ocean. Other remains, however, could have been discarded on land, buried and later removed to be used as landfill for the waterfront project. Thus, the large animal bone remains contained in the seabed deposits might be partially from the aforementioned jetty and anot directly associated with the Fiscal Mole, constructed in the same area.

It is unlikely that a significant part of the sample analyzed came from the disposal of large quantities of preserved meat supplies from steamships visiting the Fiscal Mole. Historical information emphasizes the consumption of fresh meat on board when in port while at the same time, dumping waste into sea in the area used by vessels was strictly forbidden by Harbor Regulations (Peña 1872:368). However, illegal dumping is suggested by archaeological sources. In effect, the S3-4 PV deposits contained slag, coal and diagnostic artifacts such as institutional ceramic wares of the PSNC in high frequencies (ÀRKA 2012; Rodríguez et al. 2016).

On the other hand, in the *Infatigable* faunal assemblage, cattle bones far outweigh the rest of the specimens, indicating clear taxonomic selection, and those bones display butcher marks consistent with the meat preservation process. Thus, the zooarchaeological data of the S3 PV sample is in good agreement with documentary evidence regarding the Chilean Navy regulations of the period, under which preserved salted beef was a fundamental component of the official naval diet (Gundian 1866:248-249). The paucity of natural taphonomic modifications in the sample further supports the interpretation of these elements as shipboard packed salted meat supplies.

Finally, while the butchering patterns show similarities, frequency and size of the pieces varies between the two sites. However, it is interesting to note that both the Fiscal Mole faunal assemblage and that of the *Infatigable* include meat cuts suitable for preparing soup/broth and stew dishes that would have included not only meat but fat and marrow, too. This type of food preparation is an efficient way to feed working men, both land-bound civilian workers and on board naval crews, and is also consistent with important cultural expressions like the cazuela, a South American dish of Spanish gastronomic tradition, a kind of moderately-thick flavored stock obtained from cooking several kinds of meats and vegetables together (Pereira Salas 1977:82).

Conclusion

The preliminary results of the zooarchaeological analyses suggest that the S3-4 PV sample primarily represents only land consumption refuse. While the presence of preserved meat and slaughter remains within the sample cannot be precluded, taxonomic and taphonomic evidence indicates that these elements are under-represented in the Fiscal Mole faunal assemblage. Furthermore, by integrating zooarchaeological and historical information, the remains could be interpreted as waste, probably associated with the neighboring Port Market area of Valparaiso and disposed of at the waterfront. While further research regarding fragmentation and butchering patterns in the late nineteenth is certainly required, we expect that this comparative analysis can stimulate further discussion on site formation processes of bone assemblages in harbors while providing new information on food practices both on land and at sea for this time period.

Acknowledgements

This research has benefited from the financial support of Terminal Pacifico Sur Valparaiso (TPS). The authors would like to thank Patricio López for providing access to the *Infatigable* zooarcheological study.

References

ÀRKA
2012 *Informe de Caracterización Arqueológica Subacuática Sitio S3-4 PV, Muelle Fiscal, Puerto Valparaíso.* Project "Extensión y Mejoramiento Frente de Atraque N° 1 del Puerto de Valparaíso, Comuna de Valparaíso, V Región". Report commissioned by Terminal Pacífico Sur Valparaíso S.A. REF. INF10/2012.

BAGALONI, VANESA AND LEIRE CARRASCOSA
2013 Estudio de huellas producidas con objetos de metal durante el último cuarto del siglo XIX en el sitio arqueológico La Libertad (partido de San Cayetano, Buenos Aires, Argentina). *Revista Museo de La Plata, Sección Antropología* 13(87):375-393.

BARRERA, ANA CAROLINA
2014 Análisis Arqueofaunístico: Caracterización zooarqueológica del sitio histórico sumergido S3-4 PV del Puerto de Valparaíso (V Región, Chile). *Professional Internship Report for the Department of Anthropology*, Universidad de Chile, Santiago, Chile.

BEHRENSMEYER, ANNA K.
1978 Taphonomic and Ecologic Information from Bone Weathering. *Paleobiology* 4(2):150-62.

CARABIAS, DIEGO
2015 Valparaíso: El Patrimonio bajo la Cota Cero del Puerto Principal. In *Patrimonio Cultural Subacuático en América Latina y el Caribe*. Cultura y Desarrollo N° 13. UNESCO Regional Cultural Office for Latin America and the Caribbean, Habana, Cuba.

CARABIAS, DIEGO, RENATO SIMONETTI, CARLA MORALES, AND PATRICIO LÓPEZ
2015 Investigación, conservación y análisis de los restos de un transporte del estado: la barca *Infatigable* (1855). Paper presented at the XX Congreso Nacional de Arqueología Chilena, Concepción, Chile.

COY, JENNIE, SHEILA HAMILTON-DYER, AND IAN OXLEY
2005 Meat and Fish: the Bone Evidence. In *Before the Mast: Life and Death Aboard the Mary Rose. Archaeology of the Mary Rose*, J. Gardiner, editor, pp. 564-588. Mary Rose Trust/Oxbow, England.

ECHAURREN, FRANCISCO
1871 Memoria del Intendente de Valparaíso. In *Memoria que el Ministro de Estado en el Apartamento del Interior presenta al Congreso Nacionales de 1871*, pp. 97-130. Imprenta Nacional, Santiago, Chile.

ENGLISH, ANTHONY J.
1990 Salted meats from the Wreck of the William Salthouse: Archaeological Analysis of Nineteenth Century Butchering Patterns. *Australian Historical Archaeology* 8:63-69.

ESTRADA, BALDOMERO
2000 Poblamiento e inmigración en una ciudad-puerto. Valparaíso 1820-1920. In *Valparaíso. Sociedad y Economía en el Siglo XIX*, Baldomero Estrada y Eduardo Cavieres, editors, pp. 13-53. Serie Monografías Históricas 12.Valparaíso, Chile.

FERNÁNDEZ-JALVO YOLANDA AND PETER ANDREWS
2003 Experimental abrasion of water effects on bone fragments. *Journal of Taphonomy* 1(3):147–163.

GUNDIAN, ANTONIO
1866 *Manual del Marino o Guía del Comandante y Oficial de guerra y administración de la Marina de la República. Colección de Leyes, Decretos, Reglamentos, Órdenes y Formularios que deben tenerse presenta en la Marina Militar*. Imprenta y Librería de la Independencia, Santiago, Chile.

LEONARD-PINGEL, JILL SUZANNE
2005   Molluscan taphonomy as a proxy for recognizing fossil seagrass beds. Master's thesis, Department Geology and Geophysics, Louisiana State University, Baton Rouge, LA

<https://digitalcommons.lsu.edu/gradschool_theses/1678>. Accessed 23 November 2016.

LIRA, RAMÓN
1870   Memoria del Intendente de Valparaíso. In Memoria que el Ministro de Estado en el Departamento del Interior presenta al Congreso Nacional de 1870, pp. 55-66. Imprenta Nacional, Santiago, Chile.

LÓPEZ, PATRICIO
2014   Informe de Zooarqueología y Tafonomía Sitio S3 PV. Study commissioned by ÀRKA – Arqueología Marítima.

LYMAN, R. LEE
1994   *Vertebrate Taphonomy*. Cambridge Manuals in Archaeology. Cambridge University Press, Cambridge, UK.

MANHART, HENRIETTE
1998   *Die vorgeschichtliche Tierwelt von Koprivec und Durankulak und anderen prähistorischen Fundplätzen in Bulgarien aufgrund von Knochenfunden aus archäologischen Ausgrabungen*. Doctoral dissertation, Faculty of Biologie, Ludwig Maximilians University, Munich, Germany. Documenta Naturae 116.

MACLEAN, KAITLIN
2016   Analysis of the faunal remains from the *Machault*. Master's thesis, University of Southern Denmark, Esbjerg, Denmark.

MIGAUD, PHILIPPE
2011   A first approach to links between animals and life on board sailing vessels (1500-1800). The *International Journal of Nautical Archaeology* 40(2):283-292.

NUTLEY, DAVID
2005   Underwater Archaeology. In *Maritime Archaeology: Australian Approaches*, Mark Staniforth and Michael Nash, editors, pp. 92-95. Springer, New York, NY.

PEÑA, SALUSTIO
1872   Recopilación de las disposiciones administrativas vigentes en el Departamento de Valparaíso. Imprenta del Mercurio, Valparaíso, Chile.

PEREIRA SALAS, EUGENIO
1977   *Apuntes para la historia de la cocina chilena*. Editorial Universitaria, Santiago, Chile.

RODRÍGUEZ, ANGELA, VALERIA SEPÚLVEDA AND DIEGO CARABIAS
2016   Late 19th and Early 20th Century institutional wares of the Pacific Steam Navigation Company: a preliminary assessment of the Valparaiso Fiscal Mole Assemblage, Chile. Paper presented at IKUWA6: the Sixth International Congress on Underwater Archaeology, Fremantle, Australia.

SCHMID, ELIZABETH
1972   *Atlas of Animal Bones: For Prehistorians, Archaeologist and Quaternary Geologists*. Elsevier Publishing Company, New York, NY.

. . . .

Isabel Cartajena
Capitán Ignacio Carrera Pinto 1045,
Ñuñoa, Santiago, Chile

Diego Carabias
Muelle Barón s/n,
Valparaíso, Chile

Ana Carolina Barrera
Capitán Ignacio Carrera Pinto 102 A, App. 32,
Nuñoa, Santiago, Chile

Renato Simonetti
Muelle Barón s/n,
Valparaíso, Chile

Carla Morales
Muelle Barón s/n,
Valparaíso, Chile

Landing for Water and Wood can leave a Mark: Ship Graffiti as Evidence of Visitation to Cocos Island, Costa Rica

Jason T. Raupp, Anne E. Wright, Omar Fernández López

European exploration of the Pacific Ocean resulted in the identification of abundant natural resources. Though largely undisturbed for centuries, the late eighteenth and nineteenth century activities of whaleships produced new opportunities for trade and economic development in the region. For at least two hundred and twenty years ships of exploration, whaleships, merchant vessels, and pleasure craft visited Costa Rica's Cocos Island to reprovision and their crews inscribed information onto the many stones that litter its shores. Recent investigations at Cocos produced a partial inventory of visible markings and opened a dialogue about their creation and the need for additional documentation.

Introduction

Cocos Island is a mountainous and heavily vegetated landmass located roughly 295 miles southwest of the Pacific coast of Costa Rica (Figure 1) and approximately 400 miles northeast of the Galapagos Islands (Freeman 1951:552; Dodge 1971:532). Although the majority of the small island's coastline is characterized by sheer cliff faces, access to shore is provided mainly through two bays on its northern coast where safe anchorages in deep water are found (Rose 1927:262). The tropical climate of the island produces year-round rainfall, which in turn creates numerous cascades of fresh water sources (Freeman 1951:552). Perhaps best known for the legends of treasure buried by pirates and thieves, the island has been the subject of numerous expeditions by fortune seekers. Due to its remote geographic location, Cocos has only been inhabited for short periods of time and therefore relatively few physical remains of cultural activities are found there. What is apparent, however, is the physical evidence of visitation over two hundred and twenty-four years in the form of inscriptions made on the soft stones scattered around the landing places on the island. These stones contain carvings of names, dates, religious iconography, possible communication between ships, and reports of whaling data, as well as historic and modern graffiti. This paper explores the history of the island, provides a discussion of this unique heritage type, and suggests potential methods for future research into the inscribed stones of Cocos Island.

Cocos Island Historical Background

With no known evidence of prehistoric habitation, Cocos Island is considered to have been first identified by Spanish navigator Juan de Cabezas in 1526 (Oviedo 1851). Between the sixteenth and eighteenth centuries Spanish, Dutch, and English explorers called at the island and some marked its position on nautical charts (Beebe and Rose 1926). English explorer Captain George Vancouver visited Cocos in 1795 and ascertained an exact position for the island. Vancouver later published an account of his travels which included a lengthy physical description of the island and indicated that a seemingly endless supply of fresh water and an abundance of excellent firewood could be easily obtained there (1801:181-183). In 1838 the majority of the island's coastline was accurately surveyed by Sir Edward Belcher (Belcher 1843; Beebe and Rose 1926:241).

When American and British whaleships rounded Cape Horn in 1789, they found rich sperm whale hunting grounds which led to a veritable rush to exploit these natural resources (Stackpole 1972:129; Richards 1994:26). News of these fertile whaling grounds spread quickly and the number of ships entering the Pacific grew exponentially. Beginning off the southern coast

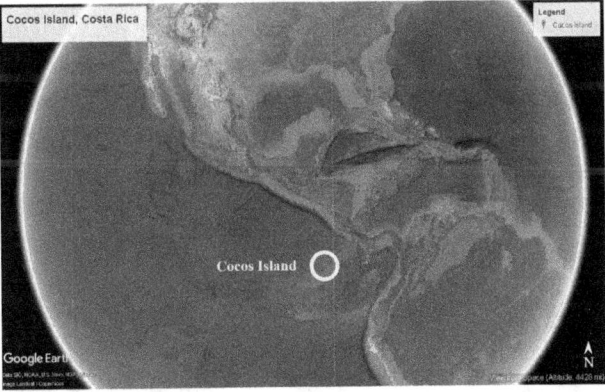

Figure 1: Location of Cocos Island indicated by yellow circle (Google Maps).

of Chile, whalers exploited cetacean populations until they were depleted. In a relatively brief time a pattern developed which saw a new hunting area identified and then rapidly depleted, which in turn led to exploration further into the largely unknown expanse of the Pacific (Raupp 2015).

Over time whaling captains developed an understanding of the migratory patterns and behaviors of their prey and a keen understanding of the physical geography of the region. With expanded operational range came an understandable lengthening of the average whaling cruise, as well as extended periods spent at sea without calls to established ports for provisions. To provide crews with fresh drinking water and produce, it was necessary to visit islands with safe anchorages to replenish supplies. Often captains drew from knowledge shared among the whaling fraternity to determine the locations for such places (Raupp 2015). Eventually certain islands became known as places to procure specific items easily and safely; with its numerous accessible cascades and ample trees, Cocos Island became synonymous with fresh water and firewood. Over the course of the nineteenth century, whaleships and merchant vessels often visited Cocos Island for reprovisioning purposes.

Although the island was claimed by Costa Rica in 1869, aside from visits by passing ships and sporadic episodes of castaways finding haven there, Cocos remained largely uninhabited (Trusty et al. 2006:252). Costa Rican authorities attempted to utilize the island for a penal colony which operated in the late 1870s, but it was short lived (Alfaro 1898; Trusty et al. 2006:252; Bergoeing 2017:229). In 1897 the government sanctioned an agricultural colony on Cocos and German adventurer and treasure hunter August Gissler acted as ex-officio governor (Rose 1926; Hogue and Miller 1981:3; Bergoeing 2017:229). Although Gissler and his wife convinced thirteen German families to work for the Cocos Island Agricultural Company, the venture was a total failure and abandoned completely by 1905 (Rose 1926; Trusty et al. 2006:252).

Scientists interested in the ecosystems of Cocos Island and its surrounding waters began conducting research missions there as early as the mid-nineteenth century (Hogue and Miller 1981; Trusty et al. 2006). The island was also the stage for numerous expeditions in search of the legendary "Treasure of Lima", which was reportedly buried there by the pirate Benno Benito in 1820 to keep it from falling into the hands of brigands (Taylor & Tevin 1880; Kirkendale 1903; Chambers and Chambers 1905; Rose 1926; Dodge 1971:532). None of the treasure hunts proved successful and the island remained largely unmolested thereafter.

In 1970, the Costa Rican government designated Cocos as an administrative district of the Province of Puntarenas (Bergoeing 2017:227). Due to its extremely remote location and the unique oceanic ecosystem in the waters surrounding it, an Executive Decree established Cocos Island as a national park in 1978. Further environmental protections were provided when it was declared a World Heritage Site by the United Nations Educational, Scientific, and Cultural Organization (UNESCO) in 1997, and incorporated as an International Important Wetland (RAMSAR site) in 1998 (Bergoeing 2017:227). For the past forty years, Cocos Island has been inhabited only by a small number of Costa Rican park rangers who manage the site and assist ecotourism ventures focused on the island's unique diving conditions.

Cocos Island Inscriptions and Cultural Heritage

Little information about the archaeological record of Cocos Island has so far been found. Although reports from scientific expeditions indicate that remains thought to be associated with the Costa Rican penal colony, colonization attempt, or treasure expeditions were previously visible (Tanner 1893:262; Rose 1926), none of these are known to have been documented in recent times. In 2014 a small team of Spanish archaeologists visited the island and documented the wreckage of a large steel-hulled sailing vessel lost in Wafer Bay in 1921 (Lozano Guerra-Librero and Fernández López 2014). Historical research conducted in association with that survey indicates several other shipwrecks have occurred around the island, however, no physical remains for those losses were identified. The survey project did identify and preliminarily document several inscriptions carved onto stones of varying sizes (Figure 2) and located at the mouth of the Genio River, which empties into Wafer Bay, as well as on stones located on the beach at Chatham Bay (Lozano Guerra-Librero and Fernández López 2014). Field analysis of these inscriptions provided dates ranging from the early nineteenth to the twenty-first century (Lozano Guerra-Librero and Fernández López 2014).

The inscriptions on the stones at Wafer and Chatham Bays have been the subject of curiosity for visitors to Cocos Island since at least the late eighteenth century. The first known historical description of this phenomena is found in Vancouver's *A Voyage of Discovery to the North*

Pacific Ocean and Round the World, in which he documented an eroded inscription which he speculated to mean that he had indeed found Cocos Island (1801:177-178). Thereafter, several visitors to the island made references to the inscriptions or the practice of making them (Belcher 1843:187; Davis 1874:116; Tanner 1893:261; Chambers and Chambers 1905:114; Wheeler 1968:8), and in some cases, undertook extensive inventories of names, dates, and other information inscribed on the stones (Rose 1926; Arias Sanchez 1993). Interestingly, Vancouver's 1794 visit to the island represents not only the first known documentation of inscriptions at Cocos Island, but also provides the earliest evidence of an order being given explicitly to create them. Upon his departure from the island Vancouver instructed members of his crew to inscribe the date of their visit, as well as the names of the vessels and their commanders, to commemorate their calling there (Vancouver 1801:189).

The fact that visitors deemed the Cocos Island inscriptions important enough to mention in their notes and musings indicates a long fascination with the act of leaving a physical mark to commemorate a visit to a remote place, as well as the historical value of graffiti. What's more is the fact that those same authors felt the need to add their own mark on the stones, thus perpetuating the practice.

Analysis & Interpretation of Inscriptions

The data collected by Lozano Guerra-Librero and Fernández López (2014) was later analyzed to better understand the depth of time represented by the inscriptions and the types of information they depict. Though not a complete inventory, this dataset represents a sample of the many visible markings that could be documented in the limited time available. The markings are carved into soft sandstone boulders and many are heavily weathered and eroded, which created difficulties in deciphering some of them. To standardize thematic categories on historical maritime graffiti, the current analysis utilized those determined by Fyfe and Brady (2014) in their study of similar historical inscriptions found on Ngiangu (Booby Island) in northern Queensland (Australia).

The sample of inscriptions recorded by Lozano Guerra-Librero and Fernández López (2014) provide information for a period of approximately 170 years (Figure 3). Based on these data, the majority of nineteenth century visitors who commemorated their calls did so between 1830 and 1870, with the decades of 1830-1850 having the highest numbers of inscriptions. Curiously, for the period of 1880 to 1920 no evidence of visitation is found in this data set. Furthermore, although the number of inscriptions dating from the early to mid-twentieth century (1920-1960) remained a relatively consistent and small number, a noticeable increase in the number of marks is seen between the years 1970 and 1999.

The inscription data were also analyzed to determine basic types of information depicted. Sub-categories for this analysis included names, ship names with dates; names of individuals with dates; initials/single letters; other inscriptions; and symbols (Figure 4). The data indicate that the markings primarily consist of the names of ships and associated dates of visitation. Names of individuals and associated dates are also a common theme, while inscriptions depicting initials or single letters, other (unidentifiable) words or letters, and symbols are only marginally represented. The information contained in the data collected by Lozano Guerra-Librero and Fernández López (2014) is interesting when considered within its proper historical context. The impact of the American whaling industry on Cocos Island is undeniable. Analysis of the names and dates inscribed from the early to mid-nineteenth century indicates that they were made by crews of whaling vessels who stopped for provisions. A cursory review of entries recorded in some of the Nantucket Historical Association Research Library's logbook collections, and which correspond to names depicted on stone, reveal stops made at Cocos Island for water or firewood (Nantucket Historical Association Research Library 2017). The fact that most of the inscriptions dating to that period were made by whalers is unsurprising given the fact that American whaling reached its peak in the late 1840s with several hundred ships roving the Pacific on voyages lasting up to six years (Raupp 2015). Furthermore, the lack of inscriptions dating from 1880 to 1920 could also be the result of the eventual waning of the American whaling industry following the discovery of petroleum in Pennsylvania in 1859 (Daum 1959:21; Raupp 2015).

Another interesting observation produced by the analysis of the 2014 dataset is that despite a consistently small number of inscriptions made during the early to mid-twentieth century, a dramatic increase occurred between 1970 and 1999. In the earlier period most of the marks appear to have been left by crews from merchant ships, military vessels, or pleasure craft. The majority of inscriptions dating from the later part of the century, however, were placed on the stones by crews

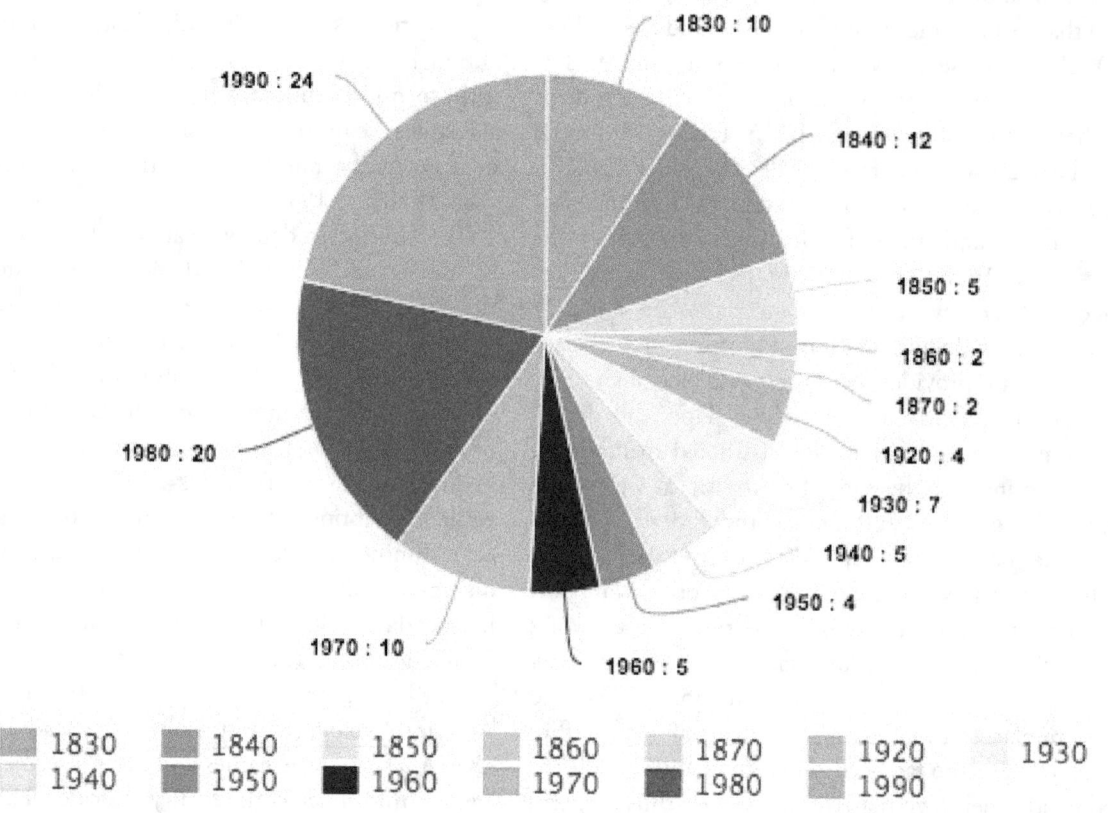

Figure 3: Chart illustrating the frequency of inscriptions by decade drawn from data collected during the 2014 investigation by Guerra-Librero and Fernández López.

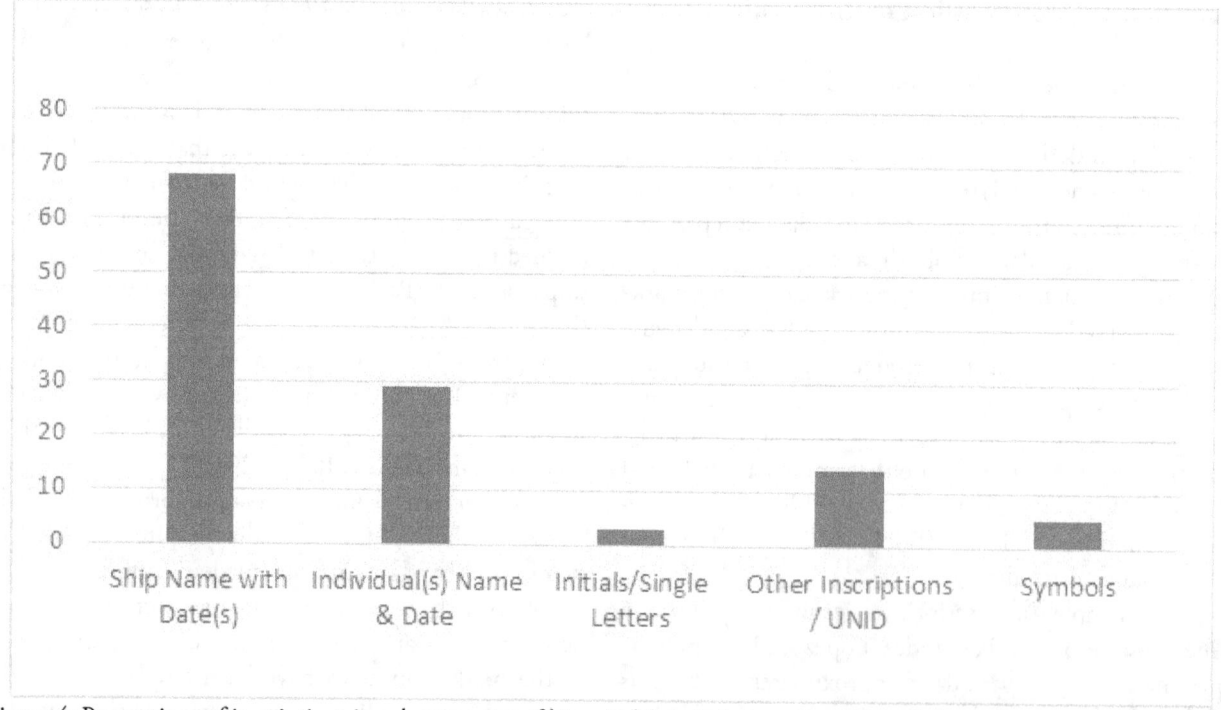

Figure 4: Proportions of inscriptions in sub-categories of historical inscriptions at Cocos Island drawn from data collected during the 2014 investigation by Guerra-Librero and Fernández López (modified from Fyfe and Brady 2014).

or passengers of pleasure craft and scientific expeditions. The fact that some of those inscriptions include stylistic symbols could also indicate a more leisurely pace for completion as opposed to those considered to have been made by working crew. An explanation for this disparity could correspond with the designation of national park status and an increase in visitation resulting from the development of tourism ventures to Cocos Island. Furthermore, the fact that the data set does not include inscriptions dating after 1999 could be a direct response to UNESCO World Heritage listing and provide evidence of efforts to forbid the practice as way of preserving the island's cultural heritage at the time of designation.

Discussion

The range of information that is included in the Cocos Island stone inscriptions brings into question the reasoning behind their creation. Similar types of inscriptions have been documented and interpreted at other locations around the world including the Canadian Arctic and the Azores (James Delgado 2018, pers. comm.) in the Atlantic, the southern coast of Africa and islands situated off its east coast in the Indian Ocean (Van Duivenvoorde et al. 2013), islands off the coast of Australia in the Torres Strait (Fyfe and Brady 2014) and Muscat Bay in the Gulf of Oman (Costa 1985). Thus, the practice of creating rupestrian communications was without doubt a worldwide phenomenon and the purpose of leaving them were multifaceted. Upon consideration of the data recovered by Lozano Guerra-Librero and Fernández López (2014), three possible explanations for the presence of those made at Cocos Island include: indications of an ocean post office onshore; postal stones; and historical graffiti left to commemorate or memorialize a visit.

One possible explanation for these collections of inscriptions is that they represent indicators that an "ocean post office" had been placed at Cocos Island. Ocean post offices were designated places in remote parts of the world where vessels engaged in long cruises dropped off mail to be sent home or those on return voyages to mainland ports collected similar mail for delivery. This practice was particularly common among nineteenth century American whalers operating in the Pacific since their cruises could last several years. Though the exact date for the beginning of this tradition is uncertain, there are several known instances in which sailors left letters in designated and marked spots. Some well-known ocean post offices were placed at specific locations in the Galapagos Islands (Hohman 1927; The *Leisure Hour* 1882:704), Tierra del Fuego (Marwick and Smith 1901:18), and the Torres Strait (The Leisure Hour 1882:703-704; Fyfe and Brady 2014). Although the establishment of an ocean post office at Cocos Island would seem logical since it was a known reprovisioning point, there is not historical or physical evidence to indicate that one operated there.

Another possible interpretation is that they represent "postal inscriptions" or "postal stones". As described by Van Duivenvoorde et al. (2013:57) postal inscriptions were notices that constituted part of a communication system established by European seamen for relaying information on the whereabouts of vessels while on distant voyages. Essentially carvings left by sailors on stone, wood, or pewter, these messages allowed sailors to communicate with vessels who would copy messages with the intent of delivering them to a sailor's home port. Often practiced by the Dutch, examples of seventeenth and eighteenth-century postal inscriptions have been documented in Australia, South Africa, Madagascar, and islands of the southern Indian Ocean (Van Duivenvoorde et al. 2013). One such postal inscription left in 1619 at Table Bay, South Africa, indicates the location of an ocean post office (Sclater 1900). While the recorded inscriptions of the stones found at Cocos Island do not explicitly state that visitors should look for letters, there is unmistakable evidence that some of the information inscribed may have been to pass on a message. Many of the inscriptions left placed there in the early to mid-nineteenth century provide the names and dates of whaleships that historically are known to have called there. Other inscriptions include information relating to whaling data, including the numbers of barrels of oil and/or the type of whale oil they contained. Thus, there is a high probability that some of the inscriptions found at Cocos Island are in fact postal stones.

The last, and most probable, explanation for the creation of the inscriptions at Cocos Island relates to the concepts of memorialization and formal commemoration. Simply put, most of the inscriptions, particularly those made in the latter part of the twentieth century, are maritime graffiti left by passengers on pleasure craft that visited Cocos while on a sea voyage. Similar activities are described in historical literature. During his visit to the island, George Vancouver gave a formal order to inscribe a stone with information to commemorate their stop (1801:189), while American whaler William Davis intimated that he spent some time engaged in the informal pursuit of "carving the name of the Chelsea among the hundreds already recorded on the rocks, and I also engraved the name of a young Pennsylvanian in whom I felt unseal [sic] interest" (Davis 1874:124-125). It is clear that the human need to "leave one's mark" is often powerful, and evidence of the practice from places around the world dates back thousands of years. At other ocean post office sites, there is evidence of graffiti inscriptions alongside postal stones and around ocean post offices. For example, the "Post Office Cave" of Booby Island (Ngiangu) contains rupestrian inscriptions which have been categorized as "other inscriptions" or "names and words with dates" (Fyfe and Brady 2014). Additionally, Fyfe and Brady interpolate phases of European presence on Booby Island based on graffiti inscriptions. It may be possible to apply similar analysis towards the carved stones of Cocos Island as well.

Future Research Potential

Although the unique nature of the Cocos Island inscriptions has made them a popular subject of photography for visitors to the island, for the most part they remain archaeologically undocumented. While the stone inscriptions recorded by Lozano Guerra-Librero and Fernández López (2014) do offer an opportunity to better understand and contextualize them, they are but a small sample of the overall collection. While so many of the stones have easily visible and very well persevered inscriptions, a considerable number of them are weathered, leaving markings largely indiscernible. Thus, this important heritage site should be systematically documented and studied further.

The use of Reflectance Transformation Imaging (RTI) would be an excellent method for preserving severely weathered stones at Cocos Island. RTI uses projected light from different knowable directions, producing a series of images of objects scanned in different highlights and shadows. The data are then mathematically analyzed to create a model, which allows the RTI image to be digitally examined from a variety of viewpoints and lighting. This process allows faded details, no longer visible to the human eye, to be seen on screen (Cultural Heritage Imaging 2017). Another recording technique that could be useful for documenting the inscriptions is photogrammetry. Photogrammetry is a low-cost method which uses a series of digital photos to generate high-quality three-dimensional (3D) spatial data. Photo-realistic 3D models can be manipulated and viewed on a variety of digital platforms. Photogrammetry has recently gained popularity among maritime archaeologists as it produces high-quality 3D images, does not require a significant amount of technical or special equipment, and is an easy and effective way to communicate with the public (Wright 2018).

Regardless of the recording method, the need for preserving the rich cultural heritage of Cocos Island is great. The history of the island is unique in that it represents a series of carved stones used for multiple purposes, some of which may indicate messages passed from ship to ship. Very few, if any, other sites in the world represent such a wide range of carved cultural material.

Conclusion

The inscriptions on the stones at Wafer and Chatham Bays present a unique type of cultural heritage that has been the subject of curiosity for visitors to Cocos Island since at least the late eighteenth century. Analysis of a sample of these inscriptions indicates their usefulness in helping to contextualize visitation to the island over the past one hundred and seventy years. While the reasoning behind their creation is still not completely understood, further investigation of them could help to better understand the tradition of maritime memorialization and commemoration.

References

ALFARO, A.
1898 Informe Sobre la Fauna de la Isla. In *Revista del Colegio Superior de Señoritas*, Year 2(4/5):12–15.

ARIAS SANCHEZ, RAUL FRANCISCO.
1993 *La Isla del Coco: Perspectiva Hitoricia y Ananlisis de una Leyenda*. Master's thesis, Department of Social Sciences, University of Costa Rica, San Jose.

BEEBE, WILLIAM AND RUTH ROSE.
1926 Cocos – The Island of Pirates. In *The Arcturus Adventure: An Account of the New York Zoological Society's First Oceanographic Expedition*, William Beebe, editor, pp. 220-249. G.P. Putnam's Sons, New York, NY.

BELCHER, EDWARD.
1843 *Narrative of a Voyage Round the World, Performed in Her Majesty's Ship* Sulphur, *During the Years 1836-1842*. Henry Colburn, London.

BERGOEING, J.P.
2017 *Geography and Volcanology of Costa Rica*. Elsevier, Inc. Amsterdam, Netherlands.

CHAMBERS, WILLIAM AND ROBERT CHAMBERS
1905   Treasure Seeking on Cocos Island. In *Chambers Journal* 8(373):113-115.

COSTA, G.G.
1985   The Ships' Names of Muscat Bay. In *The Journal of Oman Studies* 7:105-120.

CULTURAL HERITAGE IMAGING.
2017   Reflectance Transformation Imaging. http://culturalheritageimaging.org/Technologies/RTI/. Accessed 28 December 2017.

DAUM, ARNOLD R.
1959   Petroleum in Search of an Industry. In *Pennsylvania History* 26(1): 21-34.

DAVIS, WILLIAM M.
1874   *Nimrod of the Sea; or, The American Whaleman.* Harper & Brothers, New York, NY.

DODGE, ERNEST S.
1971   *Beyond the Capes: Pacific Exploration from Captain Cook to the Challenger* 1776-1877. Victor Gollancz Ltd., London, UK.

FREEMAN, OTIS W. (EDITOR).
1951   *Geography of the Pacific.* John Wiley and Sons, Inc., New York, NY.

FYFE, JANE AND LIAM BRADY.
2014   Leaving their Mark: Contextualizing the Historical Inscriptions and the European Presence at Ngiangu (Booby Island), Western Torres Strait, Queensland. In *Australian Archaeology* 78(1):58-68.

HOGUE, CHARLES L. AND SCOTT E. MILLER.
1981   *Entomofauna of Cocos Island, Costa Rica.* Atoll Research Bulletin No. 250. Smithsonian Institution, Washington, DC.

HOHMAN, ELMO P.
1926   Wages, Risk, and Profits in the American Whaling Industry. In *The Quarterly Journal of Economics* 40(4): 644-671.

KIRKENDALE, GEO.
1903   In Search of Pirate Treasure. In *The World Wide Magazine* 10:452-457.

LOZANO GUERRA-LIBRERO, CLAUDIO AND FERNÁNDEZ LÓPEZ, OMAR.
2014   Memoria de Actividad Prospección Arqueologica en Isla del Coco (Costa Rica) Primera Fase (2 Mayo – 31 Mayo 2014). Manuscript, Universidad de Huelva, Huelva, Spain and Universidad de Barcelona, Barcelona, Spain.

MARWICK, W. FISHER AND WILLIAM A. SMITH.
1901   *The World Around Us, Book X: The South American Republics.* Silver, Burdett and Company, New York, NY.

NANTUCKET HISTORICAL ASSOCIATION RESEARCH LIBRARY.
2017   Ships' Logs Collection. Collection No. 220. Nantucket Historical Association Research Library, Nantucket, MA.

OVIEDO, GONZALO FERNÁNDEZ DE.
1851   *De la Natural Historia General y Natural de la Indias.* Real Academia De La Historia, Madrid, Spain.

RAUPP, JASON T.
2015   "And So Ends this Day's Work": Industrial Perspectives on Early Nineteenth-century American Whaleships Wrecked in the Northwestern Hawaiian Islands. Doctoral dissertation, Department of Archaeology, Flinders University, Adelaide, SA.

RICHARDS, RHYS.
1994   *Into the South Seas: The Southern Whale Fishery Comes of Age on the Brazil Banks* 1765 to 1812. The Paremata Press, Wellington.

ROSE, RUTH
1926   Cocos – A Tale of Treasure. In *The Arcturus Adventure: An Account of the New York Zoological Society's First Oceanographic Expedition*, William Beebe, editor, pp. 250-281. G.P. Putnam's Sons, New York, NY.

SCLATER, W. L
1900   Notes on the So-Called "Post Office Stones" and Other Inscribed Stones Preserved in the South African Museum and Elsewhere. In *Transactions of the South African Philosophical Society* 10:189–206.

STACKPOLE, EDOUARD A.
1972   *Whales and Destiny: The Rivalry between America, France and Britain for Control of the Southern Whale Fishery, 1785-1825.* University of Massachusetts Press, Amherst, MA.

TANNER, Z.L.
1893   Report upon the Investigations of the U.S. Fish Commission Steamer Albatross from July 1, 1889 to June 30, 1891. In *Report of the Commissioner of Fish and Fisheries* 1889-891, pp. 207-342. Government Printing Office, Washington, DC.

TAYLOR & TEVIN, PRINTERS AND ENGRAVERS
1880   *History of the Buried Treasure on Cocos Island, and the Confession of the Pirates the Night before Execution, in Kingston, Jamaica.* Taylor & Tevin, Printers and Engravers, San Francisco, CA.

THE LEISURE HOUR
1882   An Ocean Post Office. In *The Leisure Hour* 31:703-704.

TRUSTY, JENNIFER L., HERBERT C. KESLER, AND GERMAN HAUG DELGADO
2006 Vascular Flora of Isla del Coco, Costa Rica. In *Proceedings of the California Academy of Sciences* 57(7):247-355.

VANCOUVER, GEORGE
1801 *A Voyage of Discovery to the North Pacific Ocean and Round the World*. John Stackdale, London, UK.

VAN DUIVENVOORDE, WENDY, MARK E. POLZER, AND PETER J. DOWNES
2013 Hoaxes and Folklore: Inscriptions Associated with the *Vergulde Draack* (1656) and *Zuiddorp* (1714) Shipwrecking Events. In *Australian Archaeology* 77:52-65.

WHEELER, ELLSWORTH H., JR.
1968 *General Narrative. Stanford Oceanographic Expedition 20*. Manuscript, Stanford University, Stanford, CA.

WRIGHT, ANNE E.
2018 *3D Printing for Maritime Cultural Heritage: A Design For All Approach*. Master's thesis, Department of History, East Carolina University, Greenville, NC.

. . . .

Jason T. Raupp
Program in Maritime Studies, East Carolina University
Admiral Eller House, 302 E. 9th Street
Greenville, NC 27858252-328-1966

Anne E. Wright
Program in Maritime Studies, East Carolina University
Admiral Eller House, 302 E. 9th Street
Greenville, NC 27858

Omar Fernández López
Área de Arqueologiá, Facultad de Filosofía y Letras, Universidad de Cádiz
Avenida Doctor Gómez Ulla

Impressions, Itineraries and Perceptions of a Coastscape: The Case of Medieval Paphos (A.D. 12th–16th Century)

Maria Ktori

The author analyzes the monumental topography of Paphos, a harbor town in western Cyprus, during the Lusignan (A.D. 1191/92-1474/89) and the Venetian periods (1474/89-1570/71). The analysis was based on narrative sources (primarily travelogues and chronicles), as well as archaeological finds. These were used to record the activities reflecting its economy, character, and geographical range, its mariculture. The process highlighted the vulnerability of the medieval monuments and the importance of creating a Cultural Heritage Management plan. Potential cultural trails can highlight new areas of cultural interest, consider others under new light, and raise awareness among the public in order to safeguard them.

Introduction

Medieval travelers and pilgrims often describe Paphos as a once glorious town that had been reduced to a mere derelict village. This short description underlines what they had encountered when visiting Paphos on their way to the Holy Land: a coastal landscape, abundant in ancient ruins and other interesting monuments without its former glory. Their travelogues are usually written in the form of diaries, furnishing the genre of travel literature with one of its main characteristics (Grivaud 1990:11). Diaries are a very personal form of writing, reflecting the author's mentality, convictions and perceptions of reality. These texts, although short when compared to other literary genres, provide information on various subjects and raise questions on the circulation of ideas in the Middle Ages.

The present work derives information from a larger project, concerning the partial reconstruction of Paphos' monumental topography during the Lusignan and Venetian periods. Paphos' medieval topography has received little attention when compared to the study of the town during other periods, such as the Hellenistic or Roman, and even less attention, compared to medieval Nicosia (Leventis 2005; Trélat 2009; Michaelides 2012) or Famagusta (Enlart 1987; Walsh, Kiss and Coureas 2014). This created a gap in understanding and interpreting the town's fragmented topography and the "umbrella" project was established to minimize it. Paphos' medieval monuments were studied both as unique entities and within the urban landscape nexus, to illustrate the evolution over time and contextualize processes often described in historical sources.

It is accepted that townscapes and their populations have strong connections with their territories, hinterlands, and natural resources, all comprising their landscape (Christie 2004). Human impact, as well as the influence of the environment on human activities, can create impressions which are often expressed in the form of short notes, lengthy travelogues or paintings. Landscape Archeology offers significant analytical possibilities in interpreting such phenomena, characterized by an integrated multidisciplinary approach (Bintliff 1999; David and Thomas 2008). The temporal and spatial variation is acknowledged and reflected in a case-dependent, flexible methodology, throughout the development of a given project (Christie 2004:4); the present study of Paphos was no different, while its coastal setting adds another layer of complexity, predicated on its being a maritime landscape (Ford 2011).

Paphos' maritime cultural landscape encompasses every activity associated with the sea and the coastline, whether far-ranging (e.g. maritime trade) or close-ranging (e.g. coastal fort maintenance). Its topography reminds one of Westerdahl's (1992:5-6) theoretical approach: the landscape is multi-faceted as attested by pre-industrial, military and religious activities. It is chronologically multi-layered, and has a profound action radius based on the exports of local wares, particularly to the Latin Kingdom of Jerusalem. Paphos' landscape evolution over time reflects local and regional developments, as per Westerdahl's notion of the cognitive landscape, contributing to the reconstruction of the town's functions, trade relations, and the flow of people and ideas.

The medieval perception of Paphos as a harbor, landing place or entrepôt, coexists with that of pilgrim itineraries, providing contextual information for secular and sacred places, as well as archaeological finds. These were used here to record the activities which reflect its economy, character, and geographical range, or, its *mariculture* (Westerdahl 1992:6). This process highlighted the vulnerability of the medieval monuments and the importance of creating a Cultural Heritage Management plan, to highlight new areas of cultural interest, consider others under new light and examine the future prospects of medieval monuments in a developing modern urban landscape.

Materials, Methods and Objectives

The methodology reflects both the data used in this study and the objectives mentioned below. Travelogues became the starting point, as they furnished information stemming from impressions, comments, and experiences, which were collected and assessed both individually and comparatively. Chronicles provided necessary data on the historical and political events, and contributed another perspective on Paphos' development. Moreover, they were used to gauge the accuracy of travelogues. The sources are dated between the 12th and 16th centuries: A.D. 1150 was the conventional cut-off point used for the texts, in order to focus on those chronologically closer to the beginning of the Lusignan period in 1191-1192.

The literary sources gave a clearer view of *loci communes* in the description of monuments, yet their combination with archaeological data was challenging. Maier and Karageorghis' (1984) general volume on Paphos' history and archeology remains the most important work to date, but there are no works focusing on the 12th-16th centuries. Several other issues plague the period's archeology: most archaeological finds come from rescue excavations, the majority of the material remains unpublished or is only partially published in brief articles, and there is a general neglect and lack of particular focus on archaeological research concerning medieval Paphos.

The substantial research on Hellenistic, Roman and Byzantine Paphos provided a good starting point to delve into its medieval topography. Młynarczyk (1990) and Vitas (2013) focused on the Hellenistic period, while Gkioles (2003) furnishes an expansive overview of Paphos in his textbook on the Early Christian and Byzantine heritage of Cyprus. Chotzakoglou's (2005) chapter on Byzantine archeology of the island focuses only on monuments, particularly their architecture and decoration, whereas Gkioles briefly discussed other forms of art (e.g. illuminated manuscripts). Various aspects of Roman Paphos have been presented elsewhere and although they do not address topography directly, they provide a background to understand the landscape evolution (Bekker-Nielsen 2004; Lysandrou 2014).

The joint consideration of literary and archaeological data has evoked a more coherent image of medieval Paphos, which resulted in the following: a) partial reconstruction of Paphos' monumental topography, b) critical assessment of the literary information on the identity of monuments, c) identification of Cultural Heritage Management issues, and, d) proposal of possible solutions to promote and safeguard medieval monuments.

Monuments across Time and Space: Interpreting Literary Sources and Archaeological Data

Harbor towns are places bustling with people who influence the natural landscape to accommodate their needs and activities. Whether the harbor is natural or artificial, military or commercial, building harbor installations is essential towards establishing a safe haven for vessels. Merchant and passenger vessels frequenting commercial harbors contribute in their development, as foreigners would engage in trading and purchase local goods. Consequently, local inhabitants and authorities profit and reinvest their gains. For example, tax revenue from trading can be redirected towards the construction or repair of administrative, storage or other buildings directly related to harbor activities. Although one can surmise that such buildings existed, it is difficult to identify them at Paphos without archaeological or other evidence.

The successful ventures of the Crusaders in the Middle East and the establishment of the Latin Kingdom of Jerusalem gave a new impetus to medieval pilgrimage. As pilgrims embarked on their journey to visit places where the events of the Bible had taken place, maritime powers such as Pisa, Genoa and Venice controlled the seaborne routes in the eastern Mediterranean and pilgrim transportation (Jacoby 1986). Many pilgrims set off from Venice to go to Acre, which had become a religious center particularly after the fall of Jerusalem to the Ayyubids in 1187 (Jacoby 1986:28). Cyprus' geographic location along the seaborne routes, between the Italian harbor cities frequented by pilgrims and Acre, was not ignored. The island was incorporated in medieval pilgrimage routes relatively quickly, initially as a stop for vessels that needed supplies to complete their journey. The early contracts between pilgrims and ship captains included a clause mentioning they could stay in Cyprus for only three days during their journey to the Holy Land (Grivaud 1990:23), while later contracts included a visit to Nicosia (Von Breydenbach 1911:xii). The primary sources provided a glimpse into Paphos' topography between 1191 and 1571. The quality of the information varied as the authors provided the amount of details they considered meaningful. Their personal perspective and the influence of the available literary sources are often difficult to distinguish, but still allowed the identification of areas of interest.

Chronicles and travelogues are the two types of narrative sources used and dated between the late 12th to 16th centuries. Travelogues provided the basis for identifying monuments, as travelers often provided detailed descriptions. A number of compilations of excerpts from travelogues mentioning Cyprus have been published by Cobham (1969 [1908]), Mogabgab (1941; 1943; 1945), Flourentzos (1977) and Grivaud (1990). These provided the basic information on monuments and the landscape itself, complemented by papal letters (Schabel 2010), and a series of chronicles written by Leontios Machairas (1932; 2003), Florio Bustron (1886; 1998), George Bustronios (1997; 2005), Francesco Amadi (Amadi and Strambaldi 1891; Coureas and Edbury 2015), Estienne de Lusignan (1580; 2004), and Pietro Valderio (1996).

Once the literary data were combined with the archaeological finds, it became possible to identify areas and types of activity: military, religious, pre-industrial, and trading. Another group of monuments emerged though, which cannot be integrated in the topography at present. These monuments are: a) known only from sources and cannot be located, b) known from their architectural remains but lack any other pertinent information, and, c) a series of unassociated finds to any monument or site (Figure 1).

Fortifications and Harbor Installations

Archaeological investigations from the 1980s onwards established that Paphos is a settlement tracing its roots to the Cypro-Archaic Period, an assertion corroborated by the existence of the 160-meter-long defensive wall at Paphos-*Marcello* (Iacovou 2008) and necropolis and tombs in the area dated to between the 11th and 3rd centuries BC (Daszewski 1985; 1987).

The harbor installations and fortifications had remained visible but changed considerably over the centuries. St. Neophytos' imprisonment in the φρουριον (*frourion*, fort) located at the ναυσταθμος (*nafstathmos*, harbor) area draws our attention (Chotzakoglou 2005:557), as Nicholas of Thingeyrar and Roger of Howden mention a castellum in the 12th century (Petre 2012:315). These texts are thought-provoking, especially in light of the finds from nearby Saranda Kolones Castle. Megaw had argued that the circular corner tower of Saranda Kolones was of Crusader origin, possibly constructed in 1192 as an independent structure and later incorporated into the castle (Megaw and Rosser 2001). A Crusader tower would only tally with Roger of Howden's testimony, as his text is dated sometime after 1191. Petre (2012:315-316) notes that it is unclear what kind of defense building is referred to, yet it must have had a military character. The location of these monuments can only be estimated at this point (Figure 1),

Figure 1: Paphos' function zones (A.D. 12th – 16th centuries).

yet one can assume they were situated somewhere in the harbor zone.

The harbor area changed significantly in the 13th century once the Saranda Kolones Castle was built, on a sloping hill overlooking the area (Figure 2). The material culture related to the Crusaders (Megaw 1972:340–343) and the castle outline were key factors in attributing it to a military order or even Aimery of Lusignan (1194-1205) (Megaw 1984; Megaw 1994; Rosser, 2010). This led to a complete reconsideration of the construction chronology, privileging the late 12th to early 13th century.

The castle is an imposing feature in the landscape but its destruction in 1222 (Department of Antiquities 1958:16; Department of Antiquities 1959:14–18; Megaw 1971:118), or, as per Von Wartburg (2001) during the 1268 earthquake, naturally prevented any later travelers from making further observations, since it was never rebuilt (Megaw 1971:130; Rosser 2004). The harbor fort and coastal tower were likely erected to defend the area after the loss of Saranda Kolones. The mid-13th-century portolan Parma Magliabecchi advised seamen to anchor their vessels east of the tower, possibly near Moulia Rocks, an anchoring location favored by the mid-14th-century portolan Il Compasso da Navigare (Gertwagen 1995:518). While the first source provides a terminus ante quem for the construction of the tower, the portolans do not indicate a military function.

The construction of the medieval fort benefited from the previous, structurally resilient harbor installations (Gertwagen 1995:518). The allied Genoese forces took over the καστελλια (*kastellia*, castles) (Machairas 1932:358–359; Machairas 2003:276, MS V, fol. 158r; O, fol. 148r; R, fol. 103r), noted in *Amadi* as *fortezze* (Amadi and Strambaldi 1891:444; Coureas and Edbury 2015:404, §899). The Genoese then raised the originally low walls and created a moat for a more effective defense, which gave the fort its present form (Machairas 1932:358–359; Machairas 2003:276, MS V, fol.158r-v). Sources of the 15th century state that Paphos had been ravaged by earthquakes to the point of being reduced to a small harbor town. Travelers referred to the 14th-century fort and tower, demonstrating that they had remained functional in the 15th century, whereas Leonida Attar's 1542 map indicates that the harbor and its fortifications were present (Cavazzana-Romanelli and Grivaud 2006:102) (Figure 3). Their condition remains unclear but the garrison stationed at the 'castle of Paphos' shows that the sea fort remained operational (Bustronios 1997:108), at least until 1566, when Fürer von Haimendorf visited Paphos and spoke of a small harbor with a castle (Młynarczyk 1990:40).

Pre-Industrial Activity and Habitation Area

Pre-industrial activities have been securely identified and dated in two locations: the Kato-Paphos *Fabrika* site, and in an underground Roman tomb which was converted into a workshop in the 13th century. A team from the University of Sydney has been excavating the ancient theater at *Fabrika* hill since 1995 (Green, Barker and Gabrieli 2004:3), and revealed a medieval building complex erected over the orchestra still under investigation (Department of Antiquities 2007:70). The pottery from closed deposits and scattered finds belongs to three occupational phases: Early / Industrial Phase (late 12th–early 14th century), Middle / Habitation Phase (late

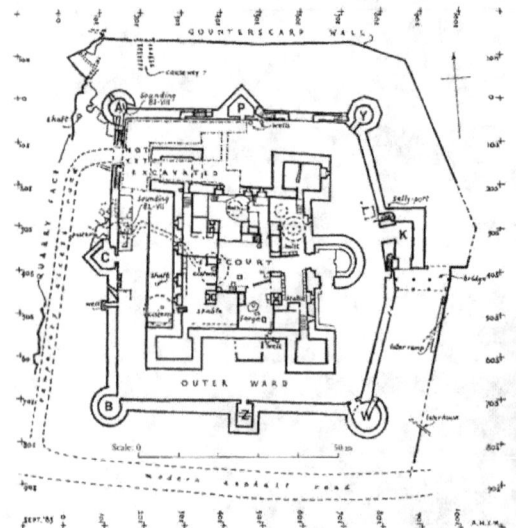

Figure 2: The Saranda Kolones Castle 1985 plan (left; Rosser 1985:83) and photo (right; author).

14th–15th century), Late / Rebuilding and Habitation Phase (16th–17th century).

The pre-industrial activities, found mainly southwest of the orchestra area, may have given the hill its toponym. The team identified those elements early on: layers of ash, burnt material, signs of metalworking (metal slag, runs from molding) and glass manufacture (Department of Antiquities 2007:70). The kilns attest to large-scale glazed pottery manufacture (Green, Barker and Gabrieli 2004:3; Green et al. 2014:15), while the system of interconnected cisterns over the eastern *parodos* area was considered to have been used for tanning leather (Department of Antiquities 2010:64; Barker 2009-2010:16–19). The discovery of a medieval farmstead adds another layer of complexity, as agriculture was simultaneously practiced at the site (Department of Antiquities 2003:55). A team of researchers from the University of Avignon has identified a possible habitation quarter during their investigation regarding the ancient walls of Nea Paphos (Balandier and Morvillez 2009:434–436), as well as a medieval hydraulics system related to a cistern (Balandier 2012:151–164).

Fabrika did not develop in isolation, but was connected with its surroundings based on the finds from the Roman tomb at Icarus Street, from a rescue excavation in 2001. They recovered 13th-century glazed wares, coarse wares and Levantine imports (Raptou 2006:319; Gabrieli 2008). The coarse wares formed an assemblage belonging to a complete household, while the absence of large storing vessels indicates that the tomb was perhaps used for only a brief period (Gabrieli 2008:423–426). The assemblage was compared with the material from *Fabrika*, Saranda Kolones, the three pit groups Megaw excavated in 1937-1939 at Nicosia, and Flourentzos' rescue excavation of a medieval well in the capital in 1988 (Megaw 1951; Flourentzos 1994:4–5; Gabrieli 2008:427–444).

The tomb at Icarus Street is connected to other underground tombs, previously discovered during rescue excavations in the 1990s (Raptou 2006:319). The pottery indicates that this underground system was perhaps established in the 13th-14th centuries (Raptou 2006:319; Gabrieli 2008; Department of Antiquities 1991:69). The complex hydraulic installations effectively converted the tombs into a type of workshop (Department of Antiquities 1991:69), showing how the locals repurposed existing structures to meet their needs. The system demonstrates that one should look for pre-industrial activities in less conventional environments, while a complete investigation would provide significant information on how the *Fabrika* area developed and what its connection might have been to the repurposed tombs.

Religious Sites

The religious sites of Paphos can be distinguished into shrines (Agia Solomoni, Agios Lambrianos), and churches (Latin cathedral at Agia Kyriaki Chrysopolitissa area, Franciscan church). The 'Catacombs' of Agia Solomoni and Agios Lambrianos show an evolution of their identity and a site repurposing process similar to the tomb at Icarus Street. These underground complexes are situated in close proximity, at the southwestern edge of *Fabrika* (Młynarczyk 1990:88–90). Evidence indicates that they were altered to accommodate ongoing sepulchral needs and converted into cult places, probably simultaneously,

Figure 3: Southeast view of the harbor fort (left; author) and a detail from Leonida p (right; Cavazzana–Romanelli and Grivaud 2006:102).

for Christian worship (Młynarczyk 1990:225–226; Papageorghiou 1996:153; Vitas 2013:157–160; Lysandrou 2014:214–215). They are mentioned more often in 15th-century travelogues, due to an increased interest in the early years of Christianity in Cyprus and the phenomenon of *interpretatio christiana* (Calvelli 2009:29).

Both shrines were a favorite stop for pilgrims. The descriptions of the grotto of the Seven Maccabees or the Seven Sleeper Saints correspond to Agia Solomoni: a stairway leading underground, niches on the walls and a fountain of healing water which is still in use even today. The Byzantine mid-14th century frescoes at Agia Solomoni (Hatfield-Young and Hatfield-Young 1978; Papageorghiou, 1966), carved crosses and Greek and Latin graffiti on the frescoes and walls indicate the diachronic religious character of the monument, with different approaches to the shrine on the part of their authors (Volanakis 2001; Meinardus 1969; Trentin and Hadjikyriakos 2007; Trentin 2010). Latin graffiti can be linked to travelogue entries mentioning visits to religious sites, and therefore elucidate the pilgrims' landscape perceptions and intended itineraries. Conversely, the Greek graffiti suggests that the Orthodox associated it with a spiritual journey, even seeking divine protection (Trentin 2010:300–302, 320).

Agios Lambrianos 'catacomb' has been linked to St. Paul's incarceration incident. According to several travelogues, his prison was supposedly located beneath the Franciscan church (Grivaud 1990:35, 89–91; Cobham 1969 [1908]:51). Ulrich Brunner described it as an underground complex with four caverns and a well (Grivaud 1990:78–79; Calvelli 2009:29), while others noted numerous caves below the Franciscan church (Grivaud 1990:98–101, 106–111). Fra Noe's late 15th-century description of the landscape provides accurate directions to the shrine: it is near a church with a fountain of healing water and the underground rooms of the Seven Sleepers, i.e. opposite Agia Solomoni (Cobham 1969 [1908]:53).

The Franciscan church, frequently associated with the incarceration of St. Paul and Barnabas in 15th-century texts, was mistaken by Enlart to be the Latin cathedral (Enlart 1987:357–358). Currently known as 'Panagia Galatiani / Galatariotissa', it is almost completely ruined. The simplicity of the single-nave edifice and its proximity to the catacombs are indicative of its identity (Olympios 2011:117). Its design was influenced by the Franciscan church of Famagusta, which had been completed in the 1290s, and together with Angelo Clareno's comment in his *Chronica septem tribulationum Ordinis Minorum*, the evidence points to a late-13th-century date (Olympios 2011:105, 118–119; Golubovich 1906:345).

The Agia Kyriaki Chrysopolitissa site is about 400 meters east of Saranda Kolones Castle and was continuously used in a religious context: the 4th century Early Christian basilica was expanded in the 6th century, the Latin cathedral was erected adjacent to it in the 14th, and a Christian Orthodox church was erected in the 15th. The space was used for both religious and secular purposes as the archaeologists found 14th century houses below the 15th-century Orthodox church (Department of Antiquities 1965:11), concurrent with the Latin cathedral based on the chronology of the pottery assemblage (Papanikola-Bakirtzis 1988:245–248) and the recovery of a coin of Hugh IV (1324-1359). The area around the churches had been used as a cemetery at the same time (Department of Antiquities 1973:14; Department of Antiquities 1974:29; Department of Antiquities 1992:60). The Early Christian mosaic floors were destroyed in the process of creating graves, and the archaeologists recovered five tombstones in total from the Latin cathedral furnishing a 14th-century date on epigraphical and stylistic grounds (Department of Antiquities 1972:22; Imhaus 2004, I:227–229).

A final area with a religious character is situated at the Porto Paphos Hotel, just outside the ancient walls. The accidental discovery of the Le Chien family tomb in 1982 under the hotel provides us the easternmost attested limit of the 14th-century urban development. The tomb was possibly related to a church known to have existed there (Imhaus 2004, I:230–232), similarly to the tombstones found at the Latin cathedral, although their relationship remains unclear.

Coastal Monuments as an Educational Tool: The 'Medieval Cultural Trails' Concept

Rogers (2013) aptly discusses the importance of applying a social approach to port and harbor studies, as harbors have a diachronic importance in travel, trade and human interaction, to name but a few areas. Harbors are integral in many of the key themes that are significant throughout history, which is evident in the case of the Paphos harbor, too. The harbor accommodated various activities, ranging from trading and travelling, to defending the town from possible incursions and pirate raids. It was further associated with the pre-industrial activities identified at *Fabrika* and Icarus Street, and provided the necessary seaborne link to perform long-distance trade and travelling. There are certain harbor facilities which are absent in the archaeological record, but must have existed nonetheless. Granaries, a customs house, docks and jetties are the primary features that come to mind when thinking of trading activities, loading and unloading goods from vessels. The presence of passing travelers would require the existence of one or more loggie, if not in the immediate harbor area, then certainly in close proximity.

The military buildings at the harbor add another layer to Paphos' daily life, as they are naturally associated with army corps. Soldiers and commanding officers were stationed there, which meant that barracks and a storage space for munitions and equipment must have been the minimum requirements to facilitate military activities. One could also entertain the possibility of having soldiers patrolling the harbor as part of their duties, signifying thus the relationship between the capital, and the ruler, with such a remote urban center. The imposing Saranda Kolones Castle could also be interpreted as a sign of the firm administrative link between Paphos and the Lusignan kings in the 13th century, when they were consolidating their rule in Cyprus. This creates questions about the location of the administrative buildings and their relationship with the military center, which apparently remained in the harbor during the Lusignan and Venetian periods.

The results further demonstrated that medieval monuments have been neglected both in terms of research and appreciation from the public. This resulted from the comparative review of the annual number of tourists visiting Cyprus (locals and foreigners), available from the Cyprus Tourism Organization (CTO), for the years 2002-2016 (Table 1). The numbers refer only to those renting accommodation, since one cannot monitor locals on a day trip or staying with family and friends. Nonetheless, it was useful to juxtapose these with the annual number of local and foreign visitors at museums and monuments, which were kindly provided by the Department of Antiquities. The total number includes both paid and free entrance tickets, the latter being only a small percentage. The emerging trends demonstrated a clear preference to visiting monuments located at Paphos city than the District Museum. Visitors pay a small

Year	Total number of tourists in Cyprus	Tourists staying at Paphos and Polis (number)	Tourists staying at Paphos and Polis (%)	Paphos district museum visitors	Paphos district museum visitors (%)	Paphos district monuments visitors	Paphos district monuments visitors (%)
2002	2,418,238	739981	30.6	76775	10.4	611887	82.7
2003	2,303,247	796924	34.6	66730	8.4	548890	68.9
2004	2,349,012	810409	34.5	60795	7.5	590400	72.9
2005	2,470,063	859582	34.8	57892	6.7	602429	70.1
2006	2,400,924	847526	35.3	56176	6.6	534589	63.1
2007	2,416,081	811803	33.6	51817	6.4	507622	62.5
2008	2,403,750	831698	34.6	55647	6.7	481751	57.9
2009	2,141,193	708735	33.1	54964	7.8	445123	62.8
2010	2,172,998	695359	32.0	51201	7.3	460949	66.3
2011	2,392,228	830103	34.7	55681	6.7	506812	61
2012	2,464,908	894762	36.3	53203	6	489789	54.7
2013	2,405,390	930886	38.7	46335	5	442485	47.5
2014	2,441,239	934995	38.3	43387	4.6	375424	41.1
2015	2,659,405	1106313	41.6	44794	4.1	406051	36.7
2016	3,186,531	1242747	39.0	49317	4	434407	35
Total:	36,625,207	13,041,823	35.6	824714	6.3	7438608	57

Table 1: Annual number of tourists at Paphos district and monument visits

entrance fee only for two monuments (Tombs of the Kings, Harbor fort), and the Kato Paphos Archaeological Park which actually encloses several more monuments (e.g. House of Aion, Saranda Kolones Castle). Since not all monuments require an admission fee, it is difficult to estimate their popularity and could not include here monuments such as Agia Kyriaki Chrysopolitissa or Fabrika hill. Some monuments are not open to the public due to ongoing excavations, whereas those located at the Archaeological Park are accessible by paying a general entrance fee which, in both cases hinders further insight on which monument(s) one may visit and the reasons for doing so.

The data showed a decrease in visitors at monuments over time, especially in the years 2012-2016, whereas museum visits dropped from 6% to 4% during the same period. There is a stark contrast in the overall number of tourists, which rose above one million in 2015 and 2016, and sparked further analysis on specialized tourism. Changing trends in the tourism industry since the 1980s promote alternative forms of tourism, especially Cultural Tourism (Du Cros and McKercher, 2015:1–3). McKercher and Du Cros (2005:211–212) aptly defined it as "a form of tourism that relies on a destination's cultural heritage assets and transforms them into products that can be consumed by tourists". Paphos is evidently a favorite tourist destination. Its cultural assets could be used to differentiate and reposition the Cypriot tourist product, and local stakeholders should be engaged in sustainable tourism development (Du Cros and McKercher, 2015:9–11).

The city offers several built heritage examples, and unlocking the 12th-16th century landscape brought forth various function zones which can be used in creating thematic cultural trails. The author performed a Strenghts-Weaknesses-Opportunities-Threats analysis which illuminated several aspects of such an attempt. Harbor installations and fortifications would be an ideal function zone to establish a cultural tourism trail, as they are easily accessible, already frequently visited and one would need to make minimal changes to accommodate a trail. The pedestrian walkway provides immediate access to harbor zone monuments and the possibility of setting up information panels from the cape to the harbor fort and the sea wall ruins. More panels could be placed around Saranda Kolones Castle, introducing new concepts to the public such as the impressions of foreign travelers while their vessel was approaching the coast. Information on medieval fortifications, pilgrim itineraries and the use of landmarks for sailing are just a few of the topics a visitor could read about.

The endeavor would take time to prepare and implement, while hiring and training staff is essential. This is currently a weakness, as the human resources of the Department of Antiquities are spread thinly and understaffing remains a critical issue. However, one may moderate it by providing short seminars to accredited CTO guides who will then facilitate future excursions related to the proposed trail. This also keeps the overall expenses very low; funds can be redirected to designing and printing customized leaflets and even a mobile phone application for a self-guided tour.

The Saranda Kolones Castle offers tremendous possibilities if used as an educational tool, for both layperson and archaeologists alike. The latter, being a specialized target group would benefit from using the castle as an educational tool: archeology students could attend short courses and receive hands-on training on harbor fortifications, military architecture, its association with Crusader castles such as Belvoir, and Paphos' historical context in the 12th-16th centuries.

All these elements were taken into consideration, to select and pilot test an easy, efficient way of conveying archaeological data to the public. To that end, a series of guided tours has been scheduled by the author, to assess the proposed cultural trail described in this paper and later connect it with the appropriate educational material. Previous research on visitors' experience to archaeological sites and monuments further demonstrated that a tour guide would need a tool to iterate all the information related to the trail; a leaflet was selected as first method to be tested and subsequently improved based on the participants' feedback (Figure 4).

The logo depicts a galleon sailing to its destination and is the visual representation of the concept behind the trail: the visitor will be guided through the Frankish and Venetian coastal landscape of a harbor city, which had been frequented by pilgrims and travelers of the time. The map marks the monuments on the modern urban nexus, and informs one of the function zones based on the monument uses between the late 12th to 16th centuries. This first instalment in a series of three leaflets focuses on the harbor installations and fortifications, thus, the short information text is about the harbor fort and Saranda Kolones Castle only.

The associations among artifacts, their location at an archaeological site, the intentions and hypotheses related to their function, are considered a medium allowing one to reconnect with the distant past (Chourmouziade

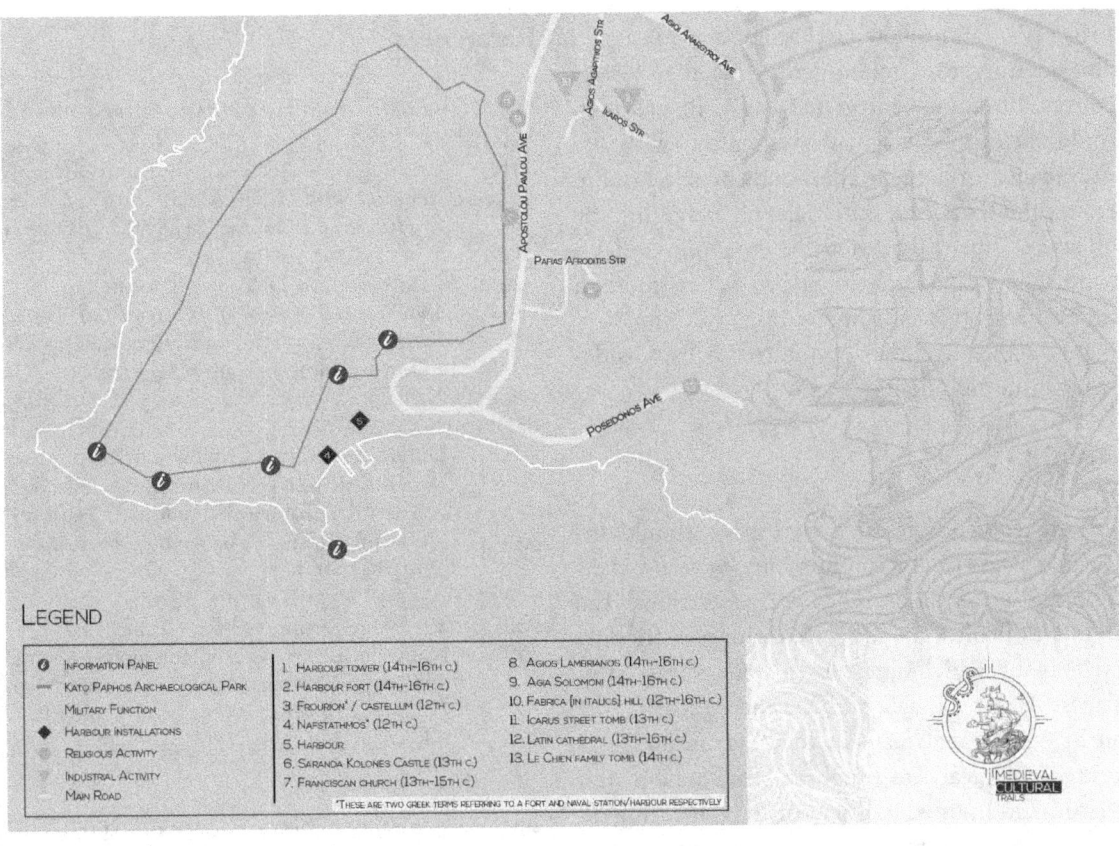
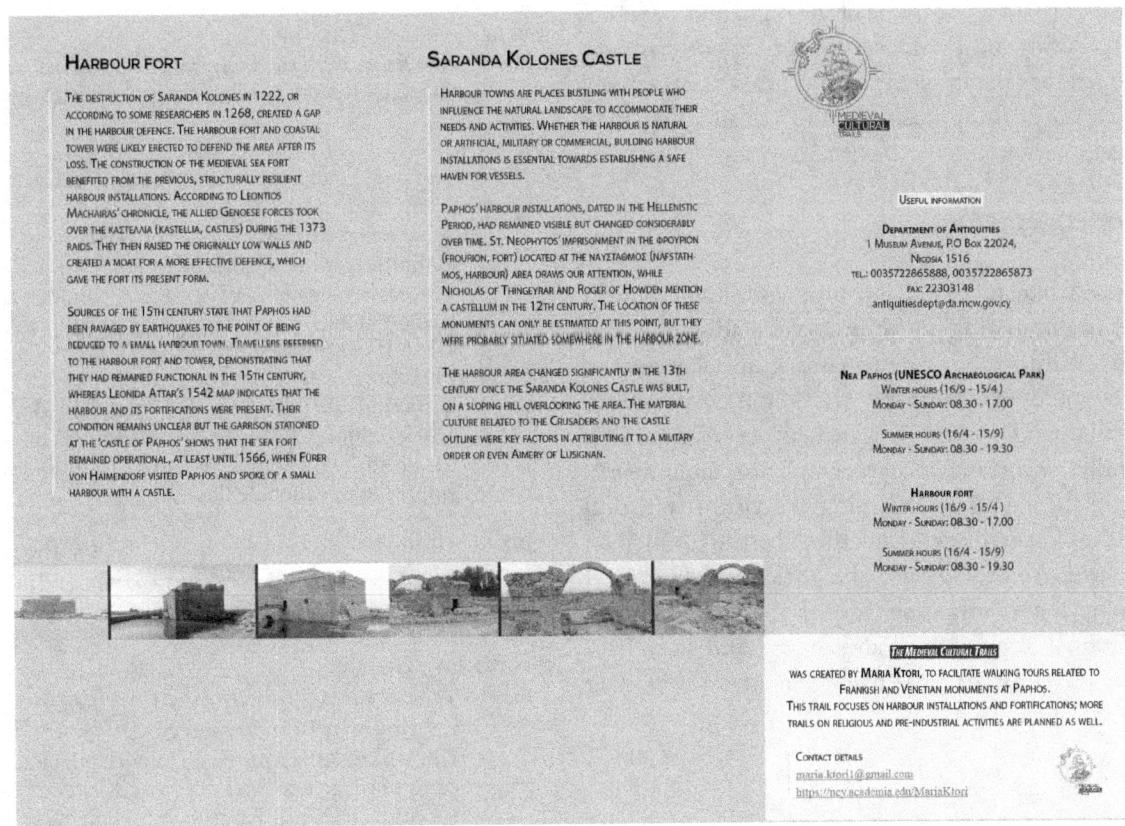

Figure 4: The proposed cultural trail and information panel locations, focusing on the harbor and fortifications.

2010:116–117), and allow archaeologists to assign a possible identity to a monument. This is a central concept that cannot be integrated easily in a leaflet, but should instead be adequately discussed with the tour participants to further understand the relationship between monuments and rationale of assigning the function zones. This will then enable the group to delve deeper into Landscape Archaeology, as well as modern and medieval perceptions of 'interesting' or 'important' monuments, which again are connected to Paphos development in the Middle Ages.

Conclusions

Future archaeological research in Paphos should include the management of its monuments, to ensure their protection and preservation for future generations. The establishment of cultural trails paired with user-friendly interactive maps which integrate historical narratives and images (Alemy, Hudzik and Matthews 2017), the creation of educational material focusing on a city as a large archaeological site (Tuğberk, Pachoulides and Makriyianni 2009), or educational material focusing on artifacts dated between the 12th to 16th centuries to be used in highschool History classes (Makriyianni et al. 2011a, 2011b), are only some of the numerous possibilities into raising local awareness about Paphos' heritage. It is hoped that the implementation of such actions will educate people in appreciating and safeguarding their heritage.

Aknowledgements

I would like to thank my supervisor Dr. Michalis Olympios for guiding my research and reading previous versions of this paper. Any remaining mistakes are my own. I would like to thank Dr. Marina Solomidou-Ieronymidou (Director, Department of Antiquities), for kindly permitting to photograph the monuments, accessing the archives, and using the visitor statistical data. I should also like to thank the Advisory Council on Underwater Archeology and the Society for Historical Archeology, for awarding me the George Fischer International Travel Award and the Ed and Judy Jelks Student Travel Award respectively to present my work at the 2018 conference.

References

Alemy, Alexis, Sophia Huzdik and Christopher N. Matthews
2017   Creating a User-Friendly Interactive Interpretive Resource with ESRI's ArcGIS Story Map Program. In *Historical Archeology* 51(2):288–297.

Amadi, Francesco and Diomède Strambaldi
1891   *Chroniques d'Amadi et de Strambaldi. Première Partie: Chronique d'Amadi*, René de Mas Latrie, editor. Imprimerie Nationale, Paris.

Balandier, Claire
2012   Du Nouveau sur la Capitale Hellénistique et Romaine de Chypre: Premiers Résultats de la Mission Archéologique Française à Paphos [MafaP] (2008-2012). In *Dialogues d'Histoire Ancienne* 38(2):151–164.

Balandier, Claire and Eric Morvillez
2009   Nouvelles Recherces Archéologiques à Paphos. in *Premiers Résultats de la Mission Française sur la Colline de Fabrika* (2008-2009). Cahiers du Centre d'Études Chypriotes 39(1): 425–447.

Barker, Clive
2009-10   Nea Paphos Theatre Excavations 2009. In *The Australian Archaelogical Institute at Athens Bulletin* 7:16–19.

Bekker-Nielsen, Tønnes
2004   *The Roads of Ancient Cyprus*. Museum Tusculanum Press, University of Copenhagen, Copenhagen.

Bintliff, John L.
1999   Regional Field Surveys and Population Cycles. In *Reconstructing Past Population Trends in Mediterranean Europe (3000 BC - AD 1800)*, John L. Bintliff and Kostas Sbonias, editors, pp. 21–34. The Archeology of Mediterranean Landscapes, 1. Oxbow Books, Oxford.

Bustron, Florio
1886   Chronique de l' Île de Chypre, René de Mas Latrie, editor. Collection des documents in-édits sur l'histoire de France, Mélanges historiques, 5. Imprimerie Nationale, Paris.

1998   Historia overo Commentarii de Cipro, Theodoros Papadopoullos, editor. Κυπριολογικ Βιβλιοθηκη 8. Nicosia.

Bustronios, George
1997   Τζωρτζης (Μ)πουστρονς (Γεωργιος Βο(σ) τρ(υ)ηνος η Βουστρωνιος). Διηγησις Κρονικας Κυπρου, Georgios Kehayioglou, editor. Πηγες και Μελετες της Κυπριακης Ιστοριας, XXVII. Κεντρο Επιστημονικων Ερευνων, Nicosia.

2005 A Narrative of the Chronicle of Cyprus 1456-1489, Nicolas Coureas, editor. In *Texts and Studies in the History of Cyprus*, LI. Cyprus Research Centre, Nicosia.

CALVELLI, LORENZO
2009 Cipro e la memoria dell' antico fra medioevo e rinascimento: la percezione del passato romano dell' isola nel mondo occidentale. In *Memorie*, 133. Istituto Veneto di Scienze, Lettere ed Arti, Venice.

CAVAZZANA-ROMANELLI, FRANCESCA AND GILLES GRIVAUD
2006 *Cyprus 1542: The Great Map of the Island* by Leonida Attar. The Bank of Cyprus Cultural Foundation, Nicosia.

CHOTZAKOGLOU, CHARALAMBOS
2005 Βυζαντινη αρχιτεκτονικη και τεχνη. Iν Ιστορια της Κυπρου, Βυζαντινη Κυπρος, volume 3, Theodoros Papadopoullos, editor, pp. 465–787. Ιδρυμα Αρχιεπισκοπου Μακαριου Γι ανδ Γραφειον Κυπριακης Ιστοριας, Nicosia.

CHOURMOUZIADE, ANASTASIA
2006 Το Ελληνικο Αρχαιολογικο Μουσειο. Ο Εκθετης, το Εκθεμα, ο Επισκεπτης. Εκδοσεις Βανιας, Athens.

CHRISTIE, NEIL
2004 Landscapes of Change in Late Antiquity and the Early Middle Ages: Themes, Directions and Problems. In Landscapes of Change. In *Rural Evolution in Late Antiquity and the Early Middle Ages,* Neil Christie, editor, pp. 1–37. Ashgate, Aldershot.

COBHAM, CLAUDE D., EDITOR
1969 [1908] Excerpta Cypria. Materials for a History of Cyprus. The Library, Nicosia.

COUREAS, NICOLAS AND PETER EDBURY, EDITORS
2015 The Chronicle of Amadi. In *Texts and Studies in the History of Cyprus*, LXXIV. Cyprus Research Centre, Nicosia.

DASZEWSKI, WIKTOR A.
1985 Researches at Nea Paphos 1965-1984. In *Archeology in Cyprus 1960-1985*, Vassos Karageorghis, editor, pp. 277–291. A. G. Leventis Foundation, Nicosia.

1987 Remarks on the Early History of Nea Paphos. In *Report of the Department of Antiquities*, Cyprus:171–175.

DAVID, BRUNO AND JULIAN THOMAS
2008 Landscape Archeology: Introduction. In Handbook of Landscape Archeology, Bruno David and Julian Thomas, editors, pp. 27–43. *World Archaeological Congress Research Handbooks in Archeology*, 1. Left Coast Press Inc., Walnut Creek, CA.

DEPARTMENT OF ANTIQUITIES
1958 Annual Report of the Director of the Department Antiquities for the Year 1957. Department of Antiquities, Nicosia.

1959 Annual Report of the Director of the Department Antiquities for the Year 1958. Department of Antiquities, Nicosia.

1965 Annual Report of the Director of the Department Antiquities for the Year 1964. Department of Antiquities, Nicosia.

1972 Annual Report of the Director of the Department Antiquities for the Year 1971. Department of Antiquities, Nicosia.

1973 Annual Report of the Director of the Department Antiquities for the Year 1972. Department of Antiquities, Nicosia.

1974 Annual Report of the Director of the Department Antiquities for the Year 1973. Department of Antiquities, Nicosia.

1991 Annual Report of the Department Antiquities for the Year 1990. Department of Antiquities, Nicosia.

1992 Annual Report of the Department Antiquities for the Year 1991. Department of Antiquities, Nicosia.

2003 Annual Report of the Department Antiquities for the Year 1997. Department of Antiquities, Nicosia.

2007 Annual Report of the Department Antiquities for the Year 2001. Department of Antiquities, Nicosia.

2010 Annual Report of the Department Antiquities for the Year 2008. Department of Antiquities, Nicosia.

DE LUSIGNAN, ESTIENNE
1580 *Description de toute l'isle de Chypre*, reprint by Jos Adam (Bruxelles, 1968). Guillaume Chaudière, Paris.

2004 Chorograffia, Theodoros Papadopoullos, editor. Κυπριακη Βιβλιοθηκη, 10. Πολιτιστικη Πδρυμα Τραπεζης Κυπρου, Nicosia.

DU CROS, HILARY AND BOB MCKERCHER
2015 *Cultural Tourism*, 2nd edition. Routledge, Abingdon.

ENLART, CAMILLE
1987 *Gothic Art and the Renaissance in Cyprus,* David Hunt, translator and editor. Trigraph and The A. G. Leventis Foundation, London.

FLOURENTZOS, PAVLOS
1994 *A Medieval Hoard of Medieval Antiquities from Nicosia*. Department of Antiquities, Nicosia.

1977 Τα Τσεχικα Οδοιπορικα της Αναγεννησης. Nicosia, n.p.

FORD, BEN
2011 Introduction. In *The Archeology of Maritime Landscapes*, Ben Ford, editor, pp. 1–9. Springer-Verlag, New York.

GABRIELI, RUTH SMADAR
2008 *Towards a Chronology-The Medieval Coarse Ware from the Tomb in Icarus Street, Kato Paphos*. Report of the Department of Antiquities, Cyprus:423–454.

GERTWAGEN, RUTHI
1995 Maritime Activity Concerning the Ports and Harbours of Cyprus from the Late 12th and 16th Centuries (1191-1571). In *Cyprus and the Crusades. Papers Given at the International Conference 'Cyprus and the Crusades',* Nicosia, 6-9 September, 1994, Nicolas Coureas and Jonathan Riley-Smith, editors, pp. 511–538. Cyprus Research Centre and Society for the Study of the Crusades and the Latin East, Nicosia.

GKIOLES, NICOLAOS
2003 Η Χριστιανικη Τεχνη στην Κυπρο. Μουσειον Ιερας Μονης Κυκκου, Nicosia.

GOLUBOVICH, GIROLAMO P., EDITOR
1906 *Biblioteca Bio-Bibliografica della Terra Santa e dell' Oriente Francescano*. Tomo I (1215-1300). Collegio di S. Bonaventura, Quaracchi.

GOODWIN, J. C.
1984 *An Historical Toponymy of Cyprus*, volume I, 4th edition. J. C. Goodwin, Nicosia.

GREEN, JOHN R., CLIVE BARKER AND SMADAR GABRIELI
2004 Fabrika: An Ancient Theatre of Paphos. Moufflon Publications, Nicosia.

GREEN, JOHN R., RUTH SMADAR GABRIELI, HOLLY K. A. COOK, EDNA J. STERN, BERNADETTE MCCALL AND ESTELLE LAZER,
2014 The Well and Its Contents. In *Paphos 8 August 1303. Snapshot of a Destruction*, Charalambos Bakirtzis, editor, pp. 15–30. The A. G. Leventis Foundation, Nicosia.

GRIVAUD, GILLES, EDITOR
1990 Excerpta Cypria Nova. In *Voyageurs occidentaux à Chypre au XVème siècle. Sources et Études de l'Histoire de Chypre*, XV. Centre des Recherches Scientifiques, Nicosie.

HATFIELD-YOUNG, SUSAN AND N. HATFIELD-YOUNG
1978 The Iconography and Date of the Wall Paintings at Ayia Solomoni, Paphos, Cyprus. In *Byzantion* 48(1):91–111.

IACOVOU, MARIA
2008 The "Palaepaphos Urban Landscape Project": Theoretical Background and Preliminary Report 2006-2007. In *Report of the Department of Antiquities*, Cyprus:263–289.

IMHAUS, BRUNHILDE
2004 *Lacrimae Cypriae. Les Larmes de Chypre. Volume I: Catalogue et planches photographiques*. Département des Antiquités, Nicosie.

JACOBY, DAVID
1986 Pèlerinage médiéval et sanctuaires de Terre Sainte: la perspective vénitienne. In *Ateneo Veneto* 24:27–58.

LYSANDROU, VASILIKI
2014 Η Ταφικη Αρχιτεκτονικη κατα την Ελληνιστικη και Ρωμαικη Περιοδο στην Κυπρο. Doctoral dissertation, Department of History and Archeology, University of Cyprus, Nicosia.

MACHAIRAS, LEONTIOS
1932 *Leontios Makhairas. Recital Concerning the Sweet Land of Cyprus Entitled 'Chronicle'*, Richard M. Dawkins, editor. Clarendon Press, Oxford.

2003 Λεοντιου Μαχαιρα: Χρονικο της Κυπρου. Παραλληλη Διπλωματικη Εκδοση των Χειρογραφων, Michalis Pieris and Angel Nicolaou-Konnari, editors. Πηγες και Μελετες της Κυπριακης Ιστοριας, 48. Κεντρο Επιστημονικων Ερευνων, Nicosia.

MAIER, FRANZ GEORG AND VASSOS KARAGEORGHIS, EDITOR
1984 *Paphos History and Archeology*. A. G. Leventis Foundation, Nicosia.

MAKRIYIANNI, CHARA (ET AL)
2011a *Learning to Investigate the History of Cyprus through Artefacts – A Teacher's Guide*. Association for Historical Dialogue and Research, Nicosia.

2011b *Learning to Investigate the History of Cyprus through Artefacts; Student's Booklet*. Nicosia: Association for Historical Dialogue and Research.

MCKERCHER, BOB AND DU CROS, HILARY
2005 Cultural Heritage and Visiting Attractions. In *Tourism Business Frontiers: Consumers, Products and Industry*, Dimitrios Buhalis and Carlos Costa, editors, pp. 211–219. Butterworth-Heinemann.

MEGAW, ARTHUR HUBERT STANLEY
1951 Three Medieval Pit-Groups from Nicosia. In *Report of the Department of Antiquities*, Cyprus, 1937-1939: 145–168.

1971 Excavations at 'Saranda Kolones', Paphos. Preliminary Report on the 1966-67 and 1970-71 Seasons. In *Report of the Department of Antiquities*, Cyprus:117–146.

1972 Supplementary Excavations on a Castle Site at Paphos, Cyprus, 1970-1971. In *Dumbarton Oaks Papers* 26:322–343.

1984   Saranda Kolones: Ceramic Evidence for the Construction Date. In *Report of the Department of Antiquities*, Cyprus:333–340.

MEGAW, ARTHUR HUBERT STANLEY AND JOHN ROSSER
2001   A Watchtower before Paphos Castle. In *Report of the Department of Antiquities*, Cyprus: 319–334.

MEGAW, PETER
1994   A Castle in Cyprus Attributable to the Hospital?. In *The Military Orders: Fighting for the Faith and Caring for the Sick*, M. Barber, editor, pp. 42–51. Ashgate, Aldershot.

MEINARDUS, OTTO F. A.
1969   Mediaeval Graffiti in the Church of St. Solomomi in Paphos, Cyprus. Δελτιον της Χριστιανικης Αρχαιολογικης Εταιρειας 5(4):105–110.

MŁYNARCZYK, JOLANTA
1990   *Nea Paphos III. Nea Paphos in the Hellenistic Period*. Éditions Géologiques, Varsovie.

MOGABGAB, THEODORE A. H., EDITOR
1941   *Supplementary Excerpts on Cyprus or Further Materials for a History of Cyprus*, volume 1. The Pusey Press, Nicosia.

1943   *Supplementary Excerpts on Cyprus or Further Materials for a History of Cyprus*, volume 2. The Pusey Press, Nicosia.

1945   *Supplementary Excerpts on Cyprus or Further Materials for a History of Cyprus*, volume 3. Zavalli Press, Nicosia.

OLYMPIOS, MICHALIS
2011   The Fransiscan Convent of Famagusta and Its Place within the Context of Early-Fourteenth-Century Cypriot Gothic Architecture. Κυπριακαι Σπουδαι 73:103–122.

PAPAGEORGHIOU, ATHANASIOS
1966   Η Παλαιοχριστιανικη και Βυζαντινη Αρχαιολογια και Τεχνη εν Κυπρω. Αποστολος Βαρναβας 26:151–173.

PAPANIKOLA-BAKIRTZIS, DEMETRA
1988   Χρονολογημενη Κεραμεικη του 14ου αιωνα απο την Παφο. Report of the Department Antiquities, Cyprus:245–248.

PETRE, JAMES
2012   *Crusader Castles of Cyprus. The Fortifications of Cyprus under the Lusignans: 1191-1489*. Texts and Studies in the History of Cyprus, LXIX. Cyprus Research Centre, Nicosia.

RAPTOU, EFSTATHIOS
2006   The Building in Icarus Street, Kato Paphos. In *Report of the Department of Antiquities*, Cyprus:317–343.

ROGERS, ADAM
2013   Social Archaeological Approaches in Port and Harbour Studies. In *Journal of Maritime Archeology*, 8(2):181–196.

Rosser, John
2004   Archaeological and Literary Evidence for the Destruction of "Saranda Kolones" In 1222. Επετηριδα του Κεντρου Επιστημονικων Ερευνων 30:39–50.

2010   Who Built Saranda Kolones?. Επετηριδα του Κεντρου Επιστημονικων Ερευνων 35:35–51.

SCHABEL, CHRISTOPHER, EDITOR
2010   *Bullarium Cyprium. Volume I: Papal Letters Concerning Cyprus, 1196-1261*. Texts and Studies in the History of Cyprus, LXIV. Cyprus Research Centre, Nicosia.

TRENTIN, MIA GAIA
2010   Mediaeval and Post-Mediaeval Graffiti in the Churches of Cyprus. In POCA 2007: *Postgraduate Cypriot Archeology Conference*, Skevi Christodoulou and Anna Satraki, editors, pp. 297–322. Cambridge Scholars Publishing, Newcastle upon Tyne.

TRENTIN, MIA GAIA AND IOSIF HADJIKYRIAKOS
2007   Graffiti nelle chiese cipriote: primi risultati della ricerca. In *Report of the Department of Antiquities*, Cyprus:449–467.

TUĞBERK, ALEV, KYRIAKOS PACHOULIDES AND CHARA MAKRIYIANNI, EDITORS
2009   *Nicosia is calling... Teacher's Book*. Association of Historical Dialogue and Research, Nicosia.

VALDERIO, PIETRO
1996   *La Guerra di Cipro*, Gilles Grivaud and Nasa Patapiou, editors. Texts and Studies in the History of Cyprus, XXII. Centre des Recherches Scientifiques: Nicosie.

VITAS, DEMETRIS
2013   Νεα Παφος – Σαλαμινα. Η Τοπογραφια και η Πολεοδομικη τους Αναπτυξη κατα την Ελληνιστικη Περιοδο. Doctoral dissertation, Department of History and Archeology, University of Cyprus, Nicosia.

VOLANAKIS, IOANNIS
2001   Η κατακομβη της Αγιας Σολομωνης στην Παφο. Επετηριδα Κεντρου Μελετων Ιερας Μονης Κυκκου 5:43–67.

VON BREYDENBACH, BERNHARD
1911   *Bernhard von Breydenbach and His Journey to the Holy Land 1483-4*, Hugh William M. Davies, editor. J. & J. Leighton, London.

Von Wartburg, Marie-Luise
2001   Earthquakes and Archeology: Paphos after 1222. In Πρακτικα του Γ Διεθνους Κυπρολογικου Συνεδριου, Λευκωσια 1996, τομος Β, Μεσαιωνικο Τμημα, Athanasios Papageorghiou, editor, pp. 127–145. Εταιρεια Κυπριακων Σπουδων, Nicosia.

Walsh, Michael J. K., Tamás Kiss and Nicholas Coureas, editors.
2014   *The Harbour of All this Sea and Realm: Crusader to Venetian Famagusta.* CEU Medievalia, 17. Department of Medieval Studies and Central European University Press, Budapest.

Westerdahl, Crister
1992   The Maritime Cultural Landscape. In *International Journal of Nautical Archeology* 21(1):5–14.

. . . .

Maria Ktori,
2, Dionysios Skylosofos street,
4159 Kato Polemidia, Cyprus

Routes of Removal: Vessel Biographies and the Island Transfer of Aboriginal and Torres Strait Islander Peoples, Queensland, Australia

Madeline Fowler

Forced relocations, known as removals, affected every Aboriginal and Torres Strait Islander community in Queensland in the 19th and 20th century. Despite the island location of many missions and stations, the watercraft engaged in removals are often implicit in the historical archives. Targeted research of these vessels offers insights into removals beyond origin and destination. The study of the maritime transport of removals enriches the biographies of the Aboriginal and Torres Strait Islander peoples involved by contextualizing human experiences beyond a series of place names. It also magnifies the biographies of the vessels plying the Queensland coast during this time.

Punishment and Protection

During the British colonial period (1788–1901), several people put forward the idea of removing Indigenous peoples to islands in Queensland, Australia (Copland 2005:66). Before 1897, governments informally condoned the forced relocations of Aboriginal and Torres Strait Islander peoples, alongside outright violence and abductions. "Protective" legislation introduced in the late 19th century created both formal legislative and administrative frameworks for the continuation of forcible removal and institutionalization (Copland 2005:6). The 1897 *Aboriginal Protection and Restriction of the Sale of Opium Act* legislated for the "better protection and care of the aboriginal and half-caste inhabitants of the colony," establishing the positions of regional Protectors and the later Chief Protector.

The Act led to the "removal" of Aboriginal and Torres Strait Islander peoples, often also described as their "transfer", to missions, stations, and reserves. Copland (2005:18) defined removal as the forcible movement of a person to a church or State-run institution, brought about or sanctioned by the State, often through the use of race-based legislation. The twin colonial policies of punishment and protection through removals affected every Aboriginal and Torres Strait Islander community—almost every family—in the State of Queensland in the 19th and well into the mid-20th century, with continued impacts of these dislocations experienced to the present (Copland 2005:15).

Previous research into Aboriginal and Torres Strait Islander removals, from the perspective of historians, focus to a large degree on quantifying the implementation and extent of this atrocity and extend our knowledge about specific aspects such as child separation in Queensland. Archival sources provide evidence of 12,576 removals in Queensland between 1859 and 1972 (Copland 2005:100). Copland (2005:7) concludes that past policies resulted in the separation of one in six Aboriginal children in Queensland from their natural families. Yet, a statistician's perspective of removals becomes clinical and neglects the lived experiences of removal (Copland 2005:45). Copland (2005) adopts a qualitative approach through analyzing removals registers, removals cards, and annual reports for the department. Removal orders, while unreliable, record surplus attempts to justify removal, changing in focus over time, from "immoral conduct", "refuses to work", "mixes with Chinese", "neglected", "for own good", and "inciting other aboriginals to strike" to "for medical treatment" and "dangerously affected by moon" (Copland 2005:28).

Routes of removal took place in an amphibious landscape. During the 19th century, the concept of islands of incarceration emerged, on which to detain Aboriginal and Torres Strait Islander people, leading to the location of missions, stations, and reserves on islands (Finnane and McGuire 2001:279; Copland 2005:209). Elsewhere, Westerdahl (2006:61) describes the sphere of maritime culture as a "social security valve", but in this case the State controlled it as a landscape of power, with 38% of total removals to islands. The practice in Queensland of using islands as places of exile and punishment for Aboriginal and Torres Strait Islander people began with the establishment of institutions on Fraser Island (K'gari) as early as 1871 (Copland 2005:79).

Official records disclose little about the situation of Aboriginal and Torres Strait Islander people, but much about the racial thinking of the time. In particular, the journey these people undertook is not well-known. The ships involved in the routes of removal are important from an archaeological perspective. As Westerdahl (2006:60) queries, "where do we find wagons, carts, roads and paths which give such concentrated information both on communication and landscape as well-preserved shipwrecks?" Aboriginal and Torres Strait Islander people removed to islands reached a transit point at one or several points along this journey. This prompted the use of a landscape approach to examine qualitative data for this paper.

A Roadless Landscape

Removals took place across vast distances and their sea routes are more variable and fluid than the land routes (Westerdahl 2006:60). Removal descriptions do not provide detailed accounts of the route followed, rather only accounting for a series of points and place names. The end point of the removal was the only certain detail. The choice of the sea route, or even the choice between a land or sea route, is the result of a transport structure—the amalgamation of the regional variety of a transport pattern that develops in a natural way and the transport system overlaid by the authorities (Westerdahl 2006:60, 62–63) (Figure 1). Political control was dependent on the transport pattern, although the transport system required permanent maintenance. Local factors determined the implementation and extent of removals to an equal, if not larger, degree than policy direction from the centralized Office of the Chief Protector of Aborigines (Copland 2005:8). The Chief Protector was reliant on local Aboriginal Protectors, usually police officers, and employers for information and advice, the latter of which were responsible for executing policies and affected the rate of removals in a major way at particular locations.

Archaeologists rarely take into account roads, road nets and systems, and transportation (Westerdahl 2006:59, 96). Yet, those that do seldom consider the close relationship to their maritime parallels—sea routes (Westerdahl 2006:59–60). Sectoring these two facets of transportation is ineffective as there is seldom a principal road on the coast that does not have a coastal sea route alternative (Westerdahl 2006:60, 100). Of particular concern is the meeting place of land and sea routes—nodal or transit points where a change to the means of transport takes place (Westerdahl 2006:102). These often occur at the "harbor", with boat causeways, landing stages, piers, and jetties (Westerdahl 2006:81; Ilves 2011:10). In the past, the coast and islands were more accessible and less isolated from various forms of communication than most inland settlements due to the rapid transmission of information, the rapidity of transport, and a greater spatial extension of communication lines (Westerdahl 2006:59, 61). Analyzing routes of removal requires assessing roads and sea routes at the same time, although maritime archaeology requires a concentration on the sea traffic as the point of departure. In many respects, routes of removal are part of the archaeology of transport and communication—the transport aspect of sociocultural space—with Queensland serving as the transport zone.

Vessel Biography

Ships are artifacts—portable objects showing evidence of manufacture, modification, and use by people (Muckle 2006:219). Thus, archaeologists can handle ships, like single

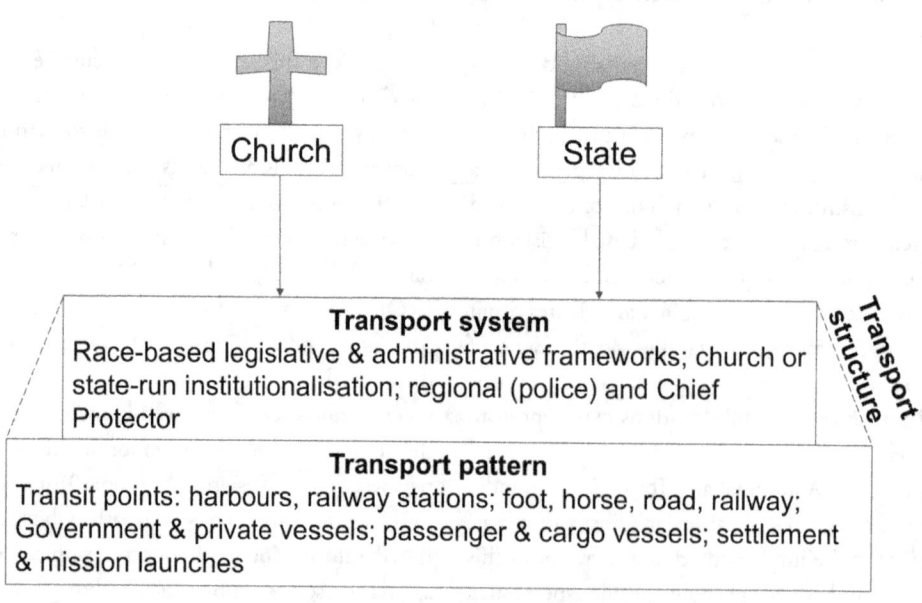

Figure 1: The relationship between the transport pattern, transport system and transport structure. (Author, after Westerdahl 2006.)

objects, through an object, or in this case vessel, biography (Colwell-Pasch 2014:22). Archaeologists rarely undertake full vessel histories, despite the potential the use of a ship has to reveal significant insights into the people associated with the vessel and their membership in wider society (Adams 2001:300; Colwell-Pasch 2014:30). Ships had, and have, social lives, allowing archaeologists to take a biographical approach to consider these social aspects alongside their function. Furthermore, the archaeological record does not reflect all activities on board, meaning historical accounts are of considerable benefit in the construction of a vessel biography. It is conceivable that ships and shipwrecks are the largest artifact of the routes of removal.

Archaeologists have employed many biographical approaches: object biography, artifact biography, life history model, life-cycle analysis, chaîne opértoire, use-life analysis, and cultural biography (Colwell-Pasch 2014:27); but here I refer to BULSI. The BULSI system uses the five core stages in the 'life cycle' of a vessel—build, use, loss, survival, and investigation—to record the history of a shipwreck (Wessex Archaeology 2011:17, 30). Use is of particular interest to the vessels involved in routes of removal, encompassing changes of use during their career, yet in other contexts it can also shed light on aspects relating to cargo, personal possessions, trade, warfare, life aboard, and social organization (Wessex Archaeology 2011:30). Information recorded includes: registration and nationality; associated companies and individuals, for example owners, managers, passengers and crew; cargo type; and ports of call and vessel routes (Wessex Archaeology 2011:30). The early stages of this research relied on newspaper archives, however Lloyd's Register, insurance records, shipwreck databases, and the archaeological record may also contain useful data.

"Handcuffed Together for a Thousand Miles"

Evans (1999b:95) describes the State's perceptions of Aboriginal and Torres Strait Islander people as people "to be 'mustered', then removed alone or in 'mobs' by dray, railway truck and steamer, to be 'herded' and 'mated' on reserves or missions." Of course, routes were also undertaken on foot. In late 1932, 11 Aboriginal people were "gathered" from the Coen police district on Cape York, particularly the Batavia goldfields (*Telegraph* 1933:8; *Townsville Daily Bulletin* 1933:3). Police constables marched these people to Laura, a journey of 232 km and taking 20 days at the height of the wet season (Copland 2005:229). Chains adjoined at the neck subdued most of the Aboriginal people who suffered repeated flogging with a stock whip (Copland 2005:222–257). Indeed, officials sanctioned the use of chains during removals (Copland 2005:248). The trek continued overland to Cooktown, to board a boat to Cairns and then take a train to Townsville (*Telegraph* 1933:8; *Townsville Daily Bulletin* 1933:3). The Palm Island Aboriginal Settlement launch then concluded the transfer to Palm Island (Bwgcolman). The number of people involved and the brutality of this 1932 removal was not exceptional.

Indeed, ordinary events such as this were not limited to land routes. In 1902, Archibald Meston, Southern Protector of Aborigines, noted the increased transportation of Aboriginal "offenders" without trial southward by steamer to Fraser Island (K'gari), "handcuffed together for a thousand miles" (cited in Evans 1999a:138, 1999b:89). The following case studies enrich the record of routes of removal by focusing on aspects of the events of moving and traveling themselves. This allows for the interrogation of those vessels involved, through the reconstruction of events based on the careful and critical use of primary sources.

QGSS Llewellyn 1897 Maryborough to Fraser Island (K'gari)

As mentioned, the 1897 Act resulted in an increase in removals and 84% of removals that year were to White Cliffs and then to Bogimbah Creek on Fraser Island (K'gari) (Copland 2005:113–114). This mission was a prototype for all later Aboriginal institutions in Queensland, with the majority of Aboriginal people transported there from the Maryborough region (Evans 1999a; Copland 2005:114). Bogimbah was a secular reserve under government control from February 1897 to February 1900 and an Anglican mission supported by State subsidy until closure in August 1904 (Evans 1999a:128).

In 1897, Meston mustered 51 Aboriginal people, 23 men, 10 youths and boys, and 18 women and girls, accompanied by a likely exaggeration of 100 dogs, from Wide Bay to Fraser Island (K'gari). The group was marshaled, clothed, and then gathered in the forecastle of the twin-screw pilot steamer *Llewellyn* (160 gross tonnage; 112 ft. length, 19.6 ft. width, 9.2 ft. depth; Australian National Shipwreck Database ID 2776) (*Queenslander* 1897:500; *Telegraph* 1897a:3; *Telegraph* 1897b:5; Department of the Environment and Energy 2018). A contemporaneous newspaper account gives the following description:

Deported to Fraser's Island. Fifty aboriginals, men, women, and children, the remnants of the once powerful Fraser's Island and Mary River blackfellows, and who of late years have, as a tattered and undisciplined brigade, been the waifs and strays of the gutters, were, on Wednesday last, embarked aboard the Llewellyn and deported to Fraser's Island, which is to be their future home (Telegraph 1897a:3).

According to newspaper reports, the Aboriginal people were "very eager and enthusiastic in the matter" (*Telegraph* 1897a:3).

Built in England in 1884, under order from the Queensland government, *Llewellyn* first served as a pilot vessel in Maryborough from 1885 to 1903 (Department of the Environment and Energy 2018) (Figure 2). Its primary role was to supply lighthouses and maintain navigational lights. This vessel was thus part of the existing transport pattern when the State requisitioned it into the removal transport system (Table 1).

Rio Loge 1904 Fraser Island (K'gari) to Yarrabah

In 1904, the closure of the Fraser Island Mission for financial reasons lead to the dispersing of Aboriginal peoples to destinations including Yarrabah Mission and Durundur (*Brisbane Courier* 1904:4; *Telegraph* 1904a:2; Copland 2005:114–115). The expenditure of the Aboriginal Department on the "cost removing Aboriginals" in 1904 was 408 pounds 15 shillings 3 pence, of which 306 pounds was for the transfer of the Fraser Island Settlement to Yarrabah (Roth 1905:22). About 30 Aboriginal people went to Durundur (*Telegraph* 1904a:2), with only two or three elderly Aboriginal people remaining at the abandoned mission station on Fraser Island (K'gari) (*Telegraph* 1904b:7). Fitzroy Island (Gabar) was an outstation of Yarrabah Mission from 1904, with approximately 144 Aboriginal peoples living there in 1907 (*Queenslander* 1907:41). By 1911, only approximately 10 of the original 117 people removed to Yarrabah from Fraser Island (K'gari) survived (Evans 1991:26–27).

The "specially-chartered" schooner *Rio Loge* (249.72 gross tonnage; also described as a brigantine; Australian National Shipwreck Database ID 10498), owned by Captain Spence, transferred those people destined for Yarrabah and the buildings and useful property (*North Queensland Register* 1904:11; *Telegraph* 1904a:2; *Truth* 1904:5; *Morning Bulletin* 1933:13; Department of the Environment and Energy 2018). Departing Fraser Island (K'gari) on 23 August, it arrived at Cape Grafton by 5 September, a 13-day, roughly 1,000-mile sea voyage (*Telegraph* 1904c:5). The Aboriginal people went from the Cape to Yarrabah Mission, although the shallowness of the water in Mission Bay resulted in the unloading of the building material cargo into shallow punts and whale boats, towed by the mission launch, taking several months to complete (*North Queensland Register* 1904:11; *Morning Post* 1905:2).

Iron-built in England in 1869, *Rio Loge* first traded sugar between New Zealand (Aotearoa), Mauritius, and the Cape before going into the labor trade (which ran from 1863–1904) among the South Sea Islands (*Brisbane Courier* 1909:5; *Clarence*

Figure 3: *Rio Loge*, Brisbane, no date. (Record No. 109676, John Oxley Library, State Library of Queensland.)

and Richmond Examiner 1909:10) (Figure 3). Undergoing overhauling at the port of Maryborough in 1895, due to the strict conditions of the *Pacific Island Labourers (extension) Act 1892* (QLD) which controlled the Queensland labor trade, the newspaper described the brig-rigged *Rio Loge* as "large and well-appointed" (*Maryborough Chronicle* 1895:2). After the banning of the Queensland labor trade, effective from 31 March 1904 under the *Pacific Islander Labour Act* 1901, the vessel was an ordinary cargo carrier on the Queensland coast (*Clarence and Richmond Examiner* 1909:10). Only months after the closure of the Queensland labor trade forced *Rio Loge* to find alternate employment, the State appropriated it for the removal transport structure (Table 1).

Palmer 1918 Hull River to Palm Island (Bwgcolman)

In March 1918, a cyclone destroyed the Hull River settlement, established four years earlier, resulting in the removal of several hundred Aboriginal people and 150 tons of houses, machinery, and fencing to Palm Island (Bwgcolman) (*Queenslander* 1918:12; *Telegraph* 1918:9; Snow 1933:9). Although gazetted as an Aboriginal reserve in 1914, Palm Island (Bwgcolman) first received those removed Aboriginal peoples from Hull River. Within 20 years, the population of the island reached 1,248, the most populous reserve in the State (State Library of Queensland 2016).

Clyde, a timber-carrying schooner owned by Rooney & Co., transported the salvaged material as part of a fleet of flat-bottomed schooners all engaged in timber freight on the coast (*Queenslander* 1918:12; *Telegraph* 1918:9; Snow 1933:9). The Queensland government auxiliary ketch, *Melbidir*, was also engaged in the demolition of the Hull River Settlement and establishment of the Palm Island Station (Bleakley 1919:4).

Palmer, a small (298 gross tonnage; 140.2 ft. length, 26 ft. width, 8.5 ft. depth; Australian National Shipwreck Database ID 2964) twin-screw steamer under the charge of Captain Broadfoot, transferred the people (*Queenslander* 1918:12; Department of the Environment and Energy 2018). After spending two days on Dunk Island (Coonanglebah) awaiting the transporting steamer, almost 100 people departed, reportedly "with cheers" (*Northern Miner* 1918:7). The Superintendent had arranged for the departure of exactly 100, but a husband and wife wandered off along the beach and failed to return in time to catch the steamer (*Northern Miner* 1918:7). The couple departed on the settlement launch with the working squad; the latter retained to ship the building materials salvaged from the cyclone (*Northern Miner* 1918:7).

Scottish-built of steel in 1844 for the then Australasian Steam Navigation Company, by 1910 the Australian United Steam Navigation Company withdrew *Palmer* from the Townsville to Cairns passenger service for employment in the company's cargo service between Townsville and the various northern sugar ports (*Telegraph* 1910:10; Department of the Environment and Energy 2018) (Figure 4). Broadfoot and Sons, who conducted a shipping service for the banana industry to the rivers between Townsville and Cairns, likely later purchased the vessel (*Townsville Daily Bulletin* 1945:5). The steamer *Palmer*, while engaged in the passenger trade between Townsville and Cairns, most often loaded bananas in the Johnstone River (*Townsville Daily Bulletin* 1945:5). It appears that the State seconded *Palmer* to its transport structure from cargo-based private employment (Table 1).

Use	QGSS *Llewellyn*	*Rio Loge*	*Palmer*
Associated companies and individuals	Queensland Government (owner), Archibald Meston (Southern Protector of Aborigines), 51 Mary River and Fraser Island Aboriginal peoples, John Evans (sea pilot), James Parker Howitt (engineer), a coxswain, four boatmen, two firemen, a cook and a boy	Captain Spence (owner), >100 Fraser Island Aboriginal peoples, Reverend E.R. Gribble and two inmates (Yarrabah Mission Station), six Europeans	Australasian Steam Navigation Co. (owner, 1844), Australian United Steam Navigation Co. (1877), Broadfoot (Captain, 1918), Broadfoot & Sons (owners), ~100 Hull River Aboriginal peoples
Cargo type	Pilot vessel; general cargo	Sugar (1868–?), labour trade (?–1904), general cargo (1904–1905)	Passenger service, cargo (sugar, bananas)
Ports of call and vessel routes	Maryborough 1885–1903	New Zealand, Mauritius, the Cape, South Sea Islands, Queensland	Townsville to Cairns, Townsville to northern ports, rivers between Townsville and Cairns (Johnstone River)

Table 1: Use of each vessel leading up to, and at the time of, removal.

Figure 4: *Palmer*, no date. (Record No. 68035, John Oxley Library, State Library of Queensland.)

Significance

Of these three case studies, the *Commonwealth Historic Shipwrecks Act* 1976 protects the *Llewellyn* and *Palmer* shipwrecks, the former of which also has a 500 m protected zone (Department of the Environment and Energy 2018). Yet no prior documentation has connected these vessels to the events of Aboriginal removals. Indeed, previous researchers attribute the social significance of *Llewellyn* to the descendants of the crew and passengers who lost their lives aboard the vessel at the time of its loss in 1919 (Hopkins-Weise 1999, 2006; Doyle 2005).

These "hidden histories" in the biographies of vessels plying the Queensland coast in the 19th and 20th centuries should inform the significance of the vessels associated with the island transfer of Aboriginal and Torres Strait Islander peoples. I argue that there were changes to the function of the vessels, regardless of duration, that are more significant than the vessels' intended function and that the particular aspects of life on board the vessel during that time add to its importance. These vessels operated as part of a wider social system, adding to their importance, and the cultural origin of the passengers adds to the interest of the shipwreck. The scale of removals, whether entire communities or small groups and individuals, suggests that the function of these vessels were somewhat common to the period, yet archaeologists have not connected vessels used for this function to the archaeological record and further investigation may reveal an underrepresentation of these sites. These vessels were thus associated with events that, while not well-known, are significant to Queensland's history and have regional associations and implications.

Of course, responses of both the enforcers and the enforced to the policy of removals were not without agency. Some Protectors worked to ensure that local Aboriginal and Torres Strait Islander people could remain in their own community and geographical location (Copland 2005:8). Aboriginal and Torres Strait Islander people demonstrated a degree of resistance to the policy and there are many recorded examples of extraordinary human endurance where they travelled large distances in difficult circumstances to return to their Country and communities (Roth 1904:16–17; Copland 2005:8).

References

Adams, Jonathan
2001   Ships and Boats as Archaeological Source Material. In *World Archaeology* 32(3):292–310.

Bleakley, John W.
1919   Aboriginals Department. — Information Contained in Report for the Year Ended 31st December, 1918. In *Report to Home Secretary's Department*, Brisbane, QLD.

Brisbane Courier
1904   Fraser Island. In *Brisbane Courier* 4 August:4. Brisbane, QLD.

1909   Missing Brigantine. In *Brisbane Courier* 16 February:5. Brisbane, QLD.

Clarence and Richmond Examiner
1909   The Missing *Rio Loge*. In *Clarence and Richmond Examiner* 13 February:10. Grafton, NSW.

Colwell-Pasch, Chelsea
2014   *From Shipyard to Seabed: A Multiphasic Vessel Biography of* Leven Lass *[1839–1854]*. Master's thesis, Department of Archaeology, Flinders University, Adelaide, SA.

Copland, Mark
2005 *Calculating Lives: The Numbers and Narratives of Forced Removals in Queensland 1859–1972*. Doctoral dissertation, School of Arts, Media and Culture, Griffith University, Brisbane, QLD.

Department of the Environment and Energy
2018 Australian National Shipwreck Database. <http://www.environment.gov.au/heritage/historic-shipwrecks/australian-national-shipwreck-database>. Accessed 21 February 2018.

Doyle, Coleman
2005 *Q.G.S.S. Llewellyn: A Management and Conservation Plan*. Report to Queensland Museum, Brisbane, QLD.

Evans, Raymond
1991 A Permanent Precedent: Dispossession, Social Control and the Fraser Island Reserve and Missions, 1897–1904. In *The Ngulag Monograph* No. 5, Aboriginal and Torres Strait Islander Study Unit, University of Queensland, St Lucia, QLD.

1999a *Fighting Words: Writing About Race*. University of Queensland Press, St Lucia.

1999b 'Steal Away': The Fundamentals of Aboriginal Removal in Queensland. In *Journal of Australian Studies* 23(61):83–95.

Finnane, Mark and John McGuire
2001 The Uses of Punishment and Exile: Aborigines in Colonial Australia. In *Punishment & Society* 3(2):279–298.

Hopkins-Weise, Jeff
1999 *A History of the Service and Loss of the Q.G.S. Llewellyn, 1884–1919*. Report to Queensland Museum, Brisbane, QLD.

2006 A History of the Service and Loss of the Queensland Government Steamer *Llewellyn*, 1884–1919. In *Memoirs of the Queensland Museum, Cultural Heritage Series* 4(1):29–51.

Ilves, Kristin
2011 Is there an Archaeological Potential for a Sociology of Landing Sites? In *Journal of Archaeology and Ancient History* 2:3–31.

Maryborough Chronicle
1895 General News. In *Maryborough Chronicle* 22 October:2. Maryborough, QLD.

Morning Bulletin
1933 Origin and History. In *Morning Bulletin* 4 February:13. Rockhampton, QLD.

Morning Post
1905 Yarrabah Mission Troubles. In *Morning Post* 26 January:2. Cairns, QLD.

Muckle, Robert
2006 *Introducing Archaeology*. Broadview Press, Peterborough.

Northern Miner
1918 Rural Homilies. In *Northern Miner*. 6 July:7. Charters Towers, QLD.

North Queensland Register
1904 Cricket. In *North Queensland Register* 12 September:11. Townsville, QLD.

Queenslander
1897 Queensland. In *Queenslander* 6 March:500. Brisbane, QLD.

1907 Northern Aboriginals. In *Queenslander* 19 October:41. Brisbane, QLD.

1918 Aboriginal Settlements. In *Queenslander* 20 July:12. Brisbane, QLD.

Roth, Walter E.
1904 *Annual Report of the Northern Protector of Aboriginals for 1903*. Report to Department of Public Lands, Brisbane, QLD.

1905 *Annual Report of the Chief Protector of Aboriginals for 1904*. Report to Department of Public Lands, Brisbane, QLD.

Snow, F.
1933 Making Towns Where Savages Roam. In *Telegraph* 5 August:9. Brisbane, QLD.

State Library of Queensland
2016 *Aboriginal and Torres Strait Islander Missions and Reserves in Queensland*. <http://www.slq.qld.gov.au/__data/assets/pdf_file/0018/82602/missions_and_reserves.pdf>. Accessed 21 February 2018.

Telegraph
1897a Wide Bay Aboriginals. In *Telegraph* 1 March:3. Brisbane, QLD.

1897b Fraser Island Blacks. In *Telegraph* 2 March:5. Brisbane, QLD.

1904a Aborigines Removing. In *Telegraph* 20 August:2. Brisbane, QLD.

1904b Removal of Aborigines. In *Telegraph* 24 August:7. Brisbane, QLD.

1904c Aborigines Removing. In *Telegraph* 5 September:5. Brisbane, QLD.

1910 Steamer Palmer. In *Telegraph* 17 May:10. Brisbane, QLD.

1918 Care of Aborigines. In *Telegraph* 17 September:9. Brisbane, QLD.

1933   Long Journey. In *Telegraph* 31 January:8. Brisbane, QLD.

TOWNSVILLE DAILY BULLETIN
1933   Cairns Notes. In *Townsville Daily Bulletin* 1 February:3. Townsville, QLD.

1945   When the N.Q. Banana Industry Boomed. In *Townsville Daily Bulletin* 3 October:5. Townsville, QLD

TRUTH
1904   About Aboriginals. In *Truth* 21 August:5. Brisbane, QLD.

WESSEX ARCHAEOLOGY
2011   *Assessing Boats and Ships 1860–1950: Methodology Report*. Report to English Heritage, Salisbury, UK.

WESTERDAHL, CHRISTER
2006   The Relationship between Land Roads and Sea Routes in the Past—Some Reflections. In *Deutsches Schiffahrtsarchiv* 29:59–114.

....

Madeline Fowler
University of Southampton,
Avenue Campus, Highfield,
Southampton, Hampshire SO15 1BF, United Kingdom

The Plantation Boat Accommodation: A Maritime Icon of the American Southeast

Daniel Mark Brown, Kathryn L. Cooper M.A., Lynn B. Harris

East Carolina University's Program in Maritime Studies traveled to the Charleston region in South Carolina for its 2010 Fall Field School to record several vessels both underwater and on land. This included the vernacular craft, Accommodation. *The vessel was donated by the Charleston Museum to Middleton Plantation on display for exhibition as an example of historic plantation associated human and cargo transportation. The Program in Maritime Studies sought to accurately record the details of the vessel's construction, lines, and features over several days.*

Introduction

Accommodation is a split-log dugout vessel and a very rare example of vernacular water craft once common in the Southeastern region of the United States from the colonial period through the 19th century. Although similar vessels were commonplace, they are minimally represented within the archaeological record. Therefore, every detail that was possible to record was significant given the lack of physical and documentary evidence and, consequently, the lack of our current understanding of this important feature of plantation logistics and the maritime economy of the American Southeast. This report will touch upon historical evidence, construction details, and formation processes to explore some of the more significant themes that concern the nature of these historic vessels that *Accommodation* represents.

Accommodation, a History

Individual vessels within a common vernacular type are by nature difficult to uncover within the historical record, but there are certain clues that shed a little light on *Accommodation's* background. Fortunately, its donation to the Charleston Museum, and afterwards to the Middleton Plantation, left documentary traces through the associated accession and de-accession records that illuminate its history of ownership. The names mentioned in the accession document provide some context within which *Accommodation* operated, these can then be compared to the more general background of similar vessels and vessel types within the historical record.

Though terse, Charleston Museum's accession record for *Accommodation* disclosed two important figures in Charleston's history that each owned the vessel. The accession reads:

Donated by W.G. Hinson 1908. Built by negro laborers, being hollowed out of two cypress logs. Brought from Pon Pon by W.W. McLeod, Sr., many years before the [Civil} [W]ar. Bought by Mr. Hinson about 1855 for $150 and used on his plantation for years. It was christened the Accommodation *by the plantation people. (Charleston Museum 1908)*

William Godber Hinson, the first person introduced, descended from the Stiles family on James Island and subsequently inherited the plantation. The plantation house was originally built by Benjamin Stiles in 1742 and was extended in 1891 by W.G. Hinson (Preservation Consultants 1989:13). Hinson (1838-1919) became a prominent Charlestonian for several key reasons. Many southern historians are familiar with his involvement in the Civil War as a lieutenant in the Seventh South Carolina Cavalry. He kept an extensive diary detailing his account through the duration of the war, which he donated to the Charleston Library Society along with most of his acquired personal and historical documents (Waring 1974:14). Nevertheless, Hinson's contributions to South Carolina's agricultural industry secured his prominent social position and are more pertinent to this study. Hinson contributed to furthering South Carolina's agricultural industry through advocating the use of commercial fertilizers and utilizing methods of scientific drainage. He was "a member and director of the Commercial club" and belonged to "the State Agricultural and Mechanical society.... the South Carolina Agricultural society," and was "president of the Farmers' Alliance" (Hemphill 1908:207). As a result, "he was recognized as the last of local planters of the long stapled cotton, for which the Sea Islands were famous" (Waring 1974:14).

William Wallace McLeod, like Hinson, was a prominent planter on James Island and rose to prominence under similar circumstances. Although there is no other reference apart from the accession document that link *Accommodation* to Pon Pon, which was on the Edisto River in Colleton County near today's Jacksonboro, the statement may refer to McLeod's origins. He bought what is now known as the McLeod Plantation in 1851 and built the current house in 1858 that was used as a Confederate unit headquarters during the American Civil War (Preservation Consultants 1989:18-21). W.W. McLeod was also known for his agricultural contributions. He attended the first World's Fair in London in 1851 promoting Sea Island cotton (*The Weekly Heral 1851:55*). Additionally, he played an active role in local politics, becoming a representative for St. Andrews Parish and a Warden at St. James church in 1856 (*Charleston Mercury 1856:2; CM 1856:2; CM 1856:2*). According to a census record from 1860, W.W. McLeod, who was currently residing in St. Andrews Parish containing his plantation, was born in Edisto.

A cypress canoe may very well be synonymous with a pirogue or periauger. The contemporary Webster Dictionary explained, "This word is variously written, periagua or pirogue. The former is the spelling of Washington and Jefferson; the latter of Charlevoix." It is defined by Chalevoix as, "A canoe formed out of the trunk of a tree or two canoes united." Also, "In modern usage in America, a narrow ferry boat carrying two masts and a leeboard" (Webster 1828,:283). As a plantation vessel, it is fair to predict that *Accommodation* was used by the Stiles Point and McLeod Plantations throughout nearby waterways, including James Creek, Wappoo Creek, and Charleston Harbor. It is necessary, however, to appeal to alternative sources that reveal the use-life of similar watercraft to gain a more comprehensive perspective of *Accommodation's* services. Split-log dugout vessels were mainly utilitarian, but one story from *Spirit of the Times,* illustrates that these vessels were also used recreationally. It chronicles the results of a regatta in Charleston during the summer of 1848, and several participating vessels were cypress dugouts. The following excerpt is particularly descriptive:

> *The Olive Branch was built in Georgia, in 1812, out of one Cypress tree. She is forty-two feet long, five feet wide. She was built during the war, to smuggle from Amelia Island to Georgia. At the termination of the war she was purchased by Mr. Clarke, for many years the proprietor of packets to Sullivan's Island; the Olive Branch having been used by him in that business under the name of the Highflyer. Mr. Lucas bought her at the sale of Clarke's effects, for $150, and has made several good runs with her. Mr. Lucas ... had ten strong oarsmen, who were assisted by sails, whenever the wind allowed them to be used in the different reaches (*Spirit of the Times 1848:319).

In addition to recreational use, vessels like *Olive Branch* were used to carry both cargo (including the smuggling reference) and passengers, and were propelled by both oars and wind.

Often, classified advertisements in contemporary newspapers give evidence for periaugers' expected functions, consistently intended for plantation use. One advertisement reads: "For Sale, A New Cypress CANOE, 37 feet long, 5 feet 6 inches beam, rows eight oars—suitable for a plantation. Enquire of Mr. Henry Stocker, Boat-builder" (City Gazette (Charleston) 1822:3). While other advertisements point to more general services, the emphasis for plantation use is persistent: "by Capers and Heyward. At private sale— Will be sold, a staunchly built and handsome Twelve Oared Cypress Canoe, Copper fastened. Rows well, and is in good condition. To Planters and Farmers near the city, the above presents a fine opportunity for serviceable investment" (Mercury, Advertisements 1856:3). The vessel type permeated through the cross section of social and economic function and ownership. *The State,* a paper out of Columbia, South Carolina, told the story of an African American, a former slave, who fished in the rivers with his dugout canoe (State 1892:4).

The *Accommodation*, as a vessel used specifically within the context of cotton plantations on Sea Island, was likely used in the waterways that were not accessible to larger vessels to transport cotton, various goods, materials, and people. This functional aspect was imperative within the larger commercial infrastructure of the Charleston region. The ubiquitous use of periaugers attested to their utility, and their high demand called for a cheap and effective solution to maintaining efficient commercial logistics. The Great Southern Convention, held in 1854 at Charleston, emphasized the need for efficient commercial logistics. In fact, McLeod attended this convention as a representative of South Carolina (*American Whig Review 1854:3*). They discussed issues such as promotion of manufacturing, mining, agriculture, railroad planning, and: "introducing commercial education among the youth of our country, ... training them up to habits of business, and thereby establishing a body of merchants whose every interest and feeling shall be identified with the country which has reared and sustained them" (*AWR 1854:7*). Nearly everything discussed at the convention was commercial in nature and sought for positive change towards that end. It proposed reducing railroad iron duties, "encouraging boys to go to sea" to improve the merchant service, exploring the Amazon, and fostering and maintaining free and direct trade with Europe (*AWR 1854:9*). Southern planters were aware of commercial reforms that were necessary to boost the Southern economy, and in many areas like Charleston, with shallow inland waterways, periaugers were essential in getting those goods to the market.

Vessels like periaugers have been recorded within the historical record of the 19th century as having been used as far north as New England (Montulé 1821:95), as far south as the Caribbean (Day 1852:201), and as far west as Ohio (Cummings 1829:7). Additionally, they were utilized by a multitude of cultural groups such as Native Americans (Montulé 1821:95; Simms 1855:280; Bigland 1811:304), Huguenots, Germans (Gerstacker 1848: 232), African Americans (State 1892:4) and wealthy planters.

South Carolina Cypress Dugouts in the Historical Record

South Carolina's 18th century newspapers regularly ran advertisements for the recovery, discovery, or sale of cypress dugouts. The pickup trucks of their day, single-log dugouts, split-log dugouts, and expanded-log dugouts carried people and cargo up and down the rivers of South Carolina's Low Country.

Boats Gone Missing

In the earliest edition of Charleston's *South Carolina Gazette* on record, Edward Scull advertised "Gone a Drift or taken from Col. Brewton's Bridge, a Cyprus Canoo, call'd the *Old Dolphin*, 26 Foot long, 3 Foot 6 Inches over…40 s Reward" (1732). It appears bridges were a common place to lose a canoe. Thomas Smith advertised in the next week's edition "Gone Adrift from *Thomas Elliot's* new Bridge… a Cyprus Canoe, 22 Foot long, lately topped…carries 4 Oars…Five Pounds Reward" (*South Carolina Gazette* 1732). The list goes on. Another ad describes "lost…from *Capt. Frankland's* wharf new canow 3 feet wide, 18 or 19 feet long, single gunnel with 4 oars" (SCG 1745). Frankland's wharf might have been an unlucky place to keep a canoe. Peter Bonneau ran a similar add two years later for a "large Cypress Canow 4 feet wide 27 feet long" lost from the same wharf at night, offering a reward of four pounds (SCG 1747). One of the most detailed adds ran two years later:

> *Stolen from my landing on Ashley River, in February last, a large cyprus canow near 30 feet long and about 4 and a half wide, a broad stern; she has 3 or 4 links of chain in a staple drove in her head to fasten rope to; she is supposed to be in some creek near Charles-Town, the rogues who stole her carried 3 barrels of rice with her….5 l.[pound] reward.* William Cattel *(1749)*

This ad ran for three weeks. Most ads ran for two or three weeks, seldom longer. Whether this reflects the success of placing such ads is uncertain. The presence of three barrels of rice attests to the small scale trade most farmers carried out alongside the larger plantations. A similar ad describing the disappearance of a "Pettiauger that carries about 30 Barrels of Rice…" fetched the same five pound reward (SCG1732) suggesting canoes were highly prized by their owners. Jacob Motte suffered a similar fate with his 16 foot long canoe "Taken or went adrift from the bluff at Mount Pleasant, near *Gray's ferry*" marked on the "head and stem IM," offering an unspecified reward (SCG 1760). *William LAWRence* ran an ad "Stolen from my landing…A CYPRESS CANOW That rows with 4 oars, about 20 feet long and 30 [3] feet wide, and has a new stern seat not finished, and is branded on the forecastle in several places M. Reward of TWO DOLLARS" (SCG 1760).

Boats Found

Just as often as cypress canoes, or cooners, disappeared, the auto theft of its day (and unlike most car theft), canoes were found by other boatmen. As per the laws of the day regarding salvage and finds, it was common for ads to appear where some of those "lost" canoes should be found. John Stuart advertised "a large Cyprus Canoe, about 5 Feet wide and 28 long…." It was customary for owners to present some form of proof of ownership, usually in description and then upon paying for the cost of the ad and some reward, receive their vessel again: "giving her true Marks (of which there are several) may have her paying reasonable Charges…" (*SCG 1738*). James Pratt ran a similar ad for a "Cypress Canoe 15 Feet 8 inches long, and 2 Feet 8 inches over, the inside painted red…" the ad ending with reference to payment of proper charges (SCG 1743). This ad was run again the following week and a third time with the canoe's latest location, suggesting the cost of advertising the find was worth the potential payment of "proper charges."

Construction Features Revealed by Ads

Similar ads offer insight into the dimensions and construction features of cypress dugout canoes. An ad run by William Fond refers to a "Cypress Canoe" 3 feet wide, 17 feet long with a locker in the stern (*SCG 1745*). Another ad run two years later merely refers to a "small canow, branded CC in Stern," owners were to apply to Elizabeth Hill (*SCG 1747*), evidence that women too partook in profiting from salvage of small cypress vessels. A 1748 ad runs, "Taken up adrift near Sullivan Island, a Cypres Canow, 4 feet 2 inches wide, 29 feet 6 inches long, and another split Head and Stern with plank in the bottom [expanded split-log] 2 feet 6 inches wide, 15 feet long…" (*SCG*). Another example of an expanded split-log was run in an ad by John Fryer, who refers to a "cypress canow that had been split and widened, near 18 feet long, 3 feet 5 inches wide" (*SCG 1749*). Such ads demonstrate not all expanded split-log boats were of larger dimensions than single log dugouts. Another ad in the same issue reveals consistent dimensions "a Cypress Canow, 3 feet wide, 20 feet long, rows with 4 oars and has a sculling place in her stern…" indicates not all logboats were equipped with rudders (*SCG 1748*). An ad run a decade later reveals detailed construction features, no doubt specified in hopes of turning up the owner and a reward.

> *A Cypress Canow, 3 feet 4 inches wide, 20 feet long, much broken at her head, live oak stem, with a chain 8 feet 4 inches long, has 6 timbers on one side 4 on the other, with 2 oars, also stern seats on each side, 3 rowing seats, 1 fore seat, and 4 row locks, but no head seat, and steers with a rudder…the owner may have her again, proving his property, paying the charges and applying to John Godfrey at Wappo* (SCG 1758).

Here the actual floors are described in a nonsymmetrical arrangement, seats for three rowers, locks for rowing, and a rudder for steering. An ad run the following year lists "a cypress canow, about 24 feet long and 4 feet broad, with long stern sheets…" demonstrating the use of sail for propulsion, hereunto yet mentioned (*SCG 1759*).

The consistent run of ads for lost and found canoes suggests such vessels, though easy to dismiss as crude, ungainly, and insignificant, were rather the contrary. The author encountered a few ads such as run in 1774, "WANTED, A CANOE, Thirty Feet long, and Four Feet Ten Inches wide" (*SCG*). Such specificity attests to both the popular use of canoes along the waterways of the Low Country and the availability and knowledge of potential buyers as to their dimensions. Rarely did ads, as one run in 1781, actually list a canoe for sale: "A Commodious CANOE, 26 feet long, and upwards of five feet wide, rows with six oars, sails…." affirming the use of sail on a small vernacular craft (*Port Royal Gazette*). A similar ad is found in 1800 placed by Nicholl Turnbull, "VERY HANDSOME Cypress Six oared CANOE" (*Georgia Gazette*).

As mentioned above, cypress wood was used in the construction of larger vessels. A packet boat, *Two Brothers*, is listed at 36 foot keel, 39 feet long, 6 feet 3 inches [beam]….Is built of cypress and cedar…." (*Savanah Gazette* 1803). The *Brown's Ferry* Wreck was comprised of pine and cypress, and the *Mempkin Abbey* Wreck utilized cypress as well, showing the utilization of the wood by Southeastern shipwrights in larger vessels (Hocker 1991:229, Vezeau 2004:68). Despite it being softwood, its famed resistance to rot and damp made it a favorable choice (*Fleetwood* 1995). One ambitious Charlestonian whose name appears in land deals and other advertisements put an ad in 1751 describing "a cypress canow about 17 feet long, 3 feet wide. Any person owning the same, may have her, on paying 40lb., which he paid for taking up the same" (*SCG*). Obviously the market for cypress canoes was strong. *Accommodation*, its age unknown at the time of sale, managed to fetch its seller 150 dollars in 1855 (Charleston Museum 1908).

Propulsion of Small Low Country Vernacular Craft

Most log boats, dugout canoes, and periaugers employed a combination of sail and rowing. Boats ranging from 25 feet to 45 feet employed four to eight oars, the former usually having a single mast, the latter two masts.

Propulsion

Even if equipped with mast and rigged for sail, dugout log boats and periaugers usually employed at least one pair of oars for navigating closer to land, beaching, docking, or when becalmed. Fleetwood mentions the universal use of oars (1995:103-107) and newspaper advertisements mention canoes' number of oars in their description (*SCG 1732:1738*). The May 1732 ad for a 22 foot long cypress canoe mentions four oars in its description (*SCG*).

As is often the case with ubiquitous water craft, the rigging of single-long dugouts, split-log dugouts, and expanded split-log dugouts is difficult to track down in the historical record. Rigging elements rarely survive deposition in the archaeological record, compounding the puzzle. This is in part from the recycling of rigging elements upon the wrecking or abandonment of a vessel. Thankfully, John Lawson, the first to mention cypress dugouts and periaugers describes them as carrying "two Masts and Bermuda Sails" (Lawson 1967:9-10). Given that such vessels were used to navigate the estuaries and sounds of the Carolinas, a shallow draft and ability to sail close hauled was certainly desirable by whoever piloted them.

Photographic evidence found in the Charleston Museum shows several examples of rigging for log boats and other small vessels that plied the rivers and harbor of Charleston (2010). Some show a Bermuda sloop style rig, with or without a boom, others are gaff rigged, sprit rigged, leg-of-mutton rigged, or other creative combinations thereof, both showing the use of and absence of gaffs, booms, and sprits. Typical of vernacular craft, the pilots of these boats used whatever they deemed fit for their environment and the weather. Michel B. Alford's drawing of a 1730 periauger shows two masts, both gaff rigged, the mainmast with a gaff and boom, the foremast without a boom, and no sprit present (1992:191).

Fleetwood's chapter on plantation boats and dugouts in the 19th century depicts several of Charles Heyward's illustrations of plantation watercraft underway (1995:104-106). Two illustrations show Bermuda rig with a spritsail, jib, and topsail, while a third shows a craft with sprit removed, sail and peak brought to the mast and tied in a "fisherman's reef" (Fleetwood 1995:104). Chapelle refers to Chapman's illustrations of Bermuda sloops with a mainmast bearing a fore-and-aft rigged sail with boom and gaff, topsails, foremast bearing a fore-and-aft triangular sail with no boom, as well as a spritsail (1967:68-69).

Certainly, there existed abundant trade between the Carolinas and Bermuda. Michael Jarvis accredits the gradual adoption of Bermuda sloop rig in the Caribbean and the Eastern United States as a reflection of Bermuda's commercial influence (2002:597). Due to large slave populations in both Charleston, South Carolina, and Bermuda, it is no wonder that the *South Carolina Gazette* regularly reported on the activities of Bermudian slaves, their owners, and slave legislation *(SCG 1758;)*. If trade itself were not enough to spread the rig, over 1,000 Bermudians emigrated to Virginia and the Carolinas in the late 1720s (Jarvis 2002:612).

Regardless of commercial or migratory influences, utilizing a rig which allows vessels navigating shallow estuaries, harbors, and rivers to sail close hauled undoubtedly benefitted both personal and commercial transportation. Their heavier bulk and cypress's tendency to absorb water, only adding to the weight of the vessels, made getting such boats underway, be it by sail or oar, a more difficult endeavor. Though heavier than skeleton constructed or bottom based boats, log boats could cut through chop once underway, offering another advantage to these frugal and hardy vernacular craft (Fleetwood 1995:111-112).

Methodology

As part of phase two of East Carolina University's Program in Maritime Studies 2010 Fall Field School, students, PI Lynn Harris, and Co-PI David Stewart, split into two groups to record historic split-log dugout vessels located at the Charleston Museum and Middleton Plantation. *Accommodation* is located under an outdoor shelter on the historic plantation grounds outside of Charleston, on the Ashley River, South Carolina. Lynn Harris led five students to record the construction details of *Accommodation*, rendering several illustrations, detailed drawings, and two scaled drawings over two days. Measurements were taken in metric (mm) and construction details, original repairs, and reconstructions were photographed on the second day of recording.

Initial observations about the vessel were made, including overall dimensions, original construction, repairs, and reconstructed elements. Students rendered three isometric drawings of the vessel from various perspectives to try and capture its overall structure. Following this, students established a baseline with the zero end beginning from the tip of the bow, running down the centerline of the boat, secured at the stern. Using baseline-offset, students recorded the shape and dimensions of the sheer, framing elements, profiles of the bow and stern, cross-sections, as well as construction detail. All data was recorded in field journals and then drawn onsite, creating scaled drawings of the plan view and profile or sheer view. The scaled drawings were done 1:10, metric. Work was carried out over two days on site.

Results

The following discusses the results of the above recording and analysis of the vessel's structure and composition.

Construction

The main hull is comprised of two log halves. The two halves appear to be joined by dowels that were driven in at a 90 degree lateral angle into the breast hook and at a 45 degree angle up through the hull into the other half. This method has been noted in the literature review as one used by Pacific North West Native Americans to join split log-dugouts (Fox 1875:404). These lateral fasteners are found in the bow and stern, the only two locations where the hull would have sufficient thickness to allow wooden fasteners to retain any structural integrity. It is possible, however, that these are merely gauging pins, used to signify when the digger of a dugout should stop removing material (Figure 1). The lack of gauging pins throughout the rest of the hull makes this seem to be a less likely interpretation. Wood analysis has revealed the logs to be of cypress, a very typical and abundant material in the Low Country. Further analysis is required to determine if the log halves are from the same tree; such was usually the practice.

Length overall is 8.68 meters with a maximum breadth of 1.58 meters, a 5:1 length to beam ratio making for a slender vessel and falling within the 5:1 to 6:1 ratios found in the historical record. *Accommodation* was most likely used for personal transport and minor commercial trade up and down the river between plantations and Charleston. A stem adjoins the two log halves and is bolted to the breast hook which is capped by a deck hook. A short span of deadwood appears in the bow but no apron is present. There is no keelson or keel plank present, ruling out this vessel from the historically prevalent periaugers popular throughout the 18th and 19th centuries. A single mast step measuring 720 mm by 90 mm is located forward beneath a lateral mast partner, simply a thwart with a circular 100 mm hole for a mast-step.

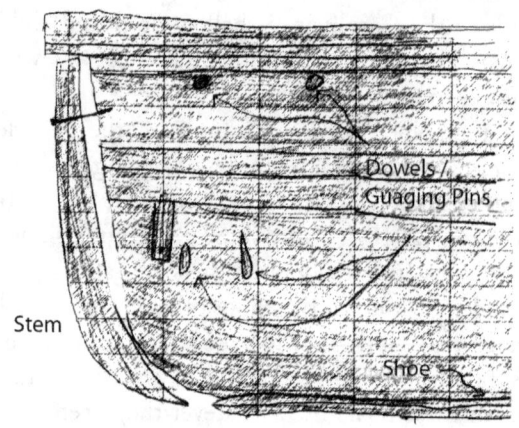

Figure 1: Bow detail sketch of Accommodation, note the near disarticulated stem, possible dowels or gauging pins and shoe. (Image by author, 2010.)

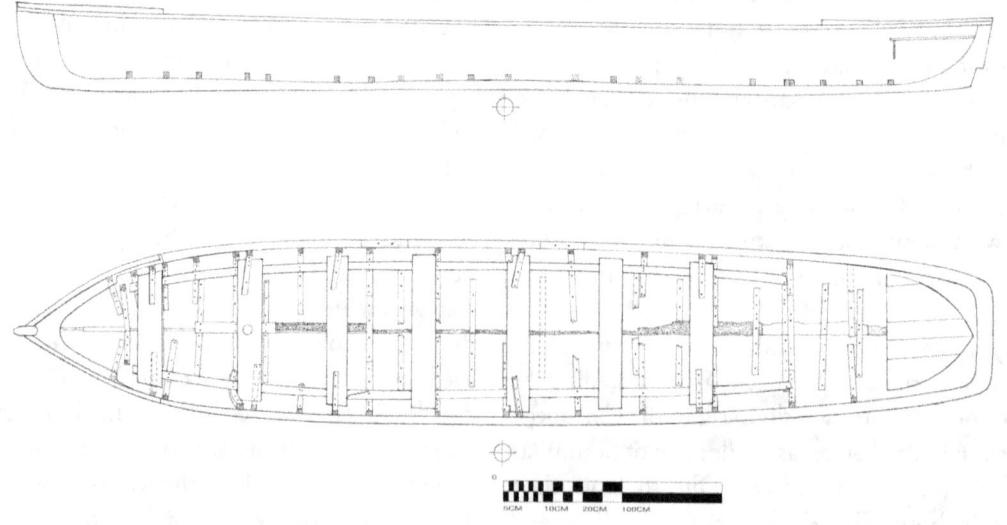

Figure 2: Site plan of plantation boat Accomodation. (Image by authors, 2010.)

The vessel has a regular, if untraditional, frame pattern totaling 23 frame stations with an average room and space between 350 mm and 400 mm. Frame elements averaged 50 mm molded and sided. Eight frame stations consist of frames with futtocks overlapping the forward face of the floor; this continues all the way down the vessel, even beyond amidships, contrary to convention. Six frames consist of floors with futtocks abutting the edge of each. Five frames consist of single floors across the centerline, the ghost of one is present, the remaining three are half-frames. Several framing elements are broken, their original dimensions discernable by ghosts and fastener holes. The first frame station's futtocks are canted, followed by an additional cant frame between station one and station two on the starboard side. Frame elements appear to be nailed directly to the hull, no lateral fastening or treenails, as can be expected on a small vessel. While unconventional, a definite pattern appears in the arrangement of different floors and futtocks. With the exception of the bow and stern, likely due to the sharper rise, the pattern consists of a single floor followed by either a floor with overlapping futtocks or abutting futtocks, and occasionally a half frame. If A represents a single floor, B a floor with overlapping futtocks, C a floor with abutting futtocks, and D a half-frame, then the pattern from bow to stern is: A B B C A D A C A C A C A D A B A C A A CA DA (the last two double frames) (Figure 2).

There are seven thwarts and a stern seat with planks angled in the same direction as a person would sit, if at the tiller. No rudder is present although the socket for a rudder is. Thwarts are reinforced by five pairs of standing knees positioned outboard on top of thwarts, none present abaft reconstructed oarlocks and reconstructed oar seats. A remnant of a shoe runs from the stem down the centerline until the mast step, abaft which deterioration has left a large hole on the inboard edge of the starboard log. There are several smaller strakes that appear to be either filler pieces or repairs over the vessel's work life. Fleetwood documented similar features that he considered to be "rising" strakes added to the gunwales (Fleetwood 1995:112), however closer investigation suggests that the strakes on *Accommodation* are more recent repairs, likely during the vessel's time at the Charleston Museum.

Conclusion

Wealthy planters, such as W.G. Hinson and W.W. McLeod, consistently sought to cut costs in the spirit of maximizing profit. Small vessels like periaugers, hollowed out of cypress trees, offered a viable option for transporting goods and people through shallow waterways inaccessible to larger cargo vessels. This became especially important as planters and merchants of the Southern states sought to cultivate the practice of free trade, especially with Europe. Periaugers were essential within the logistics of Southern commerce, and therefore featured centrally in Charleston's maritime economy.

Despite past ubiquity, periaugers exist very minimally within the archaeological record, in part because of their vernacular and extremely commonplace nature. The study of *Accommodation* is therefore crucial in adding to our understanding of this once-essential feature of South Carolina and the broader American Southeast's maritime culture. Accommodation reflects the predominance of cypress use within the Southeastern vernacular boat-building tradition, along with the ubiquitous utilization of this resource. Hinson and McLeod, as slave owning planters, had ready access to natural and labor resources necessary to take advantage of the hollowed out split-log technique, which enabled them to move their goods and remain prominent agriculturalists in the Charleston region. These two merchants are just two examples of planters who utilized cypress log boats, propelled by oars and sail along South Carolina's waterways. The prevalence of these craft, spanning over two centuries, attest to their significant place in the development of the agrarian capitalist economy of the Southeastern United States.

References

Alford, Michael B.
1992   Origins of Carolina split-dugout canoes. *The International Journal of Nautical Archaeology* 21(3):191-203.

American Whig Review. 11 vols. New York: Unknown, 1852. Sabin Americana. <http://galenet.galegroup.com>. Accessed November 29, 2010.

Art. IX. The Great Southern Convention in Charleston. *DeBow's Review and Industrial Resources, Statistics, etc. Devoted to Commerce, Agriculture, Manufactures* (1853-1864), June 1, 1854: 632. East Carolina University. <http://www.proquest.com>. Accessed November 29, 2010.

Berlin, Ira and Phillip D. Morgan, ed.
1991   *The Slave's Economy: Independent production by Slaves in the Americas.* London.

Bigland, John. *A geographical and historical view of the world: exhibiting a complete delineation of the natural and artificial features of each country.* Vol. 5. Boston, 1811. Sabin Americana. <http://galenet.galegroup.com>. Accessed 11 26, 2010.

Bowness, John. "Modern Close-Hauled Saling." *Mariner's Mirror*, 1956.

Burns, Anna C. "Frank B Williams, Cypress Lumber King." *Journal of Forrest History* (Forest History Society and American Society for Environmental History) 24, no. 3 (July 1980): 127-133.

Chapelle, Howard Irving. *The Baltimore Clipper.* New York: W. W. Norton & Company, Inc., 1930.

—. *The History of the American Sailing Navy: The Ships and Their Development.* New York: W. W. Norton & Company Inc., 1949.

—. *The Search for Speed Under Sail.* New York: W. W. Norton & Company, Inc., 1967.

CHARLESTON MERCURY
1856   Advertisements. *Charleston Mercury* 15April:3. <http://imgcache.newsbank.com> Accessed 26 November 2010.

Charleston Museum. "Accession 1686." Charleston, SC, 1908.

"Charleston (S.C.) Regatta." Spirit of the Times: A Chronicle of the Turf,

Agriculture, Field Sports, Literature and the Stage (1835-1861), August 26, 1848: 319. East Carolina University. <http://www.proquest.com> Accessed November 29, 2010.

CITY GAZETTE
1822   Advertisements City Gazette (Charleston)2 August 1822:3. <http://imgcache.newsbank.com>. Accessed 26 November 2010.

Cummings, Samuel. *The western pilot: containing charts of the Ohio river, and of the Mississippi form the mouth of hte Missouri to the gulf of Mexico.* Cincinnati: Unknown, 1829. Sabin Americana. <http://galenet.galegroup.com>. Accessed 11 26, 2010.

Day, Charles William. *Five years' residence in the West Indies.* 1 vols. London: Unkown, 1852. Sabin Americana. <http://galenet.galegroup.com>. Accessed 11 26, 2010.

"Easter Election St. James's Church James Island." Charleston Mercury, April 8, 1858: 2. Early American Newspapers Series 1 - 3, 1690-1922. <http://imgcache.newsbank.com>. Accessed 11 26, 2010.

"Election Returns." Charleston Mercury, October 15, 1856: 2. Early American Newspapers Series 1 - 3, 1690-1922. <http://imgcache.newsbank.com>. Accessed 11 26, 2010.

Fleetwood, Rusty. Tidecraft: the boats of South Carolina, Georgia, and northeastern Florida, 1550-1950. Tybee Island: WBG Marine Press, 1995.

Gerstacker, Friedrich. The wanderings and fortunes of some German emigrants. New York: Unknwon, 1848. Sabin Americana. <http://galenet.galegroup.com>. Accessed 11 26, 2010.

Hemphill, J.C. "William Godber Hinson." In Men of Mark in South Carolina, Ideals of American Life: a Collection of Biographies of Leading Men of the State, by J.C. Hemphill. Washington, D.C.: Men of Mark Publishing Company, 1908. Archive.org. <http://www.archive.org>. Accessed 11 26, 2010.

Hocker, Fred M. The Development of a Bottom-Based Shipbuilding Tradition in Northwestern Europe and the New World. PhD Thesis, College Station: Texas A&M University Press, 1991, 220-248.

Jarvis, Michael J. "Maritime Mastes and Seafarintg Slaves in Bermuda, 1680-1783." William and Mary Quarterly 59 (July 2002).

Lawson, John. A New Voyage to Carolina [1709]. Chapel Hill: The University of North Carolina Press, 1967.

"Members of the Senate and House of Representatives." Charleston Mercury, October 30, 1856: 2. Early American Newspapers Series 1 - 3, 1690-1922. <http://imgcache.newsbank.com>. Accessed 11 26, 2010.

Montulé, Édouard de. A voyage to North America and the West Indies in 1817. London: Unknown, 1821. Sabin Americana. <http://galenet.galegroup.com>. Accessed 11 26, 2010.

Moore, Alan. "Rig in Northern Europe." *Mariner's Mirror*, 1956: 17-20.

Port Royal Gazette. "Advertisement." May 30, 1781.

Preservation Consultants, Inc. *James Island and Johns Island Historical and Achitectural Inventory, Charleston, South Carolina*. Survey Report, Department of the Interior, National Park Service, Washington D.C.: National Register of Historic Places, 1989. The National Register of Historic Places - Search Records by County. <http://nationalregister.sc.gov>. Accessed 11 26, 2010.

Savanah Gazette, Savanah. "Advertisement." June 11, 1803. Sharitz, Rebecca L. and Schneider Rebecca R. "Hydrochory and Regeneration in a Bald Cypress-Water Tupelo Swamp Forest." *Ecology* 69, no. 4 (August 1988): 1055-1063.

Simms, William Gilmore. *The forayers, or The raid of the dog-days.* New York: Unknown, 1855. Sabin Americana. <http://galenet.galegroup.com>. Accessed 11 26, 2010.

South Carolina Gazette. "Advertisement." May 3, 1774.

—. "Advertisement." November 4, 1732.

—. "Advertisement." November 11, 1732.

—. "Advertisement." May 6, 1732.

—. "Advertisement." May 13, 1732.

—. "Advertisement." January 20, 1733.

—. "Advertisement." January 20, 1733.

—. "Advertisement." February 28, 1743.

—. "Advertisement." July 14, 1758.

—. "Advertisement." January 26, 1760.

—. "Advertisement." November 8, 1760.

—. "Advertisement." 1745.

—. "Advertisement." June 5, 1745.

—. "Advertisement." April 15, 1751.

—. "Advertisement." May 1, 1749.

—. "Advertisement." March 30, 1747.

—. "Advertisement." June 4, 1747.

—. "Advertisement." October 10, 1748.

—. "Advertisement." April 4, 1749.

—. "Advertisement." April 4, 1749.

"The Dr. Didn't Exceed." *State*, March 27, 1892: 4. Early American Newspapers Series 1 - 3, 1690-1922. <http://imgcache.newsbank.com>. Accessed 11 26, 2010.

"The World's Fair. The Works and Inventions of the American Sovereigns, for the Crystal Palace." The *Weekly Herald*, 15 1851, February: 55. Early American Newspapers Series 1 - 3, 1690-1922. <http://imgcache.newsbank.com>. Accessed 11 26, 2010.

United States Department of Commerce. "US Census." *HeritageQuest Online*. 1860. <http://persi.heritagequestonline.com>. Accessed 11 26, 2010.

Vezeau, Susan Lynn. *Mempkin Abbey Wreck*. Thesis, College Station: Texas A&M University, 2004.

Waring, Joseph Ioor. "The Diary of William G. Hinson during the War of Secession: April 6th, 1864 Part I." *South Carolina Historical Magazine*, January 1974: 14-23. JSTOR. <http://www.jstor.org/stable/27567225>. Accessed 11 26, 2010.

Webster, Noah. *An American dictionary of the Englsih language.* New York, NY, 1828. Sabin Americana. <http://galenet.galegroup.com>. Accessed 11 26, 2010.

. . . .

Daniel Mark Brown
Oceaneering International Inc.
6090 Dorsey Road
Hanover, MD 21076

Kathryn L. Cooper M.A.
Independent Researcher
3623 East Wilson Street
Farmville, NC 27828

Lynn B. Harris
East Carolina University
Program in Maritime Studies, Eller House 200
Greenville, NC 27858

Chebacco: The Boat that Built Essex

Leland S. Crawford

Built to save a struggling New England fishing industry, the Chebacco *boats were an amalgamation of ship features that rose to prominence after the time of the American Revolution. This is the boat that gave Chebacco Parish of Massachusetts, the power and influence to become the famous shipbuilding town of Essex. This paper will cover construction characteristics with which to compare to archaeological finds, the history of the vessel, as well as its sociopolitical impact.*

Introduction

The Coffin Beach Wreck was discovered in late spring 2014 in Gloucester, Massachusetts, and subsequently investigated by the MBUAR. The results of the investigation revealed a pre-1820's vessel believed to be the first archaeological evidence of a Chebacco boat. This in turn lead to a deeper investigation into what a Chebacco boat was and what characteristics would distinguish one in the archaeological record. This paper will be a summation of distinguishing characteristics to be used to compare against archaeological finds, as well as a historical understanding of the importance of the Chebacco Boat

Naval Characteristics

Most Recognizable Features

When the individual characteristics of a Chebacco boat are taken individually, none of them are particularly unique. The three most readily apparent features of a Chebacco boat are its mast and size. Chebaccos were easily recognized by the configuration of their two mast. The foremast "being not over 4 feet from the bow"(Hall 1884:7), which placed this mast squarely in the eyes of the bow. In the standard thirty-foot version of the Chebacco boat, the main-mast would be within eleven feet of the fore-mast, putting it amidships (Hall 1884:7). Many other contemporary vessels common to the area, such as shallops or Bermuda boats, or even some sloops, had masts pushed forward in this fashion (Baker 1966), thus this was not a new design. It was the size in conjunction to the masts of the Chebacco boat that made it visually stand out in the seascape of the time. The other vessels of the time with a similar mast orientation were generally 10-20 ft. in length (Baker 1966). In the earlier years of the Chebacco Boat's construction, before 1780, the average size was around 30 ft. and were about 5 tons (Hall 1884:7). However, by 1793 there are custom house records of Chebacco Boats already being 40 ft. long and 23 or more tons. The increasing size made them more easily distinguished from other vessels of the same mast configuration type. The last distinguishing characteristic was the lack of bowsprit. While unexpected on a vessel that was intended to head out to sea, it reduced crew needed to handle the ship.

Other Important Features

Rigging

While these first two features were the most noticeable, the new mast configuration brought about a change in the rigging as well. The boom and the gaff changed from being centered on the yard to being attached at the end of the mast, making it gaff rigged. The gaff itself was raised, lowered, and controlled by means of the halyards. As the gaff was shorter than the boom the sail tapered towards the top. The "luff, being attached to the to the mast by wooden hoops, which would slide up and down with ease"(Hall 1884:7). "The sails were fitted with booms as a rule though some Chebaccos had 'lug' or loose-footed, overlapping foresails" (Chapelle 1960:180). Howard Chapelle gives the example of a 40-ft. vessel on which he estimates that the foremast and the main mast would be 28 ft and 30 ft. respectively. The fore boom and fore gaff would be 15 ft. and 12 to 14 ft. While the main boom would be 22 to 24 ft. with a matching gaff of 14 ft. (Chapelle 1960:181). "The gaffs had only moderate peak. No forestay or shrouds were employed"(Chapelle 1960:180). The fore-and-aft style of the gaff rig was an important change because it gave most of the power of the square-rigged sail but allowed each mast to be worked by only one crew member. The lack of a bowsprit also simplified the setting of sails for a very limited crew. Chapelle mention that post War of 1812, Chebaccos were known for lacing their sails to the boom (Chapelle 1960:180).

Hull Shape

A peculiarity of the Chebacco boat is its having two similar but distinctly different hull types. The bow of both variations had a broad steep bow. Kellogg describes that the bow or stempost rose above the deck about 2 f.t (60 cm) (Kellogg 1874:264), other authors provide measurements that only vary by 6 in. at most. It is also argued that some of the shipbuilders on both variations had the stem head fall inward above deck giving rise to another regional name for the Chebacco Boat, 'Ram's Head Boat' (Chapelle 1960:180).

While the two variants were known as the "Pink" and the "Dogbody", it is clear that both types were still considered "Chebacco Boats". The Pink style of Chebacco boat is distinguished by its stern coming to a fine point (Figure 1). Initially both variations were built to the same size, however as the size of the Chebacco Boats increased it was the Pink that became the larger vessel (Chapelle 1960:164). The Pink was also the variant that would later evolve into the "Pinkie" with the addition of the bowsprit and rigged like a schooner (Davis 2012:17). Conversely, the Dogbody variant had wide square stern (Figure 2). It has been noted that the Dogbody had a larger deck space and hold when compared to a Pink of the same length and breadth (Story 1995:17). It is interesting to note that while this combination of features was documented before the Chebacco boats, the naming of the two vessels may actually indicate some connection to an older heritage. In all of the sources that have dealt with the Chebacco boat the belief is that the "pink" name comes from the French for pinched. However, the name etymology of Dogbody has eluded previous researchers. When contacted about research on other facets of the Chebacco Boat, Dr. Thjis Maarleveld of the University of Southern Denmark made a connection to two Dutch vessels. The first is the Pink Zeeboot (Maarleveld and Ginkel 1990:86) (Figure 3). The second was more striking as it was named Dogboot (Beylen 1970:162) (Figure 3). The names of both, especially the later, and the similarity in design may very well indicate that the Chebacco boat was greatly influenced by the Dutch colonists and shipbuilding tradition. Further investigation into this connection is needed.

Decks and Rooms

Early Chebacco Boats may have been an open design, like the shallops and sloops they developed from, by the time that they rose to prominence they were known for being decked. "From open boats, they came, ultimately, to be partially decked to afford protection for cargo"(Story 1995:7). As part of the deck there were two to three standing-room hatchways where the crew could stand. The standing-rooms brought a crewman's hand close to the water and allowed for minimum bending over and gaining full strength when hauling in either lines or nets. "The floor of the standing-room was about three feet below the deck the room; extended to within two feet of the waist or gunwale and was about three and a half foot wide" (Gott et al. 1888:256). As the Chebacco boats started be used for more offshore

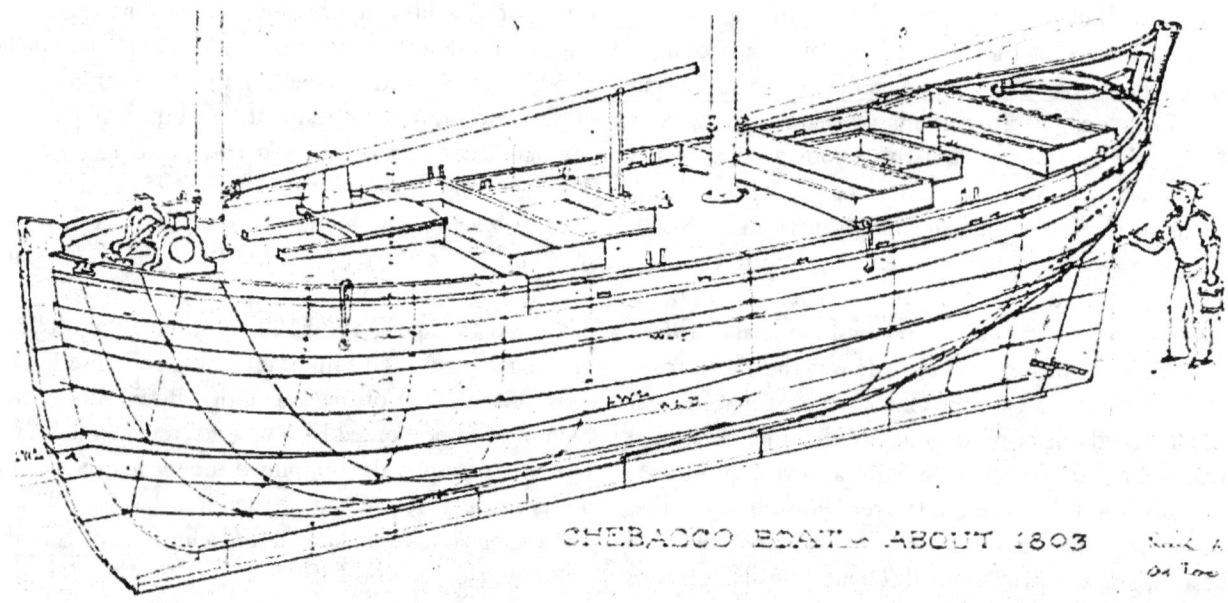

Figure 1: A drawing of a Pink style Chebacco Boat, with a man for scale. Drawn by George C. Wales. (Chapelle 1960)

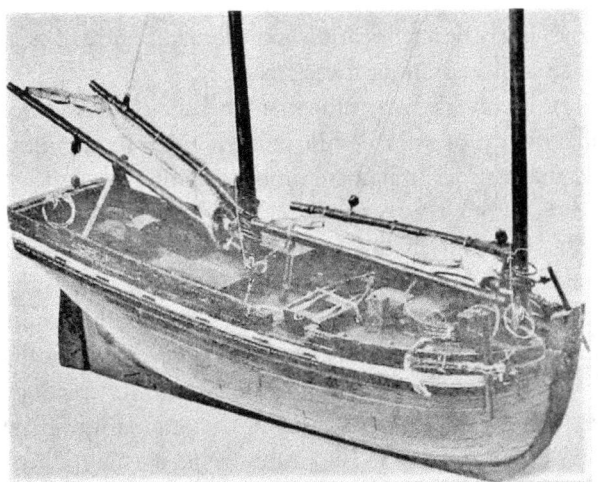

Figure 2: Model of a Dogbody style Chebacco Boat. USNM 57587. (Chapelle 1960)

fishing, they "had a little cabin, or cuddy, beneath the forward deck which served for sleeping quarters and cooking"(McFarland 1911:314).

A detailed layout of the Chebacco boat *Sea Bird*, as described by Kellogg follows: "Just after the sternpost was a small decked area that, formed the salt room and the salt was put in at a small door"(Kellogg 1874:264). After the salt room was a "standing-room: a platform was laid directly over the ballast, and on this platform a man stood to fish" (Kellogg 1874:264). Kellogg then describes a "kid" which is a room "that ran from one side of the boat to the other, with hatches to cover it"(Kellogg 1874:264). Since Kellogg also refers to them as "fish rooms" the "kid" is likely a fish hatch. It is important to clarify that the "kid" is not a standing-room. Forward of the "kid was the hold proper, which was decked over and had a small hatchway, with one hatch, aft of the main-mast and directly under the main boom; at the bottom of the hold was ballast floored over" (Kellogg, 1874: 265). After the main-mast, there is another "kid" followed by a standing room. "The deck at the sides ran entirely round the boat, being at the standing-rooms only about eighteen inches wide in order not to interfere with the man fishing. There was a break in the deck at the cuddy of nine inches to give height and there were combings round the standing-room hatchways" (Kellogg 1874:265). From the standing room, there were doors that opened into the caddy or even a cabin in later versions. Kellogg tells us that the Sea Bird had a fireplace and four berths with lockers. It is a little hard to believe that there was enough space in the cuddy for that many places to sleep. In early times, the fireplace was made of brick and took up most of the cuddy. The Chebacco boat evolved to where "the chimney would have been bricked or plastered inside" (Chapelle 1960:180). The final evolution was the incorporation of a metal chimney. The Sea Bird must have possessed a chimney, for sleeping in the caddy with no exhaust could lead to carbon monoxide poisoning. "These quarters were usually cramped. They were also dingy from the smoke of the fireplace" (Mitman 1923:132–133). There is evidence in the models and from Dana Story's *The Shipbuilders of Essex*, that the Dogbody style only had two standing-rooms, while the Pink had three (Story 1995:17). This may have been due to the added deck space in the stern of the Dogbody, however there is no historical reference to this being a steadfast rule.

The deep open hatchways and low rails, despite expectations, did not cause Chebacco Boats to take on water. The *Sea Bird* demonstrates how the boat could be made nearly water tight in times of particularly bad weather. Kellogg says, "both the standing-rooms had

Figure 3: The two pictures on the left are of Dutch Zeeboots of the Pink fashion. (Maarleveld and Ginkel 1990). The drawing on the right is of a Dutch Dogboot. (Beylen 1970)

hatches and when they were all put on she was decked over, as it were, and very little water could get in, either from spray or from a sea coming aboard and then running off" (Kellogg 1874:265). He does point out that the cabin doors could not be opened if the hatches were on. The hatches were made watertight not by caulking, but instead "they covered the whole hatch with tarred canvas and fastened it to the deck with pump tacks, thus rendering the whole water-tight and secured the main hatch in the same way" (Kellogg 1874:300). In addition, Chebacco boats often had churn pumps, like the *Sea Bird* (Kellogg 1874:301).

Steering

"Chebacco's were usually steered by a stern mounted tiller that passed under the mainsheet horse" (Chapelle 1960:1980). This is similar to the smaller types of local vessels. "The aft most standing room functioned as cockpit for the fisherman that was steering" (United States National Museum, Smithsonian Institution 1884:128). The tiller arm ran back from the "cockpit and attached to the tiller that ran along the sternpost into the water". The tiller position in conjunction with the gaff sails meant that the one crew member could handle both. "The Sea Bird was so accurately sparred that with a steady breeze she would run an hour upon a stretch without requiring the helm to be shifted"(Kellogg 1874:316). Kellogg mentions that the Sea Bird had a "notch-board" which is a section of wood that was attached to the deck with predetermined places to slot the tiller arm. Then "the helmsman might put the tiller in the notch-board, go forward, light his pipe, get biscuit or water or coffee; if tired of standing, he might sit down and smoke; and there was no work to do, as on board a square-rigged vessel" (Kellogg 1874:316).

Early History of the Chebacco Boat

The name Chebacco boat is derived from the name of the town in which they were most prolifically built. Most experts place the Chebacco Parish, now the town of Essex, Massachusetts, as the place where these vessels were first designed and built. The name of the Parish derives from the Native American name for the lake on which much of the Parish sat. From here on in Chebacco Parish and the Town of Essex will simply be referred to as Essex. There is a common story that the first Chebacco boat was built in the attic of one of the local houses (Chapelle 1960:164). At this point, most understand this to likely be a fabrication considering the size of even the smaller versions of the vessel.

It is highly likely that the first Chebacco boat was not built by a professional ship builder. Essex at this time had the facilities to prepare timber to build vessels, such as a mill, but they were not known for shipbuilding. Most of the vessels that were constructed were done so by fisherman and farmers in their off season. They used local white oak, of which there was a plentiful supply in the surrounding forests. While it is never specifically stated, the large supply of old growth white oak may very well have played a factor in the popularity of the Chebacco boat, due to the timber being such a resilient shipbuilding material. The British Naval Board claimed that American Oak was inferior to English Oak (Albion 1926:24), this was likely due to improper sorting, bundling inferior Red Oak with the White Oak, and poor transportation methods of the colonists that were selling the timber. *Quercus alba*, or American White Oak, ranks higher on the Janka hardness scale than *Quercus robur*, English Oak, 1,350 lbf to 1,120 lbf. Unlike American Red Oak, American White Oak possess the same type of rot resistance, due to its tyloses, as does the English Oak.

It is clear that Chebacco boats had been constructed and used well before they reached the height of their popularity. Many authors indicate that Chebacco Boats were built in the first part of the 18th century. However, the first clearly documented use was not until 1755. In that year when Abram Somes and Edan Sutton used "Jebacco boats" to first visit Mount Desert Island in what is now Maine (Thornton 1938:239). Again in 1762, Somes uses a Chebacco boat to move his family from Somersville, MA to the island (Sweetser 1888:94–95). This was a journey of a minimum of 160 nautical miles. Despite this being the first documented use of these types of vessels it is very clear that they were designed and built for fishing. The recessed walkways mentioned in the deck section only really make sense if one is fishing off the side. Indeed, we see that,

> *By 1770, just before the war, about 80 vessels would head out to the banks to fish, while about seventy boats fished for cod, hake and pollock on the ledges near our own coast. The latter boats were mostly Chebacco boats. There was a large fleet of them owned here and in Rockport at the commencement of the present century, but they have all disappeared (Procter Brothers 1882:6).*

The Chebacco Boat's Rise to Prominence

The Chebacco boat may have been in use much earlier but it wasn't until after the American Revolutionary War, hereafter referred to as the Revolution, that it rose in popularity with the height around 1808 and its decline starting after the American War of 1812. In the title of this paper the assertion is made that the Chebacco boat is what built the Essex shipbuilding industry. As previously mentioned, when Chebacco Boats were first being made the place was simply called Chebacco Parish. The parish belonged to the Town of Ipswich. It wasn't until 1819 that it was incorporated to the Town of Essex, which falls at the end of the height of the Chebacco Boats popularity, and the rise in Essex Shipbuilding. At first glance (Figure 4), Essex appears to be perfectly situated for shipbuilding, as it is located up a small river from a protected estuary that connects to the Atlantic Ocean. The reason that building ships in Essex is complicated is the depth of the river. Parts of the Essex River, which runs from Essex to Essex Bay, has many points where the bottom has to be dredged to keep the Mean Low Water depth at a mere 4 ft. and Mean High Water only 13 ft. (NOAA:date). Thus, making Essex a less than ideal for the building of Chebacco Boats with a draft of about 4-6 ft., let alone the great schooners for which they are most well-known.

So, what was is about the Chebacco boat that drew people to this place to buy their vessels? The answer is that the shipbuilders of Essex recognized a social-political environment and promoted a vessel that filled the niche that had been created.

Causes of the Chebacco Boats Rise

The Essex shipbuilding industry was created by the fortuitous situation of being at the right place at the right time with the right product. As previously stated, no single feature of the Chebacco boat was new to this region, nor was the Chebacco boat itself even a new design when it became popular enough to create an industry. It is easiest to see the appeal of the Chebacco boat when the sociopolitical issues are compared to the Chebacco's design answers. The Revolution hit New England particularly hard. The expense of building and maintaining a war against a large foreign power was a great burden, not to mention the cost of rebuilding a new nation. Unlike other areas of the new United States, New England relied heavily on both shipping and fishing for its economy, both of which rely on ships. Thus, is was of particular economic injury when the British fleet sank most vessels, especially non-combatants, as they

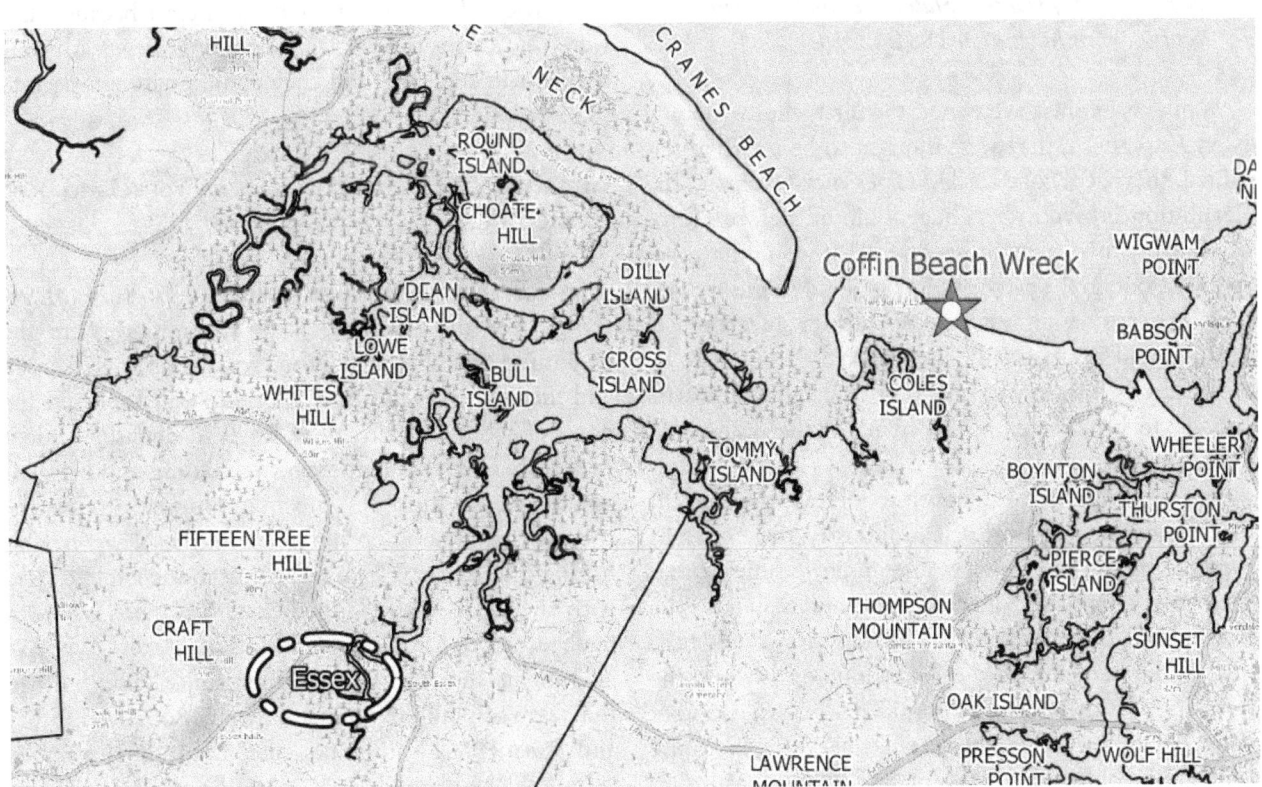

Figure 4: Map of the Essex area and Essex River out to the Atlantic. (Map by author, date.)

were leaving Boston harbor and the surrounding waters. This is not even taking into account all of the private vessels that were turned into privateers and lost during the war. Having lost their economic means or collateral for future loans, the fishing industry above all lacked the ability to rebuild the large deep sea going vessels that they had lost. While the new government recognized the importance of rebuilding the New England fishing industry when they enacted "a bounty of five cents on every quintal of dried fish or barrel of pickled fish exported" (Morison 1921:134), they didn't subsidize any way for the fishermen to get to the best fishing locations. The Chebacco boat answered this problem by being a mid-sized vessel with a decent hold that was known for being extremely seaworthy and most importantly, inexpensive to build and crew.

The next major social issue was the formation of the new United States navy. As the country built ways to protect itself and its interests, it drew heavily on crew resources of the fishing industry.

> *The larger class of fishing vessels, those which had been employed on the Grand Bank and other distant fishing grounds, were compelled to lie idle, while, in most cases, the hardy men who had composed their crews were employed in the Army or Navy (United States National Museum, Smithsonian Institution 1884:653).*

While fishermen were not the first choice of any Navy Captain, as they were thought to be poorly disciplined, they were none the less experienced seamen. The Revolution proved to be a huge drain of the work force of available fishermen, and a drain that would never be returned due to the extensive loss of life. For this reason, the Chebacco design was a perfect answer since its mast position and easily sealed decks allowed the vessel to be crewed by as little as two members while also being safe enough to be handled out to many of the deep-water fishing grounds.

Lastly, while there was a push to increase the amount of fishing done by New England industry, the embargos imposed by the US as well as foreign powers meant that there was a difficulty in producing and selling. "The Revolution, of course, put an embargo on Bank fishing, as well as an end to the exportation of fish, and the business soon dwindled to insignificant figures" (Procter Brothers 1882:6). This had the effect of destroying some generations old connections for trade, as well as losing a training ground for the next generation of fishermen

and traders. The inexpensiveness of building, maintaining, and crewing the Chebacco Boats allowed individuals with a much smaller amount of economic might to start fishing fleets. The sound nature with which they traversed the seas also allowed the humblest of entrepreneur to both collect from, and deliver to, a much wider ranger than previously possible.

Chebacco Boats for All

At the height of its popularity the Chebacco boat was used in a great many ways, despite being designed as a fishing vessel. Even before it reached the apogee of its popularity we see people like Abraham Somes, using it for personal use as he explored and transported his family. There are also accounts of merchants using a small fleet of Chebacco Boats to transport goods, since they could spread their risk with minimal or no additional overhead. There are examples of Chebacco boat being used to trade as far away as the Caribbean, some 1,200 to 1,700 nautical miles away (Kellogg 1874:296). Finally, it is clear that they were used as naval vessels in times of war. The vessel *Fame* is possibly the most well known of these even if it was refitted with a bowsprit before being used as a privateer. Even the "Royal Navy carried one on the Navy List at Halifax, Nova Scotia, as a fisheries patrol vessel or guard as late as 1815. (Chapelle 1960:180)" They were a good naval craft because they were fast, could carry a large boarding crew with only two to run the ship, and they could easily escape into shallow waters if needed.

Conclusion: Chebacco Boats as Vessels to be Remembered

It is clear that Chebacco Boats came to mean many things. For the shipbuilders of Essex, they were the beginning of a grand tradition. For the fishing industry and merchants, they stood as keys to a fortune and the hope of rebuilding. To New England and the United States, they were a platform for rebuilding and prosperity, as well as a form of protection. However, to history, they are less than a footnote. Would the New England fishing industry have ever recover from the issues caused with the birth of the United States? Maybe. Would it have recovered as quickly as it did? Not likely. We have documents showing 1,364 named ships being built in the Essex shipbuilding industry from 1860-1980 (Story and Story 1984). This is not to count all of the named vessels that were built before 1860 nor all of the unnamed vessels. Would this have been possible without the Chebacco Boat? Highly unlikely. If Helen of Troy is famous, thousands of years later, for launching a thousand ships, doesn't the Chebacco boat deserve a place in history for launching many if not thousands more?

References

ALBION, ROBERT GREENHALGH
1926   *Forests and Sea Power*. Harvard University Press, Cambridge, MA.

BAKER, WILLIAM A.
1966   *Sloops & Shallops*. 1st Ed. edition. Barre Publishing Company, Barre, MA.

BEYLEN, JULES VAN
1970   *Maritieme Encyclopedie. Vol. 2*. De Boer, Bussum, NL.

CHAPELLE, HOWARD IRVING
1960   *The National Watercraft Collection*. Smithsonian Institution, Washington, D.C..

CRAWFORD, LELAND S., AND VICTOR MASTONE
2017   A Preliminary Autopsy on Coffins Beach, Gloucester, Massachusetts. In ACUA *Underwater Archeology Proceedings 2017*, John Albertson and Frederick Hanselmann, editors, pp. 45–50. Advisory Council on Underwater Archaeology/PAST Foundation, Columbus, OH.

DAVIS, CHARLES G.
2012   *American Sailing Ships: Their Plans and History*. First edition. Dover Publications, New York, NY.

GOTT, LEMUEL, EBENEZER POOL, AND JOHN W. MARSHALL
1888   *History of the Town of Rockport*. Rockport, Mass.: Rockport Review Office, Rockport, MA.

HALL, HENRY
1884   *Report on the Ship-Building Industry of the United States*. G.P.O., Washington D.C.,

KELLOGG, ELIJAH
1874   *The Fisher Boys of Pleasant Cove*. Lee and Shepard, Boston, MA.

MAARLEVELD, THIJS J, AND EVERT J. VAN GINKEL
1990   *Archeologie onder water: het verleden van een varend volk*. Meulenhoff, Amsterdam, NL.

MCFARLAND, RAYMOND
1911   *A History of the New England Fisheries: With Maps*. University of Pennsylvania, Philadelphia, PA.

MORISON, SAMUEL ELIOT
1921   *The Maritime History of Massachusetts, 1783-1860*. Houghton Mifflin Company, Boston, MA.

NOAA
2000   *Essex River, MA Datums. Governmental. National Oceanographic and Atmospheric Administration Tides & Currents*. <https://tidesandcurrents.noaa.gov/datums.html?units=0&epoch=1&id=8441771&name=ESSEX%2C+ESSEX+RIVER&state=MA>. Accessed March 21, 2018.

PROCTER BROTHERS
1882   *The Fishermen's Own Book: Comprising the List of Men and Vessels Lost from the Port of Gloucester, Mass., from 1874 to April 1, 1882, and a Table of Losses from 1830, Together with Valuable Statistics of the Fisheries, Also Notable Fares, Narrow Escapes, Startling Adventures, Fishermen's off-Hand Sketches, Ballads, Descriptions of Fishing Trips and Other Interesting Facts and Incidents Connected with This Branch of Maritime Industry*. Procter Bros., Gloucester, Massachusetts.

STORY, DANA A.
1995   *The Shipbuilders of Essex*. 1st edition. Ten Pound Island, Gloucester, MA.

STORY, LEWIS H., AND DANA A. STORY
1992   *A List of Vessels, Boats and Other Craft Built in the Town of Essex 1860-1980*. Essex Shipbuilding Museum, Essex, MA.

SWEETSER, MOSES FOSTER
1888   *Chisholm's Mount-Desert Guide-Book*. Chisholm Brothers, City, State

THORNTON, NELLIE C.
1938   *Traditions and Records Southwest Harbor and Somesville*. Acadia Publishing Company, Bar Harbor, ME.

MITMAN, CARL WEAVER (EDITOR)
1923   *Catalogue of the Watercraft Collection in the United States National Museum*. Smithsonian Institution. United States National Museum, Bulletin 127. Smithsonian Institution, Washington, D.C.

UNITED STATES NATIONAL MUSEUM, SMITHSONIAN INSTITUTION
1884   *Bulletin of the United States National Museum*. No. 27. Smithsonian Institution, Washington, D.C.

• • • • • • • • • • • • • • •

Leland S. Crawford
1374 Main St Apt B2,
Osterville, MA 02655

Mapping the Sacramento River in 1837

Glenn J. Farris

The Sacramento River as it flows through the Carquinez Straits into San Francisco Bay is an imposing body of water. Ocean going ships could sail a considerable distance upstream. Whereas early Spanish explorers provided rough, schematic maps of the river as far back as 1824, the first professional mapping was accomplished by surveyors aboard HMS Sulphur, *commanded by Captain Edward Belcher in 1837. However, the map resulting from this survey was never published. Recent research at the United Kingdom Hydrographic Office Archives combined with journals kept by expedition naturalists has greatly enhanced our understanding of this historic survey.*

Introduction

The 1820s and 1830s were relatively peaceful for the British navy compared to the proceeding years which pitted England against France and the United States in the Napoleonic wars and the War of 1812 respectively. The Admiralty's Hydrographic Office was able to engage the use of several ships for global expeditions to explore and map many ports. In November of 1826, HMS *Blossom* under the command of Captain Frederick William Beechey arrived in California (Beechey 1832). While anchored in San Francisco harbor, a mapping survey of the bay of the same name was undertaken by Captain Beechey, Lieutenant Belcher, Thomas Elson (master), and James Wolfe (mate). Whereas the bay was well surveyed on that occasion, its main tributary, the Sacramento River, was not mapped despite representing a substantial body of water. A key member of the survey was Edward Belcher, the naval lieutenant who was assigned to the expedition as a "Supernumerary and Assistant Surveyor" (Farris et al. 2004:46). The map of San Francisco Bay was duly published in Beechey's account of the overall expedition.

Return to California in 1837 and 1839

A decade later, Captain Beechey was again asked to lead an expedition, this time aboard HMS *Sulphur* with the schooner HMS *Starling* as its consort, the latter under the command of Lieutenant Commander Henry Kellett. However, while on the coast of South America at Valparaiso, Chile, Beechey fell ill and Commander Belcher was sent to take over the expedition, meeting the two ships in Panama. HMS *Sulphur* was a Royal Navy bombship converted to duty for survey work. In fact, it was the last ship of this class built for the Royal Navy. Two other well-known converted bombships were HMS *Erebus* and HMS *Terror* which were under the command of Sir John Franklin on his ill-fated journey into the arctic in 1845. These ships were chosen because of their heavily reinforced hulls meant to accommodate heavy mortars used in naval warfare (Ware 1994:70-71). The only known drawings of HMS *Sulphur* include a cut-away image of the orlop deck of the ship. This seemed appropriate given the importance of the ships' surgeons on the expedition because the orlop deck was traditionally the location of the ship's infirmary, especially in battle.

Returning to California in October of 1837, Belcher once again entered San Francisco Bay and set up his Observatory near the port of Yerba Buena and later a second observatory in the Sacramento Delta that was located at 38°15'56.0"N 121°33'48.0"W. Such local observatories became the key datum point on which the survey of the area was based. By taking careful calculations of longitude and latitude, these observatories could be tied in to the Royal Observatory at Greenwich in England from which the British established longitudinal calculations. After spending a little time visiting the local missions and the commander of the presidio of San Francisco, Belcher sailed in HMS *Starling* with a picked crew of surveyors to the Carquinez Straits and into the large bay (Suisun Bay) beyond. On a map of the Carquinez Straits, a pencil note stated: "This rock is the rock on Capt. Beechey's 'Plan A'" (Figure 1), which indicated that Belcher was linking up the 1826 Beechey survey to his 1837 visit to the Sacramento River. As the river narrowed and became increasingly shallow, the survey crew transferred to ship's boats that could be rowed, if necessary. To date, this "Plan A" has not been found. This is unfortunate since the map of San Francisco Bay published by Beechey does not extend as far as the Carquinez Straits.

Unpublished Maps of the Sacramento River

In 1843, Belcher published his narrative of the journey of the *Sulphur* that included the trip up the Sacramento River, but the volume did not include a map of the river. As far as this author is aware, Belcher's personal daily journal recording events in real time no longer exists. Fortunately, the journals of two ship's surgeons/naturalists who were on the voyage are to be found in the Natural History Museum Archive in

Figure 1: Belcher map of Carquinez Straits showing note identifying a rock as relating to a previous map of San Francisco and San Pablo Bay. (Courtesy, UK Hydrographic Office-Archives). Photo by Glenn Farris.

London, due to their focus on botany, biology, and geology. One of these journals that was written by the surgeon aboard HMS *Sulphur*, Richard Brinsley Hinds has been published as an annotated transcription (Farris 2015:51-60). Following the voyage, Hinds had published two edited studies relative to the finds made on the trip (Hinds 1844a, 1844b).

Unpublished maps of the Sacramento River made during the 1837 survey were discovered at the UK Hydrographic Office (UKHO) Archives in Taunton, Somerset, England. Of special interest were 47 original section maps made during the expedition. These were rendered in pen and ink, often on scraps of varying shapes. These section maps show the progression downstream during which the river was continually criss-crossed for depth soundings registered in fathoms. The map sections also provided names associated with key points in the survey. These names are mostly those of animals such as "Cuyote" [sic], Lark, Tortoise, Snake, and Goose, however, there is one that stands out because it is simply named "Skull." Nearby is another designation that specifies "Skull Md."

It is interesting to note that on these rough maps someone later wrote in the names of locations such as "Sacramento City," "Rio Vista," and "Suisun" (Figure 2). These were all place names that did not come into being until later, mainly in the late 1840s and 1850s. I suspect that at the time of the Gold Rush, these maps, like many others of early California, were seized on by cartographers seeking to meet the demand of the Argonauts flooding into California.

Curious as to how accurate these maps are in comparison to current-day aerial images, I approached Dr. Jay Lund and his colleague, Alison Whipple of the Center for Watershed Sciences, at UC Davis. Alison was able to substantiate several of the locations such as the conjunction of the Sacramento

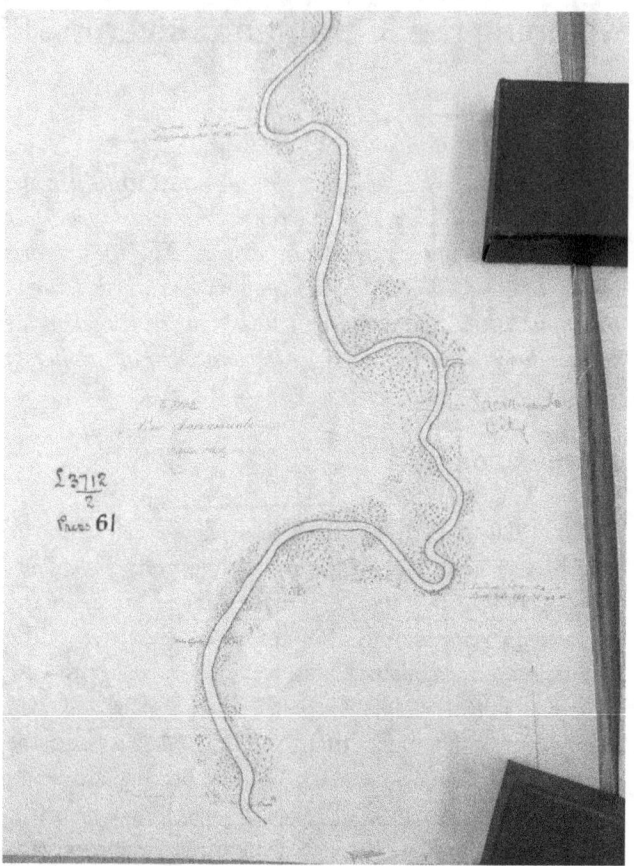

Figure 2: Belcher survey map section on which has penciled in notation for Sacramento City which must have been made around the time of Gold Rush (1849). (Courtesy, UK Hydrographic Office—Archives). Photo by Glenn Farris.

and Feather Rivers and also of the Sacramento and American Rivers. I subsequently enlisted the help of Jeff Rosenthal and Jill Bradeen of Far Western Anthropological Research Group. Jill prepared overlays of the Belcher maps which seem to show them as being most accurate in the lower Sacramento River area, but diverging more in the northern part of the survey.

Several other finished maps of locations in the Californias from HMS Sulphur expedition were also present at the UKHO Archives including maps of Bodega Bay, San Juan (Capistrano) Bay, and Magdalena Bay (in Baja California). In addition to the maps, there are copybooks of letters sent by the chief hydrographer of the time, Sir Francis Beaufort (famous for the Beaufort Scale), and portions of the log of *Starling* that add to the journal accounts.

Accounts of the Belcher Expedition

The survey of the Sacramento River commenced "on October 24, 1837 when the Starling, accompanied by the pinnace, two cutters and two gigs left the anchorage of Yerba Buena" (Hinds, quoted in Farris 2015:51). The total survey

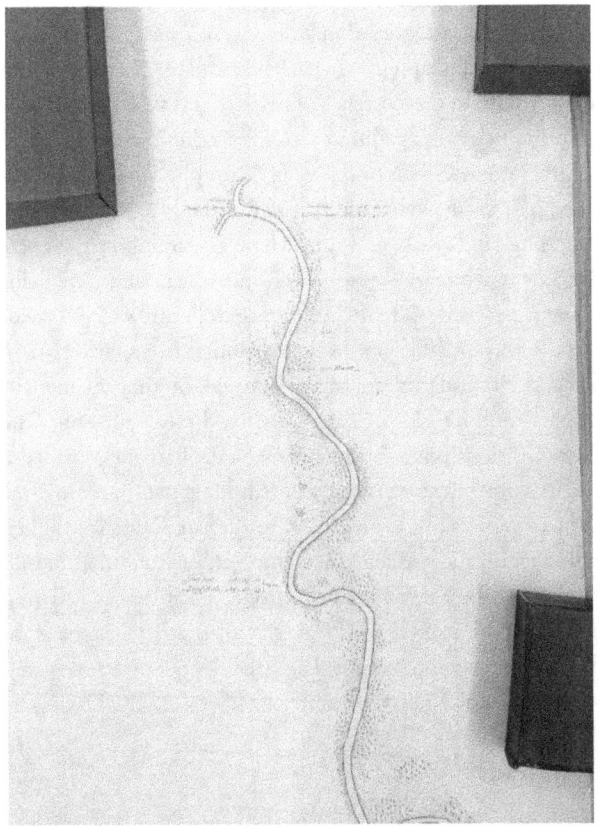

Figure 3: Belcher map section showing location of "Point Victoria" and associated native villages. (Courtesy, UK Hydrographic Office-Archives). Photo by Glenn Farris.

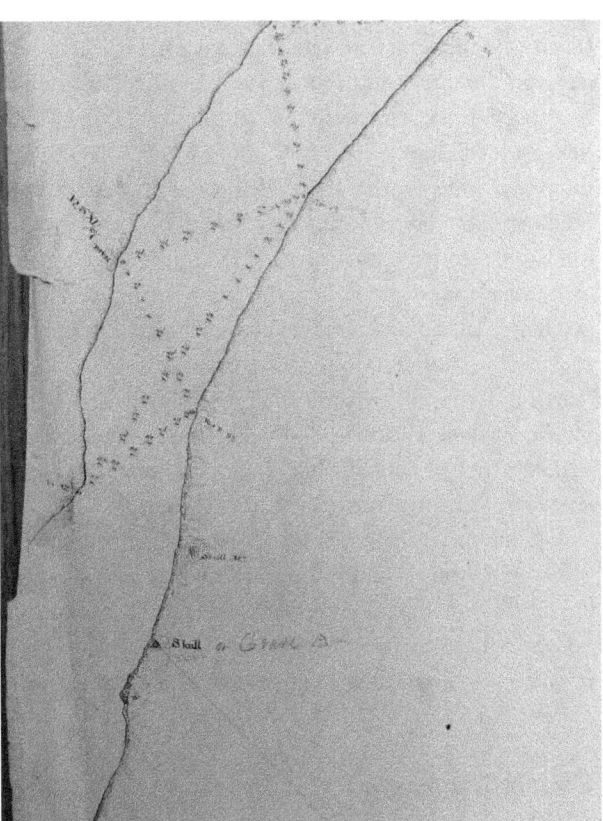

Figure 4: Belcher survey map section showing a location titled "Skull" with a nearby raised spot noted as "Skull Md." (Courtesy, UK Hydrographic Office Archives). Photo by Glenn Farris.

took 31 days. On October 26, after two days in which Starling ascended the bay and passed the Carquinez Strait to enter the lower Sacramento River travelling some 36 miles, it was necessary to transfer the gear to the other five vessels to continue further. Belcher reported that after twenty more miles the Sacramento became a narrow stream as they skirted to the north of an "archipelago" of islands (the Sacramento-San Joaquin Delta). The trip upstream was rapid, punctuated by stops at 9 a.m., Noon and 3 p.m. for "astronomical observations" (Pierce and Winslow 1969:38) using theodolites. The expedition went as far as the confluence of the Sacramento River and the Feather River which they titled Point Victoria on October 30 (Figure 3). A native village was located here. Belcher commented that he "landed at 'the fork,' which was named Point Victoria and found the natives had but shortly fled, leaving a large stock of acorns, and all their provisions, fires, etc., behind" (Pierce and Winslow 1969:39). Across the river from the spot known as Point Victoria Hinds noted: "the surface was covered with a vast quantity of human bones. I was informed there were skulls in hundreds. They were exposed on the surface, without any apparent attempt at burial" (Farris 2015:56).

This was said to be the village of the Wallocks, a name associated with the tribal village of Gualacomne, although Bennyhoff (1977:60-61) and Milliken believed it to be further south, below the city of Sacramento. Bennyhoff (1977:65) suggested that the site might be the archaeological site CA-SAC-56 which was notable for the number of contact period artifacts, especially trade beads. One reason for the discrepancy in locations might have been the displacement of Central Valley native peoples about the time of the Gold Rush and later.

Occasionally Native Americans would be met along the way. "Apart from the people living along the river, there was at least one party of *neofitos* from Mission San José on paseo with a pass signed by Mariano Vallejo" (Belcher quoted in Pierce and Winslow 1969). Only two villages were noted. One was called "Wee-shan-a-to" by Hinds. Belcher titled it "Onee-shan-a-tee" and Milliken suggests that it was the village of Guizinato, (Farris 2015:74; Milliken 2008). Hinds commented that "several human bones were lying about. On one side a skull was dug up with ashes and hair. No natives made their appearance" (Farris 2015:56). This village was very likely at the spot noted on the surveyors' map as "Skull Md"

(Figure 4). The comments on the presence of skeletal material lying on the surface associates these sites with the disastrous malaria epidemic that swept through this part of the Central Valley in 1832-33 (Cook 1955:308) which killed a huge number of Indians here. This epidemic was introduced by the Hudson's Bay Company hunting party led by John Work that came to California in the winter of 1832-33.

Another interesting observation was that in a village they saw that "a large bundle of arrows lay on the ground, they [the Indians] informed us for the Mission of San Francisco Solano" (Farris 2015:58). There they would probably have been used by the Indian auxiliaries who fought with Mariano Vallejo against a tribe of non-Christian Indians called the Sotoyomi, let by a chief named Tucumin Succara (Farris 1989).

In addition to the survey work Hinds noted a number of plants and animals along the way. Unfortunately, it being late in the year the season was not conducive to botanizing. However, Hinds did comment on the impressive Valley Oak (*Quercus lobata*) which was initially named for him as *Quercus Hindsii Benth*.

Concluding Comments

The Belcher survey of the Sacramento River in October and November of 1837 was the earliest known scientific survey in this body of water using a theodolite for accuracy. Whereas, the written description of the survey by Captain Belcher was published in 1843, the actual map of the survey was not. Copybook records of two letters from the Admiralty's chief hydrographer, Sir Francis Beaufort dated October 11 and 20, 1838 indicate a reason for the failure to publish the map as being based on a discrepancy of two minutes of latitude between the map of San Francisco Bay prepared by Captain Frederick Beechey in 1826 and the survey results submitted by Captain Belcher for his 1837 survey. Given that a "minute" of latitude would be about 70 miles, this was a substantial figure, indeed. It is uncertain, however, whether the error should be attributed to the Beechey mapping in 1826 or that of Belcher in 1837.

Modern researchers on the historic hydrography of the Sacramento River have found this earliest formal survey of the river to provide valuable baseline data for the era preceding the Gold Rush of 1849 which greatly affected the river.

Acknowledgments

I would like to thank the following individuals and organizations for their assistance in this study: First of all, it was thanks to Thomas Blackburn that I first obtained the unpublished journal of Richard Brinsley Hinds. The California Mission Studies Association, this journal was published the Hinds journal. Captain Michael Barritt, RN (Ret.), brought to my attention the existence of maps of the Sacramento River from the Belcher expedition residing in the United Kingdom Hydrographic Office Archives in Taunton, Somerset. I was aided by Adrian Webb and his staff of the UK HO Archives, including Ian Killick, and Ann-Marie Fitzsimmons. I am particularly indebted to several other individuals who were helpful to me in my study including LtCdr Andrew C.F. David, RN (Ret.), and the late Maurice Hodgson, an historian in Canada who shared an earlier journal of then-Lieutenant Belcher from his visit in 1826-27 aboard HMS Blossom. The Special Collections Library at UC Santa Barbara provided a quality copy of the 1826 map of San Francisco Bay. Finally, I want to express my appreciation to the late Randall Milliken and to nautical historian Alan Kemp. Jeffrey Rosenthal and Jill Bradeen of the Far Western Anthropological Research Group in Davis, CA created a GIS overlay of the Belcher maps on the modern day topography. I also thank Jay Lund and Alison Whipple of the Center for Watershed Service, UC Davis.

References

BEAUFORT, FRANCIS
[1838] Copies of letters sent by Sir Francis Beaufort to many correspondents. On file at the UKHO Archive, Taunton, Somerset, England.

BEECHEY, FREDERICK WILLIAM
1832 *Narrative Of A Voyage To The Pacific and Beering's Strait, to Co-Operate with the Polar Expeditions Performed in His Majesty's Ship Blossom*, Under the Command of Captain F. W. Beechey, R. N. in the Years 1825, 26, 27, 28.

BELCHER, EDWARD
1843 *Narrative of a Voyage Round the World, performed in Her Majesty's Ship Sulphur during the years 1836 to 1842, including details of the Naval Operations in China from Dec. 1840, to Nov. 1841*. Two volumes. Henry Colburn, publisher, London, UK.

BENNYHOFF, JAMES
1977 Ethnogeography of the Plains Miwok. In *Center for Archaeological Research at Davis, Publication* No. 5., Davis, CA.

COOK, SHERBURNE F.
1955 "The Epidemic of 1830-1833 in California and Oregon". In *University of California Publications in American Archaeology and Ethnology* 43(3):303-326.

FARRIS, GLENN J.
1989 *Two Peace Treaties between Mariano Vallejo and Satiyomi Chief Succara*. Paper presented at the Fifth Annual California Indian Conference, Arcata, CA.

2015 A British Naturalist in California in 1837 and 1839: The Journal of Richard Brinsley Hinds. In *Boletín, the Journal of the California Mission Studies Association* 31(1):46-78.

FARRIS, GLENN J., MAURICE HODGSON & ANDREW C.F. DAVID
2004 "The California Journal of Lieutenant Edward Belcher aboard H.M.S. Blossom in 1826 and 1827." In *Boletín, the Journal of the California Mission Studies Association* 21(1):45-67.

HINDS, RICHARD BRINSLEY (ED.)
1844a *The Zoology of the Voyage of H.M.S. Sulphur: Volume I, Mammalia, Fish and Birds*. Smith, Elder and Company, London, UK.

1844b *The Botany of the Voyage of H.M.S. Sulphur*. Smith, Elder and Company, London, UK.

MILLIKEN, RANDALL
2008 *Native Americans at Mission San José*. Edited by Thomas C. Blackburn. Malki-Ballena Press Publication, Banning, CA.

PIERCE, RICHARD A. AND JOHN H. WINSLOW (EDITORS)
1969 *H.M.S. Sulphur at California, 1837 and 1839. Being the Accounts of Midshipman Francis Guillemard Simpkinson and Captain Edward Belcher.* In *The Book Club of California*, San Francisco, CA.

WARE, CHRIS
1994 *The Bomb Vessel: Shore Bombardment Ships of the Age of Sail*. Naval Institute Press, Annapolis, MD.

· · · · · · · · · · · · · · · ·

Glenn J. Farris
2425 Elendil Lane,
Davis, CA 95616

Computer Vision Photogrammetry as a Tool for Three-Dimensional Archaeological Recording of a Sixteenth Century Spanish Shipwreck in the Dominican Republic

Kirsten M. Hawley, Matthew M. Maus, Charles D. Beeker, Samuel I. Haskell

This paper presents results of a diver-based photogrammetric survey and preliminary interpretation of a 16th-century shipwreck near Punta Cana, Dominican Republic. The photogrammetric methodology highlights the potential of this technology to rapidly assess submerged cultural resources despite constraints limiting survey time. Objects retained by the government of the Dominican Republic suggest the ship was inbound for a New World colonial port in the mid-16th century. While the site was severely disturbed by commercial salvage, the Punta Cana shipwreck remains a significant resource with in situ wrought iron artillery and anchors and possibly intact deposits that warrant protection and further investigation.

Introduction

This study applies diver-based photogrammetric techniques to record an unidentified 16th-century shipwreck located along the eastern coast of the island of Hispaniola, near Punta Cana, Dominican Republic. Based on current data, the shipwreck is tentatively classified as a merchant vessel inbound from Europe in the mid-sixteenth century. Despite extensive impacts from commercial extraction, the site retains significant potential for future archaeological research. The photogrammetric method applied in this study provides an efficient, accurate, and comprehensive means to document the visible portions of submerged archaeological sites. Potential applications of the resultant three-dimensional modeling includes site monitoring and public outreach in addition to direct research contributions.

The Punta Cana Sixteenth Century Shipwreck

The 16th-century Punta Cana Shipwreck is located offshore of Punta Cana, on the eastern coast of the Dominican Republic. This area holds high potential for early colonial shipwrecks, both because of Hispaniola's early significance in the colonization and exploration of the New World by Europeans and because of the rocky shoreline, shallow coral reefs, and prevailing northeasterly winds on this side of the island. The site is located on the interface of a coral reef ledge and a deeper sand bottom, with a maximum depth of about 7.1 meters (Beeker and Maus 2014:2). The shipwreck is in an exposed area and is often subject to rough weather from the east. On the day that the recording reported here took place there were 3-4-foot seas resulting in significant surge on the shallow site. Although the site has been severely disturbed by commercial salvage, overall the shipwreck retains sufficient significance as a 16th-century transatlantic merchant vessel to merit further research and protection. While some site distribution of artifacts may be attributed to natural depositional and post-depositional processes (Muckelroy 1978: 158), the large disarticulated scatter of ballast stones, exposed excavation trenches, and the lack of living benthic biota on the shipwreck (such as coral) are clearly a result of recent salvage operations.

The site was the subject of a two-year salvage contract between the government of the Dominican Republic and the Punta Cana Foundation, who subcontracted to the treasure hunting firm, Anchor Research and Salvage (ARS). Commercial salvage operations on the shipwreck concluded in December 2013 with the expiration of the contract. The site is known locally and among treasure hunters as "The Pewter Wreck" because of the large amount of pewter artifacts that were recovered and sold from the site. This paper refrains from using that name in order to shift the focus away from the monetary value assigned to these artifacts and focus instead on the historical significance of the site and its research potential.

Following the end of the salvage contract, the government of the Dominican Republic asked archaeologists and scientific divers from the Indiana University (IU) Center for Underwater Science to assess the site and report on its condition. The IU team submitted a report to the government which described the site as severely disturbed but retaining significant archaeological integrity. The report noted visible site features as well as an area in deeper water with the potential for undisturbed archaeological deposits. The report's recommendations included further scientific investigation, comprehensive documentation, and protecting the site as a Marine Protected Area or underwater park (Beeker and Maus 2014).

Diagnostic artifacts salvaged from the site and currently owned by the government of the Dominican Republic indicate that the Punta Cana Shipwreck likely dates to the mid-16th century, and appears to be an inbound Spanish merchant vessel. Artifacts extracted from the site include nested weights, horseshoes, customs seals, five swivel guns (versos), ceramics, and many other artifact types. Most notably, hundreds of pewter dishes were removed from the shipwreck, some of which have identifiable maker's marks. Several of these dishes exhibit the same maker's mark identified on some pewter wares from the 1545 *Mary Rose,* a mark which exhibits the letters "TC" around a rose ornamented with a crown, a motif common among Flemish pewtersmiths of the time. Although the marks from the two ships are not closely dated, they are determined to have been struck with the same punch, as the die does not appear to be damaged, worn, refreshed or re-engraved (Roberts 2013:29). It is speculated that the Punta Cana 16th-century shipwreck met its end during the same general time period as the *Mary Rose*.

Although the site has been heavily impacted by treasure hunting resulting in the irretrievable loss of archaeological data and cultural heritage, the Punta Cana shipwreck retains significant visible features and possible unimpacted deposits that merit protection and study. IU visual surveys have identified numerous anchors, bombards, and breechblocks. At least four of the anchors were located on-site, while an additional 16th-century anchor was located directly seaward of the site. In addition, iron fasteners and drift pins, thousands of large riverine basalt ballast stones, and other small artifacts—such as horseshoes, stacked dishes, and small copper fragments—are densely distributed around the bottom surface of the site. If more systematic investigation is conducted in the future, it will doubtless yield far more detailed and comprehensive data.

Photogrammetry

In the past decade, advances in software, camera, and computer processing technologies have made photogrammetry more powerful, reliable, and accessible. Photogrammetry has evolved from a technique that requires specialist equipment, manual inputs, and a high degree of technical knowledge to a quick, low-cost recording tool (McCarthy and Benjamin 2014:97). This is largely a result of a shift toward Computer Vision Photogrammetry, which comes out of efforts to design systems for the interpretation of the visual world as part of artificial intelligence systems research and therefore tasks the computer with assembling a scene as a whole in order to determine not only the measurements achieved in traditional photogrammetric methods, but the shape, appearance, orientation, and location of objects in the scene as well (Van Damme 2015:13). This approach uses structure-from-motion techniques, which utilize feature-based algorithms for the alignment of overlapping digital images. During the image alignment processing stage, the computer detects features in each image and compares them to all other features in every other image within the dataset to find matching points. If matching features are detected in at least three images, the computer is able to approximate the location and orientation of the camera in each photo (Van Damme 2015:13). This process is automatically repeated for the entire imagery dataset in order to align as many images as possible, which also generates a sparse cloud of matched points that approximates the three-dimensional shape of the target scene and/or objects. Following image alignment, the software uses known locations of the images to implement more system-intensive algorithms to generate a more detailed and accurate dense point cloud. In a typical workflow, points in the dense cloud are interpolated to create a 3D mesh, resulting in a 3D rendering of the surface of the scene (Van Damme 2015:15). Lastly, the photographs themselves are projected onto the mesh to create a final texture so that the model mimics the original scene as closely as possible (Van Damme 2015:16). In this way, 360° models of objects can be made, as well as 180° models of a planar scene, also known as orthophotogrammetry. Although it is helpful to understand the processes that the computer uses to generate the model (especially for more advanced projects), it is not entirely necessary as the programs used are largely automated and require little prompting. These programs, along with widely available, inexpensive, and high-quality digital cameras, have allowed photogrammetry to become an accurate, easy to use, fast, and cost-effective recording tool.

Methodology

Image Acquisition

The methodology used in this project for photographing the site and processing the site model were adapted from methods described in Maus et al. (2015, 2017) and Maus and Haskell (2016). Prior to image acquisition, divers deployed two scale bars and eight 12-bit coded targets, which may be automatically detected by Agisoft Photoscan (the photogrammetry software package utilized for this survey), that were themselves mounted on 8.5" x 11" polyethylene panels weighted for negative buoyancy. Both scale bars and coded targets were used to establish scale, estimate error, and orient the site to cardinal directions. Additionally, coded targets were used to assist with image alignment, as well as stitching together contiguous subject areas, or "chunks", which were photographed and processed separately.

The Punta Cana site was split into two chunks, both of which were simultaneously photographed by the authors using open-circuit SCUBA. In order to achieve this, the coded targets were placed along the border between the chunks to be included in both batches of photographs. Additionally, the distance between each set of coded targets was recorded to be used in establishing scale. The two scale bars deployed on the site were pointed north for later orientation of the site plan. Divers were each equipped with a GoPro Hero 4 camera, chosen because it comes equipped with an underwater housing, a wide-angle lens, integrated time lapse, and is relatively inexpensive. The GoPro also records metadata which is exported along with the photos, which assists Agisoft Photoscan in determining image distortion during the processing stage. For best results, the camera position should change with each image while maintaining a minimum of 60% side and 80% forward overlap with the surrounding photos (Agisoft 2016). This was achieved by divers slowly swimming closely-space parallel transects over their respective chunks while taking top-down photographs using the GoPro's two-second time lapse function. Where significant features or topographic change were present, oblique photos were also taken to record vertical complexity. In this manner, 1,000 photographs were taken of the site by two divers during a single dive. Typically, anything mobile which is not captured in at least three photographs (i.e. fish, fins, fingers) is usually excluded in the model as the algorithm can only identify matching features that are static relative to the scene. Nevertheless, mobile subjects should be avoided or masked during the processing stage as they may cause error, noise, or prevent image alignment altogether.

Processing Site Model

Before importing the photos into Agisoft Photoscan, they were batch processed in Adobe Lightroom to perform color corrections. After pre-processing, the photos were imported into Photoscan. Wherever possible, the two chunks of photographs were processed individually to reduce computer processing demands, which scale exponentially with linear increases in the imagery dataset. After importing the dataset, the coded targets were automatically detected using Photoscan's 'Detect Markers' tool. Standard workflow commands were used to generate a sparse point cloud, dense point cloud, mesh, and finally textured model of each chunk. After processing both chunk models, they were then scaled, aligned, and merged using the known locations of the coded targets to produce a single contiguous model of the site. Once merged, the model texture was reprocessed using the "color correction" option after the chunks were aligned in order to remedy color differences between the chunks. Finally, the merged chunk was also re-processed as a tiled model to further improve texture and model detail. Once the model was complete, the distances between markers and the dimensions of the scale bars and coded targets were manually entered to provide as many references as possible to establish scale. By comparing these measurements, estimated error for this model was 1.02 cm. Finally, an orthomosaic was generated from the model and was used to create a two-dimensional site plan of the Punta Cana 16th-century Shipwreck (Figure 1).

Conclusions

The site model and orthomosaic were instrumental in performing comprehensive analysis of the site's layout. While the dense (but disarticulated) ballast pile is the dominant characteristic of the site, other large features are also prominent. There is one large anchor on the shallow reef shelf which is embedded upright in the coral substrate, suggesting that the stock was assembled and it was on deck or deployed at the time of sinking. Below the large anchor, at least three stacked anchors are visible among the ballast, suggesting they may have been stowed as cargo. Furthermore, due to the location of the shipwreck at the base of a shallow reef ledge, it is most likely that the ship ran aground and sank. Unfortunately, as evidenced by the dispersed ballast stones and visible excavation trenches, the biggest conclusion that can be drawn about the site from this model is the extensive disturbance that has occurred due to salvage operations that have significantly altered the original layout of the site. It is clear that these impacts restrict the conclusions that may be drawn from the model, even preventing conclusive identification of the original shipwreck location and orientation as a result of ballast stone dispersal.

Nevertheless, the model itself may be considered a success. The strong surge complicated diver transects and reduced visibility, while time and resource constraints limited the divers to only a single on-site dive during the 2016 field season. Despite this, the detailed and accurate site model generated by this study demonstrates the effectiveness and efficiency of the image acquisition methodology in specific, and computer vision photogrammetry in general. Additionally, this model yielded a more accurate site map with far less expenditure of resources and time than would have been possible with conventional methods. As such, this technology permits much more efficient documentation of submerged archaeological sites, which may free up resources to be used for further research or investigation of other sites. The ease and speed with which these site plans can be generated also means that site records can be easily updated, allowing for detailed and accurate photogrammetric monitoring of sites over time (Maus et al. 2015, 2017).

Finally, photogrammetric models generated in this way are powerful outreach tools that may be used to improve public access to Underwater Cultural Heritage and its interpretation through digital venues by hosting three-dimensional models of shipwreck sites and artifacts on websites such as Sketchfab.com (Maus et al. 2017). Three-dimensional models are the future of archaeological documentation and analysis, and it is just as important to use these models to educate the public on the importance of the world's submerged cultural heritage and its preservation for the future.

Figure 1: Photogrammetric site plan of the Punta Cana Sixteenth Century Shipwreck created using an orthomosaic generated in Agisoft Photoscan (Indiana University, 2016, date.)

Despite degradation from commercial salvage, this shipwreck remains a remarkable historical resource. Given the paucity of shipwrecks from the early colonial period that are known to exist in the Americas, rather than permitting destructive commercial salvage to exclusively benefit private collectors, we assert that the Punta Cana 16th-century shipwreck should be recorded, studied, and protected for the public benefit to promote greater understanding of this pivotal period in world history. Due to its research potential and historical significance, the Indiana University Center for Underwater Science hopes to return to this shipwreck beginning in summer of 2018 in collaboration with other researchers and stakeholders to implement systematic archaeological investigations, assist authorities with regular site monitoring, and promote public outreach and site protection as a Marine Protected Area or underwater park. Following investigation, the Punta Cana 16th-century Shipwreck may become a prime candidate for establishment as a Living Museum in the Sea, a designation which would call for protection of both its cultural and associated biological resources as well as encouragement sustainable tourism (Figure 2). IU, in collaboration with the Dominican Government, USAID, and local stakeholders, has established a successful network of Living Museums in the Sea in the Bayahibe Region on the south coast of the Dominican Republic and hopes to do the same in the Punta Cana region, possibly with the 16th-century Shipwreck as the capstone of a regional network (Beeker et al. 2013).

References

Agisoft LLC
2016   *Agisoft Photoscan User Manual*: Professional Edition, Version 1.2. St. Petersburg, Russia.

Beeker, Charles D., Claudia C. Johnson, Loren Clark, Emily Palmer, Matthew J. Maus
2013   *Living Museums of the Sea in the Dominican Republic: Bridging the Gap Between Cultural and Biological Resources.* Poster presented at the 46th Annual Conference on Historical and Underwater Archaeology. Leicester, UK.

Beeker, Charles D. and Matthew Maus
2014   *Naufragio del Siglo 16 de Punta Cana: Informe Resumido de Evaluación Arqueologica No-Invasiva.* Report submitted to Fundación Museo Subacuático de la Republica Dominicana. Santo Domingo, Dominican Republic.

Maus, Matthew and Samuel I. Haskell
2016   *Muskegon (aka Peerless) Shipwreck (12LE 0381): Intrusive Modern Pipe Assessment.* Report to Lake Michigan Coastal Program, Indiana Department of Natural Resources and Division of Historic Preservation and Archaeology, Indiana Department of Natural Resources, Indianapolis, Indiana from Indiana University Center for Underwater Science, Bloomington, IN.

Maus, Matthew, Denise Jaffke, Samuel I. Haskell
2017   *Photogrammetry as a Tool for Monitoring Submerged Cultural Resources: The Emerald Bay State Park Workshop.* Society for California Archaeology Proceedings, Volume 31, pp.58-79.

Maus, Matthew and Samuel I. Haskell
2016   Muskegon *(aka* Peerless*) Shipwreck (12LE 0381): Intrusive Modern Pipe Assessment.* Report to Lake Michigan Coastal Program, Indiana Department of Natural Resources and Division of Historic Preservation and Archaeology, Indiana Department of Natural Resources, Indianapolis, Indiana from Indiana University Center for Underwater Science, Bloomington, IN.

Muckelroy, Keith
1978   *Maritime Archaeology.* Cambridge University Press, Cambridge, UK.

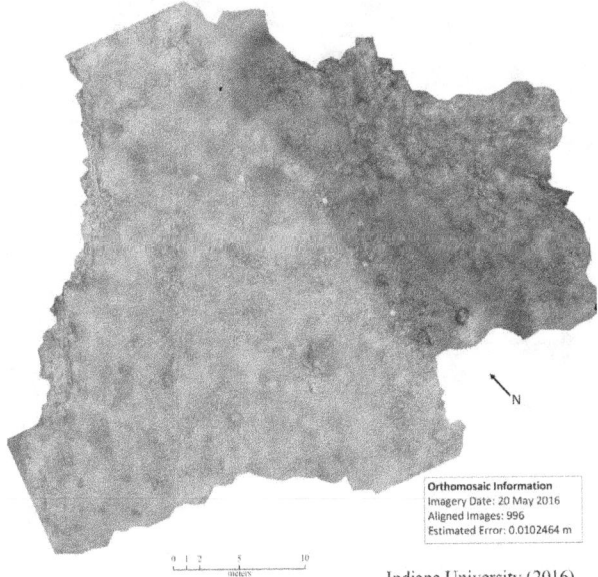

Figure 2: Indiana University Scientific Diver examines a large anchor with an endangered Acropora palmata (Elkhorn Coral) growing on the fluke (Indiana University, 2016, date.).

McCarthy, John, and Jonathan Benjamin
2014   Multi-image Photogrammetry for Underwater Archaeological Site Recording: An Accessible, Diver-Based Approach. In *Journal of Maritime Archaeology* 9(2014):95-114.

Roberts, Martin
2013   The Punta Cana Wreck: Discursions on a Discovery. In *Journal of the Pewter Society* 38:14-31.

Van Damme, Thomas
2015   *Computer Vision Photogrammetry for Underwater Archaeological Site Recording: A Critical Assessment.* University of Southern Denmark, Odense, Denmark.

....

Samuel I. Haskell
1025 E 7th St, Room 058
Bloomington, Indiana 47405

Matthew J. Maus
1025 E 7th St, Room 058
Bloomington, Indiana 47405

Charles D. Beeker
1025 E 7th St, Room 058
Bloomington, Indiana 47405

Kirsten M. Hawley
1025 E 7th St, Room 058
Bloomington, Indiana 47405

The Backyard Shipwreck: The 2017 Lake Champlain Maritime Museum Field School Exploration of a Shipwreck in Basin Harbor

Allyson Ropp

The Lake Champlain Maritime Museum coordinated investigations in 2016 and 2017 on an unknown wreck located in Basin Harbor. The ultimate aim for these projects was to develop a network of community informants and divers to participate in projects, to conduct original research on an unidentified site, and to grow a sense of stewardship among the community to protect and preserve the shipwrecks of Lake Champlain.

Introduction

The 2016 Introduction to Underwater Archaeology course and the 2017 Field School held by the Lake Champlain Maritime Museum explored an unknown wreck lying in Basin Harbor. One of the primary reasons for the start of the museum, the wreck has been known about since the inception of the Basin Harbor Club around the harbor. Yet the identity, time period, and type of vessel still remain unknown. These two projects aimed to not only answer research questions concerning the site. Basing the research design on the previous research conducted on site in 1982, the field school uncovered new information about the history and construction of the wreck. It also sought to pilot programs that would engage the community in the project through various means, including as divers and avocational underwater archaeologists and as informants on the history of the site and area.

The Lake Champlain Maritime Museum (LCMM) began as an exploratory group of divers and further expanded using community archaeology. The ideals of community archaeology have been built into the fibers of the institution. Without relying on community divers, support, and information, the LCMM crew would never have been able to conduct the work they were able to nor open their doors as a museum organization. With the 2016 and 2017 projects conducted at the Basin Harbor shipwreck site, LCMM returned to its roots. The focus of these projects required both community divers and community support and information to complete their goals as well as bring back the original ideals promoted by the museum's mission statement.

Community Archaeology

Community archaeology, as the name suggests, takes into consideration the wants and knowledge of the community and involves them in the research, whether that be historical research, archaeological research, or both. Community archaeology correlates with the rise of public interpretation of archaeology and the need to create stewards among the public, during the 1960s and 1970s when legislators began to lobby for the protection of cultural heritage sites (Jameson 2014:3). As the need arose to communicate archaeological processes and findings with the public, different models developed for how and why such a practice was necessary. The first is the deficit model which argues that as the public learns about and begins to understand archaeology they will be more likely to support the field (Merriman 2004:5). The second model, the multiple perspective model suggests that engaging the public with archaeology encourages not only self-realization of an individual's past, but also the enrichment of each one's life and stimulation of creativity and reflection upon humanity's past and our interconnectedness (Merriman 2004:7). These two models, though starkly different in their basic premise, promote the same idea of engaging the community to protect and understand the past. Recently, these two models have had to adapt to the growing participatory nature of today's culture. As today's culture has become more engrossed in consuming and participating as contributors, archaeologists have had to adjust to this. Archaeologists have found ways to "empower and motivate lay persons to more active involvement in not only archaeological fieldwork but also interpretation/dissemination processes of archaeologist/lay person collaborative relationships and multivocality" (Jameson 2014:6). This development has allowed the public to become more involved in archaeological projects in their communities both as avocational archaeologists and historical resources, and created stewards for the field and protection of cultural resources.

Archaeologists around the world, both terrestrial and underwater, have used these different ideas in running various public archaeology projects and teaching and involving the community to complete fieldwork. The following two programs are leaders in the promotion of community archaeology underwater and on land adapting all the models previously discussed to create participatory communities and stewards of the cultural heritage in their areas. The Nautical Archaeology Society (NAS), a charity formed in the 1970s, aims to protect and further interest in underwater cultural heritage in the United Kingdom. Starting in 1986, the Society began teaching courses in maritime archaeology. These courses provide not only an introduction to the field but also offered a chance to build these archaeological skills to create a group of enthusiastic avocational archaeologists to participate in projects. Since 1986, the Society has expanded internationally with advocates teaching courses around the world to teach and inspire the next generations of cultural resource stewards (The Nautical Archaeology Society 2013). The Crow Canyon Archaeological Center near Cortez, Colorado has successfully been integrating the public into their archaeological programs for years. Their success has been created by using trained archaeologists in their programs, creating experiential programs, and conducting high-quality research as well as creating a positive image of themselves in the community by bringing in local community members to participate in understanding and preserving their history. As their programs continue to use professional and avocational archaeologists to conduct high-quality research, Crow Canyon has embodied the ideas of public archaeology to their fullest to continue to attract participants and empower the local community (Heath 1997:65-72).

Creation of the Projects

Following a three-year project in conjunction with Texas A & M University (Crisman and Kennedy 2014; Kennedy 2015; Kennedy 2016; Institute of Nautical Archaeology 2018), LCMM was left in a position of attempting to figure out where their archaeological program lay regarding similar programs around the country. The museum and the lake have different offerings than other similar programs. They do not have the ocean diving and warmer waters that the St. Augustine Lighthouse Archaeological Maritime Program can offer (Martin 2014; Martin 2015; St. Augustine Lighthouse and Maritime Museum 2018) nor do they have foreshore sites accessible for a non-diving community of the Seafaring Education and Maritime Archaeological Heritage Program (Ostuni 2015a, 2015b). LCMM and Lake Champlain do have, however, almost pristine shipwreck sites visible feet above the lake bottom sediment, and an engaged diving community seeking to understand the history hidden beneath the lake's waves.

In a move to engage this community, LCMM joined forces with Waterfront Diving Center in Burlington, Vermont to offer an Introduction to Underwater Archaeology course under the auspices of the National Association of Underwater Instructors (NAUI) in the fall of 2016. Additionally, the museum revamped a program they previously offered, a field school in nautical archaeology. By using the ideals of community archaeology, these programs utilized training of community divers and researchers to examine and understand shipwreck sites as well as developing stewards to these sites and a community of avocational archaeologists and researchers to help in future projects. Though theoretical models on community archaeology were not explicitly used in the creation of the projects, the ideas promoted by these models were implicitly included in the projects to promote not only interest in engagement on a stewardship front but also to incorporate the participatory nature of today's culture to create a group of community avocational archaeologists and advocates.

Site Background

For this project to work, it had to be based on a wreck in shallow water that required few logistical necessities to access that site. Knowing that many of the divers will have never conducted an archaeological project or done task-loaded diving, a shallow, easily accessible site would add a level of ease to the divers on the projects. Ideally, the site chosen would include an exposed ship structure in the bottom sediment. The site that fit all these requirements was an unidentified wreck in Basin Harbor, Vermont.

The wreck lies in less than ten feet of water in the southern half of Basin Harbor 150 feet off the southern beach. Basin Harbor lies in the middle of the Basin Harbor Club, and is only one-half mile from the Lake Champlain Maritime Museum. Right in the backyard of the museum, the site met all the necessary requirements. The maximum depth of ten feet provided enough depth to make the site challenging but safe to work for task-loaded divers. The shallow depth also allowed divers to easily surface when they needed to discuss something they did not understand without having to deal with the time constraints of deep water diving. The ease of access further made this site a suitable candidate for the purpose of these community-based projects. Shore access and the proximity to the museum made staging the daily diving operations relatively simple. Further, shore access cut out the need for a boat and diving platform cutting not only equipment costs, but also participant costs. Additionally, the harbor is surrounded by the Basin Harbor Club and Resort. The club and its current hosts, the Beach family, offered immense help in daily dive operations.

The history of the wreck in question lying in Basin Harbor was unknown prior to beginning these projects. Part of the outlined projects, beyond training community divers, was to further explore the site in the hopes of discovering its identity and purpose. The site first became known to archaeologists in 1981 through a conversation between Bob Beach, Jr. and Arthur Cohn, the Director of the Champlain Maritime Society in which they discussed the history of the area. Local lore suggested that the vessel at the bottom of the harbor was some type of "French sloop" as the area was initially settled by the French and the Lake was the site of later conflicts between the French and English.

The vessel remains, then, were studied by a team of divers in the spring of 1982 as part of a training course. Basic documentation of the visible wreck structure took place leading to the production of a site plan and a discussion of basic observations. The visible structure only consisted of the lower portion of the hull structure including floor timbers and futtocks extending to the turn of the bilge, two small upright timbers, and the entire two-part keelson. The length of the site measured 88' 7". The keelson averaged 10 ½" sided and 11" molded. On the north end of the site, a fragmentary timber was bolted to the keelson and identified as a component of the deadwood structure, which would suggest this end was the stern. Based on their observations, Cohn and his associates and students determined the site was likely a canal schooner as they had found throughout the lake.

2016 Project

The short-term project in September 2016 encompassed two days of classroom and two days of diving. As a course offered jointly by the Waterfront Diving Center in Burlington and LCMM, the Introduction to Underwater Archaeology brought the world of underwater archaeology to the Vermont community during Vermont Archaeology Month. Six community divers attended the four-day course. The two days of lecture focused on the basics of underwater archaeology developed around four topics—discovery, documentation, conservation, and publication. The four lectures were one hour in length and introduced the basic components of each step. The remainder of the lecture component provided a hands-on mapping experience prior to diving. LCMM has a unique resource for such mapping practice, a replica of the Revolutionary War gunboat *Philadelphia* (known as *Philadelphia II*). In using a vessel to practice mapping, students were exposed to the features of a ship they were likely to find underwater as well as have a chance to discuss the various methods of recording shipwrecks without being underwater to ensure complete understanding of the methods.

The final two days of the course were spent diving on the wreck in Basin Harbor (Figure 1). Three dives were conducted in teams of two. Each team was given a task to complete while they were on the bottom to help in creating a master site plan of the exposed wreckage. One team focused on laying the baseline and recording features along the keelson. A second team focused on documenting exposed structures on the west side of the keelson, while the third focused on documenting exposed structures on the east side of the keelson. Additionally, divers photographed the site and its features and examined some of the disarticulated timbers around the site.

Results

Over the course of the three dives, data were collected that allowed for the creation of a site plan and better understanding of the overall nature of the site itself. The site measured 89 ft. in length. A scarf joint was noted

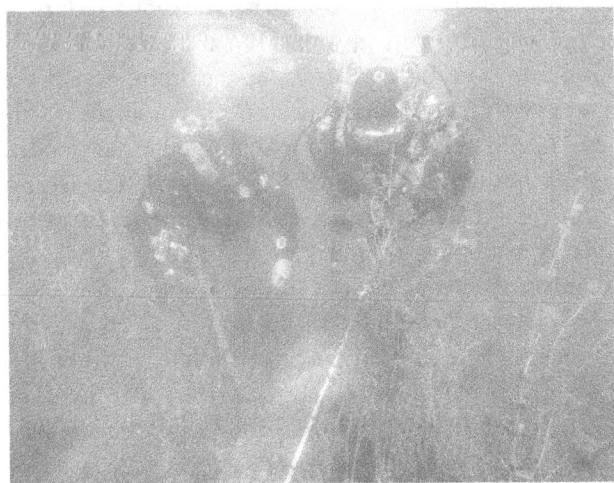

Figure 1: A team of divers documenting the keelson size on the Basin Harbor wreck in September 2016 (Pinkham 2016).

in the middle of the keelson stretching 20 ft. in length. Thirteen frames were recorded in the middle section of the keelson around the location of the scarf joint. These frames averaged 4 in. sided and 4 in. molded. Iron fasteners were observed and photographed throughout the keelson and the ends of many of the frames, but were not mapped. Additional artifacts were photographed around the site. These artifacts included large glass bottles, golf balls, disarticulated wooden pieces, and a large iron wheel. While some of these artifacts are totally unrelated to the shipwreck site, such as the golf balls coming from the surrounding resort, the remainder may be associated. This was difficult to tell after the end of this project as only two days were spent diving and the artifacts were all surface finds.

Community Roles

The community divers were the focus of the September 2016 course. The course aimed at educating recreational divers in the ways of underwater archaeology, so the instructors focused their efforts on training these divers. Data collection was secondary to the training aspect, but it was not forgotten throughout the program. In order to make a team of community divers for future utilization by LCMM, the recreational divers needed to understand the methods and meanings of conducting archaeological research as task-loaded divers. Although all the divers were well-versed in basic diving practices to manage buoyancy and air consumption, none had undergone extensive task-loaded diving.

2017 Project

The second project on the Basin Harbor wreck took place over May and June of 2017 as a field school for undergraduate and graduate students from around the country. This was the first field school conducted solely by LCMM since 2013 and built around a new model, which promoted research and learning simultaneously. Although the field school only had two participants and a part-time volunteer, seventy-three dives were conducted on the site totaling 67.5 hours on the site over a three-week period. The first two days of the project introduced the participants to the maritime history of Lake Champlain and the processes of maritime archaeology. Like the NAUI introductory course held the previous September, the students practiced mapping the replica gunboat, *Philadelphia II*, as well as a smaller vessel on the site. These hands-on lessons allowed the students to practice skills they would need underwater to record the project site. Additionally, these practices session were available opportunities to ask questions and become familiar with recording methodologies as well as ship construction techniques that would potentially be seen on the site.

The remainder of the three weeks was spent actively working on the site. The first few days involved placing a baseline on the site. The baseline was stapled into the keelson, the main feature on the site, with the zero end of the site on the north side and extending south to the other end. Detailed recordings were created of the top of the keelson documenting the fastener pattern and other keelson features observed in 2016, including the scarf joint. The frames on either side of the keelson were noted and fifteen frames around the center scarf joint were tagged for further investigation and documentation. Limited sediment removal with a dredge took place in the area on either side of the scarf joint between the frames as well as around the southern end of the wreck. These areas were chosen as it was hoped they would provide diagnostic features to aid in identifying the wreck's vessel type. Artifacts were recovered during this process. The artifacts were mapped, cataloged, photographed, and documented before being returned to the site. Throughout the project, students and staff engaged with the public as they visited the project beach. Further, the students and staff held a public lecture about the project at its close to present preliminary findings and to gain insight into what the community potentially knew about the sites and the observed artifacts.

Results

The three weeks of work on the site during the field school produced a large amount of data resulting in a report and site plan (Figure 2; Ropp 2017). The site itself consists of a keel, keelson, floors, futtocks, ceiling planking, and outer hull planking. The site extends a total of 90 ft. 11 in. The keelson lies at 350/170-degree orientation and lists significantly to the west. The keel and stern features are located at the southern end of the site indicating that the east is starboard and the west is port. Frames and hull planking are visible across much of the site stretching about 10 ft. east and west of the keelson.

Though the keel was only uncovered in certain areas, the keel extends 30 ft. past the keelson in the stern, suggesting that the known keel is 90 ft. 11 in. The southern end of the keel is fractured suggesting it has been broken off and likely extended further than its documented length. There are several other notable features on the southern end of the keel that also suggest it was the stern. Two mortises, one measuring 3 1/2 in. long by 2 1/2 in. wide and the other a fractured 13 in. long by 2 1/2 in. wide, both measuring approximately 2 1/4 in. deep were documented, as well as a stopwater 1 1/4 in. wide that is 13 in. from the southern end of the keelson, a 15 in long by 1 1/2 in. thick iron bolt that attached the keel to the keelson, and a fishplate on the starboard side of the keel that is no longer in situ. The keelson was visibly twisted from its original placement above the keel in the interpreted stern end. The keelson stretches 88 ft. 6 in. long. The average sided dimension is 9 1/8 in. and an average molded dimension of 11 3/16 in.. A vertical hook scarf joint is in the keelson between 40 ft. and 46 ft. 3 in. The hook itself is located at 43 ft. on the keelson. On either side of the keelson around the scarf joint, between 30 ft. and 55 ft. 3 in. are two sister keelsons. Each is 2 in. sided, although these pieces are extremely degraded. Four iron fasteners laterally attach the sister keelson to the scarf joint. Another 16 iron fasteners laterally attach the sisters to the keelson on either side of the scarf joint.

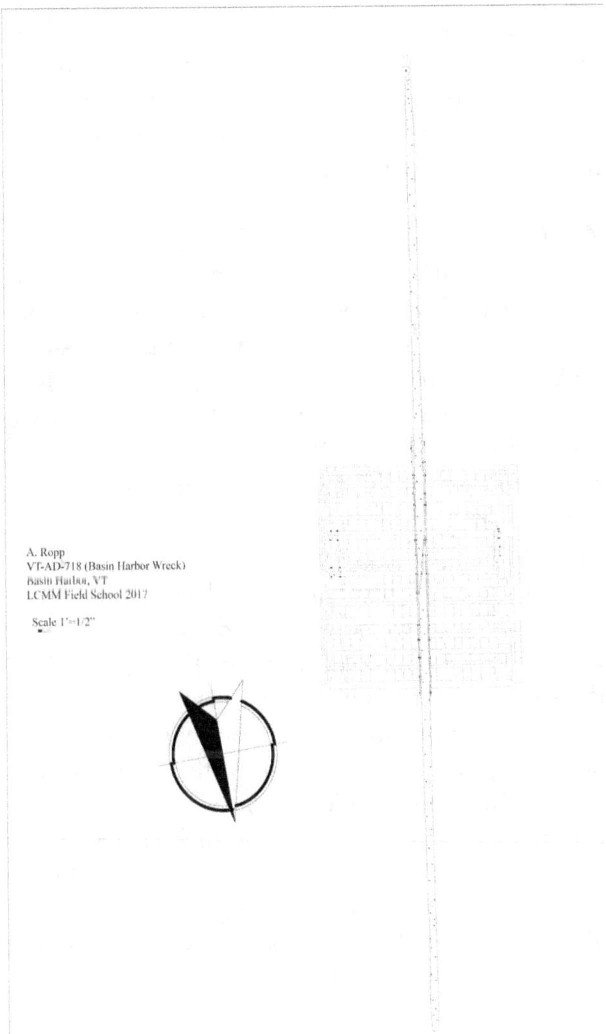

On visual inspection, 25 frames were identified on only the starboard side of the keelson, 15 frames were tagged and identified on both the port and starboard sides of the keelson. Further frame locations can be identified by looking at the fastener pattern on the top of the keelson. All frames noted were identified as floor/futtock pairs, except one directly beneath the hook in the scarf joint. This floor has no associated futtocks. The same location also reveals a shift in the position of the futtocks in relation to their floors. Forward of this floor, the futtocks are on the southern side of the floor, while aft of this floor the futtocks switch to the northern side of their associated floors. This pattern occurs on both the port and starboard sides. The floors are an average length of 15 ft. 10 in. with a sided dimension of 5 ft. 1 in.. Twenty-four outer hull planks were beneath the frames. The garboard strake average 8 1/2 in. sided and 2 in. molded. It is rabbeted into the keel. The other planks, eleven on each side, average 9 in. sided and 2 in. molded. The planks amidships are in situ. The planks are flush with the frames and the keel, except for the furthest planks on both the starboard and port side. One feature of note was a 1 in. square wooden peg stuck in the hull planking between Frames 2 and 3. It is currently unknown if the peg goes completely through the planking. The only articulated ceiling planking identified was on the port side 7 ft. 7 in. from the keel. The plank is 3 in. sided and 1 1/2 in. molded. This plank was very eroded along the edges and around iron fasteners protruding from the frames where the plank had been fastened.

Community Roles

The community played a much larger role during the 2017 field school than the 2016 NAUI course. Not only was the community involved in diving operations, but they provided information about the site, the locational history, and the artifacts discovered on side. As divers, three community members were heavily involved as students and volunteers. Further, the dive shop in Burlington actively supported the operation by providing air fills and gear maintenance throughout the project.

The other main role of the community, as informants, offered new insight into the project itself. The site was first identified through informant reporting in the 1980s by the host of the Basin Harbor Club, Bob Beach

Figure 2: Site plan of the Basin Harbor shipwreck site created from the 2016 and 2017 data (Ropp 2017).

Jr. Beach and the club itself continued to provide a flow of information about the property throughout the project. The information provided ranged from discussion of the active maritime history of the area to identifying types of materials used in the club and comparing them to uncovered artifacts from the shipwreck. One artifact originally believed to be associated with the site was a milk bottle (Figure 3). After discussion with the public, a member of the Beach family identified the bottle as a milk bottle used historically at the club. While this information did not completely dispel the possibility of it being from the shipwreck, it does provide additional information to consider. The most significant insight the community provided was a potential image of the wreck from a late nineteenth century postcard. Although the image is low resolution, timbers can be seen sticking out of the water in the harbor (Figure 4). In approximating the distance and location of the timbers to the current site, it is believed these timbers mark the bow and stern of the shipwreck. Community information provided more insight into the wreck than what was learned solely by excavating and recording the physical remains.

Overall Community Roles

The community was the focus of 2016 and 2017 Basin Harbor project. When designed, the projects were inspired to bring in community divers to the LCMM archaeological program and to create stewards of cultural resources among divers and non-divers alike to protect the lake's cultural resources. The role of the community in these two projects focused on participation in two key functions, as project divers and as informants.

As Divers

Both the 2016 NAUI introductory course and the 2017 field school brought in community members to the museum to teach them about the processes of underwater archaeology and allowed them to help in data collection on an active research project. Nine recreational divers from various fields participated in the program. While at LCMM, they participated in a total of fifteen days of diving, totaling 100 dives on the site with 94.48 hours of bottom time. Each project created data sets and information about the site. These data sets would not have been collected without the use of these divers in such a limited time. Through the dives, the participants not only gained first-hand experience in conducting underwater archaeology on an underexplored shipwreck, but they also got the chance to work on an active research project. In introducing them to the field and active research, the participants gained a deeper understanding of the process of conducting underwater archaeology and task-loaded diving safety procedures. They also learned the importance of researching cultural resources and their role in adding to the history of an area.

Figure 3: Milk bottle recovered from the center section of the shipwreck during excavation. The milk bottle is believed to be associated with the Basin Harbor Club and not the shipwreck (Corbiere 2017).

As Informants

Many more community members participated in the project without diving. These community members acted as informants on the location of the site and its history and provided information about the artifacts identified at the wreck site. By expanding the concept of participation beyond diving, LCMM was able to reach out to a larger community base that was interested in understanding and preserving submerged cultural heritage. Through these community informants, new insight was gained into the shipwreck itself. The Basin Harbor Club, and particularly Bob Beach Jr., has had an interest in the site since 1981, when the wreck was reported to Arthur Cohn. The Club has been located at Basin Harbor since before the turn of the twentieth century, and its members were able to provide a continuous history of the site. The informative nature of the community provided the project, and will continue to provide the project, with support and additional stories and clues to solving the mystery of this site and many others in Lake Champlain.

Conclusion

The two projects conducted by LCMM on the Basin Harbor Shipwreck allowed the museum to achieve its mission as a research and education institution for maritime history and archaeology on the lake, and also created an opportunity to further engage the community, both locally and nationally, in the research being conducted by the museum. Combined, the two projects had seventeen days of diving to excavate and collect data from the site. This information was processed and analyzed by the community to create a site plan and report prepared by the museum staff. Although the project uncovered information about the site, its typology, temporal period, and much of its history still remains unknown. More work is currently being planned for the site this coming summer in hopes of recording more information to identify its vessel type and temporal period, at the very least.

More importantly, the Basin Harbor projects provided the opportunity to test run community archaeology programs, create a base of avocational

Figure 4: A postcard for the Basin Harbor Club from 1898. The red oval overlaid on the postcard circles the area of the location of the project's shipwreck. Note the two timbers jutting out of the water near each end of the oval; these are believed to be the ends of the wrecked vessel sticking out of the water (Courtesy of Basin Harbor Club).

archaeological divers in the community, and encourage stewardship and participation by community divers and non-divers alike in archaeological research conducted by LCMM.

Acknowledgements

This paper, nor the projects themselves, would have been possible without the help of the following individuals and groups: Christopher Sabick, Lake Champlain Maritime Museum Archaeological Director; Jennifer Craig, LCMM Archaeologist; Bob Beach Jr. and the Basin Harbor Club hosts and staff; the staff of the Lake Champlain Maritime Museum; Waterfront Diving Center; Vermont Youth Development Corps; Vermont Division for Historic Preservation; and, of course, our students Carly Alpert, Abigail Baker, Scott Baroody, Kirk Hanley, Becky Hanley, Richard Hendren, Laura Meyer, Kreig Pinkham, Dave Potter, and Jennifer Russell for their endless enthusiasm and amazing perseverance in adverse conditions.

References

CRISMAN, KEVIN AND CAROLYN KENNEDY
2014 Shelburne Shipyard Steamboat Graveyard: A survey of four 19th-century Lake Champlain steamboats In Shelburne, Vermont. in *INA Quarterly* 41(2):16-21.

HEATH, MARGARET E.
1997 Successfully Integrating the Public into Research: Crow Canyon Archaeological Center. In *Presenting Archaeology to the Public*, John H. Jameson, Jr., editor, pp. 65-72. Altamira Press, Walnut Creek, CA.

INSTITUTE OF NAUTICAL ARCHAEOLOGY
2018 Shelburne Shipyard Steamboat Graveyard Research Project. Institute of Nautical Archaeology, Texas A & M University, College Station. < https://nauticalarch.org/projects/shelburne-shipyard-steamboat-graveyard-research-project/>. Accessed 30 January 2018.

JAMESON, JOHN H., JR.
2014 Toward Multivocality in Public Archaeology. In *Between the Devil and the Deep: Meeting Challenges in the Public Interpretation of Maritime Cultural Heritage*, Della A. Scott-Ireton, editor, pp. 3-10. Springer, New York, NY.

KENNEDY, CAROLYN
2015 Shelburne Shipyard Steamboat Graveyard: Updates on the identification of four 19th-century steamboats from the 2015 field season in Shelburne, Vermont. In *INA Quarterly* 42(2):12-17.

2016 Shelburne Shipyard Steamboat Graveyard: An update from INA's continuing study of four 18th-century steamboats in Lake Champlain, Vermont. In *INA Quarterly* 43(1/2):12-17.

MARTIN, JAKE
2014 Flagler College students use summer break to get ahead in field experience. In *The St. Augustine Record*, St. Augustine, Florida. < http://www.staugustine.com/news/school-news/2015-07-18/flagler-college-students-use-summer-break-get-ahead-field-experience>. Accessed 30 January 2018.

2015 Archaeology program offers students a hands-on learning experience. In *The St. Augustine Record*, St. Augustine, Florida. < http://www.staugustine.com/living/sunday-life/2014-06-28/archaeology-program-offers-students-hands-learning-experience>. Accessed 30 January 2018.

MERRIMAN, NICK
2004 Introduction: Diversity and dissonance in public archaeology. In *Public Archaeology*, Nick Merriman, editor, pp. 1-17. Routledge, London, UK.

THE NAUTICAL ARCHAEOLOGY SOCIETY
2013 *Discover more with the NAS Education Programme*. The Nautical Archaeology Society, Portsmouth, UK < https://www.nauticalarchaeologysociety.org/content/discover-more-nas-education-programme>. Accessed 30 January 2018.

OSTUNI, AMANDA
2015a Students to excavate Ipswich shipwreck. In *The Salem News*, Beverly, MA< http://www.salemnews.com/news/local_news/students-to-excavate-ipswich-shipwreck/article_be78e780-10cf-5e93-ab05-157955d73f47.html>. Accessed 30 January 2018.

2015b Student-based excavation on Ipswich shipwreck underway. In *The Salem News*, Beverly, MA. < http://www.salemnews.com/news/local_news/student-based-excavation-on-ipswich-shipwreck-underway/article_a108904c-98ce-587b-b068-f384547c038c.html>. Accessed 30 January 2018.

ROPP, ALLYSON
2017 *Archaeological Investigations of the Basin Harbor Wreck, VT-AD-718, in Basin Harbor, Vermont*. Manuscript, Lake Champlain Maritime Museum, Vergennes, VT.

St. Augustine Lighthouse and Maritime Museum
2018 Lighthouse Archaeological Maritime Program. St. Augustine Lighthouse & Maritime Museum, St. Augustine, FL. <http://www.staugustinelighthouse.org/LAMP/About_LAMP/LAMP_about>. Accessed 30 January 2018.

. . . .

Allyson Ropp
St. Augustine Lighthouse & Maritime Museum
81 Lighthouse Ave, St. Augustine, FL 32080

Analysis of Québec Shipwrecks: the Necessity of Integrating Local Divers to Improve the Management of Maritime Heritage

Carolane Veilleux

The province of Québec, Canada, has witnessed thousands of wrecks throughout its history. Despite this fact, the number of shipwrecks discovered remains very low. A great cultural potential is lying under the vast hydrographic system of Québec, which means that integrating the local divers to help discover and monitor sites is now becoming a necessity due to maritime archaeologists' limited time, resources and workers. There are already a few groups dedicated to wreck's conservation, but the management of maritime heritage could be tremendously improved with recent technologies and the suggestion of a GIS atlas available to the public.

Introduction

Water is at the center of the historical, cultural and natural landscape of the province of Québec, Canada. The Saint Lawrence River is the entrance to the country and was continually used since European settlers arrived, but also previously by the Natives and the Vikings. However, even though the Saint Lawrence is almost 1200 km long, it is just a part of the vast hydrographic system of the province. Indeed, the northern coastline is even bigger and that is not including the half a million lakes and 4500 rivers present on the territory (Gouvernement du Québec 2002:5).

Not all of these watercourses were easily navigable, especially the gulf of the Saint Lawrence River, greatly contributing to the thousands of wrecks throughout Québec's history. For instance, there are more than 400 recorded in the Anticosti area alone and somewhere between 500 and 1000 around the Magdalen Islands (Robitaille 2007). However, despite all those "paper wrecks", an expression referring to wrecks only known from archives, the number of shipwreck sites actually discovered remains very low. In 2009, only 49 sites had been located in Québec (Simard 2009); in 2018, the total has barely risen above 100.

In other words, a great cultural potential is lying underneath all this water, and even on land in some cases. However, with the current situation in Québec, it can't be fully preserved nor enhanced. This can be partly explained by the few trained maritime archaeologists that have to work within short field seasons, a capricious underwater environment, and limited financial resources. They must also contend with maritime heritage protection laws that could be improved.

It is argued here that maritime archaeologists need to integrate local divers to help them discover, protect and monitor shipwreck sites. Underwater heritage management would also be facilitated through better use of new technologies, especially GIS. In order to address improved management, it is first necessary to review the evolution of maritime archaeology, then summarize the different laws protecting shipwrecks in Québec and the current situation in the province. Finally, it will be possible to offer solutions that might improve underwater cultural heritage management.

The Evolution of Maritime Archaeology

Definitions

According to the UNESCO Encyclopedia of Life Support Systems, maritime archaeology is the study of the relation between humans and the sea, or any other watercourse. This definition includes shipwrecks sites found at sea or on land, and also piers, shipyards and lighthouses amongst others (Delgado and Staniforth 2002:4). In comparison, underwater archaeology is studying all submerged sites or artefacts, like inundated cities or lost aircrafts. Maritime archaeology is a specialization within archaeology, but also has its own subdivisions. The most well known is nautical archaeology that focuses on ships and shipbuilding, but also includes marine, lacustrine and riverine archaeology (Delgado and Staniforth 2002:4; McKinnon 2014:414-415)..

The Beginnings of the Discipline

The investigation of sunken ships is not a recent endeavor. Underwater recovery is known to have taken place throughout Antiquity and Medieval times. A perfect example is the salvage attempt of the *Mary Rose* by Henry V in 1549. The archives recount that the king hired professional Venetian salvage divers, but, fortunately for the archaeologists, they failed (Jones

2003). Still, these salvage operations can't be considered archaeological work since the goal was to recover and reuse whatever could be saved.

Following maritime archaeology's definition, the beginning of the discipline seems to be in the late nineteenth and early twentieth centuries, with the study of watercraft discovered in Egyptian and Anglo-Saxons tombs. In 1885, the first underwater archaeological survey took place at the Battle of Salamis site, in Greece. Fieldwork was performed by divers while archaeologists were directing the operations from the surface (McKinnon 2014:415).

Significant developments in the field followed invention of the Aqua-Lung by Emil Gagnan and Jacques-Yves Cousteau in 1940. This was the first self-contained underwater breathing apparatus, scuba in short, which gave the divers better autonomy and mobility. Until the widespread availability of SCUBA the situation had remained the same from 1885 to the 1950s: divers were doing the underwater work while archaeologists were giving instructions from the surface. In the 1960s, a shift occurred, as summarized by archaeologist John Goggin: "It is far easier to teach diving to an archaeologist than archaeology to a diver!" (Bass 2013). Archaeologists who started to dive themselves allowed maritime archaeology to soar to new heights. Even so, it was not before the early 1970s, after major field projects like the *Vasa*, that this discipline became an official academic subject in universities (Bass 2013; McKinnon 2014).

Meanwhile, in Canada and Québec

Canada started to preserve and study its underwater cultural heritage tardily, but quickly caught up with the world. In 1961, Parks Canada took actions to compile a complete underwater inventory of the siege of Louisbourg, Nova Scotia, and then to protect the shipwrecks encountered. In 1964, the Underwater Archaeology Service of Parks Canada was created and performed its first underwater excavation five years later. They partially excavated the French war vessel *Machault*, lost in 1760 in Québec's Chaleur Bay. From this project was born the first museum dedicated to maritime archaeology and a ship (Zacharchuk et Waddell 1984; Grenier 2003). Parks Canada's team learned a lot from the *Machault* and were able to improve their methods and techniques. From 1978 to 1984, the Underwater Archaeology Service completely excavated a sixteenth century Basque whaling ship in Red Bay, on the southern coast of Labrador. The team deconstructed the vessel and analyzed its smallest details. The impressive fieldwork and the synthesis that resulted gave birth to the solid reputation of Canada throughout the world in the field of maritime archaeology. The ship was even chosen as UNESCO's permanent logo (Grenier 2003, 2007).

Another important project led by Parks Canada was realized in 1993-1995 on the *Elizabeth and Mary*, a ship that was part of the Phips' fleet and was lost after a storm in 1690. Discovered by a local diver, Parks Canada decided to use voluntary divers to help during the excavations. After following the Nautical Archaeology Society (NAS) formation, and under the supervision of archaeologists, the local divers became precious collaborators (Grenier 2003). Indeed, the contribution of local divers is not to be underestimated in Canada. Most of the sites of the province of Québec were found by them. In the 1970s, some of them regrouped in organizations to help protect shipwrecks sites. These associations, like the *Groupe de Préservation des Vestiges Subaquatiques de la Manicouagan* (GPVSM) and Save Ontario Shipwrecks (SOS), are playing a critical and key role in raising awareness against looting amongst other divers (Grenier 2003; Delmas et Mercier Gingras 2016). In 2010, a public discussion took place in Rimouski during which maritime archaeologists met with government officials and local divers. Since then, voluntary divers have assisted on many projects. Such was the case with the *Projet Côte-Nord*, which aimed to record shipwreck sites only known by divers on the northern coast of the Saint Lawrence River (Delmas et Mercier Gingras 2016; Delmas 2017).

Maritime Heritage Legislation and Guidelines

Like in the United States, Canada has a patchwork of legislation where each province has its own regulations while still falling under the federal government. In Québec, there are two main laws protecting the maritime cultural heritage.

Firstly, the 2001 Canada Shipping Act is a federal law that makes it mandatory to report any wreck, or any artifacts taken from one. The finder needs to declare their discoveries to the Receiver of Wreck and follow the specified procedures. The Receiver of Wreck is required to keep a record of all the reported remains and to search for their rightful owner. The Canada Shipping Act gives power to the government to declare a shipwreck of historical importance and protect it accordingly. If it is not declared historically significant, the Receiver of Wreck decides the disposition of the find; he can either give it back to its owner, if still applicable, or to the finders (Gouvernement du Canada 2001).

Secondly, the 2011 Cultural Heritage Act is the newest provincial law in use since it replaced the Cultural Property Act introduced in 1972. It is important to note that neither of these laws were made specifically for underwater cultural heritage. The primary difference between the two laws is that the Cultural Heritage Act is designed not only to protect Québec's heritage, but also to understand, convey and enhance it. With this new law, the government is now required to provide a conservation plan for all classified heritage, which can be sites, documents, objects or buildings. To excavate a site or sample any artefact from it, it is necessary to have a permit delivered by the provincial government, and only archaeologists can obtain them (Gouvernement du Québec 2011). Finally, the UNESCO Convention on the Protection of Underwater Cultural Heritage, adopted in 2001, is a good guideline for maritime archaeologists, but it is important to note that it does not provide any legal protection. This convention fights against looting and suggests rules to standardize the archaeologists' fieldwork and reports. It also advocates for *in situ* preservation and the accessibility of sites to divers and the general public, when possible (UNESCO 2013). However, according to the actual list of member states, Canada has not signed the convention (UNESCO 2017); even so, it is still considered to be a good model of practice.

What is the Current Situation?

The actual situation in Québec is not critical, but it could be improved. Four challenges exist to improving maritime archaeology: the size of the province territory; the incomplete inventory of Québec's shipwrecks; the diminution of maritime archaeology projects undertaken; and the difficulty for students to get a complete formation inside the country.

First of all, there is undoubtedly a lack of physical protection on most sites and looting is still frequent. Fines and even jail time are prescribed against anyone found in violation of either the federal or provincial laws (Gouvernement du Canada 2001; Gouvernement du Québec 2011), but they need to get caught first. It is difficult for the Coast Guard to enforce those laws on such a vast territory. Also, as shipwrecks become archaeological sites protected by the provincial law 50 years after their wreckage (Simard 2009:21), the number of archaeological sites is growing every year.

The second problem is that the exact number of shipwrecks on Québec's territory is unknown. Between the "paper wrecks", the multiple occurrences of one ship under different but similar names, the located sites and others that are still only known to local divers, there isn't a satisfactory inventory (Robitaille 2007). The sites known by the ministry are reunited in the PIMIQ (*Patrimoine immobilier, mobilier et immatériel du Québec*) and ISAQ (*Inventaire des Sites Archéologiques du Québec*) system, and most of these are located in the Saint Lawrence River. The surveys do not cover all of the important, high potential zones, like Anticosti and the Magdalen Islands.

The third challenge is the low number of maritime archaeology projects undertaken. In Québec, most of them are conducted by Parks Canada, their small team being responsible for all of Canada's federal land and national historic sites. Some projects are developed by university teachers and a few researchers in the field. It's only recently that a non-profit organization, named *Institut de Recherche en Histoire Maritime et Archéologie Subaquatique* (IRHMAS), was created to promote maritime and underwater archaeology in Québec and develop capacity. Furthermore, IRHMAS seeks to finance new projects by professionals outside universities (Musée maritime du Québec 2017). It is a good start to bring about change in the discipline, but this organization will have a lot of work to do in order to reach the same level of stability as those focused on terrestrial archaeology.

Finally, there exists the significant challenge of training the next generation of students without them having to leave the province or even the country. In Canada, there is no specialized program, like in the United States or in England, and there are few maritime archaeology teachers. In Québec, there is only one at the University of Montreal. There are also very few field schools available for students to earn more experience in the cold and often dark waters of Québec. They can train outside the country, but they might not get experience working in the same environmental conditions, or with the same required specialized equipment, such as dry suits.

Possible Solutions

Changes are needed to improve the management of underwater cultural heritage, but also the state of maritime archaeology in the province of Québec. For instance, hiring specialized teachers in more than one university would allow a better distribution of the workload of training the new generation while also making maritime archaeology accessible to a greater number of students. Additional faculty and university programs would also allow for more university-funded projects to take place. The inclusion of mandatory dive training in Québec's rough underwater environment might be a good addition to theory classes.

For the improved management of maritime heritage, an important first step would be to complete new surveys in untapped high potential waters, like the area of the Magdalen Islands. This would lead to a better inventory of shipwrecks throughout the province. However, doing systematic surveys of every watercourse in Québec is stymied by the short field season, the few maritime archaeologists available, and the high expenses it would cause. The solution would be to integrate the local divers to help find, monitor and protect the sites.

Many shipwrecks have been found by local divers, but often, the sites were only declared years later. Was this delay because the electronic system of declarations did not exist, or was not well managed, at the time of the find? Or was the delay the result of locals not being aware of the laws or their belief that the shipwreck had already been declared? There is still confusion among the public between artifacts recovered and displayed through ethical and scientific excavations, and commercially exploited artifacts. The key is to raise the awareness of the public, so they will trust and help maritime archaeologists.

In return, archaeologists also need to trust the local divers, who can become vocal advocates for preservation and receive specialized training through programs like those sponsored by NAS. Training provides local divers with an understanding of maritime heritage importance and fragility, which the divers can carry back to their own organizations (Grenier 2003). With the help or supervision of archaeologists, avocational divers could monitor, protect and survey greater areas of the province. UNESCO argues that diving centers can become useful allies in preservation since their livelihood can depend on well-preserved patrimonial sites. They could become responsible for the maintenance of one particular wreck against some privileges on diving rights (UNESCO 2013) or even government grants.

Working against this idea is, of course, the risk of more looting occurring, but local divers often already know the positions of shipwrecks. They will obviously dive on the sites with or without the approval of archaeologists; it is arguably better to use their keen interest for wreck diving and transform it into something beneficial for the population by protecting our common maritime heritage.

It is suggested here that a GIS atlas be created that is available to the public. This idea was inspired by the MACHU (Managing Cultural Heritage Underwater) project, which is a pan-European inventory on GIS. Their interactive map includes shipwreck sites, erosion patterns, and bathymetry data, among other data sets. It is a great tool to manage underwater heritage, by making it possible to protect shipwrecks from dredging routes and constructions sites for example. However, it was only available to archaeologists and decisions makers from the government (MACHU 2008).

Using the MACHU database as a model, information could be made available to well-trained and trustworthy divers. By coordinating the efforts of local divers, protecting and monitoring known shipwreck sites after big storms or after a certain amount of time would be a lot easier. The GIS atlas would also allow the divers to organize survey dives to explore new areas. Divers could compile small reports with photos and videos and link them to a specific GPS point.

Conclusion

In conclusion, Québec has a really rich maritime heritage, but it must be defined with more precision. How many shipwrecks are there really? Where are they found in greater concentrations? From which era are they from the most? But also, what is the real extent of the local divers' implication in Québec's maritime archaeology? These are questions that need answering in order to improve shipwreck management, and potentially modify the laws to be better suited to protect underwater cultural heritage.

The idea of a GIS atlas available to the public still needs to be refined since all the consequences and possible outcomes need to be evaluated. Some measures would need to be taken in order to prevent nefarious uses of this system. However, the integration of local divers increasingly seems like a necessity.

References

Bass, George F.
2013 The Development of Maritime Archaeology. In *The Oxford Handbook of Maritime Archaeology*, Ben Ford, Bonny L. Hamilton and Alexis Catsambis, editors, pp. 1-26, England.

Delgado, James P. and Mark Staniforth
2002　*Underwater Archaeology.* The Encyclopedia of Life Support Systems. UNESCO, 19 p., Paris, France.

Delmas, Vincent
2017　L'Archéologie Maritime de la Côte-Nord: Rapport de Recherche Archéologique de 2016 In *Report of Investigations*, 105 p., Montréal, Qc.

Delmas, Vincent and Mathieu Mercier Gingras
2016　*Projet d'Inventaire des Épaves de la Côte-Nord. Activités de 2015.* Report of Investigations, vol. 1, 98 p., Montreal, Qc.

Gouvernement du Canada
2001　Loi de 2001 sur la Marine Marchande du Canada. In *L.C.* 2001, ch. 26.

Gouvernement du Québec
2002　L'Eau. La Vie. L'Avenir. In *Politique Nationale de l'Eau.* 94 p. Québec, Qc.

2011　Cultural Heritage Act. CQLR c P-9.002.

Grenier, Robert
2003　Préface - L'Archéologie Subaquatique au Québec et au Canada: Bilan et Perspectives. In *Mer et Monde : Questions d'archéologie maritime*, Christian Roy, Jean Bélisle, Marc-André Bernier and Brad Loewen, editors, pp. ix-xiii. Série Archéologiques, Hors série 1. Québec.

2007　Introduction. In *The Underwater Archaeology of Red Bay : Basque Shipbuilding and Whaling in the 16th Century*, Robert Grenier, Marc-André Bernier and Willis Stevens, editors, vol. 1, pp. 1-12. Manitoba, On.

Jones, Mark.
2003　*For Future Generations : Conservation of a Tudor Maritime Collection.* Mary Rose Trust, editor, vol. 5, 145 p., Portsmouth, England.

MACHU
2008　*MACHU Report : A Maritime Research Project Funded by the European Union Culture 2000 Programme.* Report of Investigations, vol. 1, Amersfoort, Netherlands.

McKinnon, Jennifer F.
2014　Archaeology and the Emergence of Fields : Maritime. In *Encyclopedia of Global Archaeology.* Claire Smith, editor, pp.414-420. Springer.

Musée maritime du Québec
2017　Archéologie Subaquatique. <http://www.mmq.qc.ca/archeologie-subaquatique-annonce-du-partenariat-mmq-et-irhmas/>. Accessed March 1st, 2018.

Robitaille, Michel
2007　*Évaluation du Potentiel Archéologique des Côtes de l'Île d'Anticosti.* Dissertation, Department of Anthropology, University of Montreal, Montreal, Qc.

Simard, Frédéric
2009　*Patrimoine Archéologique Maritime* : Les Épaves et les Anciens Quais. 143 p., Québec.

UNESCO
2013　*Manuel Pratique pour les Interventions sur le Patrimoine Culturel Subaquatique: Le Patrimoine Culturel Subaquatique et les Règles de la Convention de 2001 de l'UNESCO.* Thijs J. Maarleveld, Ulrike Guérin and Barbara Egger, editors, 345 p.

2017　États parties de la Convention sur la protection du patrimoine culturel subaquatique. <http://www.unesco.org/eri/la/convention.asp?order=alpha&language=F&KO=13520>. Accessed March 1st, 2018.

Zacharchuk, Walter, and Peter J. A. Waddell
1984　Le Recouvrement du Machault, une Frégate Française du XVIIIe Siècle. 74 p. Ottawa, On.

• • • • • • • • • • • • • • •

Carolane Veilleux
39 rue de Bretagne
Repentigny, Qc, Canada
J6A 1W4

Indiana's Maritime Heritage: Ongoing Investigations and Management Strategies for the 1910 *Muskegon* (aka *Peerless*) Shipwreck (12LE0381)

Samuel I. Haskell, Matthew J. Maus, Charles D. Beeker, Kirsten M. Hawley

Built in 1872 as the Peerless, *the* Muskegon *was a steamship that operated on the Great Lakes until 1911. Having functioned in a variety of roles, the* Muskegon *represents important 19th century innovations in maritime technology, becoming the first shipwreck accepted to the National Register of Historic Places in Indiana. Since 2016, Indiana University has been conducting ongoing direct diver and photogrammetric surveys to assist with management decisions and public outreach. This paper presents methodology and results of this ongoing assessment, discussing management strategies to develop the shipwreck as a marine protected area and underwater preserve for public interpretation.*

Indiana's Maritime Heritage

The state of Indiana has the smallest territorial waters of any Great Lakes state, spanning just 45 miles of Lake Michigan shoreline and containing approximately 225 square miles of bottomland (Beeker et al. 2000). Despite the state's small amount of coastline, the Indiana Department of Natural Resources (DNR) has identified the potential for 50 unique, historic vessels in Indiana territorial waters, with wrecking dates ranging from 1843 – 1936 (Ellis 1989). 14 of these shipwrecks have been located and are included in the Indiana Marine Cultural Resource Inventory (Ellis 1989).

Historic shipwrecks in Indiana territorial waters are valuable examples of Indiana's diverse and unique maritime history. These vessels offer a cross section of Indiana and Great Lakes cultural heritage and commerce, giving historians and archaeologists an intimate look into the historic use of our state's coastal waters. Archaeological investigations of these shipwrecks can answer important questions concerning maritime technology and its influence on the historical landscape of the Great Lakes (Rogers 2016). They also act as a catalyst for increasing public awareness of the importance of maritime history and fostering a sense of stewardship for the protection of cultural resources.

The *Muskegon* shipwreck site represents the remains of a medium sized passenger freighter in southern Lake Michigan, just outside of Michigan City, Indiana (Ellis 1987). The only shipwreck in the state of Indiana on the National Register of Historic Places, the *Muskegon* is a significant piece of Indiana maritime history that should be protected and preserved for future generations.

The Peerless

The *Muskegon* was originally built in 1872 under the name *Peerless* in Cleveland, Ohio by Ira LaFranier for the Chicago transportation firm of Leopold and Austrian (Runge Marine Collection [RMC] 1959). The *Peerless* was built to serve as a passenger freighter in the firm's Lake Michigan and Lake Superior Transfer Company Fleet, operating on the Chicago-Duluth Run until 1879. In 1875 the vessel is listed as having a length of 211 feet, a 40-foot beam, and 12-foot draft and was constructed from the "best Ohio oak" (*The Evening News* [TEN] 1910; RMC 1959). The *Peerless* weighed in at 1,275 gross tons, capable of carrying several hundred passenger and hundreds of tons of packaged cargo (Ellis 1988).

The *Peerless* is an excellent example of the typical 19th century Great Lakes vessel built to serve as a combination passenger/cargo freighter. At the time of the ship's sinking, Michigan City's *The Evening News* (1910) described the ship as "one of the finest passenger vessels on the Great Lakes." The *Peerless* was built with a high pressure reciprocating engine and massive, dual boilers that remained with the ship throughout its operational life (Ellis 1988). Operating at 80 revolutions per minute with a 40-inch stroke, the 47.5-inch engine cylinder was able to stand up to the high demands of Great Lakes service (RMC 1959; Ellis 1988). The advanced steam management system's twin firebox boilers were able to provide the engine with sufficient high pressure to drive the engine at 400 horsepower (RMC 1959).

In addition to the state of the art engine assembly, the *Peerless* had a set of wooden Bishop Arches to provide exceptional load carrying capacity and to facilitate the efficient movement of goods and people. The wooden arches were connected across decks by timber latticework, "limiting their lateral movement and allowing for such movement to be tempered" (Ellis 1988). While the rear 75 feet of the *Peerless* was dedicated to the engine, propulsion, and steam management, historic photographs show the original deck configuration of the ship as consisting of one main cargo deck, a spar deck, a passenger deck, and a forward wheelhouse (Figure 1) (Ellis 1988).

The *Peerless* served as the flagship of the Lake Michigan-Lake Superior Transportation Company until 1900, when it was sold to W.H. Singer of Duluth, Minnesota (RMC 1959). The *Peerless* was bought and sold several times before it was ultimately renamed the *Muskegon* in 1908 by its new owner, the Muskegon and Chicago Navigation Company.

The Muskegon (aka Peerless)

While owned by the Muskegon and Chicago Navigation Company, the newly-named *Muskegon* served as a "night boat" for a brief period of time and was alleged to have been used as a floating gambling house (RMC 1959). After being renamed in 1908, the *Muskegon* was cut down to serve as a lumber-hooker (Ellis 1987). Lumber hookers would carry precut and dressed lumber throughout the Great Lakes during the late 19th and early 20th centuries (Ellis 1988).

In 1910, the *Muskegon* was sold to the Independent Sand and Gravel Company in Chicago. The ship was moved from Michigan City, Indiana to Manitowoc, Wisconsin to be modified and reequipped as a sand mining barge. During refitting in Manitowoc, the *Muskegon's* original passenger cabins were removed. Additionally, new steel and wood composite arches were installed in place of the ship's original, iconic wooden Bishop Arches (Ellis 1988).

After the *Muskegon* left Manitowoc, Wisconsin, it returned to Michigan City, Indiana to begin its new career as a sand reclamation barge. Shortly after returning to Michigan City, an accidental fire on 6 October 1910 burned the Muskegon to just above the waterline while it was berthed in the Indiana Transportation Company's dock on the north side of Michigan City harbor (Ellis 1987). The ignition of kerosene or oil residue near the boilers is thought to have started the fire, and *The Evening News* (1910) describes it as one of the worst fires to have ever been fought in the harbor. While the fire was eventually extinguished, the volume of water used to control the flames caused the vessel to settle at dockside (Ellis 1988).

Despite efforts by the Indiana Transportation Company to have the vessel removed, the *Muskegon* remained in place for eight months following the fire.

Figure 1: Historic photograph of the Peerless, circa 1880 (Courtesy of the Great Lakes Marine Collection, Milwaukee Public Library).

In early June 1911, the Independent Sand and Gravel Company transferred the *Muskegon's* sand-sucking equipment and deck to their new, replacement ship, the J.D. Marshall (Ellis 1987). The *Muskegon* was then towed out of the harbor and sunk just west of Michigan City by the Indiana Transportation Company on 11 June 1911. Outfitted with the *Muskegon's* sand sucking equipment, the J.D. Marshall would ironically sink the following day (TEN 1911; Ellis 1986).

Archaeological Investigations

The *Muskegon* now rests in 30 – 35 feet of water, 0.28 miles offshore from the Indiana Dunes National Lakeshore's Mount Baldy. The vessel is embedded in a Pleistocene clay deposit that was once found under the ancient glacial Lake Chicago, ca. 20,000 – 12,000 B.P (Ellis 1988). The ship was discovered by recreational divers in the early 1960s and is still a popular and commonly known recreational dive site.

The first formal archaeological survey of the *Muskegon* was conducted by former Indiana State Archaeologist Gary Ellis over a three-year period, 1985-1988. Ellis (1988) and a team of divers from the Indiana Department of Natural Resources performed subsurface reconnaissance and intensive survey to determine the nature and extent of archaeological deposits. Ellis (1987) reported to Indiana's Division of Historic Preservation that the site was in relatively stable condition. At the time of the investigation, Ellis (1988) noted that the site was stable with the majority of the wreckage distributed southwest of the vessel's main frame. Ellis (1988) explained that very little of the site was likely to collapse or drift out of position, but that there is substantial wreckage covered by a thin layer of sand. This sand, Ellis (1988) observed, periodically shifts about exposing and covering units larger than 25 square feet without having a negative impact on the cultural material underneath.

The results of Ellis' initial survey were ultimately used to put together a nomination to the National Register of Historic Places in 1988. Due to its status as a historically significant shipwreck representing important innovations in engineering, commerce, transportation and industry, as well as its tremendous research potential, the Muskegon is now listed on the National Register of Historic Places (Maus and Haskell 2016).

In 2000, Indiana University's Center for Underwater Science conducted archaeological investigations relating to historic shipwrecks in Indiana territorial waters as a part of a larger scope project being conducted by the Indiana University Eppley Institute. Indiana University researchers visited the Muskegon with the goal of making recommendations on management of Indiana shipwrecks as recreational resources.

Indiana University noted little structural change in the site from Gary Ellis' initial archaeological assessment, with site features extending above the lakebed and a plethora of undisturbed cultural deposits (Beeker et al. 2000). The main exposed site features include major segments of the ship's main frame and sidewalls, steam engine, twin boilers, Bishop Arch assemblies, propeller, and propeller drive shaft. Beeker et al. (2000) identified that approximately 90% of the ship's iron components were covered with invasive Zebra mussels (*Dreissena polymorpha*).

A significant change from Ellis' initial survey that was noted during the Indiana University assessment in 2000 was the presence of a 24" intrusive, modern pipeline. At the time of the investigation, the pipeline crossed the hull of the Muskegon north of the engine and two boilers, along the port of the ship's keel (Beeker et al. 2000). Despite none of the major machinery components being impacted, the pipeline covered some of the ship's hull. University divers believed that the pipeline had been placed relatively recently, as clay sediment showed evidence of recent settling and the pipe had no attached Zebra mussels (Beeker et al. 2000). In their official report, Indiana University recommended that an updated archaeological survey of the vessel to determine the extent of damage from the pipe and determine management strategies and mitigation of potential damage (Beeker et al. 2000).

Intrusive Modern Pipe

Between 2011 and 2013, Commonwealth Cultural Resources Group (CCRG) conducted several surveys of submerged cultural resources in Indiana's territorial waters. CCRG surveys indicate that in 2011, the intrusive modern pipe appeared to have changed significantly since the 2000 Indiana University assessment and had actually become entangled under the hull of the ship (Kaufmann 2012). In 2012, CCRG conducted indirect sidescan sonar survey and direct diver reconnaissance to document the extent of the pipe and its impact on the shipwreck.

Kira Kaufmann (2012), Principle Investigator for CCRG, explained that the greatest potential for damage to the shipwreck site comes from "erosion caused by the change in water flow patterns that the pipe has created." Kaufmann (2012) recommended that the pipe be closely monitored and ultimately removed from the site to prevent further damage to the shipwreck. With funding from the Indiana DNR, CCRG created a draft stabilization plan for the site, outlining recommendations for future management in regard to the shipwreck and pipe (Kaufman and Egan-Bruhy 2013).

In 2016, the Indiana DNR approached the Indiana University (IU) Center for Underwater Science seeking further clarification of the pipe's impact on the shipwreck. While the main segment of pipe was clearly defined in CCRG's 2013 stabilization plan, there was some uncertainty surrounding a potential second segment of pipe under the shipwreck. Indiana DNR provided a grant for IU to conduct an updated survey of the intrusive modern pipe to help determine the extent of its impact with the submerged cultural resources.

In July of 2016, a team of four Indiana University divers travelled to Michigan City, IN with the objective of assessing the extent of the intrusive modern pipe on the shipwreck and recommending strategies for its removal (Maus and Haskell 2016). With funding provided by the Lake Michigan Coastal Program and marine transport provided by the Indiana DNR Division of Fish and Wildlife at the Michigan City Field Office, IU documented the pipe using direct diver survey and photogrammetric recording on 12-13 July 2016 (Figure 2). As a result of this fieldwork, IU researchers identified two pipe segments with a combined length total length of 147.46 m (483.79 ft.) currently impacting the *Muskegon* shipwreck (Maus and Haskell 2016).

The summary report of IU's 2016 assessment provides a number of recommendations for management of the *Muskegon*. The report recommended removal of all exposed pipe sections on and around the Muskegon shipwreck by a commercial diving firm, under supervision from a qualified diving archaeologist (Maus and Haskell 2016). The removal of pipe pinned underneath the hull main frame and port sidewall could cause significant damage to the shipwreck, and it is recommended that those sections be cut, left *in situ,* and permanently capped to prevent further movement (Maus and Haskell 2016). IU additionally recommended the necessity of annual monitoring according to a rapid assessment protocol conducted by divers under the guidance of a qualified archaeologist (Maus and Haskell 2016).

Figure 2: Indiana University researchers swim photo transects over the site to build a three-dimensional model of the intrusive, modern pipe's impact areas (Indiana University, 2016.).

Photogrammetry as a Monitoring Tool

Following the 2016 photogrammetric survey of the intrusive modern pipe, Indiana University returned to the *Muskegon* to create a 3D, photogrammetric model of the shipwreck for use in baseline monitoring and management. The 2017 project was marked by low visibility conditions on the first day, which deteriorated significantly thereafter. As a result, it was only possible to photograph the stern and amidships sections of the *Muskegon*. IU hopes to return to the site to complete image acquisition of the bow section.

The central data collection technique for this project was structure-from-motion photogrammetric imagery acquisition, accomplished by divers using SCUBA and cameras to collect images while swimming delineated site sections (Maus et al. 2015, 2017; Van Damme 2015a, 2015b). The ultimate objective of image acquisition was to collect sufficient overlapping imagery of the entire site in order to align images and generate a three-dimensional model and orthomosaic using computer vision photogrammetry (Agisoft 2016; Van Damme 2015a; Van Damme 2015b). These products can then be used to increase public access to the site and during annual monitoring according to a rapid assessment protocol (Maus et al. 2017).

The image acquisition and processing methods for this project were based on methods described in Maus et al. (2017; 2018). Prior to image acquisition, divers deployed 10 12-bit, coded targets to assist with image alignment, establishing scale, estimating error, and orienting the site to cardinal directions. Targets were deployed in lines, with each target line acting as a border between "chunks." These chunks were processed individually to reduce processing time and computer memory usage (Maus et al. 2017).

Three project divers were utilized to acquire photogrammetric imagery. One diver swam slow transects over the site taking the primary top-down photos using an array of two GoPro Hero 5 cameras. A second diver photographed the borders between chunks using a single GoPro Hero 4 camera to aid in processing and chunk alignment. The third project diver managed chunk size and coded target distribution. As the first two divers finished photographing a chunk, the third diver redeployed coded targets to delineate the next chunk. In this way, a team of at least three divers could "walk" imaging chunks down the length of the shipwreck to rapidly record the site. Due to poor visibility during project dives, cameras were set to take photographs at half-second intervals. This allowed for the desired 80% forward-overlap and 60% side-overlap between images (Agisoft 2016).

Images were pre-processed in Adobe Lightroom for color correction and dehazing, prior to processing in Agisoft Photoscan. Images were processed in chunks using standard workflow commands to generate a sparse point cloud, dense point cloud, textured model, and tiled model (Agisoft 2016). The final model is composed of 7,373 images and has an estimated error of 0.00320015 m (Figure 3). Poor visibility during the project inhibited image alignment in some places. While this resulted in less-than-optimal image alignment (approximately 70%

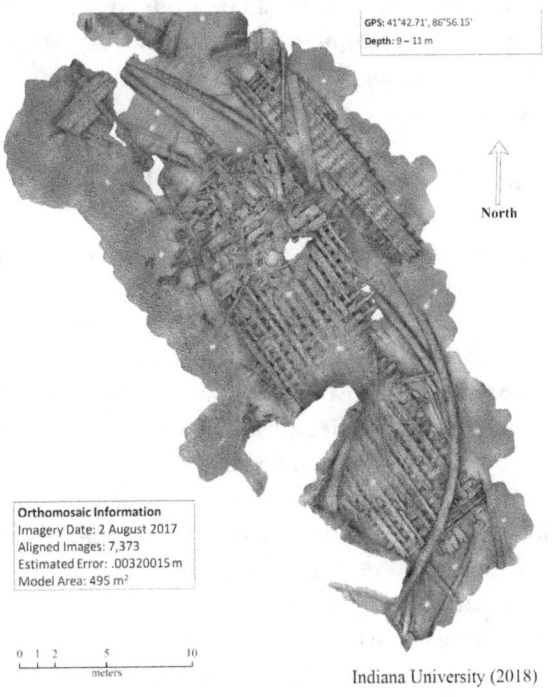

Figure 3: Photogrammetric site plan of the Muskegon's stern section created using 7,373 images aligned in Agisoft Photoscan (Indiana University, 2018.).

alignment rate), the majority of the photographed areas of the shipwreck were successfully modelled. While the stern and amidships sections, including engines, associated machinery, hull, and the intrusive modern pipe mostly rendered successfully, the complex vertical structures of the propeller and twin scotch boilers did not sufficiently resolve. To increase the rate of alignment and better resolve vertically complex structures, future projects in similar conditions should emphasize a higher density of image acquisition in these areas to compensate.

While the photogrammetric model of exposed ship remains will act as a baseline for future monitoring efforts, it is recommended that further photogrammetry be conducted on the *Muskegon* prior to the removal of the intrusive modern pipe. Computer vision photogrammetry provides a highly accurate and quantifiable method of tracking change over time and would provide archaeologists and resource managers with a cost-effective tool for damage assessment prior to and following the removal of the pipe. The ease and speed with which photogrammetric imagery can be acquired will facilitate economical monitoring and research on the *Muskegon* over time following the site's potential nomination as an underwater park.

Underwater Preserves and Park Development

Shipwrecks constitute finite resources with not just historic value to researchers and archaeologists, but an intrinsic, recreational value to the general public. Underwater parks and Marine Protected Areas (MPAs) have been shown to provide valuable recreational and economic opportunities across the world (Beeker et al. 2000; Whitehead and Finney 2003). Many U.S. states have developed successful programs establishing underwater parks and preserves; states like California, Florida, and Michigan have successful marine preservation programs that not only provide protection for shipwrecks but enhance site usage through recreation and tourism (Peterson et al. 1987; Halsey 1990; Beeker et al. 2000; Hanselmann and Beeker 2008; Maus et al. 2017).

Under federal law (Abandoned Shipwreck Act of 1987), the state of Indiana is directed to manage and protect abandoned and historic shipwrecks on Indiana lake bottomlands (United States Abandoned Shipwreck Act of 1987 1988; Beeker 2000). This law, combined with the National Park Service Federal Guidelines, give states a variety of responsibilities beyond the traditional parameters of historic preservation with regard to cultural resources (Beeker et al. 2000; National Park Service 2006). These responsibilities include dealing with a broad range of management issues, including public access to shipwrecks, recreation concerns, and the creation of underwater parks and preserves (Beeker et al. 2000; National Parks Service 2006).

Preservation of historic shipwrecks in Indiana requires the state to take an active role in facilitating protection and public access. During Indiana University's 2000 assessment, the Muskegon was determined to be the best site for an archaeological preserve in Indiana territorial waters (Beeker et al. 2000). The same criteria utilized during the establishment of the Florida Keys Shipwreck Trail were used during this assessment (Smith et al. 1990; Beeker et al. 2000). The *Muskegon*'s relatively intact features, depth, historical significance, and location give it the potential to be an exceptional park (Smith et al. 1990; Beeker et al. 2000; Kauffman and Bruhy 2013; Maus and Haskell 2016).

Indiana currently has one underwater shipwreck park, and the *Muskegon* should be extended the same designation and protection. In 2013, the *J.D. Marshall* was inaugurated as an underwater preserve under the Indiana Nature Preserves Act (1967). The *J.D. Marshall* Underwater Preserve was established with the mission to "promote understanding and appreciation of cultural values of areas by the people of Indiana" (Indiana Nature Preserves Act 1967). As the only shipwreck in the state of Indiana on the NRHP, the *Muskegon* is a prime candidate for nomination as an Indiana Nature Preserve to protect associated archaeological resources and promote cultural heritage tourism.

The first steps in successful park development involve enhancing site infrastructure to promote recreation and tourism. The *Muskegon* has been a popular location for recreational scuba divers since the 1960s, and the site currently lacks adequate infrastructure to enable and support these diving activities (Figure 4). The first step

Figure 4: Indiana University diver Charles Beeker examines the exposed engine and associated machinery. Although the Muskegon has intact and interesting features, the site currently lacks adequate park infrastructure to support recreational use (Indiana University, 2017.).

in enhancing a site for recreational use is the installation of a mooring system for boat use. An adequate mooring system is necessary to provide safe, stable anchorage for boat captains while limiting potential anchor damage to the sensitive cultural material (Hanselmann and Beeker 2008). An upright, spar buoy should be placed on the site that identifies the historic shipwreck and preserve. A monument should be placed on the site with a commemorative, bronze plaque that gives park visitors basic information about the Muskegon and its preserve (Hanselmann and Beeker 2008).

A critical component of establishing an underwater park is public outreach and education. A waterproof, interpretive guide of the *Muskegon* should be created for divers that contains a detailed site plan, significant archaeological features, jurisdictional information, and safety information. This guide could be made available from local dive centers, charter operators, and the Michigan City Field Office of the Indiana DNR's Division of Fish and Wildlife.

Additional displays should be created on land for non-diving tourists. A kiosk should be created at the nearby Indiana Dunes State Park for park visitors to learn about the *Muskegon* and build resource stewardship amongst local stakeholders. The Indiana Dunes has approximately three million visitors annually, and accessible information about the *Muskegon* and other local, historic shipwrecks will help increase public awareness of the need to protect submerged cultural resources and archaeological sites (Indiana Dunes Tourism 2018). Another land display could be located at the Old Michigan City Light. The Old Michigan City Light is a decommissioned lighthouse located in the harbor of Michigan City, Indiana and just over a mile from the site of the Muskegon (Beeker et al. 2000). The lighthouse is now a museum owned and operated by the non-profit Michigan City Historical Society, Inc. (2017) and currently displays artifacts and exhibits about Lake Michigan shipwrecks and Indiana's maritime history. These terrestrial venues would enhance tourism for shipwreck sites and would facilitate public outreach and education about Indiana's maritime heritage to the non-diving public.

The Indiana DNR (2018) currently profiles the "Indiana Lake Michigan Shipwreck Survey Project" on their website, displaying virtual tours and photo galleries of Indiana shipwrecks. The website should be enhanced with updated interpretive materials and information about active research on the *Muskegon*. The posting of photogrammetric models and detailed site plans on the website would allow visitors to experience the submerged cultural resources of Indiana's territorial waters from their own computers, building excitement and promoting cultural heritage tourism (Maus et al. 2017).

Summary and Conclusions

The results of the 2016 and 2017 Indiana University investigations demonstrate the need for improved site protection and monitoring. The intrusive modern pipe is an immediate management concern, but the site should be dedicated as a marine protected area in order to prevent further damage to the significant submerged cultural resources. Annual monitoring by a qualified professional archaeologist using structure-from-motion photogrammetry is necessary to create and modify management strategies for the *Muskegon*, as well as build resource stewardship through outreach and education. Using 21st-century technology, this 19th-century shipwreck can be made available to both the diving and non-diving public, fostering a sense of excitement and responsibility to protect and preserve archaeological sites.

In the United States and around the world, shipwrecks are of increasing interest to the diving and non-diving public. Shipwrecks spark a natural excitement and interest in archaeology and cultural heritage. Successfully nominated to the National Register of Historic Places, the *Muskegon* is representative of a specific class of steam-powered, iron-hulled passenger freighter built and used on the Great Lakes in the late 19th and early 20th centuries. For over 50 years, visitors have enjoyed this piece of maritime heritage as a recreational dive site. The Muskegon and its tangible remains should be protected as an underwater park to preserve and guarantee its availability to the public for future generations.

Acknowledgements

This project was made possible through the Indiana Department of Natural Resources and the Lake Michigan Coastal Program. The authors would like to thank the Michigan City Fish and Wildlife Office for their logistical support. In addition, the authors would like to acknowledge the important contributions of Gary Ellis, Kira Kauffman, Kathryn Egan-Bruhy, and the Commonwealth Cultural Resource Group for their extensive and excellent research on Indiana's maritime heritage.

References

Agisoft LLC
2016 *Agisoft Photoscan User Manual:* Professional Edition, Version 1.2. St. Petersburg, Russia.

Beeker, Charles, Ania Budziak, and Carina King
2000 *Assessment and Management Recommendations for the Historic Shipwrecks Located in Indiana Territorial Waters of Southern Lake Michigan.* Report to Indiana Department of Natural Resources, Indianapolis, Indiana from Indiana University Office of Underwater Science, Bloomington, IN.

Ellis, Gary
1986 *Underwater Archaeological Investigations at the* J.D. Marshall *Shipwreck Site, Indiana Dunes State Park, Porter County, Indiana.* Manuscript. Indiana Department of Natural Resources Division of Historic Preservation and Archaeology, Indianapolis, IN.

1987 Preliminary Evaluation of the *Muskegon* Marine *Cultural Resource Site No. 2, Laporte County, Indiana.* Manuscript. Indiana Department of Natural Resources Division of Historic Preservation and Archaeology, Indianapolis, IN.

1988 National Register of Historic Places Registration Form, *Muskegon* (nee Peerless)*Shipwreck Site.* Manuscript. Indiana Division of Historic Preservation and Archaeology, Indianapolis, IN.

1989 Historic Context: Marine Cultural Resources, Indiana *Territorial Waters of Lake Michigan.* Manuscript. Indiana Division of Historic Preservation and Archaeology, Indianapolis, IN.

Halsey, John
1990 *Beneath the Inland Seas: Michigan's Underwater Archaeological Heritage.* Manuscript. Bureau of History, Michigan Department of State, Lansing, Michigan.

Hanselmann, Frederick and Charles Beeker
2008 Establishing Marine Protected Areas in the Dominican Republic: A Model for Sustainable Preservation. In *ACUA Underwater Archaeology Proceedings 2008*, Langley, Susan and Victor Mastone, editors, pp. 52-61. Advisory Council on Underwater Archaeology/PAST Foundation, Columbus, OH.

Indiana Department of Natural Resources [DNR]
2018 Indiana Shipwrecks. Indiana Department of Natural Resources <https://www.in.gov/dnr/lakemich/8482.htm>. Accessed 17 January 2018.

Indiana Dunes Tourism
2018 FAQs on Indiana Dunes Tourism. Indiana Dunes Tourism <http://www.indianadunes.com/indiana-dunes-tourism/>. Accessed 8 February 2018.

Indiana Nature Preserves Act
1967 Indiana Code Title 14. *Natural and Cultural Resources.* Article 31, Section 1. Indiana General Assembly, Indianapolis, IN.

Kaufmann, Kira E.
2012 Letter to Mike Molnar, 6 November 2012. Manuscript, Lake Michigan Coastal Program, Indiana Department of Natural Resources, Indianapolis, IN.

Kaufmann, Kira E., and Kathryn C. Egan-Bruhy
2013 *Draft Stabilization Plan for the* Muskegon *(aka* Peerless) *Shipwreck (12LE0381) Archaeological Site within Indiana's Territorial Waters of Lake Michigan.* Report to Lake Michigan Coastal Program, Indiana Department of Natural Resources, Indianapolis, Indiana, from Commonwealth Cultural Resources Group, Inc., Milwaukee, WI.

Maus, Matthew, Brenda Altmeier, Charles Beeker, Samuel I. Haskell, Kirsten Hawley
2018 *Evolving Tools for Public Maritime Archaeology: From Photoshop to Photogrammetry in the Florida Keys National Marine Sanctuary.* Poster presented at the 51st Annual Conference on Historical and Underwater Archaeology, New Orleans, LA.

Maus, Matthew, Charles Beeker, Mylana Haydu, and Samuel I. Haskell
2015 *Application of Photogrammetry for Assessment and Monitoring of the 1733 San Pedro Underwater Archaeological Preserve.* Report to Florida Division of Historical Resources (Bureau of Archaeological Research), Florida Division of Recreation and Parks (Bureau of Natural and Cultural Resources), and NOAA Florida Keys National Marine Sanctuary from Indiana University Center for Underwater Science, Bloomington, IN.

Maus, Matthew, Denise Jaffke, Samuel I. Haskell
2017 *Photogrammetry as a Tool for Monitoring Submerged Cultural Resources: The Emerald Bay State Park Workshop.* In *Society for California Archaeology Proceedings*, Volume 31, Reddy, Seetha, Allika Ruby, Heather Baron, Sherri Andrews, Shelly Davis-King, Sharon Waechter editors, pp. 58-79. Society for California Archaeology, Chico, CA.

MAUS, MATTHEW AND SAMUEL I. HASKELL
2016   Muskegon *(aka* Peerless*) Shipwreck (12LE 0381): Intrusive Modern Pipe Assessment.* Report to Lake Michigan Coastal Program, Indiana Department of Natural Resources and Division of Historic Preservation and Archaeology, Indiana Department of Natural Resources, Indianapolis, Indiana from Indiana University Center for Underwater Science, Bloomington, IN.

MICHIGAN CITY HISTORICAL SOCIETY, INC.
2017   *Michigan City Lighthouse History. The Old Lighthouse Museum, Michigan City Historical Society, Inc.,* Michigan City, Indiana <http://www.oldlighthousemuseum.org/lighhouse_history.html>. Accessed 10 February 2018.

NATIONAL PARKS SERVICE
2006   *Federal Historic Preservation Laws.* Manuscript. National Center for Cultural Resources, National Park Service, Department of Interior, Washington, DC.

PETERSON, JON P., THORD C. SUNDSTROM, AND RONALD E KINNUNEN
1987   *A Profile of Great Lakes Diver Activity, Travel, and Expenditure Patterns.* Manuscript. Michigan Sea Grant Extension-Michigan Sea Grant College Program Studies, East Lansing, Michigan. U.S. Congress, Office of Technology Assessment.

ROGERS, BRADLEY A.
2016   *Vernacular Craft of the North American Great Lakes.* In *The Archaeology of Vernacular Watercraft*, Amanda M. Evans, editor, pp. 205-253, Springer, New York City, NY.

RUNGE MARINE COLLECTION [RMC]
1959   Note File No. 20470 with Photo Archive. Great Lakes Marine Collection, Milwaukee Public Library, Milwaukee, WI.

SMITH, ROGER, ROBERT FINEGOLD, AND ERIC STEPHENS
1990   Establishing an Underwater Archaeological Preserve in the Florida Keys: A Case Study. In *Association for Preservation Technology International Bulletin* 22(3):11-18.

THE EVENING NEWS [TEN]
1910   Steamer Burns at Wharf: The Muskegon Wrecked. In *The Evening News* 6 October. Michigan City, IN.

1911 Marshall Flops Over; Four Lost Their Lives. *The Evening News* 12 June. Michigan City, IN.

UNITED STATES ABANDONED SHIPWRECK ACT OF 1987
1988   42 U.S.C. 2101-2106. Public Law 100-298. 100th Congress, Washington, DC.

VAN DAMME, THOMAS
2015a *Computer Vision Photogrammetry for Underwater Archaeological Site Recording: A Critical Assessment.* Master's thesis, Maritime Archaeology Programme, University of Southern Denmark, Odense, Denmark.

2015b Computer Vision Photogrammetry for Underwater Archaeological Site Recording in Low-Visibility Environment. In *The International Archives of the Photogrammetry, Remote Sensing and Spatial Information Sciences* XL-5/W5, pp. 231-238. Piano di Sorrento, Italy.

WHITEHEAD, JOHN AND SUZANNE FINNEY
2003   Willingness to Pay for Submerged Maritime Cultural Resources. In *Journal of Cultural Economics* 27:231-240.

. . . .

Samuel I. Haskell
1025 E 7th St, Room 058
Bloomington, Indiana 47405

Matthew J. Maus
1025 E 7th St, Room 058
Bloomington, Indiana 47405

Charles D. Beeker
1025 E 7th St, Room 058
Bloomington, Indiana 47405

Kirsten M. Hawley
1025 E 7th St, Room 058
Bloomington, Indiana 47405

Past and Present Research in the Underwater Archaeology of Saint-Pierre, Martinique, (FWI)

Jean-Sébastien Guibert, Max Guérout, Laurence Serra

This paper presents underwater archaeology research being conducted in Saint-Pierre Martinique (FWI) since the 1970's focusing on port dump and shipwrecks vestiges. Doban port dump site as well as the identified Biscaye *and unidentified Guinguette wreck sites are presented. Both the dump and wreck sites demonstrate the importance of maritime activity at the main port of Martinique and of the French West Indies in general, that stopped because of the eruption of Mount Pelée in 1902. Archaeological research has traditionally focused on the wrecks from this tragic event, but there is also real potential for research into more ancient sites.*

Introduction

Saint-Pierre is famous worldwide for the 8th of May and the 30th of August 1902 volcanic eruptions and their consequences: a town totally wasted and the death of around 28,000 people. Saint-Pierre is also famous for being one of the main ports and towns of the Lesser Antilles during the French colonial period. The town was the economic hub of the French West Indies during the 17th, 18th, and 19th centuries. Saint-Pierre is located along the North West coast of Martinique on the Caribbean Sea. Its flourishing situation since the colonization in 1635 until the 1902 Mount Pelée eruption gave the town the nickname of Lesser Antilles Little Paris.

Despite this, research into the history, archaeology, nor underwater archaeology is as developed as its great potential warrants. The bay has been frequented since the 17th century by ships coming from all over the Atlantic and the Caribbean. The first publication produced by Veuve in 1999 emphasized the lack of research into both underwater and terrestrial archaeology. Since Veuve's publication, terrestrial archaeology in Saint-Pierre has developed significantly, primarily due to development-led projects, however, the development of underwater archaeology has lagged behind.

This paper focuses on underwater archaeological research conducted in Saint-Pierre since the late 1970's dealing with shipwreck site identification and a study of port dump (Figure 1). It is part of an overview dealing with maritime archaeology in the French West Indies (Guadeloupe and Martinique) that is to be published in a broader article (Guibert et al. [2019]).

Actors

The pioneers who first paid attention to the underwater heritage in Saint-Pierre were divers and fishermen. Among them, Michel Météry first focused on the 1902 shipwrecks in the 1970's (Météry 2002). In the 1990's

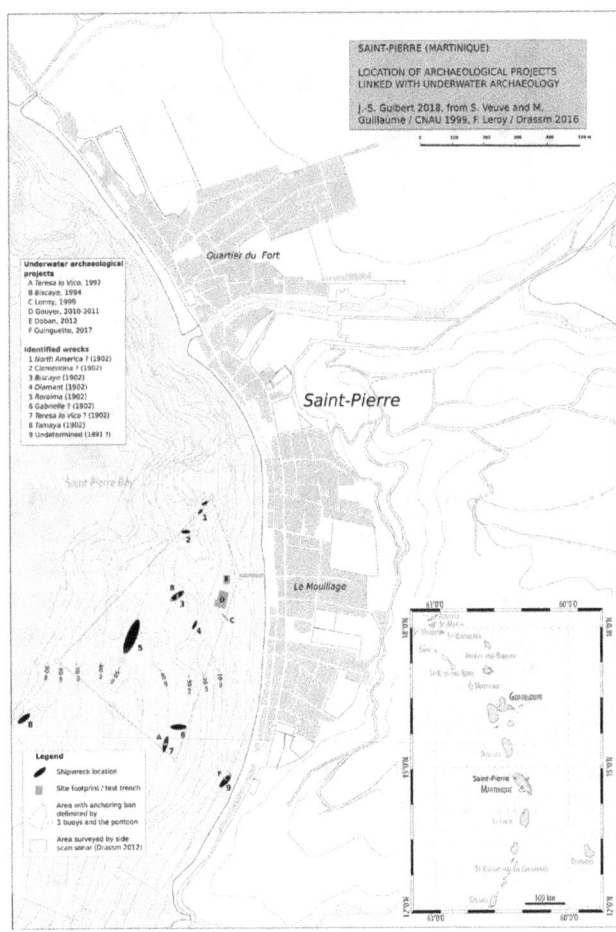

Figure 1: Map showing location of underwater sites and projects in Saint-Pierre (Map by author, 2017.)

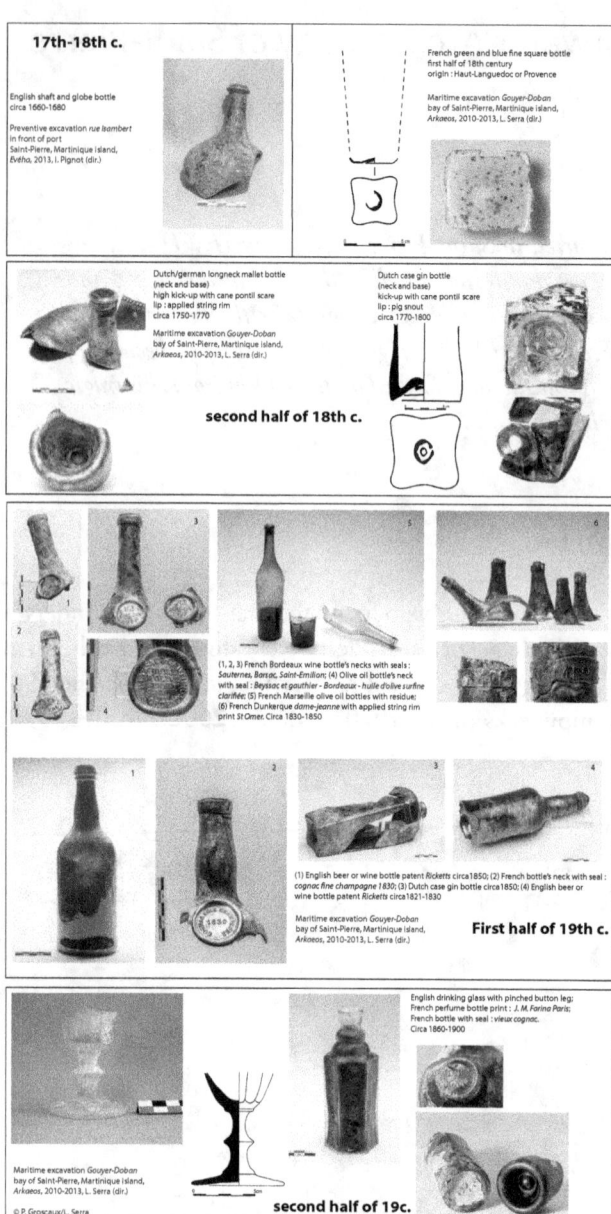

Figure 2: Glass artifacts found in the Doban site (Photos by Philippe Groscaux, 2012.)

a non-profit organization called Groupe de Recherche en Archéologie Navale (GRAN) led by Marc Guillaume and Max Guérout set up several projects in Martinique, particularly in Saint-Pierre. Since this period collaborative projects between non-profit organizations and Universities have included a partnership between Aix-en-Provence University and Arkaeos in 2010-2012, and the French West Indies University and L'Asso-Mer in 2017. In 2012 a side scan sonar survey was undertaken by Department des recherches archéologiques subaquatiques et sous-marines (DRASSM) a division of the French Ministry of Culture.

Port Dump Sites

Research focused on port dump sites first occurred in 1999 after hurricane Lenny permitted the discovery of a site originally thought to be shipwreck due to a large amount of ceramics from the late 19th century. The site was reinvestigated in the 2010's (Serra et al. 2010, 2012). At this time, two distinct dumping areas were identified: Gouyer and Doban sites. It was determined that there was not a shipwreck, but instead a large dump site associated with part of a Saint-Pierre's anchorage for merchant ships.

The Doban Site

Five test pits were excavated to a depth of 1.80 m, which was the maximum depth divers could safely trench. They revealed the existence of coherent stratigraphic units sealed by several ballast layers. The first layer contained material that could belong to a ship cargo; mainly bricks, ceramics, and glass coming from the same production centers as well as organic material. Recovered artifacts date this layer between 1840 and 1870. The second layer was composed of stone ballast and sand. Although few artifacts were recovered, this strata was dated from 1820 to 1830 because of glass sherds found within this layer. The third layer dates to the end of the 18th century and is well preserved containing a diverse range of material culture resulting from transatlantic trade (Figure 2) (Serra et al. 2012).

The Erosion Phenomenon in Saint-Pierre Bay through the Doban Site

One of the other topics that interests the archaeologists is the complex site formation processes within the Bay. Deposits are 1.80 meters thick, accumulated in less than 150 years. Due to the bay topography and lack of coral reef, the team hypothesized that the dominant site formation processes were underwater erosion due to swell and cyclonic waves (Serra et al. 2012). Layers of successive ballast discharge and artifact loss are both the result of more than 120 years of human activity in this area as well as natural erosion.

Material Culture from Port Dump Doban Site

A large quantity of objects dating mainly from the 19th century but also from the 18th century (mainly ceramics and glass) were linked to the economic exchanges and daily life of Saint-Pierre. Raw materials are bricks and tiles. Ceramics used as pots and pans come from Vallauris and Aubagne-Saint-Zacharie in the South of France. Glass was used as wine and beer bottles, oil, liqueurs, and perfumes (Figure 2). Other products such as cod have been found in large quantities. Some of these artifacts can be dated accurately, due to the presence of in situ diagnostics such as Customs seals or coins (Serra et al. 2012). This study of material culture reveals a concentration of artifacts related to a merchant ship anchorage as well as Place Bertin, heart of Saint-Pierre's economic activities, and more generally to the consumption of one of the main ports and cities of Martinique.

Archaeology of Shipwrecks in Saint-Pierre Bay

The interest in underwater archaeological research in Saint-Pierre begun in the 1970's with diving development in Martinique. The first interest in shipwrecks in Saint-Pierre was associated with the 1902 wrecks that sunk during the Mount Pelée eruption. The discovery of wrecks and the involvement of pioneers such as Michel Métery, attracted archaeologist to Saint-Pierre Bay in the 1990's. Max Guérout and Marc Guillaume conducted magnetometer surveys and dived on the resulting anomalies in order to precisely locate the 1902 wrecks and delineate other sites. Archaeological research has been undertaken in 1992 and 1993 in order to protect the shipwreck sites (Guillaume et al. 1994). Those researches focused first on site identification followed by field investigations and archival research in order to document the 1902 shipwrecks. One can see that research has been motivated by sites identification and preservation.

The State of Research on 1902 Shipwrecks

A publication was produced in 1999 detailing the result of a decade of research on Saint-Pierre's shipwrecks (Guillaume 1999). Wrecks identified from this work include: the *Biscaye*, a three-masted, 159 ton vessel built in the Basque region of Spain in 1878; the *Diamant*, a local steamer linking Saint-Pierre and Fort-de-France; the *Roraima*, a 2,700 ton, 110 m long propeller ship with a 6 m draft built by Aitken & Maud shipyard of Glasgow for the Quebec Steamship Company in 1883; and the *Tamaya*, a 495 ton Cape Horner, built in 1862 and identified thanks to the recovery of the bell in 1985. Four other wooden built sailing ships are referenced that have not been conclusively identified: *Teresa Lo Vico*, *North America*, *Clementina*, and *Gabrielle* (Guillaume 1999). St. Pierre Bay is a unique ship cemetery in the West Indies containing a concentration of ships built from the 1860's to 1880's representing maritime activity at the end of the 19th century during the second period of globalization.

The Biscaye Site

Additional research was initiated on *Biscaye* in 1994. The wreck is 29 m deep at bow, 39 m at stern and measures 31 meters long. Three trench tests have been undertaken: the central trench test gave good results, several barrels have been excavated filled with cod fishes. Naval construction was also studied. Three elements contributed to the identification of the site as *Biscaye*: the size of the ship; the sheathing type; and the cod fish cargo All those elements corresponded to the archival data (Guillaume et al. 1994). The ship was built in Bilbao, Spain in 1878 and francized in 1895 by a merchant from Bayonne. He left France in 1902 to Saint-Pierre and Miquelon to load cod fish in order to bring it to Martinique where the ship was finally lost in Mount Pelée's eruption.

The 2013 DRASSM Survey

In 2013, a new archaeological survey was undertaken by DRASSM of the French Ministry of Culture in order to pinpoint the sites of shipwrecks and analyze anomalies in the bay (Leroy 2016). The team used a side scan sonar and was able to check much of the area. The survey was concentrated in water depths from four to 30 m, but other deeper areas were investigated in the vicinity of the deepest known site: the *Tamaya* at 85 meters. The result is a main document mapping most of the bay and showing the main anomalies and targets. The wrecks of 1902 are precisely located and can be visualized (orientation of the ships, shape of the wrecks, and dispersion of the remains). The survey provided more than 50 targets to be tested by diving. These are assumed to be anchors, other structures, or unknown wrecks. As a result of the broader attention payed to underwater heritage in 2012, the main concentration of ship remains was protected from ship moorings and anchors by buoys indicating the wreckages area (Mornet et al. 2012).

The Guinguette Wreck Site

Another recent line of research has been undertaken in Saint-Pierre in order to work on earlier shipwreck sites. A project took place on a shipwreck in the area of the beach called the Guinguette (Guibert et al. 2018). The site was discovered in 2009 in a sublittoral location and could not be reached by side scan sonar (Figure 3). The portion closest to shore, in 4 to 5 meters of water, was investigated by archaeological diving methods. Two trench tests have been conducted. The first was at what is supposed to be the stern, the second at the central part of the ship. A third test was supposed to be conducted at the bow of the ship, but this has been delayed due to hurricane Maria.

The potential at this site is great in spite of the limited field work. Material culture and hull structures are quiet well preserved in 4 to 5 meters of water. In trench Test 1 a number of artifacts are linked to personal items (thimble, buttons, a locker, syringe element, beads) and in the trench Test 2 we discovered what can be interpreted as collapsed upper deck structure (Figure 4). In between the upper and lower deck planking, several areas contained artifacts in very good state of preservation including, rope, pulley and dead eyes (Figure 4). These objects look like they were stored in an upper deck and stuck during its collapse as a result of post-depositional site formation process. The artifacts are dated from the end of the 19th century but many of the ceramics and glass sampled within the ballast were worn out. In spite of their French origin these artifacts may not be relevant to identifying the ship's origin. One of the brass gudgeon in trench Test 2 has a mark "Birmingham" suggesting an English construction. Analysis of fauna and dendrochronology are underway to provide additional data.

In order to identify additional candidates for the Guinguette beach wreck, archival research was conducted around four hurricanes that occurred at the end of the 19th century. Archives indicate five ships that were lost in the area of the south anchorage as a result of a hurricane on the 9th of September, 1883. In French ships anchorage they are listed as: *P.-A.-J.* French three-masts, captain Metaireau loaded for Bordeaux ; *Tapageur*, Captain Gombeaud coming from Bordeaux loaded ; *Bayardère*, Captain Letestu being loaded for Le Havre; *Mysore*, Captain Mahé loaded for Le Havre; *Lemnos*, Captain Lampoignard loaded for Bordeaux ; *Misti*, Captain Landgrain coming from Guadeloupe loaded with rice (Journal officiel de la Martinique 7/9/1883). Seven ships were lost in the Saint-Pierre area due to the hurricane on the 18th of August, 1891. These reportedly include at Grosse Roche: French ship *Persévérant*, French schooner

Figure 3: Map of Guinguette site (Map by Émilie Lagahé, 2017.)

Figure 4: Diver recording structures in Trench test 2, highlighting rigging, pulley, dead eyes, and paunch matting (Photo by Claude Michaud, 2017.)

Mouette; at anchorage: French ship *H.-L.*, French ship *Alphonsine-Zélie*, Italian ship *Rosanna*, French schooner *Émilie-L.*, and English boat *Golimangne* (Journal officiel de la Martinique 22/8/1891). One of those could be the remains of the Guinguette beach wreck. Initial results indicate that the Guinguette beach wreck was a large wooden vessel, possibly three-masted and at least 40 meters in length. It may have wrecked as a result of the 1883 or 1891 hurricanes which had a large impact in Martinique.

Conclusion

The site of Saint-Pierre's bay is an interesting site in order to develop underwater archaeology programs and heritage management in the Lesser Antilles. Areas of potential future research include: systematic coring to study the distribution and chronology of port deposits and possibly to find other wrecks; surveys with specialized equipment to search for older wrecks; site identification with test trenches; and 3D modelling of the 1902 wrecks utilizing photogrammetry methods.

To date, archaeological projects in the region have mainly dealt with the end of the 19th century or the 1902 sites. In spite of this, there is the potential for more ancient sites due to the history of the city and the climatic hazards that occurred in Saint-Pierre since the period of colonization. Archival research indicates that hurricanes and flooding impacted Saint-Pierre and its port during the 18th and 19th centuries. For example, the great hurricane of 1766 and hurricane of 1822 both caused substantial damages and resulted in a number of shipwrecks. It remains to be seen whether these events left wrecks in Saint-Pierre's harbor and what the dynamics of the formation of these sites were.

References

ARCHIVES DE LA COLLECTIVITÉ TERRITORIALE DE MARTINIQUE [CTM]
1891   In *Journal Officiel de la Martinique* 1883, 1891.

GUIBERT, JEAN-SÉBASTIEN (ET AL)
2018   Rapport de sondage archéologique, Épave de la Guinguette, Saint-Pierre, Martinique, AIHP-GEODE / L'ASSO-MER, Schoelcher, France.

GUIBERT, JEAN-SÉBASTIEN (ET AL)
2019   Overview of Research in Maritime Archaeology of the Colonial Period (17th-19th centuries) in the French Antilles (Guadeloupe and Martinique). In *International Journal of Nautical Archaeology*.

GUILLAUME, MARC, MAX GUÉROUT, AND EVELYNE JAY
1994   *Travaux préparatoires à la constitution de dossiers de protection des épaves de navires coulés en Baie de Saint-pierre lors de l'éruption de la Montagne pelée en 1902*, Schoelcher, France.

GUILLAUME, MARC
1999   Saint-Pierre et la mer. In *Saint-Pierre de la Martinique*, Serge Veuve, Document d'évaluation du patrimoine archéologique des villes de France, pp. 145-150, Paris, France.

LEROY, FRÉDÉRIC
2016   Prospection en rade de Saint-Pierre. In *Bilan Scientifique du Drassm*, pp. 128-129 Ministère de la culture, Paris France.

MÉTÉRY, MICHEL 2002
2002   *Tamaya Les épaves de Saint-Pierre*, Institut Océanographique. Paris, France.

MORNET, OLIVIER, SYLVIE GUENOT-REBIÈRE, LIONEL HOUILLIER, AND HERVÉ BARREDA
2012   *Balisage de protection des épaves historiques de la baie de Saint-Pierre de la Martinique*. Fort-de-France, France.

SERRA, LAURENCE, HENRI AMOURIC, AND LUCY VALLAURI
2010   Rade de Saint-Pierre Site Gouyer et épave Doban, Aix-en-Provence, France.

SERRA, LAURENCE, YVES BILLAUD, GAËLLE DIEULEFET, AND FABRICE LAURENT
2012   *Zone de dépotoir portuaire de la Rade de Saint-Pierre Secteur Doban 1780-1860*, Aix-en-Provence, France.

VEUVE, SERGE
1999   *Saint-Pierre de la Martinique*, Document d'évaluation du patrimoine archéologique des villes de France. Paris, France.

• • • • • • • • • • • • • • • •

Jean-Sébastien Guibert
AIHP-GÉODE EA 929 Université des Antilles
UFR Lettres et Sciences Humaines
Campus de Schoelcher

Max Guérout
Groupe de recherche en archeologie navale (GRAN)
Laboratoire d'histoire et d'archéologie maritime (FED 4124 : Sorbonne Université – Musée de la Marine)
4 rue Antoine Condorcet – 34500 – Béziers

Laurence Serra
LA3M Université Aix-Marseille CNRS UMR 7298
5 rue du chateau de l'Horloge 13100 Aix-en-Provence

Parallels in History: Shipwreck Salvage and Exploitation of Archaeological Resources in Florida and Aruba

Melissa R. Price

Beginning in the 1950s, Florida witnessed a fascinating and tumultuous series of events concerning salvage of historic shipwrecks. Before the Abandoned Shipwreck Act, many wrecks in Florida were actively salvaged with little regard for their archaeological value. Currently, Aruba is experiencing similar salvage activity coupled with a lack of comprehensive legislation that protects terrestrial and submerged archaeological sites. This paper draws parallels between mid-20th century Florida and present-day Aruba regarding legal frameworks that protect cultural resources. It examines Florida's legislative accomplishments and presents a potential model for the future of Aruba's cultural resources laws pertaining to submerged and terrestrial sites.

Florida

It could be argued that underwater archaeology in Florida came out of early salvage of historic shipwrecks, which gained ground in the 1920s (Roger Smith 2014, pers. comm.). Art McKee, known as the father of modern treasure diving, worked as a salvage diver off the Florida Keys and had a hand in popularizing treasure hunting. As diving and scuba technology evolved, many historic wrecks were discovered. With Florida's rich history and countless stories of ships lost on shallow reefs, something distinctive to Florida began: a frenzied search for treasure. With a few rare yet spectacular finds, many people were eager to take to the waters themselves and search for their own "booty."

The State of Florida realized regulation of salvage activities was needed, especially since these ships were historic in nature, and declared that archaeological sites and artifacts located in state waters were property of the state (Florida Bureau of Archaeological Research, Division of Historical Resources [BAR, DHR] 1994). Sites could not be salvaged without proper permission in the form of leases, under which salvage companies recorded their finds and provided the state with a percentage of artifacts for public display. As a result of accelerated salvage activities in the 50s, the state hired its first underwater archaeologist in 1964 (Murphy 1990:6). The underwater archaeologist operated as a field agent and oversaw salvage activities to ensure companies complied with contracts, which replaced leases. This became known as the Exploration and Salvage Program and was the state's attempt to control the massive consumption of archaeological resources taking place offshore (Roger Smith 2014, pers. comm).

With more restraints placed on the salvage community and pushback from the state, treasure salvors became vocal in their fight for what they believed were their shipwrecks. As the state asserted title to historic shipwrecks in its waters, treasure salvors used two laws to argue that what they were doing was not only legal, but their right. The first, salvage law, is a "service voluntarily rendered in relieving property from an impending peril at sea or other navigable waters by those under no legal obligation to do so" (Wilder 2000:92). Originally, it existed as an incentive for salvors to rescue lost cargo and return it to the original owner for a reward (Wilder 2000:93–94). This reward was determined by the risk the salvor took in rescuing the cargo. Salvage law allowed a salvor to claim rights to a reward for perilous services from the owner of the lost property. The salvor never held rights to the actual property. The second law is known colloquially as finders keepers, or the law of finds. It differs from salvage law in that the finder received title to property (i.e. a vessel) because it was abandoned. To claim title, the finder had to first prove the property was abandoned. In order for a vessel to be considered abandoned, it had to be left or deserted intentionally by those who originally owned or were in charge of it, without the hope of recovering or returning to it (Wilder 2000:94). Under law of finds, however, if a wreck was embedded in sand or other sediments, it belonged to the owner of the land in which it was embedded. Furthermore, if a vessel was lost at sea, it was not necessarily abandoned.

Salvage law and the law of finds fall under admiralty law, or laws that govern maritime matters. In the United States (U.S.), admiralty law falls under the jurisdiction of the federal courts (Bederman 1998:103). The Supreme Court set forth the principles of maritime salvage in 1869 (Wilder 2000:92), and under the Submerged Lands Act, the power to regulate these activities rests with Congress (Bederman 1998:105). As Florida's state government attempted to curb salvage activities on historic shipwrecks, treasure salvors appealed to the Federal Government and claimed title to shipwrecks, winning in many cases. This was called an "admiralty arrest," in which the treasure salvor arrested title to a shipwreck. Unfortunately, the Federal Government could override the state's claim of title to a shipwreck (Elia 2000:48).

Historically, artifacts located underwater had fewer protections than those on land. With salvage law and law of finds used by treasure hunters to exploit historic shipwrecks, Florida and other states needed more comprehensive legislation to protect submerged resources, especially after issues with Federal admiralty arrests (Roger Smith 2014, pers. comm). The imperfect answer was the Abandoned Shipwreck Act of 1987 (ASA), passed by Congress and enacted into law in 1988 (Elia 2000:46–47). It stated that title to an abandoned shipwreck rested with the U.S. for the following three categories of abandoned shipwrecks: those embedded in a State's submerged lands; those embedded in coralline formations protected by a State on its submerged lands; and those located on a State's submerged lands and included in or determined eligible for inclusion in the National Register of Historic Places. The ASA granted states legal title to shipwrecks within their territorial waters, with the goal of ending the admiralty jurisdiction of these sites and the issue of treasure salvors seeking to override the state's authority. Existing admiralty arrests were allowed to continue (Mary Glowacki 2014, pers. comm). Treasure hunters did not stop after the ASA: before the act, treasure hunters argued they owned the wrecks under finders keepers. Afterwards, they argued the shipwrecks were in marine peril and therefore should be salvaged under salvage law (Bederman 1998:104–106). Archaeologists argued that salvage law should not apply to historic shipwrecks because the wrecks were not in marine peril. They argued that traditional maritime law failed to consider the historical significance of shipwrecks found at sea. Florida's treasure hunting past caused the loss of valuable archaeological data. Most endeavors were not scientific archaeological expeditions, did not have appropriate research designs, and did not follow professional archaeological standards and guidelines (Figure 1) (Murphy 1990:2–3). They also did not maintain public minded goals of preserving shared cultural history. In the 1970s, during rampant salvage of historic shipwrecks, an underwater archaeologist in Florida at the time noted that many wrecks were completely destroyed as a result of these activities, with little public benefit since the ships were not excavated in a scientific manner (Cockrell 1977). Furthermore, the ASA was not a perfect solution: it only protects wrecks on a state's lands; beyond those boundaries, wrecks are free-for-all (Elia 2000:46). It also only protects shipwrecks, not other submerged archaeological resources.

Today, Chapter 267, *Florida Statutes*, governs archaeological resources in Florida. The Exploration and Salvage Program is now the Exploration and Recovery Program and has gone through many changes (Florida Department of State 2009). Permits are required in order to conduct surveys or excavations on state submerged lands. 1A-31 permits govern salvage activities and the state must be provided with a research design, daily logs, reports, and raw data. With the conclusion of each field season, the state claims title to a portion of the artifacts for curation and research purposes. Currently, there are active permits on Florida's east coast, as well as

Figure 1: 1950s/60s treasure hunter excavations on historic shipwreck (Photo by Peter Stackpole, Courtesy of State Archives of Florida, Florida Memory).

legacy admiralty arrests. Though many companies comply with 1A-31 requirements, there are still issues with noncompliance and lack of professional standards, especially concerning reports, photographs, and raw data. The 1A-31 program is in stark contrast to the 1A-32 program, which governs professional archaeological surveys. Permits are awarded to universities and other professional archaeological entities. 1A-32 requirements are stricter; archaeologists must provide the state with a research design and credentials, and eventually provide all data, forms, reports, and artifacts to the state. No artifacts are kept personally by the researcher; they are held in the public trust. The 1A-32 program is research based, for the public benefit, and archaeologists must follow a strict set of ethics and standards.

Florida continues to move forward to combat misconceptions concerning underwater archaeology by focusing on education and outreach. The Bureau of Archaeological Research (BAR) hosts archaeology days, provides public talks around the state, and maintains websites that discuss the importance of protecting archaeological sites. BAR coordinates with citizen scientist groups, such as the Florida Public Archaeology Network, to conduct annual training seminars for divers who want to learn about, record, and protect sites. BAR currently has five underwater archaeologists who serve the state and take a proactive approach to the management and protection of Florida's submerged cultural heritage. From the 1950s onwards, Florida has come a long way concerning underwater archaeological resources.

Aruba

Aruba, an island in the Caribbean, is experiencing similar issues concerning its cultural heritage. Located 30 kilometers (km) (18 miles) north of Venezuela's Paraguanà Peninsula and measuring 10 km (6 miles) wide and 31 km (20 miles) long, the geography consists of limestone overlain by igneous rock and fringed with coral reefs (Dijkhoff and Linville 2004:11–14). Aruba has a desert environment with cacti, shrubs, and trees, and is fairly low in elevation. An island roughly the size of Washington D.C., its current population is around 105,000. Aruba became a self-governing part of the Kingdom of the Netherlands in 1986. Historically, Aruba's economy included horse breeding, aloe farming, phosphate mining, and most importantly, oil refinery beginning in the 1920s, but today relies primarily on the tourism industry.

As of 2004, there were 171 documented archaeological sites in Aruba (Dijkhoff and Linville 2004:50); at least 33 were Archaic and dated between 2500 B.C. and A.D.1000 (Kelly and Hoffman in press:5). The estimated date of arrival for Aruba's first inhabitants is around 4500 years ago (Kelly and Hoffman in press:3). Humans most likely reached the island in canoes in the area now known as Spaans Lagoen, an inland bay with a 1.5 km channel traversing into Aruba's mainland and providing a gateway for early inhabitants to access inland resources (Figure 2). This is supported by the oldest radiocarbon dates, obtained from shell middens along the channel and dating to 3440±30 BP and 3450±30 BP (Kelly and Hoffman in press:10–13). Burials and habitation areas are distributed around the island, including at Malmok (2000±150 and 1940±140 BP), Arashi (2580±30 BP), Sero Colorado (1930±30 BP), and Canashito (1960±95 BP). Rock art consisting of red, white, and brown geometrical figures is documented at 22 sites around the island, though that number was once higher; a pigment sample from the rock art dated to A.D. 1000 (Kelly 2009:175–176; Dijkhoff and Linville 2004:48).

Aruba's contact period began in the early 1500s, and remnants of 1700s Dutch and Spanish ships are purported to exist offshore (Dijkhoff and Linville 2004:37). Historic anchors have been located by avocational divers, and other evidence of this period is likely to exist elsewhere on the island (Jensen 2004). Other historic period (1515-1880) sites include the Bushiribana gold mill ruins, used during Aruba's brief gold rush that began in 1824, as well as remnants of phosphate mining from 1879 to 1914 in Sero Colorado. The oil refinery, used especially between 1929 and 1985 and important

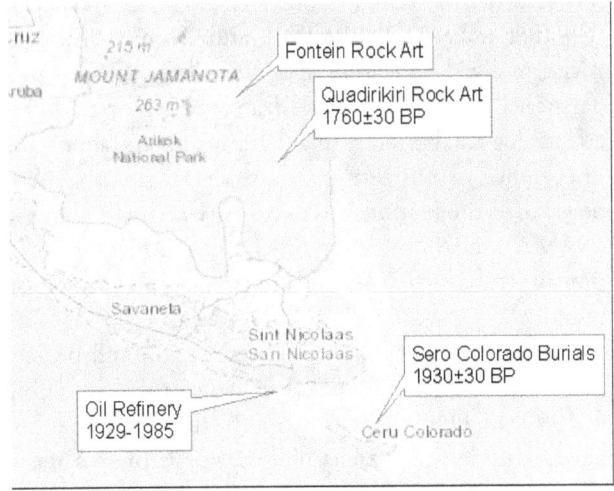

Figure 2: Aruba with selected site distribution (Melissa R. Price, 2018).

during WWII, is located northwest of Sero Colorado. The submerged archaeological record is equally intriguing, with ten identified shipwrecks dating from the 1770s to 1943 (Dijkhoff et al 2012:41). There is potential for more wrecks to exist, especially in deeper waters that are more difficult to access. The potential for submerged prehistoric sites is also great, especially in Spaans Lagoen, where archaic sites on shore likely continue into the water.

Interest in Aruba's archaeological record began in the late 1800s, during which avocationals and amateurs collected surface materials and conducted limited excavations (Dijkhoff and Linville 2004:37–51). In the 1920s, archaeology was characterized by accidental finds, which ultimately led to important steps to establish an archaeological practice on the island. The field of archaeology grew in the 1960s and received institutional support, with publications in professional outlets becoming more frequent. From 1970 to 1987, the Lesser Antilles received funding from the Netherlands Antilles government for a permanently stationed archaeologist in the area, bringing a period of sustained investigations on Aruba and the founding of the Archaeological Museum Aruba (AMA) in 1981. AMA housed archaeological materials and facilitated investigation and conservation of Aruba's cultural heritage (Dijkhoff and Linville 2004:44,50–51). Between 1988 and 1998, a collective of professionals, students, and specialized researchers from diverse backgrounds contributed to the growth and long-term management of Aruban archaeology.

In 1999, Raymundo Dijkhoff, a native Aruban trained in the professional methods and theory of archaeology, became head of the scientific department of AMA. He was joined in 2003 by another Aruban, Harold Kelly, the other archaeologist for the island. Around this time, AMA received education specialists and various other personnel who strive to investigate and preserve Aruba's archaeological heritage, and educate others about the importance of protecting archaeological sites. AMA is now called the National Archaeological Museum Aruba (NAMA) and is the only official government institution in Aruba that manages and protects archaeological resources.

Attention was given to the preservation and protection of submerged cultural heritage in Aruba beginning in 1999 (Dijkhoff 2011). Currently, the island does not have an underwater archaeologist, nor is there a maritime museum or infrastructure to manage submerged cultural resources. Coupled with this, NAMA was justifiably preoccupied with establishing an archaeological program between 1970 and 1998. Since 1999, however, NAMA spearheaded an initiative to manage and protect all archaeological resources, including those underwater. The museum maintains a few artifacts that originated from submerged sites; these were collected by amateurs and include historic bottles and two Spanish unglazed jars. There are also private collections that were created by those who recovered artifacts as they dove, though these have not been investigated in detail, and no comprehensive list of objects or their conditions exists.

In 2009, a disconcerting situation arose regarding submerged cultural heritage in Aruba (Dijkhoff 2011). A group known as the *SS Oranjestad* Memorial Committee began to remove propellers, anchors, and artifacts under the guise of erecting the objects as monuments that attested to the WWII history of the island (Jensen 2009). The *SS Oranjestad* was an oil tanker lost in 1942 after it was torpedoed by a German U-boat (Figure 3). It was from this very ship that the group of divers removed its first object: the propeller. NAMA attempted to halt these actions but was met with resistance and little legislative support (Dijkhoff 2011). NAMA discovered the Coast Guard helped the committee remove the propeller and supplied the permit allowing disturbance of the site. NAMA advised the Coast Guard permit division of the gravity of the situation, and the director at the time agreed to halt any future permits for removal of archaeological objects. Regardless, the committee removed anchors from other sites. The committee members were lauded as heroes, though they removed objects without regard for current professional archaeological standards and conservation practices, much like in Florida in the

Figure 3: *SS Oranjestad* in 1927 (HOYFM.HW.2379, © National Museum NI, Collection Harland & Wolff, Ulster Folk & Transport Museum).

1950s and 1960s. The media and the governor were in support of the committee's actions, further contributing to misconceptions concerning removal of submerged archaeological resources (Sweetnam 2009). This situation echoes the popularization of treasure hunting in Florida and hints at future of salvage activities in Aruba if appropriate action is not taken.

Submerged sites are not the only ones in danger. Terrestrial sites are at risk due to development and, to a lesser extent, looting. For example, investigations into a burial of a shipwrecked individuals that dated to 1886 revealed a number of bones were scattered or missing, suggesting looters likely searched for associated grave goods (Dijkhoff et al. 2012:25,35–39). Many Archaic sites included urn burials; pot hunting is a threat to such sites (Dijkhoff and Linville 2004:42). In terms of development, mining and bulldozing caused drastic impacts to archaeological sites in Aruba; the Aruba Phosphate Company disturbed Archaic burials in Sero Colorado, some of which contained associated turtle carapace grave goods (Figure 4) (Dijkhoff and Linville 2004:40; Harold Kelly 2017, pers. comm). Intact burials were located by archaeologists, and it is likely that others exist in the area. Intensive urbanization of San Nicolas from the 1920s onward created an archaeologically "empty" area; there is no knowing what sites were devastated during this time period (Harold Kelly 2017, pers. comm.). Modern development threatens archaic sites in Malmok, and as recently as spring 2017, construction of a bridge over Spaans Lagoen excavated through an Archaic midden on the western bank of the channel. Unfortunately, there are no requirements to conduct archaeological surveys prior to construction, nor must an archaeologist be contacted if a site is located.

Figure 4: Harold Kelly points to a disturbed burial in Sero, Colorado (Photo by Melissa R. Price, May 2017).

The island contains a fascinating archaeological record, and it is important to establish adequate protections to preserve its cultural heritage. Currently, however, legislation is lacking and Aruba is experiencing issues similar to Florida in the 1950s and 1960s. The only legislation to protect archaeological sites is the Monument Ordinance of Aruba, implemented in 1966, which states that those monuments 50 years or older with aesthetic, scientific, historic, or folkloric significance are protected and not to be disturbed or excavated without permission (Dijkhoff 2011). Under the ordinance, a permit must be acquired from the government prior to excavation or research of monuments. The protections offered by the Monuments Ordinance are marginal and limited. For example, a monument must first be established as "protected" before the Ordinance can be applied to safeguard sites or artifacts from destruction and before violators can be prosecuted for disturbing a site. Archaeologists attempted to stretch the Ordinance to shipwrecks and prehistoric sites, but the language hindered their inclusion. Under the Ordinance, terrestrial and submerged sites and artifacts have no inherent legal protection; it is a reactive rather than proactive ordinance. Sites must first be nominated, the Council must evaluate the nominations and if in agreement, propose them to the Minister of Culture, who then makes a decision. Presently, there are few protected monuments on the island, all of which are more recent and architectural in nature.

Aruban archaeologists attempted to encourage the Department of Legislation and Juridical Affairs (DWJZ) to consider implementing legislation that prohibits removal of archaeological objects from Aruba's territorial seas, though these efforts have been unsuccessful so far (Dijkhoff 2011). There have also been efforts to establish a marine park in Aruba to protect submerged sites in territorial waters and coastal sites located up to 50 meters inland. This would be an immense stride forward and protect sites most at risk of disturbance. Archaeologists also strived to implement principles set forth in the Valletta Treaty, formally known as the European Convention on the Protection of the Archaeological Heritage and also known as the Malta Convention (Kwast 2015:7). The purpose of the 1992 treaty was to protect terrestrial and submerged European archaeological heritage, including on those Caribbean islands that are part of European territory or follow European government, like Aruba. Aruba's ratification of the Malta Convention would provide another layer of protection and preservation of archaeological resources.

Aruban archaeologists continue to move forward to protect their cultural heritage by working nationally and internationally to promote the research and protection of their cultural heritage. Their long-term goals include establishing a formal archaeological department that extends beyond NAMA, implementing a management strategy for all of the island's archaeological resources, and pressuring the DWJZ to create legislation to protect archaeological sites. Outreach and education concerning the importance of preserving archaeological sites continues, as well as a presence at professional conferences and meetings. Stakeholders continue to pressure the Netherlands government to ratify the UNESCO Convention on the Protection of the Underwater Cultural Heritage, which would allow the island to ratify it as well. Dijkhoff and Kelly strive to further their training and education to be able to survey, study, and manage submerged cultural resources.

Conclusion

While Aruba is currently experiencing similar challenges to those in Florida during the height of treasure hunting, the island can learn from Florida's mistakes. Florida provides a warning to the island of what could happen if unchecked salvage or disregard of cultural heritage continues. As this article demonstrated, underwater archaeology and protective legislation in Florida has come a long way since the 1950s, though there is still room for improvement. Even today, the state faces repercussions of the treasure hunting frenzy: admiralty arrests of historic shipwrecks are still attempted. Legislation for protection is often a slow process, but Florida's accomplishments in this realm present a potential model for the future of Aruba's cultural resources laws pertaining to submerged and terrestrial sites.

Acknowledgments

My deepest gratitude goes to Aruban archaeologists Raymundo A.C.F. Dijkhoff and Harold Kelly for taking time out of their busy schedules in May 2017 to show me their fascinating archaeological sites on the island. Furthermore, this paper would not have been possible without their input and expertise, and for that, I am extremely grateful.

References

BEDERMAN, DAVID J.
1998 Historic Salvage and the Law of the Sea. In *Inter-American Law Review* 30(1):99–129.

COCKRELL, W.A.
1977 Comments presented at Conference on Florida Historic Shipwreck Archaeology Florida Atlantic University

DIJKHOFF, RAYMUNDO A.C.F.
2011 *Towards a Sustainable Underwater Cultural Heritage Management in Aruba.* Presentation at the UNESCO Underwater Cultural Heritage congresses, Mexico and Jamaica.

DIJKHOFF, RAYMUNDO A.C.F. (ET AL)
2012 A Sailor's Grave at Boc'i Brik/Puente: Skeletal Remains of a Mariner of the German Brig Hero Lost to the 1886 Hurricane Disaster. In *Ceque: Journal of the National Archaeological Museums Aruba* issue no. 2.

DIJKHOFF, RAYMUNDO A.C.F. AND MARLENE S. LINVILLE
2004 *The Archaeology of Aruba: The Marine Shell Heritage.* Archaeological Museum of Aruba, Oranjestad, Aruba.

ELIA, RICARDO J.
2000 U.S. Protection of Underwater Cultural Heritage Beyond the Territorial Sea: Problems and Prospects. In *The International Journal of Nautical Archaeology* 29(1):43–56.

FLORIDA BUREAU OF ARCHAEOLOGICAL RESEARCH, DIVISION OF HISTORICAL RESOURCES (BAR, DHR)
1994 Draft for Outside Review: Management Plan for Florida's Submerged Cultural Resources. In *Report to State of Florida, Department of Community Affairs*, Tallahassee, in Partial Fulfillment of the Requirements for Florida Coastal Zone Management, from Florida Bureau of Archaeological Research, Tallahassee.

FLORIDA DEPARTMENT OF STATE
2009 Rule Chapter: 1A-31. Florida Administrative Code and Florida Administrative Register. <https://www.flrules.org/gateway/ChapterHome.asp?Chapter=1A-31>. Accessed 4 April 2018.

JENSEN, DAN
2004 Lago Colony & Lago Refinery, Aruba. <lago-colony.com>. Accessed 6 February 2018.

2009 *SS Oranjestad* Propeller. Lago Colony & Lago Refinery, Aruba. <lago-colony.com>. Accessed 6 February 2018.

Kelly, Harold J.
2009 Rock Art of Aruba. In *Rock Art of the Caribbean*, Michele H. Hayward, Lesley-Gail Atkinson, and Michael A. Cinquino, editors, pp. 175–187. University Alabama Press, Tuscaloosa.

Kelly, Harold J. and Corinne L. Hoffman
2018 *The Archaic Age of Aruba: New Evidence on the First Migrations to the Island.*

Kwast, Sonja Maria
2015 *The Malta Convention in the Caribbean.* Master's thesis, Faculty of Archaeology, Leiden University, Leiden, Netherlands.

Murphy, Larry E.
1990 *8SL17: Natural Site-Formation Processes of a Multiple-Component Underwater Site in Florida.* Southwest Cultural Resources Center Professional Papers No. 39, Santa Fe, NM.

National Museums Northern Ireland Picture Library
HOYFM.HW.2379. Collection Harland & Wolff, Ulster Folk & Transport Museum. National Museums Northern Ireland Picture Library, Cultra, Holywood, County Down, Northern Ireland.

Stackpole, Peter
1965 Treasure diver Art McKee recovering a coral encrusted flintlock pistol from the "El Capitana" wreck - Florida Keys, Florida. Between 1955 and 1965. Black & white photonegative, 5 x 4 in. State Archives of Florida, Florida Memory. <https://www.floridamemory.com/items/show/63257>. Accessed 6 February 2018.

Sweetnam, Percy
2009 Recovery of Propeller from *SS Oranjestad*. Aruba Forum. <http://www.aruba.com/forum/f7/recovery-propeller-ss-oranjestad-38461/>. Accessed 6 February 2018.

Wilder, Mark A.
2000 Application of Salvage Law and the Law of Finds to Sunken Shipwreck Discoveries. In *Defense Counsel Journal* 67(1):92–105.

• • • • • • • • • • • • • • • •

Melissa R. Price
Florida Department of State
Division of Historical Resources
Bureau of Archaeological Research
1001 DeSoto Park Dr.
Tallahassee FL 32301

War on the Homefront: A Survey of South Africa's WWII Heritage at Risk

Ian Harrison

Sixteen World War II sites throughout South Africa's Cape Peninsula are surveyed and documented. Several metrics are identified for each, including structural integrity, legal status, and accessibility. By comparing these sites, conclusions regarding long-term survivability are drawn. Structures with active protection are generally healthy, while those with only passive legal protection are found to be as degraded as those with no legal protection. Remote sites suffered disproportionately from natural destructive forces, while more accessible sites suffered greater cultural impacts. Overall, natural weathering is found to be significantly more destructive, necessitating stronger protection for remote, yet legally protected sites.

Introduction

Throughout the Second World War (1939-1945), South Africa's strategic position on the oceanic trade lanes connecting Britain to the resources of its Commonwealth forced the Union of South Africa into a role of paramount importance. With its armed forces majorly downsized during the lean years of the Great Depression, the Union Defense Force (UDF) was largely resigned to a defensive posture in the control of its vulnerable waterways (Zukowski 2016:30). As casualties from Axis submarines and surface raiders mounted, the UDF began establishing a network of Range and Direction Finding (RDF) stations (known in the United States as RADAR), and High-Frequency Direction-Finding (Huff-Duff) installations along the Union's coastlines (Hewitt 1975).

As the war progressed, these RDF and Huff-Duff stations provided an increasingly effective network for detecting and countering hostile activity at sea (Wessels 2000). At the same time, gun batteries, observation posts, and other defensive fortifications were constructed around the nation's principal harbors (Bizley 1998). Following the end of the war however, these installations gradually fell into disrepair. According to archival research, by the 1960s nearly all of these legacy stations and fortifications had been demolished or abandoned. Of those that survived the initial demolition, few have received meaningful protection. The remainder have largely been left to the mercy of destructive forces, both natural and cultural.

Despite this lack of protection, many of these sites still possess sizeable remains from which significant information and historic value may yet be gleaned. Further, they possess unique cultural and national importance due to their operation and control by women and non-white personnel. At the time, women and non-white persons were only allowed to serve in in the armed forces within an unarmed auxiliary capacity (Stott 1998). The classified RDF and Huff-Duff stations were the first facilities to recruit non-Europeans as professional armed soldiers (the Cape Corps), as well as women as ranked staff officers and operators (the Special Signals Services). Further, as white soldiers were being increasingly sent to the northern theatres, native African troops and female artillery specialists were increasingly relied upon to operate the gun batteries and defensive installations at home (Weidman 2004). In this way, these coastal installations previewed political and societal changes decades before they could be seen throughout the rest of South African society. As such, they possess substantial cultural value that should not be so easily left to its inevitable demise.

This project was conducted by the author over six weeks during the summer of 2017, with funding from East Carolina University, under the advisement of Dr. Lynn Harris. Local assistance was provided by the Simon's Town Historical Society, and South African RDF historian Dr. Mike Inggs. Its purpose was to survey and document as many of these sites as possible. Through the creation of a digital record, this WWII heritage can be assessed for current integrity and active site formation processes, as well as preserved in digital form for future generations. Further, by noting differences in structural integrity between sites, it is possible to draw baseline associations between the different natural and cultural factors impacting each location. With an understanding of the factors that have varyingly aided and hampered the survival of each site, broader conclusions can then be drawn regarding best practices for the long-term conservation of these structures.

Methodology

Known sites were located utilizing directions from area residents and GPS locations, while the locations of unknown (or "forgotten") sites were inferred from archival documentation and satellite imagery. The survey area was the extent of the Cape Peninsula, within the Western Cape Province of the Republic of South Africa (formerly the Union of South Africa). Once a site was found, survey teams were sent to ground-truth and document the remaining structures utilizing the Historic American Building Survey (HABS) field methodology, and American Society for Civil Engineers guidelines (ASCE 2000). Documentation was conducted non-invasively with several differing priorities. Foremost, survey teams utilized scaled photographs, video, and architectural drawings to obtain the most accurate and complete coverage of historic structures in their present state. Throughout this process, any type of natural or cultural damage to the appearance or integrity of structures was noted and recorded. Artifacts and surface scatter both within the remaining structures as well as throughout the site generally were also photographed and documented. The layout of each site was mapped, with particular attention given to maintaining the relationship of buildings to one another as well as to pertinent topographic features; GPS points were used to aid in this process.

After recording structures, sites were then surveyed for active site formation processes. Particularly for sites located in remote locations, the area surrounding each structure was searched for signs of wildlife activity. Tracks and spall belonging to various animals could often be identified, giving insight into the types of wildlife in and around the site that may be impacting preservation. Further, sites were ranked for their proximity to centers of modern occupation and overall accessibility as follows: 1. *Within an Inhabited Area*, 2. *Nearby an Inhabited Area (along main roads or otherwise easily accessible)*, and 3. *Distant from Inhabited Areas* (off the beaten path, requires concerted effort to reach). This metric serves as a rough indicator for the frequency of human visits and the general impact of cultural processes. Sites were then ranked into three categories depending on the state of their physical and legal conservation: 1. *Active Restoration or Conservation* (any site undergoing active conservation, protection, or restoration), 2. *Passive Conservation* (sites within national parks or wildlife reserves, but that are not otherwise protected), and 3. *No Protection*. Finally, sites were assigned a measure of overall integrity from 1 (Healthy) to 5 (only foundations remain). Utilizing these metrics, sites can be broadly categorized and compared according to the natural and cultural factors that most meaningfully impact site preservation.

Results

A total of 16 sites were surveyed utilizing this methodology throughout six distinct geographic locations. Due to meaningful topographical and geological features, sites were often concentrated within nearby locations, but were considered separate if they possessed a unique name, and/or were not part of the same contiguous

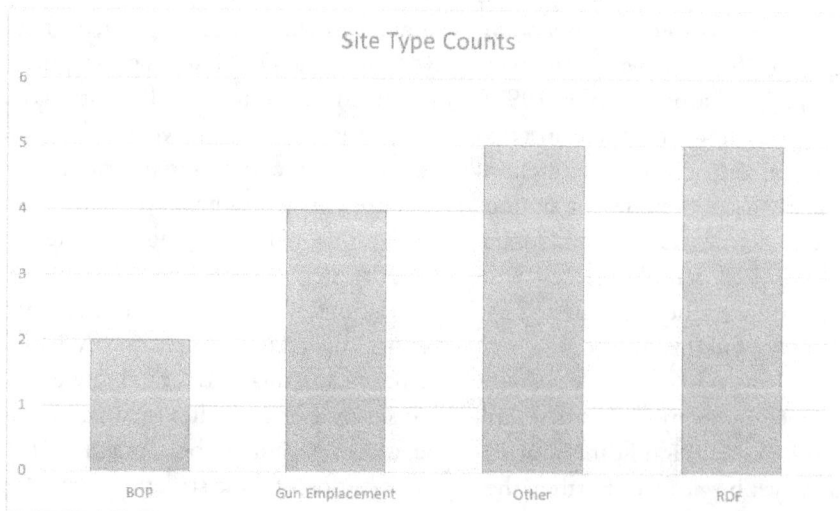

Figure 1: Number of sites surveyed of each type. RDF (Radio Direction Finding), BOP (Battery Observation Post). Other includes all other WWII and non-WWII historic sites. (Image by author, 2017.)

structure complex. Of the 16 sites surveyed, 5 (31%) were RDF stations, 4 (25%) were gun batteries, 2 (12.5%) were Battery Observation Posts (BOP), and 5 (31%) were other historic WWII and non-WWII sites (Figure 1).

While the vast majority of sites surveyed were those utilized throughout the Second World War, several were located on or in close proximity to fortifications constructed during the First World War and earlier colonial periods. In this way the *Other Sites* category includes a crude stonework observation post from the Dutch colonial period, as well as an early limestone kiln used to supply mortar and construction materials. In addition, other miscellaneous WWII sites are included within this category, including a former army relief station that would later become the Simonstown Town Hall, a training school for the Special Signals Services, and an unidentified WWII concrete structural foundation.

Protection Status

Six (37%) of the sites surveyed were considered actively conserved. This category includes any sites undergoing active conservation, protection, or restoration. Nearly every site receiving this type of conservation is a former gun battery. In most cases, these batteries serve as local tourist attractions, or are historic sites located within functioning naval bases. Sites within this category were commonly known about by local residents, easily found through online resources, and often had posted signs describing the history and purpose of the site itself.

Seven (44%) of sites surveyed were considered to be passively protected. (Figure 2) While each of these sites is located within a national park or wildlife reserve of some kind, they do not receive any other form of physical conservation or protection. This category comprises all of the RDF stations surveyed, as well as the unidentified WWII concrete foundation, and historic limestone kiln. Sites within this category were virtually unknown to local residents, including to tour guides and rangers for the parks these sites were located within. Further, records of these sites were either vague or non-existent in online resources. The location of these sites was only possible through the utilization of archival documentation from the war, satellite imagery, and the assistance of a local RDF historian. Only one site had any posted signs to indicate the function or history of the structures, and even this merely referred to them as "WWII foundations" (Cape Point National Park Placard 2017).

The remaining three (19%) sites were located on municipal or private land, and had no protection whatsoever. This category comprises both of the BOPs as well as the historic Dutch observation post. Similar to the passively protected sites, those within this category were unknown to local residents, were non-existent in online resources, and were only located with the assistance of historic documentation and satellite imagery. Not only did none of these sites have any posted signage to indicate their existence or purpose, but in one instance a large sign for a historic quarry neglected to mention the WWII BOP located less than 500ft away.

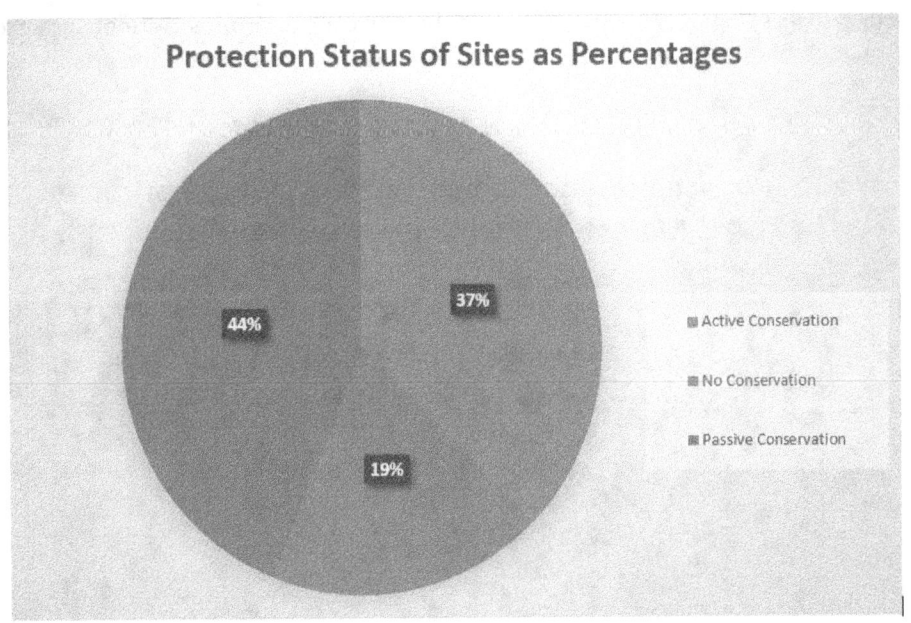

Figure 2: Protection status of sites surveyed as percentages. (Image by author, 2017.)

Accessibility

Four (25%) of the sites surveyed are located within zones of modern occupation. These sites, such as the former army relief station and several of the gun batteries located within active naval bases have become integral parts of daily life, and see the greatest volume of human interaction on a day to day basis. Eight (50%) of the sites surveyed are located near zones of modern occupation. While this is a rough metric, sites were considered to be located nearby inhabited areas if located along main roads, off of highly-trafficked hiking trails, near other major tourist destinations such as the Cape-Point Lighthouse, or were otherwise readily accessible. These sites see moderate foot-traffic, though require somewhat more effort to reach than those located directly within towns or cities. This is a diverse category, including two of the RDF stations, as well as both BOPs, and one gun battery. For example, the Slangkop RDF station is located within Table Mountain National Park, yet is less than a 15 minute hike along popular foot-paths from the town of Kommetjie, resulting in appreciable foot-traffic and noticeable cultural impacts on the site.

Finally, four (25%) of the sites surveyed are considered to be distant from zones of modern occupation. This includes several of the RDF stations, as well as the historic Limestone Kiln. These sites are only found by following backroads or hiking trails that are significantly out of the way. Reaching these sites commonly requires hikes of an hour or more over rough terrain, making them unlikely destinations for many people. As such, they see relatively little foot-traffic, and are thus the least impacted by human activities (Figure 3).

Structural Integrity

While it is difficult to quantify structural integrity, especially considering that sites were commonly comprised of between five and 15 individual structures, each site was ranked as a whole on a scale of one (healthy) to five (only foundations remain) to give a general sense of its overall state. Six (37%) of the sites surveyed are in a healthy condition, with good preservation and maintenance. Three (19%) have only minor aesthetic damage. Two (12%) have moderate structural damage (cracking and checking in concrete, some missing roofs). Three (19%) have sustained major structural damage, compromising their integrity and making them extremely unsafe, with most or all structures missing roofs. Finally, two (13%) of the sites surveyed had only foundations and rubble from the original structures remaining (Figure 4).

Discussion

It comes as no surprise that the 37% of sites found to be in a healthy state of preservation are the same sites that are being actively protected and conserved. All four of the gun batteries, as well as the army relief station, and Special Signals Services training school remain in good condition due to ongoing use and protection. Further, because of their protected status, their location within or nearby inhabited towns makes them valuable tourist destinations as well as readily accessible for security and maintenance.

As for the remaining 63% of sites that had sustained some amount of structural damage, the relationship between effective preservation, distance from modern occupation, and protection status seems somewhat

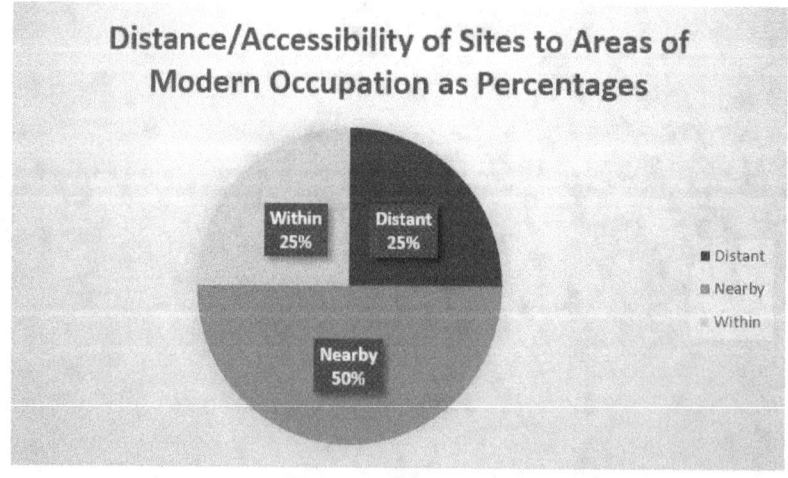

Figure 3: Distance/Accessibility of sites to zones of modern occupation expressed as percentages. (Image by author, 2017.)

paradoxical. The three (19%) sites with no protection status whatsoever are ironically the ones with the least amount of damage, whereas the seven (44%) passively protected sites were among those with the most severe degradation.

In general, sites located nearby towns and cities have been significantly impacted by cultural processes, but less so by natural forces. Graffiti is prolific throughout these sites, commonly covering both interior and exterior surfaces of nearly every structure present. In addition, one BOP displayed evidence of active, and current human inhabitation. Although these processes substantially impact sites in an aesthetic sense (altering/destroying the original appearance of the structures), they do not impact the structural integrity of the buildings themselves as severely. In fact, sites displaying substantial graffiti seemed to be more structurally sound than those without, potentially indicating a protective effect of the paint coating on the survival of the concrete superstructure.

Conversely, passively protected sites seemed to be in significantly worse condition. Though their more distant locations protect them from the deleterious effects of cultural processes (as evidenced by a reduction in, or the absence of modern trash and graffiti), these sites have nevertheless sustained substantially more meaningful damage. Including all of the RDF stations, these sites are typically located along remote coastlines at high altitudes. Exposed to high winds, rain, salt, and wildlife, their long-term prospects for survival are grim. Most have already sustained enough damage to collapse roofs and make critical structural elements unsound. Thus, despite the protection gained from being located within a national park, this passive protection ignores the much more significant natural and environmental forces that are the preeminent causes of structural damage. In this way, the results of this study indicate that there is no effective benefit in the long-term conservation of historic structures located within the Cape Peninsula's national parks, compared to those with no legal protection status whatsoever.

Conclusion

Given the small sample size of sites surveyed for this study, these results must be regarded as preliminary. Nevertheless, enough sites have been documented to demonstrate the significant damage sustained by these historic structures since their abandonment (Table 1). Though many are legally protected within the boundaries of national parks and wildlife reserves, it is obvious that this status alone is not enough to ensure their long-term survival. Many gun batteries and other buildings from the war have already been successfully preserved across a number of towns and cities in the Cape thanks to active conservation and restoration policies. These successes should serve as a guide for the RDF stations and observation posts located in the more distant (and lesser known) corners of the peninsula's national parks. These structures represent an important part of South Africa's national heritage, embodying the social and political struggles that continue in many aspects of daily life even today. As such, if these monuments are to be saved, it will require both a greater awareness by the general population, and a more active commitment from relevant authorities.

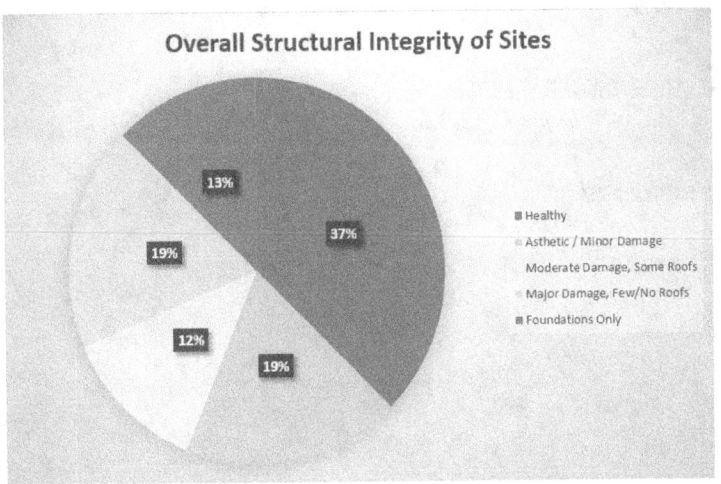

Figure 4: Generalized structural integrity of sites expressed as percentages. (Image by Author, 2017.)

References

AMERICAN SOCIETY OF CIVIL ENGINEERS (ASCE)
2000   *Guideline for Structural Condition Assessment of Existing Buildings: An ASCE Standard 11-90.* American Society of Civil Engineers, ASCE/SEI 11-99

BIZLEY, W. H.
1998   The Sinking of the U-197: A Flashpoint in German and South African Surveillance Politics, 1942-3. In *Military History Journal* 11(2).

CAPE POINT NATIONAL PARK
2017   Placard indicating the foundation of a WWII observation post at the Cape Point Lighthouse, Cape Peninsula, RSA. http://capepoint.co.za/ Viewed June 2017.

HEWITT, F. J.
1975   South Africa's Role in the Development and Use of Radar in World War II. In *Military History Journal* 3(3). <http://samilitaryhistory.org/vol033fh.html accessed 3/8/17>. Accessed 8 March 2017.

STOTT, N. A.
1998   South Africa's Secret War: The War against Enemy Submarines, 1939-1945. In *Military History Journal* 11(1). <http://samilitaryhistory.org/vol111ns.html>. Accessed 8 March 2017.

WEIDMAN, MARINDA
2004   Robben Island's Role in Coastal Defense 1931-1960. In *Military History Journal* 13(1). <http://samilitaryhistory.org/vol131mw.html> Accessed 7 March 2017.

WESSELS, ANDRE
2000   The First Two Years of War: The Development of the Union Defense Forces (UDF) September 1939 to September 1941. In *Military History Journal* 11(5) <http://samilitaryhistory.org/vol115aw.html> Accessed 7 March 2017.

ZUKOWSKI, ARKADIUSZ
2016   The Union of South Africa Towards the Outbreak of the Second World War. In *Politeja* (42)17-32.

• • • • • • • • • • • • • • • •

Ian Harrison
1807 South Elm St.
Greenville NC, 27858

Shore to Ship: The application of KOCOA to a Maritime Military Environment

Terence Christian, Kristen McMasters

As part of its mission to advance the understanding and preservation of U.S. battlefields, the National Park Service's American Battlefield Protection Program (ABPP) is investigating the use of military terrain analysis on maritime engagements. Limited research has been completed on the variable landscapes associated with maritime battlefields. However, additional research is desirable as the ABPP, research partners, and stakeholders develop best practice. The standardization of battlefield terrain analysis across the terrestrial-maritime divide allows for inter-site and inter-environment comparison. A condensed maritime KOCOA military terrain analysis of the Battle of Mobile Bay for 5 August 1864 is presented.

Introduction

Created in 1991 (American Battlefield Protection Program 2018a), the American Battlefield Protection Program (ABPP) is the only federal program congressionally mandated "to assist citizens, public and private institutions, and governments at all levels in planning, interpreting, and protecting sites where historic battles were fought on American soil" (54 U.S.C. 308101-308103). Under this broad remit, the ABPP works

> to protect battlefields and sites associated with armed conflicts that influenced the course of our history, ... to encourage and assist all Americans in planning for the preservation, management, and interpretation of these sites, and ... to raise awareness of the importance of preserving battlefields and related sites for future generations (American Battlefield Protection Program 2018b).

Considering the 13:1 area ratio of the terrestrial United States (9,158,022 km²) to US waters (699,284 km²) (United States Census Bureau 2012), it is understandable that much of the ABPP's past focus has been dedicated to developing best practice in the preservation of terrestrial battlefields. This is not to say that maritime sites are omitted from the ABPP's program vision, rather a recognition that much of the methods and theory used to identify, inventory, and preserve maritime sites has been transferred from terrestrial site experience. The ABPP recognizes that the historical and physical characteristics of maritime sites often differ from terrestrial sites and that a specific best practice should be developed for their planning preservation, management, and interpretation. The ABPP first began this work with the development of the *Submerged Battlefield Protection Manual* (Sabick and Dennis 2011) in 2008. Mirroring congressional policy for periodically revising the ABPP's two landmark theme studies (the Civil War Sites Advisory Commission's 1993 *Report on the Nation's Civil War Battlefields* with its 2009-2011 update and the ABPP's 2007 *Report to Congress on the Historic Preservation of Revolutionary War and War of 1812 Sites in the United States* with its in-progress update), the ABPP currently is assessing its past underwater protection guidelines. The revised best practice document is set for completion by 2022. This paper introduces current thought experiments, theories, and thought processes undertaken by ABPP staff on the subject of maritime battlefield mapping using KOCOA military terrain analysis. The Battle of Mobile Bay is presented as a case study to demonstrate the applicability of KOCOA in maritime environment. It does not introduce, advance, or endorse specific methods as best practice; these will be published in the final, peer-reviewed update to the *Submerged Battlefield Protection Manual* (Sabick and Dennis 2011).

Military Terrain Analysis

Central to the ABPP's ability to provide accurate assessments on the preservation of our nation's battlefields is an accurate understanding of individual battlefield history and their respective archaeological inventories. The ABPP's two theme studies highlight 1,061 conflict sites of national significance. Of nearly 3,000 total recorded sites from the Revolutionary War and the War of 1812 and some 10,500 total recorded sites from the Civil War, 677 and 384, respectively, were highlighted by the studies (Civil War Sites Advisory Commission

1993; American Battlefield Protection Program 2007:9). However, the Program's enabling legislation provides an unbounded time frame. The large data set this unbounded remit provides requires methodological standardization across wide geographies and chronologies. Completion of military terrain analyses is the method by which the ABPP reduces diverse battlefield terrains and tactics to a uniform standard. Military terrain analysis is defined, from a purely military perspective, as:

> *The collection, analysis, evaluation, and interpretation of geographic information on the natural and man-made features of the terrain, combined with other relevant factors, to predict the effect of the terrain on military operations* (Office of the Joint Chiefs of Staff 2017:GL-7, 2018:232).

The collective, extensive literature on military terrain analysis and its use in historical/archaeological research projects refines both "other relevant factors" (Office of the Joint Chiefs of Staff 2017:GL-7, 2018:232) and the analysis end product. Generally, a historically-focused military terrain analysis combines historical and archeological evidence to understand combatant decision making and to identify possible locations of military operations for the purpose of site preservation and interpretation.

Military terrain analysis as a means of assessing military options has an established pedigree in the United States. The ABPP advocates the use of KOCOA for the mapping and analysis of historic battlefields. KOCOA was developed by the US Army following the Second World War and first used by the National Park Service as a historic preservation tool in Gettysburg National Military Park's 1999 *General Management Plan and Environmental Impact Statement* (Gettysburg National Military Park 1999:45-49, 102). KOCOA military terrain analyses, undertaken either as a military planning exercise or as a cultural resource assessment, are structured under five characteristics: Key Terrain, Observation and Fields of Fire, Cover and Concealment, Obstacles, and Avenues of Approach (and Withdrawal) (Scott and McFeaters 2011:115; Christian and American Battlefield Protection Program 2017). The ABPP advances KOCOA as best practice both because of the large body of work establishing its functionality as an interrogative methodology and because of its flexible scaling (McNutt 2014; Parker 2016). In support of KOCOA's use as Phase I battlefield assessment best practice, the ABPP developed and maintains both an in-house *Battlefield Survey Manual* (American Battlefield Protection Program 2016) and a guidance document for KOCOA military terrain analyses of historic battlefields (Christian and American Battlefield Protection Program 2017). The ABPP's advocacy for KOCOA as best practice for Phase I historic battlefield assessments has seen KOCOA included in state historic preservation office archaeological guidelines throughout the United States (Virginia Department of Historic Resources 2017:47-48). In tandem with providing technical assistance to external partners and stakeholders, the ABPP promotes inclusion of a KOCOA analysis within ABPP Battlefield Planning Grants for which a military terrain analysis has not yet been completed. The ABPP maintains a bibliography of projects which employed KOCOA; access to the bibliography and specific project reports can be obtained through consultation with ABPP leadership.

While KOCOA has become a central tool in Phase I historic battlefield assessments, the ABPP recognizes that its development and implementation has had a terrestrial focus as a result of project focus. A review of the ABPP's own grant awarding history reflects the terrestrial focus with 73 grants with terrestrial archaeology tagged as a secondary project type/product and 17 grants with underwater archaeology tagged as a secondary project type/product since 1997. Refining the dataset further reveals that 59% of underwater archaeology grants were awarded from 2010-2017 (American Battlefield Protection Program 2018c). While there are projects which have successfully applied terrestrial KOCOA analyses to the maritime environment (Mastone et al. 2011; Maryland Maritime Archaeology Program 2013), such projects are generally the exception rather than the norm. The aforementioned *Submerged Battlefield Protection Manual* (Sabick and Dennis 2011), which the ABPP helped craft, does translate much of KOCOA to meet the needs of naval combat but also reflects the terrestrially-focused milieu in which KOCOA was defined and refined. For example, the *Manual* identifies that Key Terrain in pre-steam ship naval combat may equate to the direction of the wind or current relative to the combatants. However, the *Manual* dismisses Observation as having "only nominal application to ship-on-ship conflict" (Sabick and Dennis 2011:13) and Avenues of Approach and Withdrawal as having "little application to the naval battlefield ... there is very little that will influence the path of the combatants" (Sabick and Dennis 2011:13). The implied conclusion that the planar naval battle space is equivalent to a featureless terrestrial battle space, where troops can move unencumbered, is a dated assessment of how historical naval assets occupy and use the maritime environment. Through the following case study, it shall be argued that all aspects of KOCOA military terrain analysis have application to naval combat so long as a wider interpretation of KOCOA characteristics is adopted.

Case Study: The Battle of Mobile Bay (AL003)

To demonstrate the fluidity, complexities, and idiosyncrasies of a maritime KOCOA (in comparison to the terrestrial standard used for much of battlefield archaeology), attention is turned to Admiral Farragut's reduction of Mobile Bay as a strategic base of operations for both the Confederate navy in the Gulf and the larger Confederate military cause. The use of Mobile Bay [ABPP Battlefield Code: AL003] as a maritime military terrain analysis case study is deliberate. Not only is the Battlefield Boundary (formerly labeled the Study Area in CWSAC and ABPP reports) 92% water (Figure 1) but the 1999 ABPP *Update to the Civil War Sites Advisory Commission Report on the Nation's Civil War Battlefields* specifically highlights consideration of the maritime environment in future battlefield preservation planning (American Battlefield Protection Program 2011:13, 34-36). The battlefield landscape, therefore, provides an excellent example of KOCOA's application to the maritime environment.

An exhaustive historical summary of Mobile Bay is not undertaken both for brevity and as the CWSAC's *Report on the Nation's Civil War Battlefields* provides a concise historical summary as evidence for the Battle of Mobile Bay's national significance:

> *A combined Union force initiated operations to close Mobile Bay to blockade running. Some Union forces landed on Dauphin Island and laid siege to Fort Gaines. On August 5, Farragut's Union fleet of eighteen ships entered Mobile Bay and received a devastating fire from Forts Gaines and Morgan and other points. After passing the forts, Farragut forced the Confederate naval forces,*

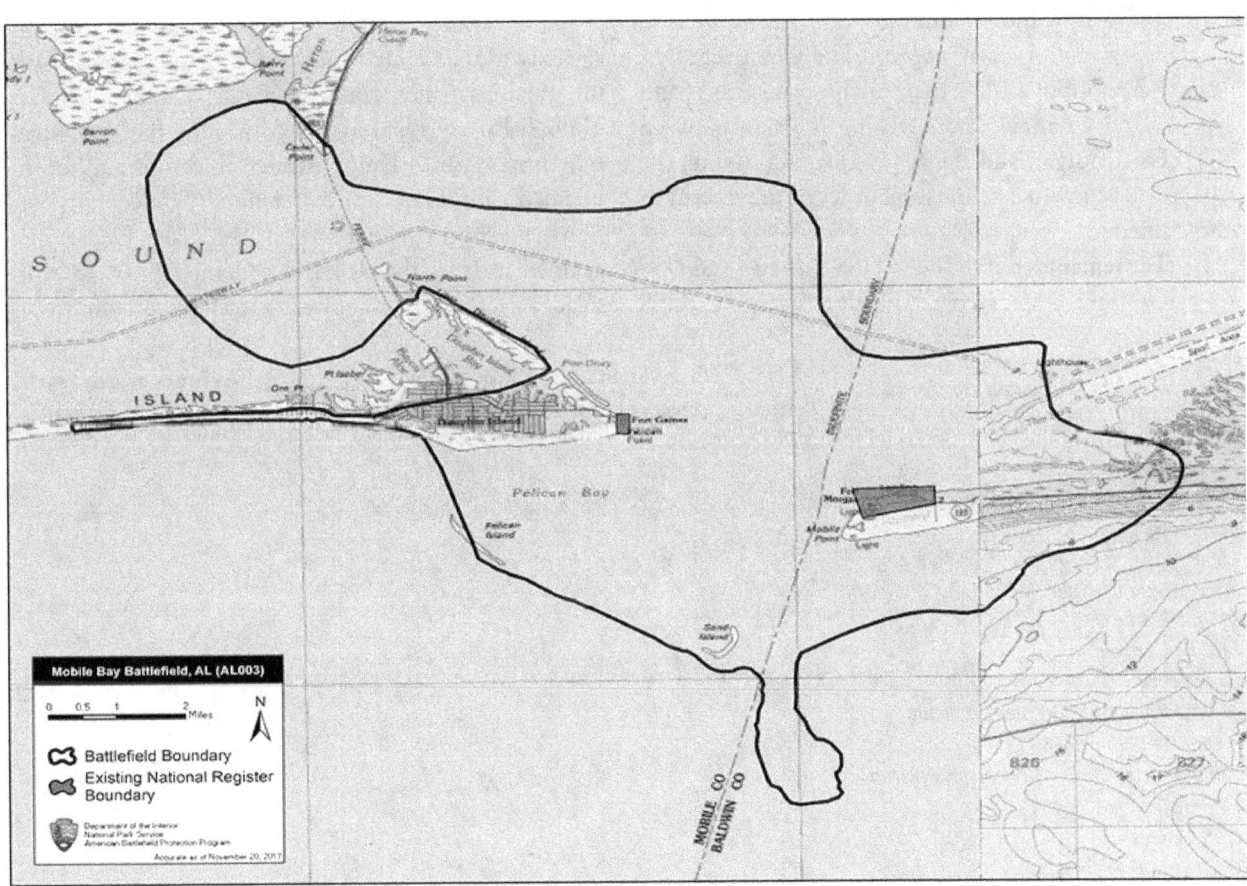

Figure 1: The Battlefield Boundary (formerly labeled Study Area in CWSAC and ABPP reports) and Existing National Register Boundary of AL003: Mobile Bay (T. Christian and K. McMasters after American Battlefield Protection Program 2011:13, 34-36).

under Adm. Franklin Buchanan, to surrender, which effectively closed Mobile Bay. By August 23, Fort Morgan, the last big holdout, fell, shutting down the port. The city, however, remained uncaptured (Civil War Sites Advisory Commission 1997).

Of critical supplement to the CWSAC battle description is recognition of Farragut's objectives and planned movements. Farragut launched his plan to effect entrance into Mobile Bay on 5 August 1864. His plan centered on three objectives and three primary movements (Figure 2) (Johnson and Buel 1888:381-385):

Objectives
1. Force entry into the Bay to close the port of Mobile to civilian and military maritime traffic;
2. Neutralize the threat of the CSS *Tennessee*; and
3. Cut off possible avenues of escape for the forts' garrisons.

Movements
1. The four Union monitors USS *Tecumseh*, USS *Manhattan*, USS *Winnebago*, and USS *Chickasaw* were to move from their anchorage in the Sand Island Channel to a blocking position between Fort Morgan and the Main Channel. (Note: the order of names reflects the order of movement in line.)
2. The remainder of the fleet (USS *Brooklyn* and USS *Octorara*, USS *Hartford* and USS *Metacomet*, USS *Richmond* and USS *Port Royal*, USS *Lackawanna* and USS *Seminole*, USS *Monongahela* and USS *Kennebec*, USS *Ossipee* and USS *Itasca*, USS *Oneida* and USS *Galena*), Farragut's less robust wooden vessels, were to assemble in the Outer Bar and move in lines of two up the eastern side of the channel (to the east of the red buoy) avoiding the emplaced obstructions. (Note: the first ship of each pairing is located on the starboard side of the line.)
3. The assembled force were to capture or sink the CSS *Tennessee* and then proceed to anchor in the Outer Bay.

There was no plan to capitalize on the capture of the Outer Bay by pushing toward Mobile itself. More detailed accounts of the battle can be obtained from a variety of primary and secondary sources (Hearn 1998; McPherson 2012:207-223; Friend 2014). Focus now is given to codifying the battle characteristics according to the KOCOA system (Table 1).

Key Terrain

Action against Mobile was directed at reducing the capacity of the Confederate navy to launch new, powerful warships which could challenge Union blockades. Though Farragut had identified Mobile Bay as strategically important to Union theater objectives and recommended capture of lightly defended Confederate positions as early as January 1864, the Navy Department decided to back the Red River Campaign of 1864 instead. As a result, Farragut was forced to contain Mobile

Description	Key Terrain	Observation and Fields of Fire	Cover and Concealment	Obstacles	Avenues of Approach (and Withdrawal)
Mobile Bay	X				X
Fort Gaines	X	X	X		
Fort Morgan	X	X	X		
Fort Powell	X	X	X		
Outer Bar					X
Sand Island Channel	X				X
Main Channel	X				X
Middle Channel	X				X
Grant Pass	X				X
Mobile Bay Coastal Waters (outside navigable channels)				X	
Piling Obstructions & Torpedoes (Main Channel)				X	
CSS Tennessee	X	X	X		
Confederate fleet	X	X	X		
Union fleet	X	X	X		
Battle resultant smoke/haze				X	

Table 1: Battle of Mobile Bay (AL003) Battlefield Defining Features identified by the maritime environment KOCOA analysis.

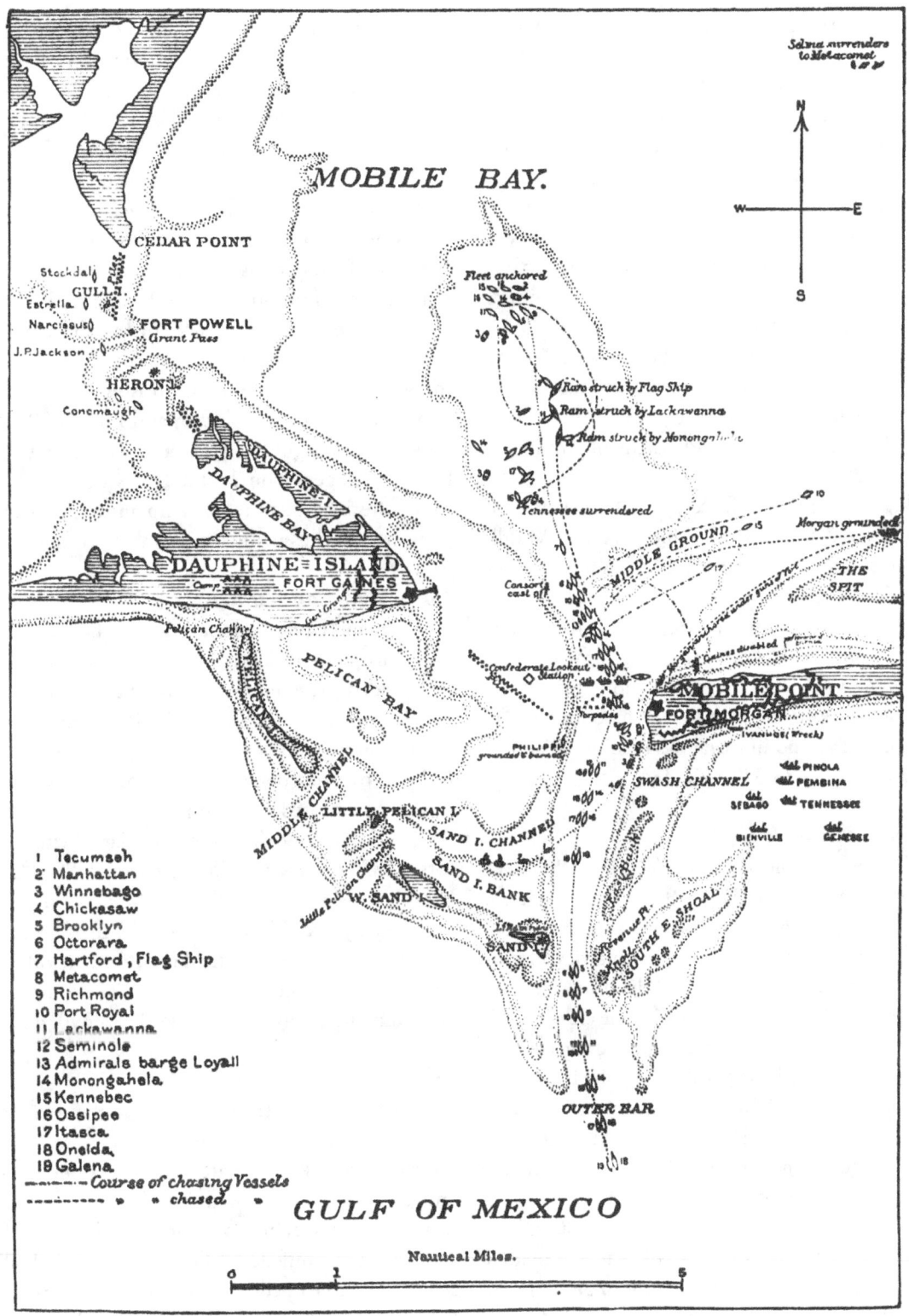

Figure 2: Traditional cartographic narrative of the Battle of Mobile Bay, 5 August 1864 (Johnson and Buel 1888: 384).

Bay and its increasingly powerful naval garrison from May to July 1864 using the wooden vessels he had at his command (Johnson and Buel 1888:379-381).

Confederate leadership similarly realized Mobile, Alabama and Mobile Bay's strategic importance. The Bay was protected by a series of brick forts, obstructions, and naval assets. Fort Morgan, positioned on Mobile Point east of the Main Channel, was the centerpiece of Confederate defenses. Supporting Fort Morgan was Fort Gaines on Dauphine Island (west of the Main Channel) and Fort Powell (positioned to block the shallower channel between Gull Island and Heron Island). Fort Gaines and Fort Powell were fortified positions mounting three and eight guns, respectively (Johnson and Buel 1888:381; United States War Department 1892:428; England et al. 2000).

In addition to fixed defenses, the four navigable channels (Main Channel, Sand Island Channel, Middle Channel, and Grant Pass) and each navies' fleet can be considered Key Terrain. The channels dictated the flow of battle while the capture/sinking of the fleets were both strategic and tactical objectives. Additionally, it is argued that the CSS *Tennessee*, as an individual vessel, is Key Terrain due to its prominence in both the defense of Mobile Bay and in Farragut's mission objectives (Johnson and Buel 1888:379-382, 384-385).

Observation and Fields of Fire

Fort Morgan was the keystone for the defense of Mobile Bay. At a reported 3.2 to 9.8 m above natural ground level, the pentagonal star fort with central citadel provided defending forces with a dominating viewshed of the Main Channel and Mobile Point (Historic American Buildings Survey 1933). In tandem with the elevated citadel and the approximately 40 guns (including 10-inch columbiads and 7-inch Brooke rifles) that the interior of the fort mounted, Fort Morgan also emplaced artillery in a shore battery. The additional 29 guns in exterior batteries provided additional, independent observation and long-range engagement capability (Johnson and Buel 1888:381; England et al. 2000; Tucker 2013:861). The 10-inch columbiads and 7-inch Brooke rifles provided a near level range of approximately 1,650–2,300 m and 1,900–2,400 m, respectively (Scott 1861:69, 164-165; Abbot 1867:121; Drury and Gibbons 1993:79). Fort Morgan outranged the whole of the Main Channel. Similar observation considerations can be hypothesized for Fort Gaines's 27 guns (Johnson and Buel 1888:381; Tucker 2013:2275) and Fort Powell's 8 guns (United States War Department 1892:428), though with reduced fire accuracy on the Main Channel due to their location. The respective fleets were similarly well armed with a range of approximately 1,900–2,400 m at near level elevation (Abbot 1867:121; Tucker 1989:220; Drury and Gibbons 1993:79); a longer maximum effective range could be achieved by elevating the gun tubes.

The Union and Confederate fleets maintained comparable observation advantages due to similar ship designs. However, Farragut's use of US Army signal officers—intended for communication with Army assets planning to isolate/besiege the forts following the Union navy's entrance to the Outer Bay—to communicate between individual ships/elements comprising his fleet provided a marked advantage (Johnson and Buel 1888:381, 386, 396-397). Farragut likely began the battle with not only better intelligence on Mobile Bay's defense, but could more effectively command ship movements after first contact with the enemy force.

Cover and Concealment

Cover and Concealment is divided between terrestrial and maritime considerations. The masonry, earthwork, and sandbag revetments and ramparts of Fort Morgan certainly qualify as both characteristics. For the naval assets it is more complex. The lashing of Union vessels together provided a degree of cover for one vessel while the other was exposed (Johnson and Buel 1888:386, 391-392). Additionally, the armor associated with the monitors (CSS *Tennessee*, USS *Tecumseh*, USS *Manhattan*, USS *Winnebago*, and USS *Chickasaw*) provided cover from enemy fire. More sporadically, the residual smoke which hung on the battlefield may have provided a modicum of concealment in an otherwise devoid maritime environment (Johnson and Buel 1888:390, 406-407).

Obstacles

Of primary concern to both Union and Confederate commands was the presence of natural obstacles. Mobile Bay's relatively shallow waters are compounded by shoals and sandbars which bound and constrict movement in the Bay to specific corridors. In addition to natural obstacles, the Confederate defenders deployed piling obstructions and torpedoes between Fort Morgan and Fort Gaines. The obstructions were marked with black buoys, the easternmost of which (the famed red buoy) marked the beginning of unobstructed navigation (Johnson and Buel 1888:382, 384-385, 387). Used together, for example around the Main Channel, the natural and emplaced obstacles forced maritime traffic within range of Fort Morgan's substantial armament.

Avenues of Approach and Withdrawal

Avenues of Approach and Withdrawal primarily are restricted by natural and emplaced obstacles to the four navigable channels (Main Channel, Sand Island Channel, Middle Channel, and Grant Pass) and regions of deeper water (largely the Outer Bay) (Johnson and Buel 1888:381, 384-385). Following the Union navy's passage up the Outer Bar and its rendezvous with the four Union monitors at the Main Channel–Sand Island Channel junction, the planar battlefield environment of maritime engagements necessitates examination of Avenues of Approach and Withdrawal using time slices to isolate ship-to-ship and ship-to-shore relative positions. This micro-level analysis has not been conducted here due to space consideration. However, such an analysis would likely be completed using 30-minute intervals considering the battle's relatively short timeline (0545 hrs to 1000 hrs) (Johnson and Buel 1888:386, 398).

KOCOA in the Maritime Environment

KOCOA both is applicable and advantageous to historic maritime battlefield assessment because the maritime battlefield is multifaceted. The general battlefield environment can be located in brown water, brackish water, littoral, blue water, or a combination thereof while the localized battlefield environment is ever changing; planar on the macro-scale, the battle space takes on the properties of terrain on the micro-scale and when military asset characteristics are compared against one-another (for example, the disparate heights of ships' masts can be equated to the disparate height of high ground). Following an abbreviated discussion of KOCOA characteristics in the maritime environment, brief examples of maritime KOCOA characteristics are provided (Table 2).

Key Terrain

Key Terrain in the maritime landscape varies according to the battlefield environment in which naval forces are engaged. As naval assets move away from the constricted interior and coastal waters, where interaction with terrestrial military objectives necessitates KOCOA analyses adopt a more terrestrial hybridization, it is argued that Key Terrain becomes more fully linked with the ever-changing relationship between geographic position, weather systems, opposing force locations, and ship specifications. Limited geographical relief removes terrain relief from contest; dynamic Key Terrain, based on maneuvering for spatial advantage and relative position, replaces the fixed Key Terrain typical of terrestrial KOCOA analyses.

Observation and Fields of Fire

One of the most critical facets for the successful use of KOCOA in a maritime environment, Observation and Fields of Fire are inter-linked with Key Terrain and Avenues of Approach and Withdrawal. In the planar maritime environment, the ability to identify and rapidly engage the opposition is often the marker for victory. Observation is most particularly embodied by ship/mast height, the height of surrounding terrain/built structures, and the difference in height between ships and terrain/structures. However, more general evaluation of the role Observation plays in an expansive, planar battlespace may see natural and artificial illuminants (for example, the sun, moon, and stars or illumination rounds, navigation lanterns, and spotlights) considered. Fields of Fire, like terrestrial military analyses, are linked to gun platform altitude, elevation angle, maximum and minimum range, and munitions used.

Cover and Concealment

Cover and Concealment can benefit from wider interpretations for a maritime environment. The armor thickness of vessels vis-à-vis the weapons deployed against them is a parallel assessment of Cover as the field fortification-munitions comparisons conducted on terrestrial battlefields. Concealment characteristics can reflect similar considerations as blue water Obstacles; the wide interpretation of Concealment to include purposeful and expedient obscurants (for example, lingering gun smoke, burning vessels, smoke screens, etc.) is especially beneficial in interrogating maritime battlefield landscapes.

Obstacles

Obstacles often play a central role in brown, brackish, littoral, and coastal maritime conflict. Much like characteristics of Avenues of Approach and Withdrawal in the same zones, the presence and/or deployment of Obstacles in these terrain environments can be considered similar to obstacle functionality in terrestrial battlefield landscapes. A strict reading of Obstacles in blue water contexts limits their influence. However, a wider interpretation could see the inclusion of such varied factors as time of day and weather systems if used to specifically deny areas to the opposing force, defend unprotected areas, and/or spoil opposition planning.

Initial	Characteristic	Definition	Terrestrial Examples (Christian and American Battlefield Protection Program 2017)	Maritime Environment Examples
K	Key Terrain	"any locality, or area, the seizure or retention of which affords a marked advantage to either combatant" (U.S. Joint Chiefs of Staff 2014: GL-6)	- High ground with good observation and clear fields of fire" (2017: 1). - "Transportation choke point such as a water crossing, defile, road junction" (2017: 1).	- Naval assets (individually and/or relative to other naval/terrestrial assets) - Forts, gun emplacements - Navigable marine zones
O	Observation and Fields of Fire	"the ability to see (or be seen by) the adversary either visually or through the use of surveillance devices" and "the area that a weapon or group of weapons may effectively cover with fire from a given position" (U.S. Joint Chiefs of Staff 2014: III-3).	- Observation: High ground, sight corridors, general viewshed (2017: 1). - Fields of Fire: Directly linked to Observation, the weapon's design characteristics, and its method of deployment use (2017: 1).	- Height of vessel/mast, terrain, structures, and difference in height between the same - Natural and artificial illuminants (e.g., sun/moon, illumination rounds, navigation lanterns) - Weapon and munitions specifications; theory and method of use
C	Cover and Concealment	"...protection from observation, and can be provided by features such as woods, underbrush, snowdrifts, tall grass, and cultivated vegetation" and "...protection from direct and indirect fires" (U.S. Joint Chiefs of Staff 2014: III-3).	- Cover: "Ditches, riverbanks, buildings, walls, entrenchments" (2017: 1). - Concealment: "Forests, ravines, dense vegetation, reverse slopes" (2017: 1).	- Vessel design, construction materials, and armor characteristics - Localized terrain features, weather systems, time of day - Structures or vessels in the area of operation - Natural and artificial obscurants
O	Obstacles	Any natural or man-made obstruction designed or employed to disrupt, fix, turn, or block the movement of an opposing force, and to impose additional losses in personnel, time, and equipment on the opposing force. (U.S. Joint Chiefs of Staff 2014: III-3).	- "Existing obstacles...already present on the battlefield...natural (swamp, forest, river) or cultural (town, railroad, bridge)" (2017:2). - "Reinforcing obstacles...include such things as entrenchments, earthworks, and abatis" (2017: 2).	- Natural obstacles (e.g., sand banks, shoals, shallow waters, unfavorable tidal forces, weather systems, time of day) - Emplaced obstacles (e.g., pilings, torpedoes/mines, anti-shipping chains or booms, chevaux de frise, sunken ships/hulks)
A	Avenues of Approach (and Withdrawal)	"an air or ground route of an attacking force of a given size leading to its objective or to key terrain in its path" (U.S. Joint Chiefs of Staff 2014: III-6)	- Road over a natural or built causeway, hill path, railroad line (2017: 2).	- Road, trail, and path networks - Navigable marine zones (e.g., rivers, bays, channels, and larger bodies of water) - Shipping channels and harbors

Table 2: The five characteristics of KOCOA military terrain analyses with a comparison of terrestrial and maritime examples.

Avenues of Approach and Withdrawal

In terrestrial conflict, Avenues of Approach and Withdrawal are largely linked to terrain. Terrain—along with anthropogenic modifications to the landscape which reduce or enhance terrain's impact—either hinders or helps circulation through the battlefield landscape. As such, unit movement is primarily dictated by the interaction between defined military objectives and viable terrain; the specific position of enemy forces is often a supporting, but secondary, factor for planning approaches and withdrawal. The relative absence of large-scale terrain features in maritime environments provides more unrestricted movement within the battlefield landscape. Certainly, the shoals, shallows, currents and tides of brown water and littoral zones provide an overlapping space in which terrestrial and maritime KOCOA considerations overlap. However, as conflict moves to deeper, blue waters these smaller terrain features give way to a larger planar space punctuated by the occasional navigable channel which provides access to the inner coastal zone. In this deeper maritime environment, Avenues of Approach and Withdrawal are no longer governed by existing and/or modified terrain. On the planar maritime battlefield, it is advanced that the spatial relationship between opposing vessels becomes the primary factor in how the opposing forces approach and withdraw from a fight. Design and armament characteristics of ships (such as their speed, turning ability, and fields of fire) combine with culturally-based military theory to impose an artificial, mind's eye terrain on the maritime plane.

Conclusion

This paper highlights on-going thought experiments and hypotheses undertaken by the ABPP on maritime battlefield mapping using KOCOA military terrain analysis. The use of military terrain analyses to provide intra-site analysis and inter-site comparison has established value for terrestrial historic preservation planning. KOCOA's application to the maritime environment shows comparable results to its use on terrestrial battlefields. However, the application of a terrestrial military terrain analysis system to a maritime environment necessitates wide interpretation of system characteristics. A developing field within conflict archaeology and historic preservation methodological best practice (Parker 2016), the dialogue resulting from the ABPP's revision of the *Submerged Battlefield Protection Manual* (Sabick and Dennis 2011) will support both the refinement and the increased application of military terrain analyses to the maritime battlefield environment.

Acknowledgments

The authors are grateful to Paul Hawke, Chief, American Battlefield Protection Program and the ABPP staff for their support of this on-going research. Specific thanks to Elizabeth Marlowe and Dr. Amanda Charland for their assistance in theory development and historical research. The authors would also like to thank the 2018 ACUA *Underwater Archaeology Proceedings* editors, *Proceedings* reviewers, and our colleagues in the discipline for their assistance in preparing this paper for publication.

Any opinions, findings, and conclusions or recommendations expressed in this material are those of the authors and do not necessarily reflect the views of the Department of the Interior or Temple University.

References

ABBOT, HENRY
1867 *No. 14. Professional Papers of the Corps of Engineer, United States Army. Siege Artillery in the Campaigns Against Richmond: With notes on the 15-inch Gun, Including an Algebraic Analysis of the Trajectory of a Shot in its Ricochets upon Smooth Water*. Corps of Engineer, United States Army, Washington, D.C.

AMERICAN BATTLEFIELD PROTECTION PROGRAM
2007 *Report to Congress on the Historic Preservation of Revolutionary War and War of 1812 Sites in the United States*. National Park Service, U.S. Department of the Interior, Washington, D.C.

2009-2011, *Update to the Civil War Sites Advisory Commission Report on the Nation's Civil War Battlefields*. National Park Service, U.S. Department of the Interior, Washington, D.C.

2011 *Update to the Civil War Sites Advisory Commission Report on the Nation's Civil War Battlefields: State of Alabama*. National Park Service, U.S. Department of the Interior Washington, D.C.

2016 *Battlefield Survey Manual*. National Park Service, U.S. Department of the Interior, Washington, D.C.

2018a *American Battlefield Protection Program: What We Do*. National Park Service, U.S. Department of the Interior, Washington, D.C. <https://www.nps.gov/orgs/2287/whatwedo.htm>. Accessed 25 March 2018.

2018b   *American Battlefield Protection Program.* National Park Service, U.S. Department of the Interior, Washington, D.C. <https://www.nps.gov/orgs/2287/index.htm>. Accessed 25 March 2018.

2018c   *CABIN: ABPP Internal Grants Management Database.* National Park Service, U.S. Department of the Interior, Washington, D.C.

CHRISTIAN, TERENCE AND AMERICAN BATTLEFIELD PROTECTION PROGRAM
2017   *KOCOA (Military Terrain Analysis) Information Sheet.* American Battlefield Protection Program, Washington, D.C.

CIVIL WAR SITES ADVISORY COMMISSION
1993   *Report on the Nation's Civil War Battlefields.* Civil War Sites Advisory Commission, Washington, D.C.

1997   Mobile Bay. *Report on the Nation's Civil War Battlefields. Technical Volume II: Battle Summaries.* <https://www.nps.gov/abpp/battles/al003.htm>. Accesssed 25 March 2018.

DRURY, IAN AND TONY GIBBONS
1993   *The Civil War Military Machine: Weapons and Tactics of the Union and Confederate Armed Forces.* Smithmark, New York, NY.

ENGLAND, BOB, (ET AL)
2000   *Fort Morgan.* Arcadia, Charleston, SC.

FRIEND, JACK
2014   *West Wind, Flood Tide: The battle of Mobile Bay.* Naval Institute Press, Annapolis, MD.

GETTYSBURG NATIONAL MILITARY PARK, NATIONAL PARK SERVICE
1999   *Final General Management Plan and Environmental Impact Statement.* National Park Service, U.S. Department of the Interior. Gettysburg, PA.

HEARN, CHESTER
1998   *Mobile Bay and the Mobile Campaign: The Last Great Battles of the Civil War.* McFarland, Jefferson, NC.

HISTORIC AMERICAN BUILDINGS SURVEY
1933   *Fort Morgan, Gulf Shores, Baldwin County, AL* (HABS AL-101) [Photograph of drawn plan]. Library of Congress, Washington, D.C.

JOHNSON, ROBERT AND CLARENCE BUEL
1888   *Battles and Leaders of the Civil War.* Vol. 4. The Century Company, New York, NY.

MARYLAND MARITIME ARCHAEOLOGY PROGRAM, MARYLAND HISTORICAL TRUST AND NEW SOUTH ASSOCIATES, INC.
2013   *Naval Engagements of the Revolutionary and 1812 Wars in Maryland (ABPP Grant Agreement No. GA-2255-09-015).* Maryland Maritime Archaeology Program, Maryland Historical Trust, Crownsville, MD.

MASTONE, VICTOR, CRAIG BROWN AND CHRISTOPHER MAIO
2011   *Chelsea Creek – First naval engagement of the American Revolution. Chelsea, East Boston, Revere, and Winthrop. Suffolk County, Massachusetts* (ABPP Grant Agreement No. GA-2255-09-018). Massachusetts Board of Underwater Archaeological Resources, Executive Office of Energy and Environmental Affairs and University of Massachusetts at Boston, Boston, MA.

MCNUTT, RYAN
2014   "Finding Forgotten Fields: A Theoretical and Methodological Framework for Historic Landscape Reconstruction and Predictive Modelling of Battlefield Locations in Scotland, 1296-1650". Doctoral dissertation, Subject of Archaeology, University of Glasgow, Glasgow, Scotland.

MCPHERSON, JAMES
2012   *War on the Waters: The Union and Confederate Navies, 1861-1865.* University of North Carolina Press, Chapel Hill, NC.

OFFICE OF THE JOINT CHIEFS OF STAFF, U.S. DEPARTMENT OF DEFENSE
2017   *Joint Publication (JP) 2-03, Geospatial Intelligence in Joint Operations.* J7 Directorate for Joint Force Development, Office of the Joint Chiefs of Staff, U.S. Department of Defense, Pentagon, VA.

2018   *Joint Publication (JP) 1-02, DOD Dictionary of Military and Associated Terms* Office of the Joint Chiefs of Staff, U.S. Department of Defense, Pentagon, VA.

PARKER, ADAM
2016   *Dash at the Enemy!: The Use of Modern Naval Theory to Examine the Battlefield at Elizabeth City, North Carolina.* Master's Thesis, Department of History, East Carolina University, Greenville, NC.

SABICK, CHRISTOPHER AND JOANNE DENNIS
2011   *Submerged Battlefield Protection Manual.* Lake Champlain Maritime Museum, Vergennes, VT.

SCOTT, DOUGLAS AND ANDREW MCFEATERS
2011   The Archaeology of Historic Battlefields: A History and Theoretical Development in Conflict Archaeology. In *Journal of Archaeological Research* 19(1):103-132.

Scott, Henry
1861   *Military Dictionary: Comprising Technical Definitions; Information on Raising and Keeping Troops; Actual Service, Including Makeshifts and Improved Matériel; and Law, Government, Regulation, and Administration Relating to Land Forces.* D. Van Nostrand, New York, NY.

Tucker, Spencer
1989   *Arming the Fleet: U.S. Navy Ordnance in the Muzzle-loading Era.* Naval Institute Press, Annapolis, MD.

2013   *American Civil War: The Definitiive Encyclopedia and Document Collection.* Vol. I:A-C. ABC-CLIO, Santa Barbara, CA.

United States Census Bureau
2012   *State Area Measurements and Internal Point Coordinates.* United States Census Bureau, U.S. Department of Commerce, Washington, D.C. <https://www.census.gov/geo/reference/state-area.html>. Accessed 25 March 2018.

United States War Department
1892   *The War of the Rebellion: A Compilation of the Official Records of the Union And Confederate Armies. Series 1, Volume 39, In Three Parts. Part 1, Reports.* United States War Department, Washington, D.C.

Virginia Department of Historic Resources
2017   *Guidelines for Conducting Historic Resources Survey in Virginia.* Virginia Department of Historic Resources, Richmond, VA.

. . . .

Terence Christian
Department of History
Temple University
Gladfelter Hall, Room 928
1115 W. Berks Street
Philadelphia, PA 19122

Kristen McMasters
National Park Service, American
Battlefield Protection Program
1849 C Street NW–Room 7228
Washington, DC 20240

"Unidentified Planes Sighted": The Application of KOCOA Military Terrain Analysis to Aerial Combat

Madeline Roth, Jennifer McKinnon

KOCOA military terrain analysis is used to analyze terrestrial and naval battlescapes; there has been little experimentation, however, with the application of KOCOA analysis to aerial combat. Renewed interest in the 1942 attack on Midway Atoll presented researchers with an opportunity to expand KOCOA definitions, incorporating aerial combat into terrain analysis. The resulting terrain features were used to reconstruct the events which took place in June 1942, adding new dimension to narratives associated with the attack. As the atoll's isolation limits engagement with historic resources, the KOCOA data were used to create digital outreach materials which address the atoll's heritage.

Introduction

On 4 June 1942, the Imperial Japanese Navy (IJN) launched an attack on U.S. Naval Air Station Midway Islands to destroy the base and draw the remaining American carrier fleet in the Pacific into battle. Only seven months after the attack on Pearl Harbor, the four-day engagement ended with the withdrawal of Japanese forces and American retention of the base. While the engagement has been portrayed as a decisive turning point for American victory in the Pacific, the battle was not without sacrifice; over 2,400 Japanese and 300 Americans gave their lives in defense of their countries (Office of Naval Intelligence 1943:54; Thompson 1986).

Following the battle, the story of Midway became synonymous with American victory. Depicted in scaled dioramas of the attack, the events of the battle were retold across the country on the pages of LIFE (LIFE 1942a, 1942b, 1942c). In the decades following the attack, books, memoirs, and even a 1976 blockbuster starring Charlton Heston, continue to draw attention to the battle and keep the engagement at the forefront of American memory (Layton et al. 2006; Parshall and Tully 2007; Symonds 2011).

Given the significance of the battle, World War II (WWII) era structures on Midway have been placed on the U.S. National Register of Historic Places (NRHP). The atoll itself is protected as a National Wildlife Refuge and a National Memorial (FWS 2000). As part of the larger Papahānaumokuākea Marine National Monument (PMNM) and United Nations Educational, Scientific, and Cultural Organization (UNESCO) World Heritage Site, the atoll's significance, both natural and cultural, is recognized on a global scale (NOAA 2017).

While there are parties who share an interest in preserving and promoting cultural heritage at Midway, the atoll's physical isolation—1,300 miles northwest of Oahu—remains the largest barrier to ongoing research and outreach. Historic buildings at the atoll are maintained by a skeleton crew of U.S. Fish and Wildlife Service (FWS) staff; however, public visitation to these structures ended with budget cuts in 2008 (FWS 2016). Furthermore, as the battle took place both at the atoll and at the location of the carrier fleet (stationed 400 miles to the northwest), much of the associated submerged material culture has not been located.

In December 2016, East Carolina University was invited to collaborate on a joint U.S. National Oceanic and Atmospheric Administration (NOAA) and National Park Service (NPS) exploratory remote sensing survey of Midway Atoll. The survey took place in 2017, coinciding with the 75th anniversary of the Battle of Midway. ECU's archival and historical research contributed to the project's reconstruction of the physical battle. As the actions and decisions made in June 1942 continue to impact families and communities on a global scale, the project's aim was to not only reconstruct the physical features of the battle on paper, but build digital content addressing the main battle narrative to be shared with the public.

KOCOA Military Terrain Analysis

KOCOA military terrain analysis is one of several methodologies employed in battlescape analysis; moreover, it is a requisite of grants funded by the NPS American Battlefield Protection Program (ABPP) (NPS 2016). While the 2017 fieldwork was not funded through the ABPP, the high volume of ongoing ABPP research has established KOCOA analysis as industry standard. Subsequently, over the past decade researchers have placed emphasis on expanding KOCOA analysis, which was primarily terrestrial, to include naval and aerial engagements (Babits et al. 2011, Frye and Resnick 2013).

KOCOA analysis is used in ABPP grants to delineate core, battlefield, and potential NRHP boundaries (NPS 2016). As the WWII-era structures located at Midway Atoll are already recognized on the National Register, the focus of the historical analysis was to expand KOCOA use to identify human actions which shaped the events of the battle. Although the story of Midway is often retold chronologically, the decisions prior to and during the engagement were made spatially. Through expansion of KOCOA analysis, the battle of Midway was retold spatially using the ArcGIS Story Maps platform (see below) in hopes of recognizing the actions of aviators, sailors, and commanders who shaped the battle and the associated material record.

KOCOA analysis developed in the U.S. armed forces to collect and analyze geographic intelligence prior to battle (Department of Army 1994). The analysis, which uses primary and secondary battle histories, identifies five terrain feature groupings which either facilitate or hinder an engagement: Key/decisive terrain, Observation and fields of fire, Cover and concealment, Obstacles, and Avenues of approach/withdrawal (Table 1) (Department of Army 1994; NPS 2016). The U.S. Army (1994) published considerations for intelligence preparation of an aerial battlespace in the 1990s, while work conducted by Babits et al. (2011) expanded the terrestrial analysis to include historic naval. Both these expanded sets of parameters are presented with examples in Table 1.

Compared to terrestrial terrain analysis, many of the KOCOA naval attributes have new, often-situational, parameters due to the restrictions of naval technologies (Babits et al. 2011). Aerial KOCOA attributes share similar situational environmental parameters, such as weather or time of day. Other technological considerations for aerial combat, such as fuel consumption limits and flight ceiling, also impact parameters by dictating the placement of terrestrial features such as anti-aircraft artillery, refueling areas, and rendezvous points.

Before discussing examples of aerial KOCOA attributes, there are a few considerations involving aerial terrain features which should be mentioned. When compared to terrestrial analyses, aerial engagements take place over a larger geographical area, which emphasizes the need for increased surveillance capacity and mobile fields of fire. Aircraft restrictions and technology can, in some cases, severely limit observation, areas of approach/withdrawal, and cover. Finally, many of the aerial KOCOA attributes have temporal components related to weather, time of day, and topography (Department of Army 1994).

Key Terrain and Area of Observation

Analysis of primary sources for KOCOA key terrain features indicated that aviators stationed at Midway were familiar with an expanded battlescape across the northwestern Hawaiian Islands, which included landing zones, refueling stops, and rendezvous points at nearby atolls (Figure 1). Each of these features played a significant role in decisions made by aviators and shaped the battle's material record.

Prior to the battle, it was known that the atoll's islands—Sand and Eastern—and the U.S. aircraft carriers were the main objectives of the Japanese fleet (Office of Naval Intelligence 1947:3). U.S. forces patrolled the determined decisive terrain—a 700 mile radius of navigable waters surrounding the island and airspace around the carriers (Office of Naval Intelligence 1947:2). Radar supplemented this search area by providing continuous coverage of the 100 miles around the atoll (Simard 1942:2). At 6 a.m. on 4 June, the Midway radar

Attribute	Terrestrial	Aerial Parameters	Maritime Parameters	Examples
Key and Decisive Terrain	Features that dominate immediate surroundings by relief or some other quality that enhances attack/defense	Enemy held areas, forces, and infrastructure including landing zones, drop zones, and refueling areas.	Navigable waterways offer access to terrestrial targets.	High ground, transportation choke points, landing/loading and refueling areas, navigable waterways.
Observation and Fields of Fire	The ability to see friendly and enemy forces. Also, areas that weapons may cover/fire upon effectively.	Aircraft and ground forces need large clearings for visibility. Maximum firing range of artillery limits aerial combat.	Coastal defenses and vessels are high-visibility structures. Vessel armament defines field of fire but will fluctuate with environment and enemy defenses.	High ground, sloping ground, entrenched positions, ship superstructure, observation towers, radar, some terrestrial coastal defenses.
Cover and Concealment	Protection from enemy fire, observation, and surveillance.	Surveillance equipment, cloud cover, time of day, and topography impact visibility.	Defenders often know navigable waters and create defenses to protect/obstruct waterways. Vessels provide cover.	Ditches, buildings, walls, forests, ravines, reverse slopes, radar, cloud cover, night, vessels.
Obstacles	Natural or man-made landscape features that prevent, impede, or divert movement.	Weather/time of day limit visibility. Flight ceiling, fuel consumption, and enemy artillery limit maneuverability.	Set and temporally variable obstacles such as weather exist. Water is an obstacle itself to terrestrial forces.	Swamps, rivers, bridges, reefs, earthworks, sandbars, navigable channels, fog, anti-aircraft artillery.
Avenues of Approach and Withdrawal	Relatively unobstructed route that leads to and/or away from an objective or key terrain.	Approach from staging area for fixed wing aircraft is limited by terrestrial terrain features, fuel load, and flight ceiling.	Navigable channels are avenues of approach, however tides and wind may stall withdrawal along same route.	Roads, paths, creek beds, navigable channels, air channels, valleys and low altitude areas.

Table 1: KOCOA Attribute Definitions. (After Department of Army 1994; Babits et al. 2011; NPS 2016).

operator alerted pilots on the runway to the encroaching Japanese squadron with the words "Unidentified Planes Sighted" (Shannon 1942:1). American Buffalo fighters and Douglas SBD Dauntless scout bombers patrolled Midway's airspace while Japanese bombers and fighters strafed visible key terrain at the atoll, targeting the power plant, hangars, and fuel storage areas (Shannon 1942:2; Nimitz 1942:8). The attack disrupted communications and caused substantial damage to the seaplane base. Consequently, the "columns of smoke rising" from Midway became a beacon for bomber pilots unable to return to the American carrier fleet (Cummings 1942:1). When a squadron of 13 SBD Dauntless scout bombers was unable to return to USS Hornet, they successfully located the burning silhouette of the atoll. Although 2 bombers wrecked in the atoll's lagoon before reaching the runway, the other 11 successfully landed and continued to participate in flight operations (Cummings 1942:1; Shannon 1942:3).

Fields of Fire and Obstacles

Modifications, including beach fortifications and reinforced anti-aircraft (AA) batteries were constructed at the atoll in May 1942, yet during the attack it was discovered that their firing speed was unable to keep up with that of Japanese aircraft (Irwin 1942:35). American fighter and bomber pilots, too, were consistently out-flown by their Japanese counterparts. For example, the American Consolidated PBY-5 Catalina bomber's flight ceiling was severely limited compared to that of the Japanese Aichi D3A Type 99 bombers, while the American Brewster F2A-3 Buffalo fighters were too slow to attack the Japanese A6M Zero fighters (Bellinger 1942:2). The resulting narrative is one of both failure and perseverance—of the twenty-seven fighter planes defending the base, only a handful returned unharmed following the Japanese attack (Office of Naval Intelligence 1943). Captain P.R. White (1942:2) later stated in his report that "any commander that orders pilots out for combat in a F2A-3 should consider the pilot as lost before leaving the ground."

The severe spatial restrictions for aircraft (speed and flight ceiling) as well as the atoll's fixed artillery range limited the efficacy of the islands' defenses. Second Lieutenant D.D. Irwin (1942:2), a Brewster pilot during the attack, later testified "the Japanese had little regard for our ground anti-aircraft fire, which almost always burst behind the plane fired upon."

As the Japanese attack progressed, the Motor Torpedo (PT) Boat squadron stationed at the atoll became the

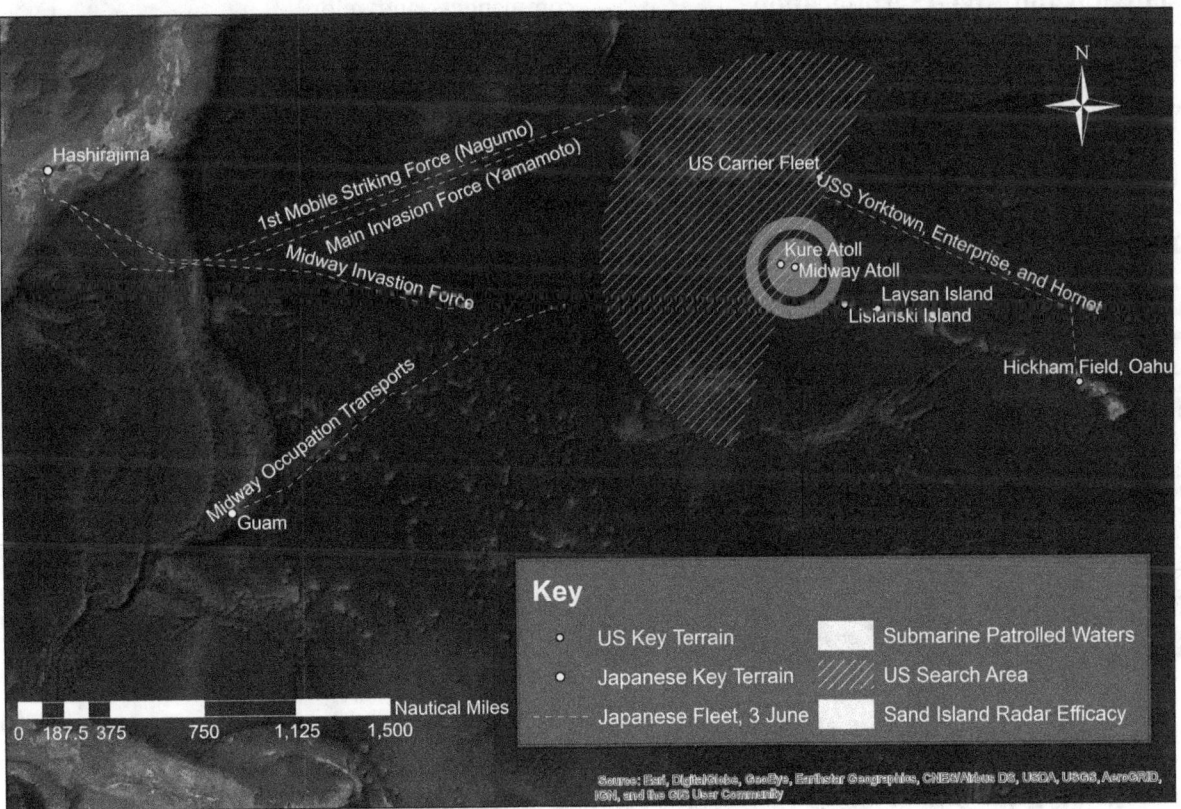

Figure 1: Battle of Midway Key Terrain and Area of Observation.

unsung heroes of the battle. The PT vessels' fields of fire could be repositioned relative to Japanese dive bombers, and were significantly more effective than terrestrial anti-aircraft fire during the battle (Nimitz 1942). Following the attack, the PT boats continued to patrol the atoll's waters for crash survivors and served a vital role in enhancing observation of friendly forces post-battle (Tyler 1942:4).

Cover and Concealment

Extensive cover was constructed at the atoll prior to the battle. Batteries were reinforced with sandbags and cribbed sand embankments, while armor and leak proof fuel tanks were added to American bombers to decrease damage from enemy fire (Pye 1942:5; Shannon 1942:4). Unfortunately, this cover was of little use during the attack—Japanese Zero fighters consistently outflew American planes while ground anti-aircraft fire was "inefficient against a multiplicity of targets" (Pye 1942:2; Nimitz 1942:25). Concealment using cloud cover became the primary means of protection for American bombers during the attack as American forces could scout Japanese planes without detection if they rode changing weather fronts (Kimes 1942:3; Pye 1942:2).

Discussion and ArcGIS Application

The above-mentioned examples of KOCOA features illustrate the immaterial heritage of the battle of Midway. Intangible KOCOA features, such as routes and temporal conditions, shaped human action while physical cultural heritage, such as targeted buildings and wreck sites, offers insight into the experiences of those who served. Midway has remained inhabited since the war and the terrestrial landscape has been heavily modified, which has resulted in the loss of terrestrial cultural heritage (LIFE 1942c). As contemporary WWII buildings on the atoll are already on the NRHP, the historic research component shifted towards presenting intangible aspects of the battle to the public, emphasizing the stories of those involved.

ESRI's ArcGIS Story Maps application became the preferred platform for public outreach associated with historic research. Story Maps was chosen because the versatile workspace can display interactive geospatial data alongside static text, images, and video. Concepts addressing large geographic areas, such as key terrain central to the battle narrative, were displayed with interpretive text, historic images, and personal accounts (Figure 2). Abstract terrain features identified in the KOCOA analysis, such as flight ceiling and radar efficacy, were also portrayed spatially, adding another level of analysis to the ongoing narrative. Perhaps more importantly, the reader could interact with the spatial data sets at various scales, linking the experiences and decisions on the ground with those of Japanese and American aviators, commanders, and sailors.

Finally, while the aim of the KOCOA analysis was to retell the battle through spatial, rather than temporal means, the Story Map facilitated an understanding of the battle of Midway by linking the past with the present. Results from the 2017 NOAA/NPS field survey

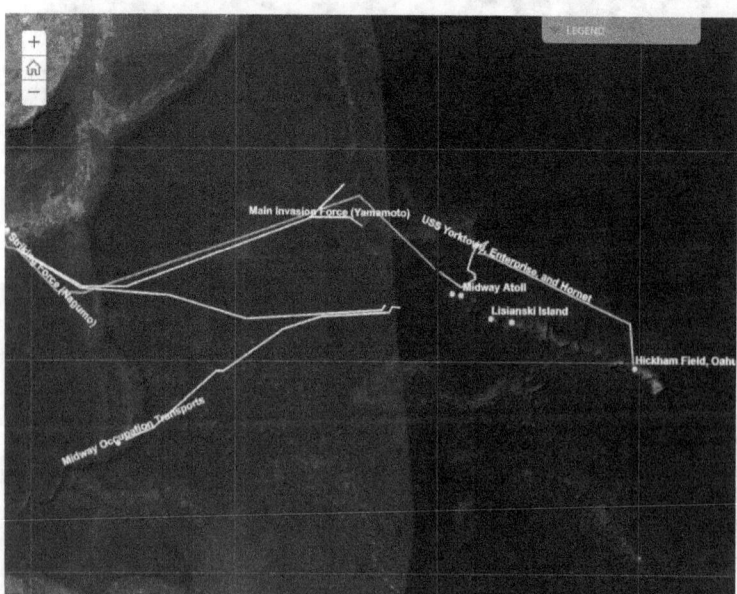

Figure 2: Key Terrain displayed through the ArcGIS Battle of Midway Story Map.

project, as well as previous archaeological work, were incorporated to provide readers with access, albeit digital, to tangible remains of the battle.

Conclusion

KOCOA attributes have been used for site detection and preservation of historic battlefields, both terrestrial and submerged. When re-assessed for aerial engagements, attributes often adopt situational parameters, while the battlefield grows in vertical and horizontal scale to accommodate aerial warfare. KOCOA analysis of aerial engagements at Midway brought new light to terrestrial terrain features and demonstrated the scale and significance of resources underemphasized in chronological works. Yet despite an expanded battlescape, human actions at Midway were still shaped by the atoll's terrain features, which today provide a tangible link to intangible aviation heritage. While this research is ongoing, the geospatial data generated from KOCOA analysis led to the creation of digital content through the ESRI ArcGIS Story Maps application. The Battle of Midway Story Map, while still evolving, has helped to bridge tangible and intangible heritage with preservation and community outreach.

Acknowledgements

Many thanks to Dr. Kelly Keogh at Papahānaumokuākea Marine National Monument, National Oceanic and Atmospheric Administration, and Bert Ho, Submerged Resources Center, National Park Service for spearheading this research. Their feedback, contributions, and support were invaluable throughout the project. East Carolina University's Program in Maritime Studies also donated significant resources to this project and provided ample technological support. Special thanks also to Lynker Technologies for their administrative support and expertise.

References

BABITS, LAWRENCE, CHRISTOPHER T. ESPENSHADE, AND SARAH LOWRY
2011 *Battlefield Analysis: Six Maritime Battles in Maryland Revolutionary War and War of 1812.* New South Associates, Final Report. Stone Mountain, GA.

BELLINGER, P.N.L.
1942 *Employment of Aircraft in Connection with Enemy Attack on Midway.* Manuscript, U.S. Navy, Midway Island, HI.

CUMMINGS, DANIEL L.
1942 Statement of Second Lieutenant Daniel L. Cummings, USMCR(V). *Report of Enemy Action, Midway Island, United States Marine Corps*, editor, pp. 55–56. Marine Aircraft Group Twenty One, Second Marine Aircraft Wing, Fleet Marine Force, Report of Enemy Action. U.S. Marine Corps, Midway Island, HI.

DEPARTMENT OF ARMY
1994 *Intelligence Preparation of the Battlefield.* U.S. Army, Field Manual. Washington, D.C.

FRYE, LORI, AND BENJAMIN RESNICK
2013 *National Register of Historic Places Registration Form: Ewa Plain Battlefield.* GAI Consultants, Inc., National Register of Historic Places Registration Form. Homestead, PA.

IRWIN, D. D.
1942 *Statement of Second Lieutenant D. D. Irwin, USMCR. Report of Enemy Action, Midway Island, United States Marine Corps*, editor, pp. 34–35. Marine Aircraft Group Twenty One, Second Marine Aircraft Wing, Fleet Marine Force, Report of Enemy Action. U.S. Marine Corps, Midway Island, HI.

KIMES, IRA L.
1942 *Battle of Midway Islands, Report Of. Marine Aircraft Group Twenty-Two, Report.* U.S. Marine Corps, Midway Island, HI.

LAYTON, REAR ADMIRAL EDWIN T., CAPTAIN ROGER PINEAU, & JOHN COSTELLO
2006 *And I Was There: Breaking the Secrets - Pearl Harbor and Midway.* Naval Institute Press, Annapolis, MD.

LIFE
1942a "U.S. Fleet Wins Victory at Midway." In *LIFE* 12(25):24-25.

1942b "Midway Battle: Navy Releases First Complete Story." In *LIFE* 13(4):32-34.

1942c "Life on Midway: On a Pacific Outpost, Marines Make a Home." In *LIFE* 13(21): 118-130.

NATIONAL PARK SERVICE (NPS)
2016 *Battlefield Survey Manual American Battlefield Protection Program.* Revised. National Park Service, Washington, DC <https://www.nps.gov/abpp/SurveyManual_NEW%202016%20Reviewed.pdf>. Accessed 25 February 2018.

NATIONAL OCEANOGRAPHIC AND ATMOSPHERIC ADMINISTRATION (NOAA)
2017 Papahānaumokuākea Marine National Monument. Papahānaumokuākea Marine National Monument <http://www.papahanaumokuakea.gov/new-about/>. Accessed 19 April 2017.

NIMITZ, C.W.
1942 *Battle of Midway*. Manuscript, U.S. Navy, Pearl Harbor, HI.

OFFICE OF NAVAL INTELLIGENCE
1943 *Combat Narratives Battle of Midway June 3-6, 1942*. U.S. Navy, Washington, DC.

1947 *The Japanese Story of the Battle of Midway, a Translation*. U.S. Navy, Washington, DC.

PARSHALL, JONATHAN, AND ANTHONY TULLY
2007 *Shattered Sword: The Untold Story of the Battle of Midway*, reprinted from 2005 edition. Potomac Books, Washington, DC.

PYE, W.S.
1942 *Commander in Chief, U.S. Pacific Fleet Report of Action, The Battle of Midway, June 3-6, 1942, Comments On*. Manuscript, Naval War College, Newport, RI.

SHANNON, H.D.
1942 *Report of Action on Morning of 4 June, 1942, and Night of 4-5 June, 1942*. Manuscript, U.S. Marine Corps, Midway Island, HI.

SIMARD, C.T.
1942 *Report of Engagement with Enemy, Battle of Midway 30 May to 7 June, 1942*. Manuscript, United States Naval Air, Midway Island, HI.

SYMONDS, CRAIG L.
2011 *The Battle of Midway*. Oxford University Press, UK.

THOMPSON, ERWIN N.
1986 *World War II-Era Military Facilities, Midway Islands National Register Nomination*. National Park Service, National Register of Historic Places Inventory Nomination Form. Washington, DC.

TYLER, M.A.
1942 *Report of Activities of VSMB-241 during June 4 and June 5, 1942*. VSMB-241, Activity Report. U.S. Marine Corps, Midway Island, HI.

US FISH AND WILDLIFE SERVICE (FWS)
2000 *Midway Atoll National Wildlife Refuge*. U.S. Fish and Wildlife Service, Washington, DC.

2016 Virtual Visitation. In *Midway Atoll National Wildlife Refuge and Battle of Midway National Memorial*. <https://www.fws.gov/nwrs/threecolumn.aspx?id=2147597177>. Accessed 25 February 2018.

WHITE, P. R.
1942 Statement of Captain P.R. White, USMC. *Report of Enemy Action, Midway Island, United States Marine Corps*, editor, pp. 22–23. Marine Aircraft Group Twenty One, Second Marine Aircraft Wing, Fleet Marine Force, Report of Enemy Action. U.S. Marine Corps, Midway Island, HI.

・・・・・・・・・・・・・・・・

Madeline Roth
302 E. 9th St.
Greenville, NC 27858

Jennifer McKinnon
302 E. 9th St.
Greenville, NC 27858

Lost at Sea: The Archival and Archaeological Investigation of Two Submerged F8F Bearcats

Hunter W. Whitehead

Naval Air Station (NAS) Pensacola, renowned as the 'Cradle of Naval Aviation', has been a fundamental pilot training facility for the U.S. Navy since its establishment in 1914. World War I ensured aviation would remain an important aspect of U.S. naval warfare, and led to an increased influx of prospective aviation cadets at NAS Pensacola. Subsequent decades of training led to hundreds of training accidents, and the loss of naval aircraft in the waters off Pensacola, Florida. Two F8F Bearcat wreck sites are discussed here, including the methods involved in aircraft investigation, and the historical documents utilized in their identification.

Introduction

It has taken archaeologists some time to realize the significance of aviation cultural resources, a change illustrated by numerous theses and dissertations (Capelotti 1996; Goldstein 1997; Ford 2006; Jung 2008; Bell 2010; Burgess 2013; Daly 2015; Pruitt 2015; Ortiz 2016). Archaeologist Richard Gould (1983) may have been the first to point out this potential. In the 1990s, U.S. federal and state agencies began inventorying aircraft wreck sites (Grant et al. 1996; Neyland and Grant 1999), and creating management plans (Diebold 1993; Whipple 1995; Milbrooke et al. 1998). This push for management and study of historic aircraft sites was a further application of cultural heritage management to resources beyond shipwrecks, likely induced by legislation such as NHPA, ARPA, etc. Over the last two decades there have been numerous studies of aircraft wreck sites worldwide (Coble and Van Tilburg 1998; Beeker and Smith 2005; Chenoweth et al. 2006; Ford 2006; Petrey et al. 2008; Bell 2015). Despite a growing number of investigations, some posit that there is still a lack of cohesive standard methodology or theoretical framework (Fix 2011). A recent study of naval aircraft sites in Pensacola adds to the body of aviation archaeology research, and discusses methods of identifying submerged naval aircraft.

The following is the investigation of historical documents pertaining to two Grumman F8F Bearcats located in the Gulf of Mexico off Pensacola, Florida (Figures 1 and 2). Submerged naval aircraft research requires both archaeological and archival inquiry. University of West Florida (UWF) archaeologists' initial site assessments (Whitehead and Mauro 2016) of the two submerged aircraft revealed the aircraft type through comparisons of site features with the plethora of WWII aircraft literature (Ireland 1998; Mondey 2002). To answer the crucial question of aircraft identification, UWF archaeologists explored various historical Navy documents and examined the histories of Naval Air Station (NAS) Pensacola, and the F8F Bearcat.

Historical Background

Known as the cradle of naval aviation, Pensacola, Florida played a crucial role in the development of naval air technology and strategy. There, the Navy established the nation's first Naval Aeronautical Station in 1914, with a unit that consisted of nine officers, twenty-three enlisted men, seven aircraft, portable hangars and other gear (Pearce 1980:132). The aviation training facility produced few aviators prior to WWI; upon entry, the Naval Aviation Unit had 38 qualified pilots, 163 enlisted men, and 54 airplanes. By the conclusion of the war, this number expanded to 2,049 pilots, 43,452 enlisted men, and 2,107 airplanes (U.S. Navy 1958:17). Naval Air Station (NAS) Pensacola, thus designated 17 December 1917, was not the only air station but certainly the largest station of its kind. Flight training included aerial gunnery, bombing, navigation, photography, signaling, radio, aircraft rigging, and orientation in plane and engine structure. Flight-school classes were small during the 1920s and early 1930s, the latter partially due to the Great Depression. The impending U.S. entry into WWII restored the naval aviation training program and pushed the limits of existing Naval Air Stations.

President Franklin Roosevelt began expanding the U.S. military in the mid-1930s due to German and Japanese aggression. For the Navy, this meant exploring ideas of utilizing aircraft aboard aircraft carriers and increased training of naval pilots. The War Department approached the Navy about starting a training program under the Naval Aviation Cadet Act, and the first class of aviation cadets began their training in July 1935. Due to the large number of students, NAS Pensacola was unable to sustain the training program and similar programs were installed at NAS Corpus Christi and NAS Jacksonville. These programs produced a substantial number of naval aviators; when the U.S. entered the war, 7 December 1941, the Navy counted 5,900 pilots to fly its 5,233 planes (Wynne and Moorhead 2010:98). The need for more pilots and planes was clear, and by the end of the war, NAS Pensacola's program produced over 28,000 naval aviators. (Wynne and Moorhead 2010:98-99).

The level of growth resulting from WWII at NAS Pensacola certainly surpassed that of WWI. Prior to World War II, the navy constructed and utilized Chevalier (formerly Station Field), Corry, and Saufley Fields for training exercises. In 1941, to assist the war-incurred increase of flight students, Ellyson Field was commissioned, followed by Bronson and Barin Fields in 1942, and Whiting Field in 1943 (Wynn and Moorhead 2010:109). The Navy utilized these fields for various training exercises including, though not limited to, navigation, night flying, and carrier landing qualifications. As pointed out by historian, George F. Pearce (1980), the growth of NAS Pensacola's facilities would have seemed incredible to those pioneer naval aviators that erected tent hangars on the beach in 1914.

F8F Bearcat

The Grumman Aircraft and Engineering Corporation, later changed to Grumman Aerospace Corporation, opened in 1930 and quickly became a leading aircraft contractor with the Navy. Grumman's first aircraft design contract with the Navy was in 1931, when the company began developing the XFF-1 (Thruelsen 1976). Navy aircraft designations, for standardization and continuity, had specific meanings for each letter and number. The 'X' stands for experimental, the 'F' for fighter, the latter 'F' is the manufacturer code for Grumman, and the '-1' is the variant of aircraft (Campbell 2012:7-9). Once an aircraft was put into production, the designation would lose the 'X', and when different variants of the aircraft were designed, the designation would be sequential: '-1', '-2', '-3', etc. Grumman continued to design and produce aircraft for the Navy in a rather evolutionary fashion. The Grumman design, especially from the F4F Wildcat, the F6F Hellcat, and the F8F Bearcat, maintained a distinct 'bumblebee' shape not seen in other aircraft prior. Of note, Grumman requested the family

Figure 1: A. Burkhard recording the cockpit of F8F Bearcat 1.

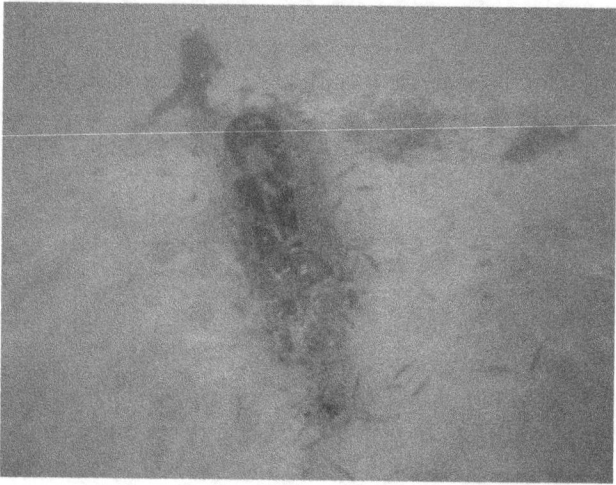

Figure 2: Aft Side of F8F Bearcat 2, Diver A. Van Slyke for Scale.

name of 'cats' for their future aircraft, just as Douglas Aircraft Company requested 'sky' (Cagle 1963).

The F4F Wildcat and F6F Hellcat served the Navy well during WWII, although Navy planners as well as Grumman employees were certainly trying to stay one step ahead of Japanese aircraft designs. Therefore, in the summer of 1943, Grumman submitted the designs for a lighter and more maneuverable aircraft: the F8F Bearcat (Figure 3). The Bearcat design utilized the Pratt & Whitney R-2800 Double Wasp engine used in the F6F Hellcat, and the Vought F4U Corsair (Mondey 1982). It also saw improvements such as a bubble canopy, allowing for a better field of view, and revolutionary breakaway wing tips. This concept was to allow the aircraft to reach 9Gs of force without requiring as heavy of an aircraft. Once the aircraft reached 9Gs the wing tips would automatically break off, potentially allowing for a safe return home (Aerodata International

Figure 3: Grumman F8F Bearcat Fighter NH 80-G-K-15898 (Courtesy of the Naval History & Heritage Command).

1987:100). The Navy was impressed and ordered two XF8F-1 prototypes in November 1943. After successful flight demonstrations, the Navy ordered 2,023 F8F-1 Bearcats in October 1944. Due to wartime demands, it was common for aircraft companies to subcontract their designs, therefore the Navy ordered an additional 1,876 F3M-1 (F8F-1) Bearcats from General Motors in February 1945 (Mondey 1982:147).

Grumman quickly began production of the F8F-1, and the Navy's carrier qualification training began soon after. The first Bearcat squadron, VF-19, was formed at NAS Santa Rosa in May 1945 and was soon headed to the Pacific theater onboard the USS Langley (Maloney 1969). Before arrival, VJ day transpired and the F8F Bearcat never saw combat with the U.S. Navy. The Navy reduced Grumman's Bearcat contract to 770 planes and General Motors' was cancelled altogether. The Bearcat did play a role in the Navy's postwar plans, however, its role was minimal due to arising jet technology. A delay in jet production allowed F8F Bearcats to serve in nine squadrons by the end of 1946. In the same year, Grumman tested the XF8F-2; the prototype that had changes such as a new R-2800 engine variant and an enlarged vertical stabilizer (Maloney 1969). By 1949, the F8F Bearcat flew in 28 squadrons, but was soon phased into the Naval Air Reserve and by June 1950 the F8F-1 replaced the F6F Hellcat as the Navy's principal advanced trainer fighter. While the Bearcat primarily served as a carrier qualification trainer, it did see combat when the Navy gave 100 F8F-1s and F8F-1Bs to the French Aeronavale during the French Indochina War. Understanding the historical background of NAS Pensacola and the role of the F8F Bearcat is essential to conducting site-specific research on potential submerged cultural heritage sites.

Methods

Naval aircraft research requires archaeological investigation and archival inquiry. Archaeological fieldwork is necessary for the two-part equation of identifying the aircraft, but it is first essential to understand which documents are likely to hold the information needed to identify the aircraft, and to determine the archival repository in which those documents may reside.

Archival Phase of Research

A variety of archives around the nation may hold naval historical documents, including the National Archives and Records Administration (NARA), Naval History and Heritage Command (NHHC) archives, aviation museums, and an assortment of other repositories. UWF archaeologists contacted the NHHC's Underwater Archaeology Branch (UAB), to first notify the intent to study naval aircraft, but also to seek the advice of their aviation resource specialists. Unfortunately,

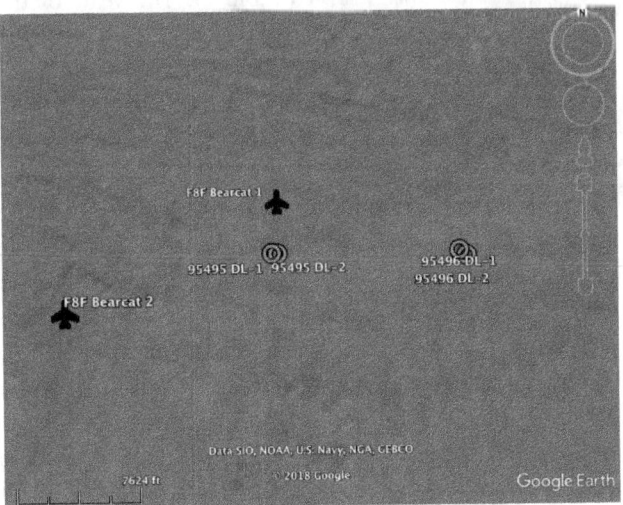

Figure 4: Comparison of Actual, Deck Log, and Aircraft Accident Report Locations (Google Earth).

Date of Accident	Aircraft Model	BuNo	Last Name	First Name	Accident Location	Pilot Recoverd
2/13/50	F8F-1	95495	Hosemann	Leland S.	USS Cabot	Yes
11/7/50	F8F-1	95496	Shade	Lester L.	USS Wright	No
4/18/51	F8F-1	94901	Gulshen	Francis J.	USS Monterey	Yes
4/21/52	F8F-1	95134	Spaeth	Stanley, Milton	USS Cabot	No

Table 1: Accident Reports Of F8f Bearcats 'Lost At Sea' In Pensacola, Florida (Nhhc Aircraft Accident Report Microfilm Collection)

a quintessential document that reveals all necessary identifying elements does not exist. According to Pruitt and McKinnon (2016:46), "Researchers are still required to travel to multiple archives and sift through countless primary sources, crosschecking facts and drawing on secondary sources." Therefore, the first step in the current investigation was to visit Washington D.C. and request the assistance of the respective archivists.

The NHHC holds microfilm copies of the Navy's Aircraft Accident Reports (AAR), which are organized by aircraft type, making it difficult to find records based on geographical information or Bureau Number (BuNo). Therefore, it was necessary to examine each F8F Bearcat AAR to determine if the aircraft was operating near Pensacola, and if the accident resulted in the loss of the aircraft at sea. The AARs hold a range of data regarding the accident, including, though not limited to, pilot name, time, flight purpose, and various accident analyses. They also contain varying geographical data that generally includes the flight origin and location of accident and possibly the approximate latitude and longitude coordinates. This type of data allows for a narrowing of aircraft possibilities and leads to the cross-examination of other primary documents such as deck logs of the aircraft carriers which lost F8F Bearcats at sea in Pensacola.

The NARA archives contain a plethora of naval aviation documents; e.g., general correspondence, courts of inquiry, and naval deck logs, etc. It should be noted that NARA also retains the physical copies of naval AARs, which hold additional correspondence and analyses attached to the original. Unfortunately, the documents are organized by aircraft type and at this time have not been fully examined by the author. Instead, investigators solely examined the deck logs of those aircraft carriers identified by the NHHC AARs. The aircraft carrier deck logs contain activity reports from on board the vessel, including locational information, inspections, daily routines, and occasionally aircraft accidents.

The AARs and deck logs, when compared to one another, provide the most valuable locational contexts. Other documents may provide valuable background information, if and when the aircraft in question are identified. In this case, the historic *Pensacola Journal* allowed for cross-examination of accident events, and provided valuable personal information not included in Navy reports, such as the names of family members, former education, etc. A number of other documents may be examined to answer additional research questions, though at this time locational information is of principal importance.

Results

In a order to place a submerged aircraft wreck site within its archaeological and historical context it is necessary to identify the aircraft type. UWF archaeologists discerned the aircraft type of the two submerged F8F Bearcats through archaeological research, visual comparisons with secondary sources, and discussion with aircraft specialists. It was then necessary to determine how many F8F Bearcats crashed off Pensacola through Navy AARs.

Aircraft Accident Reports

The author discovered four AARs (U.S. Bureau of Naval Aeronautics 1950a, 1950b, 1951, 1951) indicating F8F-1 Bearcats that were 'Lost at Sea' in Pensacola. These reports indicated aircraft with BuNos 95495, 95496, 94901, and 95134 (Table 1). The years of the accidents ranged from 1950 to 1952, and occurred during carrier qualification training on three different aircraft carriers: USS Cabot, USS Monterey, and USS Wright. Each pilot and aircraft was attached to the Carrier Qualification Training Unit 4 at Corry Field. Each accident occurred during landing procedures, suggesting the difficulty of this maneuver. Lester L. Shade and Stanley Milton Spaeth, pilots of BuNos 95496 and 95134 respectively, were both 'Lost at Sea'. The two surviving pilots, Leland S. Hosemann and Francis J. Gulshen, reported making over-corrections at the time of crash when they believed their aircraft to be stalled (U.S. Navy Bureau of Aeronautics 1950a, 1951). The AARs for BuNos 94901 and 95134 contained general latitude and longitude coordinates, which were used to identify the known wreck sites. To gain data on the other

BuNos' locations, the deck logs of corresponding aircraft carriers were referenced.

Aircraft Carrier Deck Logs

By cross-referencing the dates of aircraft accidents with aircraft carrier deck log entries, researchers revealed some locational data. The deck logs (U.S. Department of the Navy 1950a, 1950b, 1951, 1952) exposed coordinates for the two BuNos lacking coordinates on the AARs; 95495 and 95496. The deck log's locational information for BuNo 95134 corresponded with the AAR, but for BuNo 94901, the deck log entry caused some confusion. The coordinate data on the 94901 AAR and deck log entry did not coincide. The latitudinal coordinates on each document have a difference of roughly 31 minutes, a wide error. This difference likely is a result of contemporary clerical errors. The deck log is recorded as events are happening aboard the ship, and the AAR is recorded after an analysis of the event is complete. Unfortunately, one cannot be sure which information is correct; therefore, both coordinates should be considered.

Pensacola Journal

The historic news articles did not disclose locational data but added some brief background information that may be utilized for future in-depth analyses of the pilots. Only the accidents pertaining to pilots' deaths appeared in the journal (*Pensacola News Journal* 1950, 1952). This may be due to Navy disclosure, and likely because of the large amount of aircraft losses during training. Lester L. Shade had only reported to duty in Pensacola in 1949 for flight training before his death in 1950 (U.S. Navy Bureau of Aeronautics 1950b). The other reported accident did not include the pilot's name pending notification of next of kin, but corresponds with Stanley Milton Spaeth's accident resulting in his death. While the articles do not add to the locational analyses of the accidents, they provide important background information on the importance of the Navy's presence in Pensacola, and key information on the pilots.

Locational Analyses

The author plotted the latitude and longitude coordinates from the assorted documents into Google Earth to determine their proximity to the known Bearcat sites (Figure 4). The black aircraft symbols indicate the two known Bearcats, labeled F8F Bearcat 1 and F8F Bearcat 2. The red aircraft symbols indicate the coordinates found in the deck logs (DL) and Aircraft Accident Reports (AAR). Because some coordinates lacked 'seconds', the minimum and maximum values were substituted and are indicated in the figure by a -1 or a -2 respectively. For example, a latitudinal coordinate labeled 30 06' N would be substituted by 30 6.00 N and 30 6.59 N. One second is equal to 101 feet, so 59 seconds difference would a range of just under 1 nautical mile, therefore the difference between the -1 and -2 values is relatively minimal.

The known Bearcat sites correlate most closely with the locational data from BuNos 95495 and 95496, although it may be difficult to discern one site from the other due to their close proximity. The deck log referencing BuNo 94901 indicated that the crash occurred roughly 18 miles inland, and thus may be disregarded as the identity of a potential submerged site. BuNos 94901 and 95134, as shown by the deck logs and AARs, plot too far away from the wreck sites to be considered likely candidates; they are located roughly 12 and 25 miles away, respectively. Therefore, the use of historical documents allowed for a process of elimination, and narrowed the possible aircraft identities to two BuNos. The sites' proximity, roughly 3.5 miles apart, combined with the vague recorded coordinates, may cause further identification to be difficult, if not impossible.

Conclusions

While it is probable that the two submerged Bearcats correspond to BuNos 95495 and 95496, the possibility must be considered that not all lines of archival evidence have survived. During a research internship in 2016, the author discovered that aircraft losses occasionally do not have a corresponding AAR in the NHHC archives (Whitehead 2016). The project involved identifying a WWII-era aircraft engine that had been salvaged by Japanese fishermen. Cross-referencing documents, in a similar fashion as this project, led the author to documents called Aircraft Carrier Action Reports. One such report indicated a F4U Corsair 'Lost at Sea' that did not have a corresponding AAR. Thus, one should be aware of discrepancies within the archives.

Presuming that the archival evidence is complete, and the two submerged aircraft are the corresponding BuNos, it is still unlikely that these aircraft will be identified beyond this level without additional fieldwork. Each aircraft contains a BuNo plate, usually within the cockpit. If this plate survived on either of the planes, identification would be possible. Unfortunately, at this time UWF archaeologists have been unable to see or find such a plate. Further locational evidence or methods may assist archaeologists in the future, however, there will always be a shred of doubt without physical evidence.

Recommendations for Future Research

As aforementioned, aircraft identification is a prerequisite for aviation archaeological research. Without this key information, further in-depth research would be difficult, if not impossible. While identification may generally be acquired through AARs and deck logs, some other documents that may reveal additional locational information include: courts of inquiry, general correspondence, and Action Reports (wartime accidents). Some supplementary information may be found in Navy Aircraft Allotments documents, which designate how many aircraft are allotted to each NAS, aircraft carrier, etc. This would provide a terminus post quem and terminus ante quem for when training squadrons at NAS Pensacola, auxiliary fields, and attached aircraft carriers utilized the F8F Bearcat for training. Each of these documents must be cross-examined to discern a true understanding of the aircraft accident event. As has been shown, clerical errors and misplacement of documents may have a significant effect on the outcome of naval aviation research.

Acknowledgements

This research is supported by the UWF Division of Anthropology and Archaeology. Funding was also provided by the Pensacola Archaeological Society, and the UWF Scholarly and Creative Activity Committee. The author would like to show gratitude to the employees of the NHHC Underwater Archaeology Branch and National Archives for their time and expertise. Finally, this research would not be possible without the passion of Pensacola SCUBA divers whom over the years have spent generous time and money searching for naval aircraft 'Lost at Sea.'

References

AERODATA INTERNATIONAL
1987 *U.S. Navy Carrier Fighters of WWII*. Squadron/Signal Publications.

BEEKER, CHARLES AND SHELI SMITH
2005 *Crystal Cove F-4U Corsair Airplane Wreck Scuba Maintenance and Survey Dive Summer 2005 Close of Field Work Interim Report*. Department of Parks and Recreation, California State Parks.

BELL, SAMANTHA
2010 *I Can Ex-Plane: A Study of Site Formation of Submerged Aircraft in Saipan*. Master's Thesis, Flinders University, Dept. of Archaeology, Adelaide, Australia.

2015 In the Drink: Sunken Aircraft of the Battle of Saipan. In *Underwater Archaeology of a Pacific Battlefield*, Jennifer F. McKinnon and Toni L. Carrell, editors, pp. 49-52. Springer International Publishing.

BURGESS, ANTHONY
2013 *Underwater Aviation Archaeology: What is its Place and Value Within Archaeology, and in Particular Maritime Archaeology?*. Master's Thesis, University of South Hampton.

CAGLE, MALCOLM
1963 *The Naval Aviator's Guide*. United States Naval Institute, Annapolis, Maryland.

CAMPBELL, DOUGLAS E.
2012 *BuNos! Disposition of World War II USN, USMC and USCG Aircraft Listed by Bureau Number*. Syneca Research Group, Inc.

CAPELOTTI, PETER
1996 *A Conceptual Model for Aerospace Archaeology: A Case Study from the Wellman Site, Virgohamna, Danskøya, Svalbard*. Doctoral Dissertation, Rutgers University.

CHENOWETH, BOB (ET AL)
2006 Lake Mead's Cold War Legacy: The Overton B-29. In *People, Places, and Parks: Proceedings of the 2005 George Wright Society Conference*: 461-467.

COBLE, W., B. ROGERS AND H. VAN TILBURG
1998 The Lost Flying Boat of Kaneohe Bay: Archaeology of the First U.S. Casualties of Pearl Harbor. In *Historical Archaeology* 32(4):8-18.

DALY, LISA M.
2015 *Aviation Archaeology of World War II Gander: An Examination of Military and Civilian Life at the Newfoundland Airport*. Doctoral Dissertation, Memorial University of Newfoundland.

DIEBOLD, PAUL C.
1993 Aircraft as Cultural Resources: The Indiana Approach. In *CRM bulletin* 16(10):1-3.

FIX, PETER
2011 From Sea to Sky: The Case for Aeronautical Archaeology. In *The Oxford Handbook of Maritime Archaeology*, Alexis Catsambis Ben Ford, and Donny L. Hamilton, editors, pp. 989-1009. Oxford University Press.

FORD, JULIE
2006 *WWII Aviation Archaeology in Victoria, Australia.* Master's Thesis, Flinders University, Dept of Archaeology. Adelaide, Australia

GOLDSTEIN, JEREMY
1997 *The Archaeology of the Moment: Aviation Archaeology as a Sub-field.* Master's Thesis, Wake Forest University, Winston Salem, North Carolina.

GOULD, RICHARD A.
1983 The Archaeology of War: Wrecks of the Spanish Armada of 1588 and the Battle of Britain, 1940. In *Shipwreck Anthropology*, Richard A. Gould, editor, pp. 105-142. University of New Mexico Press, Albuquerque.

GRANT, DAVID, COLT DENFELD AND RANDALL SCHALK
1996 *US Navy Shipwrecks and Submerged Naval Aircraft in Washington: An Overview.* International Archaeological Research Institute.

IRELAND, BERNARD
1998 *Jane's Historic Military Aircraft Recognition Guide.* Collin's Reference.

JUNG, SILVANO
2008 *Australia's Undersea Aerial Armada: The Aviation Archaeology of World War II Flying Boats Lying in Roebuck Bay, Broome, Western Australia.* Doctoral Dissertation, Charles Darwin University.

MALONEY, EDWARD T.
1969 *Grumman F8F Bearcat.* Aero Publishers.

MILBROOKE, A., P. ANDRUS, J. COOK AND D. WHIPPLE
1998 Guidelines for Evaluation and Documenting Historic Aviation Properties. US Department of the Interior, National Park Service, National Register of Historic Places.

MONDEY, DAVID
2002 *The Hamlyn concise guide to American aircraft of World War II.* Chartwell Books.

NEYLAND, ROBERT S. AND DAVID GRANT
1999 Navy Aircraft as Artifacts. In *Underwater Archaeology*, Adriane Askins and Matthew A. Russell, editors, pp. 46-51. Society for Historical Archaeology.

ORTIZ, AGUSTIN
2016 *Perceptions and Research Potential of Submerged WWII Aircraft as Archaeology and Beyond.* Master's Thesis, Maritime Archaeology Department, University of Southern Denmark.

PEARCE, GEORGE F.
1980 *The U.S. Navy in Pensacola: from sailing ships to naval aviation*, 1825-1930. University Presses of Florida.

THE PENSACOLA NEWS JOURNAL
1950 Gulf Crash Fatal for Navy Pilot, 8 November. In *The Pensacola News Journal*, University of West Florida John C. Pace Library, Microfilm Collection, Pensacola, Florida.

1952 Crashes Kill Two Navy Pilots Here, 22 April. In *The Pensacola News Journal*, University of West Florida John C. Pace Library, Microfilm Collection, Pensacola, Florida.

PETREY, WHITNEY, JEFF KUWABARA, CINDY HUNTER AND HANS VAN TILBURG
2008 *A World War Two Underwater Plane Wreck: The History of a P-47*, University of Hawaii at Manoa.

PRUITT, JAMES
2015 *PB2Y Coronado Flying Boat Archaeology and Site Formation Studies,* Tanapag Lagoon, Saipan. Master's Thesis, East Carolina University.

PRUITT, J. AND J. F. MCKINNON
2016 Go in close, and when you think you are too close, go in closer: Finding Historical records of downed US naval aircraft. In *Interdisciplinary Journal of Maritime Studies* 6(1):45-60.

THRUELSEN, RICHARD
1976 *The Grumman Story.* Praeger.

U.S. DEPARTMENT OF THE NAVY
1950a Deck log of the U.S.S. Cabot, 1 February. National Archives and Records Administration, College Park, Maryland.

1950b Deck log of the U.S.S. Wright, 1 November. National Archives and Records Administration, College Park, Maryland.

1951 Deck log of the U.S.S. Monterey, 1 April. National Archives and Records Administration, College Park, Maryland.

1952 Deck log of the U.S.S. Cabot, 1 April. National Archives and Records Administration, College Park, Maryland

U.S. NAVY BUREAU OF AERONAUTICS
1950a Navy Aircraft Accident Report of F8F-1 Bearcat, BuNo 95495, 13 February. Naval History and Heritage Command Archives, Microfilm Collection, Washington D.C.

1950b Navy Aircraft Accident Report of F8F-1 Bearcat, BuNo 95496, 7 November. Naval History and Heritage Command Archives, Microfilm Collection, Washington D.C.

1951 Navy Aircraft Accident Report of F8F-1 Bearcat, BuNo 94901, 18 April. Naval History and Heritage Command Archives, Microfilm Collection, Washington D.C.

1952 Navy Aircraft Accident Report of F8F-1 Bearcat, BuNo 95134, 21 April. Naval History and Heritage Command Archives, Microfilm Collection, Washington D.C.

W̲ʜɪᴘᴘʟᴇ, D̲ᴀᴠɪᴅ
1995 Aircraft as Cultural Resources. The Navy Approach. In *Cultural Resource Management* 18(2):10-12.

W̲ʜɪᴛᴇʜᴇᴀᴅ, H̲ᴜɴᴛᴇʀ ᴀɴᴅ N̲ɪᴄᴏʟᴇ M̲ᴀᴜʀᴏ
2016 An Initial Site Assessment of Submerged Naval Aircraft off Pensacola, Florida. In *ACUA Underwater Archaeology Proceedings*, Washington D.C.

W̲ʜɪᴛᴇʜᴇᴀᴅ, H̲ᴜɴᴛᴇʀ
2016 *Naval History and Heritage Command Artifacts: Identification, Historical Background, and Assessment. Report* on file with Naval History and Heritage Command's Underwater Archaeology Branch, Washington D.C.

W̲ʏɴɴᴇ, N̲ɪᴄᴋ ᴀɴᴅ R̲ɪᴄʜᴀʀᴅ M̲ᴏᴏʀʜᴇᴀᴅ
2011 *Florida in World War II:* Floating Fortress. Arcadia Publishing.

• • • • • • • • • • • • • • • •

Hunter W. Whitehead
The Division of Anthropology and Archaeology
University of West Florida
11000 University Parkway
Pensacola, FL 32514

www.ingramcontent.com/pod-product-compliance
Lightning Source LLC
Chambersburg PA
CBHW081444070526
44586CB00019B/2220